JUN 0 2 2009

005.72 SEO
Ledford, Jerri L.
SEO Bible : search engine

D1542451

SEO
Search Engine Optimizat Bible

DATE

5/25

Jerri L. Ledford

Demco, Inc. 38-294

BICENTENNIAL
1807
WILEY
2007
BICENTENNIAL

Wiley Publishing, Inc.

Middleton Public Library
7425 Hubbard Avenue
Middleton, WI 53562

For James — Because your faith was strong even when mine began to fail.

Search Engine Optimization Bible

Published by
Wiley Publishing, Inc.
10475 Crosspoint Boulevard
Indianapolis, IN 46256
www.wiley.com

Copyright © 2008 by Wiley Publishing, Inc., Indianapolis, Indiana

Published simultaneously in Canada

ISBN: 978-0-470-17500-2

Manufactured in the United States of America

10 9 8 7 6 5 4 3

Library of Congress Cataloging-in-Publication Data is available from Publisher.

No part of this publication may be reproduced, stored in a retrieval system or transmitted in any form or by any means, electronic, mechanical, photocopying, recording, scanning or otherwise, except as permitted under Sections 107 or 108 of the 1976 United States Copyright Act, without either the prior written permission of the Publisher, or authorization through payment of the appropriate per-copy fee to the Copyright Clearance Center, 222 Rosewood Drive, Danvers, MA 01923, (978) 750-8400, fax (978) 646-8600. Requests to the Publisher for permission should be addressed to the Legal Department, Wiley Publishing, Inc., 10475 Crosspoint Blvd., Indianapolis, IN 46256, (317) 572-3447, fax (317) 572-4355, or online at http://www.wiley.com/go/permissions.

Limit of Liability/Disclaimer of Warranty: The publisher and the author make no representations or warranties with respect to the accuracy or completeness of the contents of this work and specifically disclaim all warranties, including without limitation warranties of fitness for a particular purpose. No warranty may be created or extended by sales or promotional materials. The advice and strategies contained herein may not be suitable for every situation. This work is sold with the understanding that the publisher is not engaged in rendering legal, accounting, or other professional services. If professional assistance is required, the services of a competent professional person should be sought. Neither the publisher nor the author shall be liable for damages arising herefrom. The fact that an organization or Website is referred to in this work as a citation and/or a potential source of further information does not mean that the author or the publisher endorses the information the organization or Website may provide or recommendations it may make. Further, readers should be aware that Internet Websites listed in this work may have changed or disappeared between when this work was written and when it is read.

For general information on our other products and services or to obtain technical support, please contact our Customer Care Department within the U.S. at (800) 762-2974, outside the U.S. at (317) 572-3993 or fax (317) 572-4002.

Trademarks: Wiley and related trade dress are registered trademarks of Wiley Publishing, Inc., in the United States and other countries, and may not be used without written permission. All other trademarks are the property of their respective owners. Wiley Publishing, Inc., is not associated with any product or vendor mentioned in this book.

Wiley also publishes its books in a variety of electronic formats. Some content that appears in print may not be available in electronic books.

About the Author

Jerri Ledford is the author of more than a dozen technology books and hundreds of articles about business and technology subjects. Her books and articles have been published in many languages throughout the world. Jerri also writes and teaches technology courses online for organizations such as HP, Forbes, AOL, and Sony. When she's not buried in a writing project, Jerri spends all of her time working on other writing projects or on the Alabama and Florida beaches with her children.

About the Technical Editor

Micah Baldwin is recognized as a leader in the search engine marketing industry, having helped author several books on search engine marketing and often speaking at industry events. Micah started Current Wisdom, a full-service search marketing agency, in 2003 after building ServiceMagic's search marketing initiative. In January 2007, Micah sold Current Wisdom to Indigio Group, a Denver-based interactive agency, where he currently works as senior vice president, media strategy.

Credits

Acquisitions Editor
Katie Mohr

Development Editor
William Bridges

Technical Editor
Micah Baldwin

Production Editor
Angela Smith

Copy Editor
Kim Cofer

Editorial Manager
Mary Beth Wakefield

Production Manager
Tim Tate

**Vice President and
Executive Group Publisher**
Richard Swadley

Vice President and Executive Publisher
Joseph B. Wikert

Project Coordinator, Cover
Lynsey Osborn

Compositor
Laurie Stewart, Happenstance Type-O-Rama

Proofreader
Sossity Smith

Indexer
Johnna VanHoose Dinse

Anniversary Logo Design
Richard Pacifico

Acknowledgments

After having written more than a dozen books, there is one thing that I can say for sure: no book is written without a ton of helpful people guiding, pushing, and providing for the author. Before even acknowledging that team, though, I must say thanks to God for giving me a talent that few people possess and the means by which to use that talent.

There is an entire team at Wiley that I owe a huge thank-you to. These people — Katie Mohr, Mary Beth Wakefield, Tom Dinse, and a good dozen or so other people whom I never get to speak to — are responsible for making this book a reality. They handle production from beginning to end, and without them, there would be no book.

My favorite development editor in the world is among those I owe thanks to as well. Bill Bridges has worked with me on several books now, and he's the reason that my words are spelled and ordered correctly and not full of clichés. Without Bill, the book would be half the quality that it is now. Thanks, friend!

And then there's Micah Baldwin. Micah put lots of hours into ensuring the technical accuracy of the text within these pages. His suggestions (and saves) have kept my facts true. Thanks, Micah.

All the interviews included in Appendix B were also gifts to me. Thanks to each of you who took the time to talk to me, to answer my sometimes dumb questions, and to allow me to pass your wisdom on to our readers. Your help provided valuable insight for me, as I hope it will for the reader as well.

Thanks, too, to my Mobile family. Big Jennifer and Little Jennifer, Rick, and James — you're my support system. And you're there when I need you; you leave when I need space, and you understand that brain drain from writing is a temporary situation and love me still. Without you and our weekly dinners, I wouldn't be able to function nearly as effectively. Thanks, guys!

And thanks to you for reading the book. I hope you find all the information you seek.

Contents at a Glance

v

Contents at a Glance

Contents

Contents

Part III: Optimizing Search Strategies   209

Appendices   279

Introduction

Welcome to the *Search Engine Optimization Bible*. Search engine optimization has come to mean a lot of things to a lot of different people. In the strictest sense, SEO is about the on-page and off-page design strategies you can use to improve your search engine ranking. This usually means tweaking your web site, using design elements and content. And in most cases, it also means spending no money at all.

SEM, or Search Engine Marketing, is not just SEO. More accurately, SEM includes PPC or pay-per-click advertising. Search engine marketing is about doing whatever you need to do to ensure that your web site ranks as high as possible in search engine results. This means not only that you make the needed changes to your web-site design, but that you also employ other tactics, like using a paid advertising program or investing in content strategies.

I lump them all into one category. The ultimate goal of SEM is to bring more people to your web site. And you can do that by improving your search engines results. You can also do that by taking advantage of a growing phenomenon on the Web, social media. Social media is a viral form of sharing information on the Web. You might think of it as a more sophisticated method of sharing your favorites or information that you think will interest other people. And using social media to improve the traffic to your web site is called Social Media Marketing, or SMM.

I vote we do away with the alphabet soup completely. All these marketing efforts have one thing in common: reaching your target audience. And today anyone who is not an SEO purist places all these marketing methods under the SEM umbrella. All of them are methods for optimizing your web site for the audience that you're trying to reach. And as social media grow in popularity, they're going to be affected by and included in search engine results as well.

Every now and then, you need to step away from the crowd and stop doing what everyone else is doing. In SEO, stepping out alone is usually rewarded with better traffic results. Everyone is doing the same thing. And that doesn't mean that you shouldn't. What it means is that you should do the same thing in a different way. And that's where the *Search Engine Optimization Bible* comes in.

Throughout the pages that follow, I'll show you the best practices for search engine optimization and provide insight into the theory behind the strategies that you'll learn. These strategies are tested. They work. For thousands of web sites. Use them to build on. Follow the best practices of search engine optimization but do it creatively. Try something different. That's how blogs became such a huge phenomenon. It's how social bookmarking and social communities caught on. Someone looked at marketing in a different way and came up with a new angle.

So, use the information that you'll find in the following pages to improve your search engine ranking. Use it to improve the traffic to your web site. But most importantly, use it to reach highly targeted customers who will take the actions you desire them to take on your web site. That customer audience is always first. Remember this as you market, keep the audience as your focus, and your efforts will be successful.

Who Should Read This Book

Search engine optimization is not for the faint of heart. It requires a lot of time and a lot of hard work. But what it doesn't require is a professional. Anyone with time and the desire to do it can learn the most successful strategies of SEO. And that's probably why there are so many SEO consultants in the world today.

Anyone can be an SEO consultant. No official certification programs exist, and no industry standards guide the development of an SEO consultant. And from one aspect, that's good news for you. It means that you can become your own SEO consultant. And a good first step is to learn the information you'll find in the following pages.

Of course, not everyone wants to be an SEO consultant. Your goal in picking up this book might be simply to learn about the SEO process so that you can be certain your SEO consultant, or the SEO firm you're considering hiring, is doing the job they should be doing to help your web site rank high. That's good.

Two types of people will get the most out of the *Search Engine Optimization Bible* — people who are interested in being their own SEO consultants and people who just want to know how SEO works. If you're an SEO expert, you'll likely find that you're already familiar with the information contained in these pages. There might be a few tidbits that are worth your while, though, so if you need a refresher course, keep reading.

For those of you who are new to SEO, you'll find the information you need to understand and begin implementing SEO strategies that will help improve your search engine rankings and drive better targeted visitors to your site.

How This Book Is Organized

Search engine optimization can be a complex process, but there are distinct areas of the process that can be addressed on their own. And that's how you'll find this book divided. It has four parts, each of which represents a portion of the SEO process.

Within each part are chapters that address different pieces for that step in the SEO process. And within each chapter, there are sections to help you work through that piece of the process. You'll also find four separate appendices, which provide guidelines and support for the various strategies and actions that are recommended.

Part I: Understanding SEO: Understanding search engine optimization is half the battle in planning and implementing an effective SEO plan. It's also the place where you need to start. The two chapters in this part of the book will help you to understand SEO and then to work through creating an SEO plan. Chapter 1 covers the introduction by breaking down a search engine and explaining how search engine optimization works. Chapter 2 explains why you need SEO and walks you through creating your SEO plan.

Part II: SEO Strategies: SEO strategies are the various ways in which you can implement SEO both on and off your web site. Chapter 3 covers the SEO factors that you should consider in web-site design. Chapter 4 introduces you to keywords and keyword strategies. Chapters 5–10 help you take keywords to the next level by explaining pay-per-click advertising and how you can leverage it to improve your web-site traffic. Chapter 11 helps you understand how HTML tags can improve your SEO rankings. And Chapter 12 provides insight into why content is so important in SEO strategy. To round everything off, Chapter 13 provides information and strategies for using links to improve your search engine traffic.

Part III: Optimizing Search Strategies: Once you understand the basics of search strategies, you can begin to improve upon those strategies to gain attention from people and from search engines. In Part III you'll find six additional chapters that help you hone your SEO efforts. Chapter 14 includes information about adding your web site to indexes and search engines. Chapter 15 demystifies pay-for-inclusion services. Chapter 16 provides a closer look at the different requirements of search engine crawlers. In Chapter 17, you'll learn how to avoid using spamming (or spam-like) techniques. Social-media optimization is covered in Chapter 18. And automating elements of optimization is explained in Chapter 19.

Part IV: Maintaining SEO: Search engine optimization is not a do-it-and-forget-it strategy. It's an ongoing process that must be maintained. In Chapter 20, you'll learn what to devote time to after the SEO launch is over. And Chapter 21 will show you how to analyze your SEO efforts to learn what's working and what must be changed.

Appendices: The appendices in this book offer additional insight into and tools for the SEO process. Appendix A is an overview of how to optimize your web site for each of the three major search engines (Google, MSN, and Yahoo!). In Appendix B you'll find a collection of interviews with industry leaders who are actually in the trenches, working with site optimization each day. Appendix C contains a large list of the SEO software and tools that are available online, and Appendix D contains worksheets and checklists that should help you as you work through the process of planning and implementing SEO strategies.

A lot of information is covered in these pages, so take your time getting through everything. This book is also a great reference tool that you should keep on your desk so that, as you're working through SEO strategies, you can refer to the different strategies for clarification on what actions you should take.

Conventions and features

As you read through these pages, you'll also find different icons that indicate important information. You should pay close attention to these special notes. They stand out from the rest of the text because it's information that you don't want to miss. The icons that you'll find include:

- **Note** — Notes including information that's not necessarily part of the section, but that will help you understand either a process or a theory in search engine optimization.

- **Tip** — Tips can be shortcuts, an easier way of doing something, or a short bit of information that will help you better comprehend the strategies and actions that are covered. In general, a Tip will make your SEO efforts easier.

- **Caution** — Pay particular attention to cautions. A caution includes information and advice that could, if not followed, have less than pleasant repercussions. If there's something you shouldn't do or should use care in doing, it's included in a Caution.

- **Cross-Ref** — Stands for a cross-reference, something of interest in another part of the book.

Each of these features is designed to make the process of learning about SEO easier for you. So if you see one of them, take the time to read through it in the context of where it's located. The additional information should help you better understand the SEO process.

Where to Go from Here

Before you even finish reading the *Search Engine Optimization Bible*, you'll be itching to start putting some of the strategies that are covered here into place. Go for it. Just keep the book handy to refer to. And remember to come back and finish reading the sections that you haven't completed.

Also remember that implementing SEO is an ongoing process. You can start immediately, but you have to keep it up, even once the desired increases are achieved. The effort you put into it will pay off in terms of the traffic increases to your site. And even better than the traffic increases is the improved conversion rate you should experience. In other words, more people will show up at your site and take the actions that you want them to take while they're there.

It's not easy to achieve, but if you work at it, you can expect to see major improvements over time.

Good luck!

Part I

Understanding SEO

Search engine optimization (SEO) is such a broad term. It can be quite overwhelming if you try to take the whole of it in a single bite. There are so many facets of search engine optimization, from how search engines work (and they all work a little differently) to how a web page is designed. There are enough elements to worry about that you could spend far more time than you can afford to invest in trying to achieve the SEO you have in mind. However, search engine optimization doesn't have to be such an onerous task that it can't be accomplished. Not if you understand what it is and how it works.

Part I explains the basics of search engine optimization. This part includes an explanation of what search engines are and how they work. There is also an explanation of the concept of an SEO plan. Together, these two elements will have you up to speed and ready to begin implementing the right SEO strategies to build the web site traffic that you need.

Chapter 1

Search Engine Basics

What do you do when you need to find something on the Internet? In most cases, you pop over to one of the major search engines and type in the term or phrase that you're looking for and then click through the results, right? But of course search engines weren't always around.

In its infancy, the Internet wasn't what you think of when you use it now. In fact, it was nothing like the web of interconnected sites that's become one of the greatest business facilitators of our time. Instead, what was called the Internet was actually a collection of *FTP (File Transfer Protocol)* sites that users could access to download (or upload) files.

To find a specific file in that collection, users had to navigate through each file. Sure, there were shortcuts. If you knew the right people — that would be the people who knew the exact address of the file you were looking for — you could go straight to the file. That's assuming you knew exactly what you were looking for.

The whole process made finding files on the Internet a difficult, time-consuming exercise in patience. But that was before a student at McGill University in Montreal decided there had to be an easier way. In 1990, Alan Emtage created the first search tool used on the Internet. His creation, an index of files on the Internet, was called Archie.

If you're thinking Archie, the comic book character created in 1941, you're a little off track (at least for now). The name Archie was used because the file name Archives was too long. Later, Archie's pals from the comic book series (Veronica and Jughead) came onto the search scene, too, but we'll get to that shortly.

Archie wasn't actually a *search engine* like those that you use today. But at the time, it was a program many Internet users were happy to have. The program basically downloaded directory listings for all of the files that were stored on *anonymous FTP* sites in a given network of computers. Those listings were then plugged into a searchable database of web sites.

The search capabilities of Archie weren't as fancy as the *natural language capabilities* you'll find in most common search engines today, but at the time it got the job done. Archie indexed computer files, making them easier to locate.

In 1991, however, another student named Mark McCahill, at the University of Minnesota, decided that if you could search for files on the Internet, then surely you could also search plain text for specific references in the files. Because no such application existed, he created Gopher, a program that indexed the plain-text documents that later became the first web sites on the public Internet.

With the creation of Gopher, there also needed to be programs that could find references within the indexes that Gopher created, and so Archie's pals finally rejoined him. Veronica (Very Easy Rodent-Oriented Net-wide Index to Computerized Archives) and Jughead (Jonzy's Universal Gopher Hierarchy Excavation and Display) were created to search the files that were stored in the Gopher Index System.

Both of these programs worked in essentially the same way, allowing users to search the indexed information by keyword.

From there, search as you know it began to mature. The first *real* search engine, in the form that we know search engines today, didn't come into being until 1993. It was developed by Matthew Gray, and it was called Wandex. Wandex was the first program to both index and search the index of pages on the Web. This technology was the first program to crawl the Web, and later became the basis for all search crawlers. And from there, search engines took on a life of their own. From 1993 to 1998, the major search engines that you're probably familiar with today were created:

- Excite — 1993
- Yahoo! — 1994
- Web Crawler — 1994
- Lycos — 1994
- Infoseek — 1995
- AltaVista — 1995
- Inktomi — 1996
- Ask Jeeves — 1997
- Google — 1997
- MSN Search — 1998

Today, search engines are sophisticated programs, many of which allow you to search all manner of files and documents using the same words and phrases you would use in everyday conversations. It's hard to believe that the concept of a search engine is just over 15 years old. Especially considering what you can use one to find these days!

What Is a Search Engine?

Okay, so you know the basic concept of a search engine. Type a word or phrase into a search box and click a button. Wait a few seconds, and references to thousands (or hundreds of thousands) of pages will appear. Then all you have to do is click through those pages to find what you want. But what exactly is a search engine, beyond this general concept of "seek and ye shall find"?

It's a little complicated. On the back end, a search engine is a piece of software that uses applications to collect information about web pages. The information collected is usually key words or phrases that are possible indicators of what is contained on the web page as a whole, the URL of the page, the code that makes up the page, and links into and out of the page. That information is then indexed and stored in a database.

On the front end, the software has a user interface where users enter a search term — a word or phrase — in an attempt to find specific information. When the user clicks a search button, an algorithm then examines the information stored in the back-end database and retrieves links to web pages that appear to match the search term the user entered.

CROSS-REF   You can find more information about web crawlers, spiders, and robots in Chapter 14.

The process of collecting information about web pages is performed by an agent called a crawler, spider, or robot. The crawler literally looks at every URL on the Web, and collects key words and phrases on each page, which are then included in the database that powers a search engine. Considering that the number of sites on the Web went over 100 million some time ago and is increasing by more than 1.5 million sites each month, that's like your brain cataloging every single word you read, so that when you need to know something, you think of that word and every reference to it comes to mind.

In a word . . . overwhelming.

Anatomy of a Search Engine

By now you probably have a fuzzy picture of how a search engine works. But there's much more to it than just the basic overview you've seen so far. In fact, search engines have several parts. Unfortunately, it's rare that you find an explanation for just how a search engine is made — and that information is vitally important to succeeding with *search engine optimization (SEO)*.

Query interface

The query interface is what most people are familiar with, and it's probably what comes to mind when you hear the term "search engine." The query interface is the page that users see when they navigate to a search engine to enter a search term.

There was a time when the search engine interface looked very much like the Ask.com page shown in Figure 1-1. The interface was a simple page with a search box and a button to activate the search.

Today, many search engines on the Web have added much more personalized content in an attempt to capitalize on the real estate available to them. For example, Yahoo! Search, shown in Figure 1-2, allows users to personalize their pages with a free e-mail account, weather information, news, sports, and many other elements designed to make users want to return to that site to conduct their web searches.

One other option users have for customizing the interfaces of their search engines is a capability like the one Google offers. The Google search engine has a customizable interface to which users can add different *gadgets*. These gadgets allow users to add features to their customized Google search home that meet their own personal needs or tastes.

FIGURE 1-1

The Ask.com search page shows how most search engine interfaces used to look.

FIGURE 1-2

Yahoo! Search allows users to make their search page more personal.

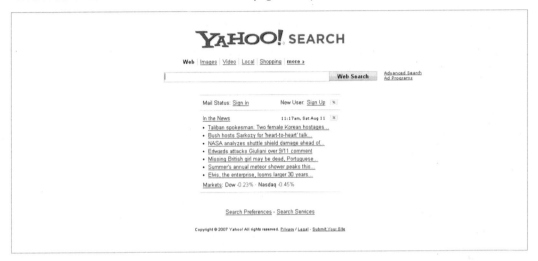

When it comes to search engine optimization, Google's user interface offers the most ability for you to reach your target audience, because it does more than just optimize your site for search; if there is a useful tool or feature available on your site, you can allow users to have access to this tool or feature through the *Application Programming Interface (API)* made available by Google. This allows you to have your name in front of users on a daily basis.

CROSS-REF   You can find more information about Google APIs in Appendix A in the section "Optimization for Google."

For example, a company called PDF24.org has a Google gadget that allows users to turn their documents into PDF files, right from their Google home page once the gadget has been added. If the point of search engine optimization is ultimately to get your name in front of as many people as possible, as often as possible, then making a gadget available for addition to Google's personalized home page can only further that goal.

Crawlers, spiders, and robots

The query interface is the only part of a search engine that the user ever sees. Every other part of the search engine is behind the scenes, out of view of the people who use it every day. That doesn't mean it's not important, however. In fact, what's in the back end is the most important part of the search engine.

CROSS-REF   There's more in-depth information about crawlers, spiders, and robots in Chapter 14.

If you've spent any time on the Internet, you may have heard a little about spiders, crawlers, and robots. These little creatures are programs that literally crawl around the Web, cataloging data so that it can be searched. In the most basic sense all three programs — crawlers, spiders, and robots — are essentially the same. They all "collect" information about each and every web URL.

This information is then cataloged according to the URL on which they're located and are stored in a database. Then, when a user uses a search engine to locate something on the Web, the references in the database are searched and the search results are returned.

Databases

Every search engine contains or is connected to a system of databases, where data about each URL on the Web (collected by crawlers, spiders, or robots) is stored. These databases are massive storage areas that contain multiple data points about each URL.

The data might be arranged in any number of different ways, and will be ranked according to a method of ranking and retrieval that is usually proprietary to the company that owns the search engine.

Search algorithms

All of the parts of the search engine are important, but the *search algorithm* is the cog that makes everything work. It might be more accurate to say that the search algorithm is the foundation on which everything else is built. How a search engine works is based on the search algorithm, or the way that data is discovered by the user.

In very general terms, a search algorithm is a problem-solving procedure that takes a problem, evaluates a number of possible answers, and then returns the solution to that problem. A search algorithm for a search engine takes the problem (the word or phrase being searched for), sifts through a database that contains cataloged keywords and the URLs those words are related to, and then returns pages that contain the word or phrase that was searched for, either in the body of the page or in a URL that points to the page.

This neat little trick is accomplished differently according to the algorithm that's being used. There are several classifications of search algorithms, and each search engine uses algorithms that are slightly different. That's why a search for one word or phrase will yield different results from different search engines. Some of the most common types of search algorithms include the following:

- **List search:** A list search algorithm searches through specified data looking for a single key. The data is searched in a very linear, list-style method. The result of a list search is usually a single element, which means that searching through billions of web sites could be very time-consuming, but would yield a smaller search result.

- **Tree search:** Envision a tree in your mind. Now, examine that tree either from the roots out or from the leaves in. This is how a tree search algorithm works. The algorithm searches a data set from the broadest to the most narrow, or from the most narrow to the broadest. Data sets are like trees; a single piece of data can branch to many other pieces of data, and this is very much how the Web is set up. Tree searches, then, are more useful when conducting searches on the Web, although they are not the only searches that can be successful.

- **SQL search:** One of the difficulties with a tree search is that it's conducted in a hierarchical manner, meaning it's conducted from one point to another, according to the ranking of the data being searched. A SQL (pronounced See-Quel) search allows data to be searched in a non-hierarchical manner, which means that data can be searched from any *subset* of data.

- **Informed search:** An informed search algorithm looks for a specific answer to a specific problem in a tree-like data set. The informed search, despite its name, is not always the best choice for web searches because of the general nature of the answers being sought. Instead, informed search is better used for specific queries in specific data sets.

- **Adversarial search:** An adversarial search algorithm looks for all possible solutions to a problem, much like finding all the possible solutions in a game. This algorithm is difficult to use with web searches, because the number of possible solutions to a word or phrase search is nearly infinite on the Web.

- **Constraint satisfaction search:** When you think of searching the Web for a word or phrase, the constraint satisfaction search algorithm is most likely to satisfy your desire to find something. In this type of search algorithm, the solution is discovered by meeting a set of constraints, and the data set can be searched in a variety of different ways that do not have to be linear. Constraint satisfaction searches can be very useful for searching the Web.

These are only a few of the various types of search algorithms that are used when creating search engines. And very often, more than one type of search algorithm is used, or as happens in most cases, some proprietary search algorithm is created. The key to maximizing your search engine results is to understand a little about how each search engine you're targeting works. Only when you understand this can you know how to maximize your exposure to meet the search requirements for that search engine.

Retrieval and ranking

For a web search engine, the retrieval of data is a combination activity of the crawler (or spider or robot), the database, and the search algorithm. Those three elements work in concert to retrieve the word or phrase that a user enters into the search engine's user interface. And as noted earlier, how that works can be a proprietary combination of technologies, theories, and coding whizbangery.

The really tricky part comes in the results ranking. Ranking is also what you'll spend the most time and effort trying to affect. Your ranking in a search engine determines how often people see your page, which affects everything from revenue to your advertising budget. Unfortunately, how a search engine ranks your page or pages is a tough science to pin down.

The most that you can hope for, in most cases, is to make an educated guess as to how a search engine ranks its results, and then try to tailor your page to meet those results. But keep in mind that, although retrieval and ranking are listed as separate subjects here, they're actually part of the search algorithm. The separation is to help you better understand how search engines work.

Ranking plays such a large part in search engine optimization that you'll see it frequently in this book. You'll look at ranking from every possible facet before you reach the last page. But for now, let's look at just what affects ranking. Keep in mind, however, that different search engines use different ranking criteria, so the importance each of these elements plays will vary.

- **Location:** Location doesn't refer here to the location (as in the URL) of a web page. Instead, it refers to the location of key words and phrases on a web page. So, for example, if a user searches for "puppies," some search engines will rank the results according to where on the page the word "puppies" appears. Obviously, the higher the word appears on the page, the higher the rank might be. So a web site that contains the word "puppies" in the *title tag* will likely appear higher than a web site that is about puppies but does not contain the word in the title tag. What this means is that a web site that's not designed with SEO in mind will likely not rank where you would expect it to rank. The site www.puppies.com is a good example of this. In a Google search, it appears ranked fifth rather than first, potentially because it does not contain the key word in the title tag.

- **Frequency:** The frequency with which the search term appears on the page may also affect how a page is ranked in search results. So, for example, on a page about puppies, one that uses the word five times might be ranked higher than one that uses the word only two or three times. When word frequency became a factor, some web site designers began using hidden words hundreds of times on pages, trying to artificially boost their page rankings. Most search engines now recognize this as *keyword spamming* and ignore or even refuse to list pages that use this technique.

- **Links:** One of the more recent ranking factors is the type and number of links on a web page. Links that come into the site, links that lead out of the site, and links within the site are all taken into consideration. It would follow, then, that the more links you have on your page or leading to your page the higher your rank would be, right? Again, it doesn't necessarily work that way. More accurately, the number of relevant links coming into your page, versus the number of relevant links within the page, versus the number of relevant links leading off the page will have a bearing on the rank that your page gets in the search results.

- **Click-throughs:** One last element that might determine how your site ranks against others in a search is the number of *click-throughs* your site has versus click-throughs for other pages that are shown in page rankings. Because the search engine cannot monitor site traffic for every site on the Web, some monitor the number of clicks each search result receives. The rankings may then be repositioned in a future search, based on this interaction with the users.

Page ranking is a very precise science. And it differs from search engine to search engine. To create the best possible SEO for your site, it's necessary to understand how these page rankings are made for the search engines you plan to target. Those factors can then be taken into consideration and used to your advantage when it's time to create, change, or update the web site that you want to optimize.

Characteristics of Search

Understanding how a search engine works helps you to understand how your pages are ranked in the search engine, but how your pages are found is another story entirely. That's where the human element comes in. Search means different things to different people. For example, one of my colleagues searches the Internet using the same words and phrases he would use to tell someone about a topic or even the exact question that he's trying to get answered. It's called *natural language*. Another, however, was trained in search using *Boolean search techniques*. She uses a very different *syntax* when she's creating a search term. Each of them returns different search results, even when each is using the same search engines.

The characteristics of search refer to how users search the Internet. This can be everything from the *heuristics* they use when creating a search term to the selection the user makes (and the way those selections are made) once the search results are returned. One interesting fact is that more than half of American adults search the Internet every time they go online. And in fact, more people search the Internet than use the yellow pages when they're looking for phone numbers or the locations of local businesses.

This wealth of search engine users is fertile ground for SEO targeting. And the better you understand how and why users use search engines, and exactly how search engines work, the easier it will be to achieve the SEO you're pursuing.

Classifications of Search Engines

With a decent understanding of how search engines work and how people use those search engines, you can now concentrate on some more detailed information about these engines. For example, you know that all search engines aren't created equal, right? But did you know that there are different types, or classifications, of search engines? There are.

Search engines can be broken down into three different types (in the broadest of terms): primary, secondary, and targeted.

Primary search engines

A *primary search engine* is the type you think of most often when search engines come to mind. Some index most or all sites on the Web. For example, Yahoo! Google, and MSN are primary (also called major) search engines.

Primary search engines will generate the majority of the traffic to your web site, and as such will be the primary focus of your SEO efforts. Each primary search engine differs slightly from the others.

For example, Lycos has been around much longer than Google, yet Google is the most popular search engine on the Web. Why is that? Most likely because people find that, when searching the Web, Google provides better search results.

The difference in those search results is all in the search algorithm used to create the search engine.

Most primary search engines are also more than just search. Additional features such as e-mail, mapping, news, and different types of entertainment applications are also available from most of the primary search engine companies. These elements were added long after the search was established, as a way to draw more and more people to the search engine. Although those features don't change the way people search, they might affect which search engine people choose.

Overview of Google

Each of the major search engines differs in some small way. Google is the king of search engines, in part because of the accuracy with which it can pull the results from a search query. Sure, Google offers all kinds of extras like e-mail, a personalized home page, and even productivity applications, but those value-added services are not what made Google popular.

What turned Google into a household word is the accuracy with which the search engine can return search results. This accuracy was developed when the Google designers combined keyword searches with link popularity. The combination of the keywords and the popularity of links to those pages yields a higher accuracy rank than just keywords alone.

However, it's important to understand that link popularity and keywords are just two of hundreds of different criteria that search engines can use in ranking the relevancy of web pages.

Overview of Yahoo!

Most people assume that Yahoo! is a search engine, and it is. But it's also a *web directory*, which basically means that it's a list of the different web pages available on the Internet, divided by category and subcategory. In fact, what few people know is that Yahoo! started as the favorites list of the two young men who founded it. Through the acquisition of companies like Inktomi, All the Web, AltaVista, and Overture, Yahoo! gradually gained market share as a search engine.

Yahoo!, which at one time used Google to search its directory of links, now ranks pages through a combination of the technologies that it acquired over time. However, Yahoo!'s link-ranking capability is not as accurate as Google's. In addition, Yahoo! also has a paid inclusion program, which some think tends to skew search results in favor of the highest payer.

Overview of MSN

MSN's search capabilities aren't quite as mature as those of Google or Yahoo! As a result of this immaturity, MSN has not yet developed the in-depth link analysis capabilities of these other primary search engines. Instead, MSN relies heavily on web-site content for ranking purposes. However, this may have a beneficial effect for new web sites that are trying to get listed in search engines.

The link-ranking capabilities of Google and Yahoo! can preclude new web sites from being listed for a period of time after they have been created. This is because (especially where Google is concerned) the quality of the link may be considered during ranking. New links are often ignored until they have been in place for a time.

Because MSN relies heavily on page content, a web site that is tagged properly and contains a good ratio of keywords will be more likely to be listed — and listed sooner — by the MSN search engine. So, though it's not the most popular of search engines, it is one of the primaries, and being listed there sooner rather than later will help increase your site traffic.

Secondary search engines

Secondary search engines are targeted at smaller, more specific audiences, although the search engine's content itself is still general. They don't generate as much traffic as the primary search engines, but they're useful for regional and more narrowly focused searches. Examples of secondary search engines include Lycos, LookSmart, Miva, Ask.com, and Espotting.

Secondary search engines, just like the primary ones, will vary in the way they rank search results. Some will rely more heavily upon keywords, whereas others will rely on reciprocal links. Still others might rely on criteria such as *meta tags* or some proprietary criteria.

Secondary search engines should be included in any SEO plan. Though these search engines might not generate as much traffic as the primary search engines, they will still generate valuable traffic that should not be overlooked. Many users of secondary search engines are users because they have some loyalty to that specific search engine. For example, many past AOL users who have moved on to broadband Internet service providers still use the AOL search engine whenever possible, because it's comfortable for them.

Targeted search engines

Targeted search engines — sometimes called topical search engines — are the most specific of them all. These search engines are very narrowly focused, usually to a general topic, like medicine or branches of science, travel, sports, or some other topic. Examples of targeted search engines include CitySearch, Yahoo! Travel, and MusicSearch, and like other types of search engines, ranking criteria will vary from one to another.

When considering targeted search engines for SEO purposes, keep in mind that many of these search engines are much more narrowly focused than primary or secondary search engines. Look for the targeted search engines that are relevant to your specific topic (like pets, sports, locations, and so on).

Putting Search Engines to Work for You

All this information about search engines has one purpose — to show you how they work, so that you can put them to work for you. Throughout this book, you'll find various strategies for optimizing your web site so it appears high in search engine rankings when relevant searches are performed. But this requires that you know how to put search engines to work for you.

Search engine optimization is essentially the science of designing your web site to maximize your search engine rankings. This means that all of the elements of your web site are created with the goal of obtaining high search engine rankings. Those elements include:

- Entry and exit pages
- Page titles
- Site content
- Graphics
- Web site structure

In addition to these elements, however, you also have to consider things like keywords, links, HTML, and meta-tagging. Even after you have all the elements of your page optimized for search-engine friendliness, there are other things to consider. For example, you can have all the right design elements included in your web pages and still have a relatively low search engine ranking. Factors such as advertising campaigns and update frequencies also affect your SEO efforts.

All of this means that you should understand that the concept of search engine optimization is not based on any single element. Instead, search engine optimization is based on a vast number of elements and strategies. And it's an ongoing process that doesn't end once your web site is live.

SEO is a living, breathing concept of maximizing the traffic that your web site generates, and because it is, that means that it's a constantly moving target. If you've ever played a game of Whack-a-Mole, you can understand how difficult search engine optimization is to nail. In the game, a little mole pops up out of a hole. Your job is to whack the mole on the top of the head before it disappears back down the hole and appears in another.

Search engine optimization is much the same concept. Search engines are constantly changing, so the methods and strategies used to achieve high search engine rankings must also change. As soon as that little mole pops up in one hole, he disappears and then reappears in another. It's a frustrating game, but given enough time and concentration, you can become very good at it.

Manipulating Search Engines

There's one more topic to touch on before this chapter is finished. SEO is about manipulating search engines — to an extent. Beyond that, the manipulation becomes something more sinister and you run the risk of having your web site removed from the search engine rankings completely. It's true. It happens.

So what exactly can and can't you do? There's a list. Here is part of it.

You can:

- Create a web site that contains meta tags, content, graphics, and keywords that help improve your site ranking.
- Use keywords liberally on your site, so long as they are used in the correct context of your site topic and content.
- Include reciprocal links to your site from others as long as those links are legitimate and relevant.
- Encourage web site traffic through many venues, including keyword advertising, reciprocal links, and marketing campaigns.
- Submit your web site to search engines manually, rather than waiting for them to pick up your site in the natural course of cataloging web sites.

You can't:

- Trick search engines by imbedding hidden keywords in your web site. This is a practice that will very likely get you banned by most search engines.
- Artificially generate links to your site from unrelated sites for the purpose of increasing your ranking based on link analysis. Most search engines have a built-in mechanism that will detect this type of deceptive practice.
- Artificially generate traffic to your web site so that it appears more popular than it is. Again, there are safeguards in place to prevent this from happening, and if you trip those safeguards, you could end up on the banned list for many search engines.
- Force your web site to appear in search engine rankings by submitting the site repeatedly for inclusion in the rankings. A good general rule of thumb is that you should submit your site once and then wait at least six weeks before submitting it again. Submitting it repeatedly will, again, only lead to something nasty like being banned from the search engine.
- Expect search engines to automatically rank you at the top of your topic, category, or keyword as soon as the site is picked up. It could take a little time to build the "status" that you need to reach a high search engine ranking. Remember, SEO is a process.

These are just basic rules for putting search engines to work for you. There are many more, which you will discover in the coming chapters. As you get started, however, keep these in mind, because you'll see them over and over again throughout the course of this book and any other research that you might be doing on search engine optimization.

Chapter 2

Creating an SEO Plan

Before you can even begin to optimize your web site for search engines, you need to have a search engine optimization plan in place. This will help you create SEO goals and keep those goals in focus as the purpose of your site changes, and as the methods for search engine optimization change — and they will change.

Your SEO plan will help you see where you need to concentrate your efforts at any given time. This need will change over time. In the beginning, you're most likely to be focusing on getting started with SEO. However, after you've put all of your SEO strategies into place, the focus of your SEO activities will change.

Note that I said they will change, not that they will end. Once you've started SEO, if you plan to continue using it, you'll need to constantly monitor and update your SEO plan, strategies, and activities. There was a time when the only thing you had to worry about was which keywords or links would be most effective for getting your site ranked high in relevant search results. Today, very few search engines focus on a single aspect of search engine optimization. This means that over time those who focused only on keywords or only on links have found themselves with diminished SEO effectiveness.

Search engines will naturally change and mature, as the technologies and principles that enable SEO and the engines themselves change. For this reason, the SEO plan should be considered a dynamic, changing document. To keep up with that document, you need to be evolving or changing as well. And that's where your SEO plan will help you stay on track.

Using the SEO plan, you can quickly and easily tell where you are and where you need to be with your search engine optimization efforts.

Understanding Why You Need SEO

Before you can understand the reasons for using SEO, it might be good to have a definition of what SEO — search engine optimization — is. It's probably a safe assumption that if you've picked up this book, you have some understanding of SEO, so I'll keep it simple.

SEO is the science of customizing elements of your web site to achieve the best possible search engine ranking. That's really all there is to search engine optimization. But as simple as it sounds, don't let it fool you. Both internal and external elements of the site affect the way it's ranked in any given search engine, so all of these elements should be taken into consideration. Good SEO can be very difficult to achieve, and great SEO seems pretty well impossible at times.

But why is search engine optimization so important? Think of it this way. If you're standing in a crowd of a few thousand people and someone is looking for you, how will they find you? In a crowd that size, everyone blends together.

Now suppose there is some system that separates groups of people. Maybe if you're a woman you're wearing red and if you're a man you're wearing blue. Now anyone looking for you will have to look through only half of the people in the crowd.

You can further narrow the group of people to be searched by adding additional differentiators until you have a small enough group that a *search query* can be executed and the desired person can be easily found.

Your web site is much like that one person in the huge crowd. In the larger picture your site is nearly invisible, even to the search engines that send crawlers out to catalog the Web. To get your site noticed, even by the crawlers, certain elements must stand out. And that's why you need search engine optimization.

By accident your site will surely land in a search engine. And it's likely to rank within the first few thousand results. That's just not good enough. Being ranked on the ninth or tenth page of search results is tantamount to being invisible. To be noticed, your site should be ranked much higher.

Ideally you want your site to be displayed somewhere on the first three pages of results. Most people won't look beyond the third page, if they get even that far. The fact is, it's the sites that fall on the first page of results that get the most traffic, and traffic is translated into revenue, which is the ultimate goal of search engine optimization.

To achieve a high position in search results, your site must be more than simply recognizable by a search engine crawler. It must satisfy a set of criteria that not only gets the site cataloged, but can also get it cataloged above most (if not all) of the other sites that fall into that category or topic.

Some of the criteria by which a search engine crawler determines the rank your site should have in a set of results include:

- Anchor text
- Site popularity

- Link context
- Topical links
- Title tags
- Keywords
- Site language
- Content
- Site maturity

There are estimated to be at least several hundred other criteria that could also be examined before your site is ranked by a search engine. Some of the criteria listed also have multiple points of view. For example, when looking at link context, a crawler might take into consideration where the link is located on the page, what text surrounds it, and where it leads to or from.

These criteria are also different in importance. For some search engines, links are more important than site maturity, and for others, links have little importance. These weights and measures are constantly changing, so even trying to guess what is most important at any given time is a pointless exercise. Just as you figure it out, the criteria will shift or change completely.

By nature, many of the elements are likely to have some impact on your site ranking, even when you do nothing to improve them. However, without your attention, you're leaving the search ranking of your site to chance. That's like opening a business without putting out a sign. You're sure to get some traffic, but because people don't know you're there, it won't be anything more than the curiosity of passersby.

Setting SEO Goals

Okay, so you understand how important it is to put time into SEO. Now, how exactly do you go about it? One thing you don't do is begin trying to implement SEO strategies without some sort of goal for what you want to accomplish.

One of the greatest failings of many SEO plans, like all technology plans, is the lack of a clearly defined goal. The goal for your SEO plan should be built around your business needs, and it's not something every business requires. For example, if you run a simple blog, SEO might be more expense than it's worth. But if your plans for that blog are to turn it into a brand, then the simplest of SEO strategies might be just what you need to build the traffic that begins to establish your brand.

If you have a larger business, say a web site that sells custom-made silk-flower arrangements, one way to increase your business (some estimate by more than 50 percent) is to invest time, money, and considerable effort into optimizing your site for search. Just don't do it without a goal in mind.

In the case of the silk-flower web site, one goal might be to increase the amount of traffic your web site receives. Another might be to increase your exposure to potential customers outside your geographic region.

Those are both good reasons to implement an SEO plan. One other reason you might consider investing in SEO is to increase your revenues, which you can do by funneling site visitors through a sales transaction while they are visiting your web site. SEO can help with that, too.

So before you even begin to put together an SEO plan, the first thing you need to do is determine what goal you want to achieve with that plan. Be sure it is a well-articulated and specifically defined goal, too. The more specific, the closer you will come to hitting it.

For example, a goal to "increase web site traffic" is far too broad. Of course you want to increase your web site traffic. That's the overarching goal of any SEO plan. However, if you change that goal to "increase the number of visitors who complete a transaction of at least $25," you are much more likely to implement the SEO that will indeed help you reach that goal.

Make sure the goal is specific and attainable. Otherwise, it's very easy to become unfocused with your SEO efforts. In some cases, you can spend all your time chasing SEO and never accomplish anything. Search engines regularly change the criteria for ranking sites. They started doing this when internal, incoming, and external links became a factor in SEO. Suddenly, every webmaster was rushing to add as many additional links as possible, and often those links were completely unrelated to the site. There was a sudden and often meaningless rise in page links. It wasn't long before the linking criteria had to be qualified with additional requirements.

Today, link strategies are quite complex and must abide by a set of rules or your web site could be banned from some search engines for what's called *SEO spam*, or the practice of targeting a specific element or criteria of search engine ranking, with the intention of becoming one of the highest ranked sites on the Web. If an SEO goal has been established, however, you're more likely to have a balanced traffic flow, which will improve your search engine ranking naturally.

In addition to well-focused goals, you should also consider how your SEO goals align with your business goals. Business goals should be the overall theme for everything you do with your web site, and if your SEO goals are not created with the intent of furthering those business goals, you'll find the SEO goals ultimately fail. Be sure that any goal you set for optimizing your site for search is a goal that works well within the parameters that are set by your overall business goals.

Finally, remain flexible at all times. Get a goal, or even a set of goals. And hold tightly to them. Just don't hold so tightly that the goals get in the way of performing great SEO activities. SEO goals and plans, like any others, must be flexible and must grow with your organization. For this reason, it's always a good idea to review your SEO goals and plans periodically — at least every six months, and quarterly is much better.

Creating Your SEO Plan

Once you have a goal or set of goals in mind for your web site, it's time to create your SEO plan. The SEO plan is the document that you'll use to stay on track as you try to implement SEO strategies on your site.

For many people, the thought of implementing SEO on a web site that includes dozens or even hundreds of pages is overwhelming. It doesn't have to be, though.

Prioritizing pages

Look at SEO in small, bite-size pieces. For example, instead of looking at your site as a whole, look at each page on the site. Prioritize those pages, and then plan your SEO around each page's priority. Taking a single page into consideration helps to eliminate the "everything has to happen right now" issue and makes it possible for you to create an SEO plan that will maximize your web site's potential in the minimum amount of time.

Top priority pages should be the ones that your visitors will most naturally gravitate to, such as your home page, or pages that will generate the most in terms of traffic or revenue. When prioritizing pages, you're also creating a roadmap for your marketing efforts. If three of the pages on your site are your top priority, those three will have the lion's share of time, capital, and effort when it comes to SEO and marketing.

Site assessment

After you have prioritized your site, you should assess where you stand and where you need to be with your current SEO efforts. Again, assess each page individually, rather than the site as a whole. In SEO, individual pages are equally important (if not more so) than the entire site. All of your efforts are designed to rank one page above all others in search results. Which page is the most important should be determined by your business needs.

Your SEO assessment should be a document that outlines the current standing of the main SEO elements of each page. It should contain columns for the element of the site you're assessing, the current status of that element, what needs to be improved in that element, and the deadline for improvement. It's also helpful if you have a check box next to each item that can be marked when improvements are completed and a column for follow-up, because SEO is a never-ending process.

The elements that should be considered during an assessment include:

- **Site/page tagging:** The meta tags that are included in the coding of your web site are essential to having that site listed properly in a search engine. Tags to which you should pay specific attention are the title tags and description tags, because these are the most important to a search engine.

- **Page content:** How fresh is your content? How relevant is it? How often is it updated? And how much content is there? Content is still important when it comes to search results. After all, most people are looking for a specific piece of content, whether it's information or a product. If your content is stale, search engines could eventually begin to ignore your site in favor of a site that has fresher content. There are exceptions to this generalization, however. And one exception is if your content is, by nature, very rich but not very dynamic. Because of the usefulness of the content, your site will probably continue to rank well. But it's a difficult case to determine. In most cases, fresh content is better.

- **Site links:** Site links are essential in SEO. Crawlers and spiders look for the links into and out of your site in order to traverse your site and collect data on each URL. However, they also look for those links to be in-context, meaning the link must come from or lead to a site that is relevant to the page that is being indexed. Broken links tend to be a large problem when it comes to search engine ranking, so be sure to check that links are still working during the assessment process.

- **Site map:** Believe it or not, a site map will help your web site be more accurately linked. But this is not the ordinary site map that you include to help users quickly navigate through your site. This site map is an XML-based document, at the root of your HTML, that contains information (URL, last updated, relevance to surrounding pages, and so on) about each of the pages within a site. Using this XML site map will help to ensure that even the deep pages within your site are indexed by search engines. If you don't have a site map, you should create one. If you do have one, make sure it's accurate and up to date.

> **CROSS-REF** You can find an example SEO Assessment worksheet in Appendix D of this book. Use this worksheet to create an accurate assessment of your web site.

Finishing the plan

With the site assessment out of the way, you should have a good idea of what areas need work and what areas are in good shape. Don't assume the areas that don't currently need work will always be perfect, however. That's not how it works. At the least, changes to the pages will require changes to the SEO efforts that you're putting forth; at most they may require that you begin SEO efforts for that page all over again.

You can now take the time to put together all of the information that you've gathered into a cohesive picture of the SEO efforts you should be making. Your SEO plan is more than just a picture of what's there and what's not, however. This is the document that you use to tie everything together: current standing, marketing efforts, capital expenditures, time frames — all of it.

The document should look much like any other plan that you'll create, for instance your business plan. In this plan, you should have an area for background information, marketing information, plans for growing the business, and plans for managing problems that may arise.

An SEO plan is very similar. You'll have your current standings, the goals that you plan to hit, and the marketing efforts that you plan to make for each page (or for the site as a whole). You'll even have the capital expenditures that you plan to encounter as you implement your SEO plan.

You'll also want to include the strategies you plan to use. Those strategies can be efforts such as submitting your site or pages from your site to directories manually and planning the content you'll use to draw search crawlers, or they can be keyword marketing plans or pay-per-click programs you plan to use. Also be sure to include a time line for the testing and implementation of those efforts as well as for regular follow-ups.

Follow-up

Follow-up is also an essential part of your SEO plan. Many people believe they can develop and implement an SEO plan and then just walk away from it. The truth is, however, that SEO is not just a one-time event. It's an ongoing process that requires testing, monitoring, and often re-building.

A good plan for conducting follow-ups is to plan for them quarterly. Some companies will choose to follow up and reassess their SEO bi-annually, but to be truly effective quarterly is much better. One thing to keep in mind, however, is that following up on your SEO efforts too soon is non-productive. In many cases, it takes at least three months to get a clear picture of how successful your efforts are. Conducting an evaluation before that three-month mark could have you chasing after an elusive SEO goal that doesn't really exist. Or worse, it could lead you away from a successful strategy.

Give your plan at least three months but no more than six between checkups. Once you create the habit of re-evaluating your SEO efforts on that time schedule, it will be much less time consuming than you assume.

Understanding Organic SEO

All this talk about planning for SEO is great, but what about *organic SEO*. You don't have to put any efforts into that, do you?

Don't go foolin' yourself. Organic SEO is just as much work as any other type of SEO. It's just a little different method of creating a site optimized for search ranking, without having to implement any new technologies or spend a lot of time submitting your site to different primary and secondary search engines. And really, the distinction here is a very general one. Only SEO purists consider "real SEO" as being strictly organic — meaning you use no fee-based services whatever. Most people are happy with "just plain SEO," which usually means a combination of organic and fee-based. It's best if you just think of SEO as just SEO; then you don't have to worry about distinctions that aren't really important in optimizing your web site.

The definitions of organic SEO vary a little, depending on whom you talk to. Some SEO experts think it's all about optimizing the content of your web site to catch the attention of the crawlers and spiders that index sites. Others think it's the number of quality links you can generate on your site. But in truth, organic SEO is a combination of those and other elements, such as site tagging, that will naturally place your web site in search engine rankings. How high in those rankings depends on how well you design your site.

But before you go thinking that organic SEO is just the solution you've been looking for, take a step back. What organic SEO is not is an easy way to land in a search engine. Basically, if you put a web site online and spend a little time getting it ready for the world to see, you will have probably achieved some measure of organic SEO without really trying.

That's because your site will probably end up listed in some search engine somewhere, without too much time and effort from you. Elements that naturally occur on a web site — like the title of the site, the URL, included web links, and even some of the content — will probably land you in a search engine (unless those elements are *black-hat SEO* efforts, in which case the engine could permanently exclude you). The question is where in the results will you land? Without attention from you, that might not be as high in the rankings as you would like.

Organic SEO maximizes those naturally occurring elements, building upon each element to create a site that will naturally fall near the top of the *search engine results pages (SERPs)*. One of the most attractive features of organic SEO is that the methods used to achieve high SERPs rankings are of no cost — other than the time it takes to implement these ideas.

However, there is a trade-off. Achieving organic SEO can take anywhere from three to six months. For web site owners impatient to see results from their SEO efforts, this can seem like an eternity. But it's worth the extra time if the budget is an issue.

Achieving Organic SEO

Achieving organic SEO can take time, but it also takes targeting the right elements of your web site. You can spend a lot of time tweaking aspects of your site, only to find that it still ranks below the third page of search results. If your attention is focused on the right elements, however, you'll find that organic SEO can be a fairly effective method of achieving a higher search engine ranking.

Make no mistake, however; organic SEO alone is not as effective as organic SEO combined with some form of *pay-per-click* or keyword advertising program. Though organic SEO is good, adding the extra, more costly programs can be what you need to push your site right to the top of the SERPs.

A good first step in search engine optimization is to ensure that the organic elements of your site are as optimized as possible. Although these elements are covered in detail in future chapters, here is a look at some of the basics.

Web-site content

Web-site content is one of the most highly debated elements in search engine optimization, mostly because many rather unethical SEO users have turned to black-hat SEO techniques, such as *keyword stuffing* to try to artificially improve search engine ranking. Despite these less-than-honest approaches to search engine optimization, however, web-site content is still an important part of any web-site optimization strategy.

The content on your site is the main draw for visitors. Whether your site sells products or simply provides information about services, what brings visitors to your site is the words on the page. Product descriptions, articles, blog entries, and even advertisements are all scanned by spiders and crawlers as they work to index the Web.

One strategy of these crawlers and spiders is to examine just how the content of your page works with all of the other elements (like links and meta tags) that are examined. To rank high in a selection of search results, your content must be relevant to those other elements.

Some search engines will de-list your page or lower your page rank if the content of your site is not unique. Especially since the advent of blogs, search engines now are examining how frequently the content on pages is updated and looking for content that appears only on your web site. This doesn't mean you can't have static content on your page. For e-commerce sites, the product descriptions may rarely change.

But including other elements on the page, like reviews or product updates, will satisfy a crawler's requirement that content change regularly. Content is an important part of your site and the ranking of your site in search engine results. To achieve organic SEO, take the time to develop a content plan that not only outlines what should be included on each page of your site, but also how often that content will be updated, and who will do the updates.

One other element you might want to consider when looking at your page content as part of SEO is the keywords that you plan to use. Ideally, your chosen words should appear on the page several times. But again, this is a balancing act that might take some time to accomplish.

CROSS-REF Chapter 4 contains additional information about keywords and how to use them to improve your search engine ranking.

Keywords are part of your site content, and as such require special attention. In fact, the selection of the right keywords is a bit of an art form that takes some time to master. For example, if your web site is dedicated to selling products for show dogs, you might assume that "show dogs" would be a perfect keyword. You might be wrong. Selecting the right keywords requires a good understanding of your audience and what they might be looking for when they want to find your web site. People looking for products for show dogs could search for "grooming products," "pedigree training," or just "dog supplies." It could even be something entirely different, like the name of a product that was featured at the most recent dog show.

Learning which keyword will be most effective for your site will require that you study your audience, but it also requires some trial and error. Try using different keywords each quarter to learn which ones work the best.

It's also advised that you use a tracking program such as *Google Analytics* to monitor your web site traffic and to track the keywords that most often lead users to your site.

Google Analytics

Google Analytics is a free web site statistics application that you can use to track your web site traffic. You can access Google Analytics by going to `http://www.google.com/analytics`. You are required to have a Google user name to access the program.

If you do not have a Google user name, you can create one when you sign up for the application. It's simple. Provide your e-mail address and a password, type the verification word from the graphic provided, and then read the Terms of Service and click "I accept. Create my account."

Once you've created your user name and password, accessing the tracking capabilities of Google is no problem. You'll need to copy a snippet of text that Google provides into the coding of your web site. Once you've added the code to your site it will take a few days for Google to gather enough information to provide reports about your site, and as much as two months to gather enough data to give you real insight into your site. But once there is enough data, you'll have access to the keywords that most often lead visitors to your site.

Google Analytics can also be combined with Google's AdWords program to provide paid keyword tracking and information. To learn more about Google Analytics, check out the book *Google Analytics 2.0* by Mary Tyler and Jerri Ledford (Wiley, Aug 2007, ISBN: 978-0470175019). It should be noted that Google Analytics doesn't track spiders and crawlers at this time, however, so there may be some limitations to its SEO functionality. Still, if you need a (free) tool to help you examine some of the metrics surrounding your SEO efforts, Google Analytics is a good starting point.

Internal and external links

Another element of organic SEO that's just as important as your web-site content is the links on your pages. Links can be incoming, outgoing, or internal. And where those links lead or come from is as important as the context in which the links are provided.

When links first became a criteria by which crawlers ranked web sites, many black-hat SEO users rushed to create *link farms*. These were pages full of nothing but web links, some of which led to relevant information and some of which led to sites in no way related to the topic of the web site. It didn't take long for search engine designers and programmers to catch on to these shady practices and change the way that crawlers use links to rank sites.

Today, links must usually be related to the content of the page, and they must link to something relevant to that content. In other words, if your links don't go to or lead in from pages that match the keywords that you're using, they will be of little value to you.

The balance of links that are included on your page is also relevant. Too many links and your site could be labeled as a link farm. Too few and you'll lose out to sites that have more and better-targeted links.

Your best option when including links on your web site is to link to the pages you know for sure are relevant to your site content. Don't include a link unless you're sure it will have value to your users, and then take the time to pursue links into your site from them as well.

One other type of link, the *internal link*, is also important. This is a navigational link that leads users from one page to another on your site. The navigation of your site (which is what these links are, essentially) should be intuitive, and natural in progression. And you should also include a site map.

CROSS-REF You can find more information about links and linking in Chapter 11.

Your site map not only makes it easier for crawlers to index every page of your site, but it also makes it easier for users to find their way around in it. Ideally, users will never have to rely on the site map; however, it's nice for it to be there in the event that they either need it or simply want to click directly to the page they're seeking.

How you design your site map is a matter of preference. Some organizations create site maps that only include the top two levels of pages. Others include ones that go three levels down or deeper. Whatever level of depth you think will be required by the majority of users is how deep your site map should go. One thing to keep in mind, however, is that site maps can become just as overwhelming as any other navigational structure if there are hundreds of pages in your site.

Design your site map so it's easy to decipher and will take users to the pages they are seeking without difficulty and confusion.

User experience

User experience is a little harder to quantify than other site-ranking elements. It's easy to say that users will find your site simple to use, that they will find the information or products that they're seeking, or that they will have reason to return to your site. But in practice, that's a little more difficult to achieve.

So, how in the world can a site gain search engine ranking by user experience? It's fairly simple really. Search engines today are smarter than they have ever been. They may not be able to make you a grilled cheese sandwich, but they can certainly keep track of what results users click when they run a search. Those result selections are essential to adding to the organic ranking of your site.

Here's a scenario. Say you search for something like health-insurance information. When the search results come up, how are you going to choose which results to look at? Most users read the small descriptive lines that are included with the search engine ranking and select from those.

In most cases, the sites that are visited are those sites that are highest in the rankings. But search engines also monitor which sites are actually clicked on, so let's say you search through the results and click a link on the fifth page. And suppose several other people do so as well.

That link on the fifth page is going to show more traffic than links that are higher in the results, so smart search engines will move that page higher in the rankings. It may not jump right up to the number one position, but it's entirely possible for the site to move from the fifth page of rankings to the second or third. This is part of the equation used when user experience is taken into consideration.

Another part of that experience might be how quickly the user jumps back to the search page. Maybe when you click that link on the fifth page, you can tell when you hit the site that it's not the page you were looking for (or doesn't contain the information or product that you were looking for). You click the back button, and you're taken back to the page of search results.

This is called *bounce*, and the rate at which users bounce off your site is an indicator of the usability of the site in terms of how relevant it is to what users are searching for. This relates directly to the keywords the user searched for, which relates directly to how your site matches those keywords. To maximize the usability of your site, make sure the keywords you choose and the description of your page are as accurate as possible.

It may take some time for you to learn how to make all of these elements work together, especially when it comes to elements like descriptions and keywords. Be patient, and be willing to experiment with different combinations of words or descriptions until you hit on the ones that combine to send your site rank closer to the top search results. Just remember, it's an art more than a science, and it takes time (usually two to three months) to see the most accurate results.

Site interactivity

When the Internet first came into being, web sites were all about disclosing information. The only interaction between a web site and a user was the reading the user did while on the site. Today, reading is still important. Users search for web sites to learn more about products, services, or topics. However, there's much more to web sites today than just text on a screen.

We now live in the Interactive Age. Most of us want to interact with the web sites we're visiting. That interaction might take the form of a poll, the ability to comment on a blog post, the downloading of a file, or even a game that relates to the site content. No matter what the type of interaction, users expect it, and search crawlers look for it.

Site interactivity is essential to achieving a high SEO ranking. Sure, you can garner a high ranking without interaction, bit it won't happen nearly as fast, and the ranking will likely be lower than that of a site that has some form of interaction with the user.

Why is interaction so important? Simple. If you can influence a user to interact with your site, you have more of a chance of gaining a *goal conversion*. Goal conversions are the completion of some form of activity designed to gather further information about your user. A goal conversion can be something as simple as enticing users to sign up for a newsletter, or it can be more specific, like persuading them to make purchases.

No matter what goal conversion you're seeking, the way to achieve it is through interactivity. And the more frequently the user interacts with your site, the more likely it is that this person will reach that goal conversion page that you're monitoring so closely.

Goal conversion is the purpose of many web sites. For example, the target goal conversion for an e-commerce web site might be for the user to make a $25 purchase. If you can entice a user to purchase from your site — that is, meet the goal conversion — you have more of a chance of getting them back to your site for a future purchase, to find additional information, or simply to interact with your site some more.

All of these are important aspects of your web site's traffic patterns. And search engines will look for elements of interactivity to judge the value of your site to users. One goal of search engines is to provide value to users. Those users turn to the search engine for help in finding something specific.

Just as it's important for your site to land high in the search results, it's important for the search engine to provide the information that a user seeks within the first page or two. Making the user happy is one way search companies make their money. Another way is through the dollars that advertisers will pay to have their pages ranked high in the search results or their advertisements shown according to the keywords for which the user was searching.

In other words, search engine optimization is two-way street. It's also a business, and search engine companies are always trying to find ways to improve their business. For that reason, these elements, and many others, are an essential part of search engine optimization.

Organic SEO is certainly not easy to achieve. One way to achieve it is to have a solid SEO plan that outlines where you are and what needs to be added to your site design or content to make it more visible to users. It also takes a lot of time and effort to create and implement the right SEO plan. However, if you use your SEO plan as a stepping stone, even for organic SEO, you'll stay focused and eventually, you'll achieve the search engine ranking that you've been working toward.

Part II

SEO Strategies

SEO is hard work. It takes much effort to optimize just the right elements of your web site so search engines will not only find you, but will also index your site so that it appears high in search query results. And all of that effort must be attended to by you. There are currently no tools that will put all of the elements of SEO in place for you.

Instead, you have to build your web site with SEO in mind, choose all the right keywords, and use them in the right places and balance on your site, determine if pay-per-click and paid-inclusion programs are for you, use the right meta tags in the right places, create great content, and add all the right links. Sounds like a lot of work, doesn't it?

It is. But don't let the amount of work overwhelm you. Consistent effort and the strategies included in this part of the book will have you working toward your SEO goals in no time. Each of the chapters in this section contains an explanation of how these elements affect SEO, and how you can create and implement strategies to help you leverage that element to reach your SEO goals.

Chapter 3

Building Your Site for SEO

S earch engine optimization is a collection of strategies that improve the level at which your web site is ranked in the results returned when a user searches for a key word or phrase.

By now, that's a definition you should be pretty familiar with. What you probably don't know (yet) is how to achieve SEO. You can't do it all at once. Instead, SEO has to happen in stages. If you try to implement too many strategies at one time, two things are going to happen.

First, you won't be able to tell which of your efforts are successful. Implementing one strategy at a time makes it possible for you to pinpoint which strategies are working and which are not.

Second, when you try to implement too many strategies at one time, your efforts — even the successful ones — could be lost in the shuffle. It's like having too many children running around the house on the weekend. If you're not paying complete attention to all of them (and that's virtually impossible), at least one is bound to get into something.

SEO is most successful when you concentrate on one effort at a time. A great place to start concentrating is on the way your site is built. One of the first things that attracts a search engine crawler is the actual design of your site. Tags, links, navigational structure, and content are just a few of the elements that catch crawlers' attention.

Before You Build Your Site

One of the most common misconceptions about SEO is that it should be implemented after a web site has been built. It can be, but it's much harder. A better option is to consider SEO even before you begin to build your web site, if that's at all possible. It may not be. But if that's the case, you can still implement SEO strategies in the design of your site; it will just require a lot more work than building it in at the beginning.

Know your target

Before you even start contemplating how to build your web site, you should know in what types of search engines it's most important for your site to be ranked. Search engines are divided into several types, beyond the primary, secondary, and targeted search engines that you learned about in Chapter 2. In addition, search engine types are determined by how information is entered into the index or catalog that's used to return search results. The three types of search engines are:

- **Crawler-based engines:** To this point, the search engines discussed fall largely into this category. A crawler-based search engine (like Google) uses an automated software agent (called a crawler) to visit, read, and index web sites. All the information collected by the crawler is returned to a central repository. This is called indexing. It is from this index that search engine results are pulled. Crawler-based search engines revisit web pages periodically in a time frame determined by the search engine administrator.

- **Human-powered engines:** Human-powered search engines rely on people to submit the information that is indexed and later returned as search results. Sometimes, human-powered search engines are called directories. Yahoo! is a good example of what, at one time, was a human-powered search engine. Yahoo! started as a favorites list belonging to two people who needed an easier way to share their favorite web site. Over time, Yahoo! took on a life of its own. It's no longer completely human-controlled. A newer search engine called Mahalo (www.mahalo.com) is entirely human-powered, however, and it's creating a buzz on the Web.

- **Hybrid engine:** A hybrid search engine is not entirely populated by a web crawler, nor entirely by human submission. A hybrid is a combination of the two. In a hybrid engine, people can manually submit their web sites for inclusion in search results, but there is also a web crawler that monitors the Web for sites to include. Most search engines today fall into the hybrid category to at least some degree. Although many are mostly populated by crawlers, others have some method by which people can enter their web site information.

It's important to understand these distinctions, because how your site ends up indexed by a search engine may have some bearing on when it's indexed. For example, fully automated search engines that use web crawlers might index your site weeks (or even months) before a human-powered search engine. The reason is simple. The web crawler is an automated application. The human-powered search engine may actually require that all entries be reviewed for accuracy before a site is included in search results.

In all cases, the accuracy of search engine results will vary according to the search query that is used. For example, entries in a human-powered search engine might be more technically accurate, but the search query that is used will determine if the desired results are returned.

Page elements

Another facet of SEO to consider before you build your web site is the elements needed to ensure that your site is properly indexed by a search engine. Each search engine places differing importance on different page elements. For example, Google is a very keyword-driven search engine; however, it also looks at site popularity and at the tags and links on any given page.

How well your site performs in a search engine is determined by how the elements of your page meet the engine's search criteria. The main criteria that every search engine looks for are the site text (meaning keywords), tags — both HTML and meta tags — site links, and the site popularity.

Text

Text is one of the most important elements of any web site. Of particular importance are the keywords within the text on a page, where those keywords appear, and how often they appear. This is why keyword marketing has become such a large industry in a relatively short time. Your keywords make all the difference when a search engine indexes your site and then serves it up in search results.

Keywords must match the words and phrases that potential visitors will use when searching for your site (or for the topic or product that's listed on your site). To ensure that your keywords are effective, you'll need to spend some time learning which keywords work best for your site. That means doing keyword research (which you learn more about in Chapter 5) and testing the keywords that you do select to see how effective they really are.

Tags

In search engine optimization, two kinds of tags are important on your web site: meta tags and HTML tags. Technically, meta tags *are* HTML tags, they just appear in very specific places. The two most important meta tags are the keyword tag and the description tag.

The keyword tag occurs at the point where you list the keywords that apply to your web site. A keyword tag on a search engine optimization page might look something like this:

```
<meta name="keywords" content="SEO, search engine optimization, page rank">
```

The description tag gives a short description of your page. Such a tag for the search engine optimization page might look like this:

```
<meta name="description" content="The ultimate guide to search engine optimization!">
```

Not all search engines take meta tags into consideration. For that reason, you site should use both meta tags and other HTML tags. Some of the other HTML tags that you should include on your web site are the title tag, the top (or H1) heading tags, and the anchor tags.

The title tag is the tag that's used in the title of your web site. This tag will appear like this:

```
<Title>Your Title Here</Title>
```

Once you've tagged your site with a title tag, when a user pulls the site up, the title that you entered will appear at the very top of the page if the user is using an Internet Explorer browser (IE) earlier than IE7, as shown in Figure 3-1. In IE7 and the Firefox browser, the title will appear on the browser tab, shown in Figures 3-2 and 3-3.

High-level headings (H1s) are also important when a crawler examines your web site. Your keywords should appear in your H1 headings, and in the HTML tags you use to create those headings. An H1 tag might look like this:

```
<h1>High-Level Heading</h1>
```

Anchor tags are used to create links to other pages. An anchor tag can point users to another web page, a file on the Web, or even an image or sound file. You're probably most familiar with the anchor tags used to create links to other web sites. Here's what an anchor tag might look like:

```
<a href="http://www.targetwebsite.com/">Text for link</a>
```

FIGURE 3-1

The reverse bar in Internet Explorer versions below IE7 will show the title that you've entered in the HTML title tag.

Title-tag display

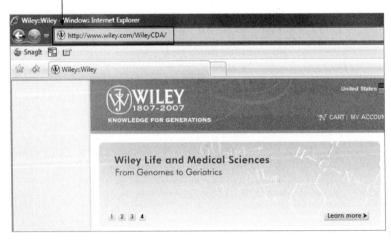

FIGURE 3-2

In IE 7 browsers, the HTML title tag you entered will appear on the browser tab.

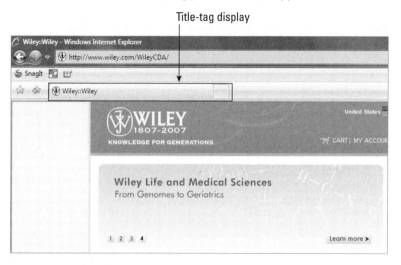

FIGURE 3-3

The Firefox browser shows the title tag in the browser tabs.

Figure 3-4 illustrates how that link might appear to users as they navigate a web page.

A link tag is combined with the anchor tag above. That link can be text-based, and that text is where search engine optimization comes into play. How many times have you seen a web site that includes text with underlined words, all of which are related to the topic covered on the site? Those links are tagged for optimization. When a search engine crawler examines your web pages, it will look for links like the one in the illustration.

FIGURE 3-4

The anchor tag is used to create links to other pages, files, or images on the Web.

Anchor tags appear as links to users.

Places you never thought you would visit

3/12/2007 06:56:00 AM
Posted by James Leape, Director General, WWF International

Not long ago, after tending to official meetings in Yaounde, Cameroon, I had an opportunity to drive seven hours southwest of the capital to one of WWF's project sites the Campo-Ma'an National Park—which you can now visit on Google Earth.

Created in 2000, the Campo-Ma'an park is a nature lover's paradise with 80 species of mammals, including endangered elephants, gorillas and

Links

To be of value, the links on your web pages must be related to the content of the page, and they must be active links to real web sites. *Broken links* can lower your search engine ranking. Links have always been an important factor in how web sites rank on the Web, but the abuse of linking that we see so often today started just a few years ago, about the time that Google became the big name in search.

When links became a ranking criterion, many black-hat SEOs began building *link farms*, which are sites that are nothing more than pages full of links designed to gain high search engine rankings.

It didn't take long for search engine administrators to figure out this sneaky optimization trick, so they changed the criteria by which links are ranked. Now link farms are fairly ineffective, but links on your web site are still important. Links show an interactivity with the community (other sites on the Web), which points to the legitimacy of your web site. Links aren't the only, or even the highest, ranking criteria, but they are important all the same.

Popularity

One other consideration, even before you build your site, is the site's popularity. Many search engines include a criterion for the number of times users click on web sites that are returned in search results. The more often the site is selected from the search results, the higher in the ranking it climbs.

For you, that means you should begin building the popularity of your site, even before it is built. Begin building buzz about the site through advertisements, info-torials, and even newsletter or other e-mail announcements. Then redouble those efforts as soon as the site goes live to the public.

It's a riddle to which there is no easy answer. You optimize your web site for search engines in order to build popularity, but your ranking in the search engine can be determined by how popular your site is. There is no magic formula that helps you solve the riddle. It requires time and consistent effort to draw visitors to your site.

Other criteria to consider

In addition to the four main elements you should plan to include on your site, there are a few others. For example, the body text on your web site will be examined by the crawler that indexes your site. Body text should contain enough keywords to gain the attention of the crawler, but not so many that it seems the site is being "stuffed' with such words.

Alternative tags for pictures and links are also important. These are the tags that might appear as a brief description of a picture or graphic on a web site that fails to display properly. The alternative tags — called alt tags — display a text description of the graphic or picture, so that even if the actual image doesn't appear, there's some explanation of what should be there. Alt tags are a good place to include additional keywords.

Understanding Web-Site Optimization

Web-site optimization is all about creating a site that is discoverable by search engines and search directories. It sound simple enough, but there are many aspects of site optimization to consider, and not all of them are about the keywords, links, or HTML tagging of your site.

Does hosting matter?

That question comes up frequently when a company or individual is designing a web site. Does it matter who hosts your site? The answer is no, but that's not to say that domain hosting is unimportant. Elements of the hosting have a major impact on how your site ranks in search results.

One of the biggest issues that you'll face with domain hosting is the location of your hosting company. If you're in the United States and you purchase a domain that is hosted on a server in England, your search engine rankings will suffer. Geographically, search engine crawlers will read your site as being contradictory to your location. Because many search engines serve up results with some element of geographical location included, this contradiction could be enough to affect your ranking.

The length of time for which you register your domain name could also affect your search engine ranking. Many hackers use *throw away domains*, or domain names that are registered for no more than a year, because they usually don't even get to use the domain for a full year before they are shut down. For this reason some search engines have implemented ranking criteria that give priority to domains registered for longer periods. A longer registration also shows a commitment to maintaining the web site.

Domain-naming tips

The question of what to name a web site is always a big one. When selecting a name, most people think in terms of their business name, personal name, or a word or phrase that has meaning for them. What they don't think about is how that name will work for the site's SEO. Does the name have anything at all to do with the site, or is it completely unrelated?

Have you ever wondered why a company might be willing to pay millions of dollars for a domain name? The domain name `business.com` was purchased for $7.5 million in 1999, and was recently thought to be valued at more than $300 million. `Casino.com` went for $5.5 million and `worldwideweb.com` sold for $3.5 million. What's so important about a name?

Where SEO is concerned, the name of your web site is as important as many of the other SEO elements that you concentrate on. Try this test. Use your favorite search engine to search for a topic, perhaps "asphalt-paving business." When your search results are returned, look at the top five results. Most of the time, a web site containing those words will be returned in those top five results, and it will often be in the number one slot.

So, if your company name is ABC Company, but your business is selling nutmeg graters, consider purchasing the domain name NutmegGraters.com, instead of ABC Company.com — ABC Company may not get you in the top of search rankings, but the very specific nature of your product probably will. And both the content of your site and your domain name will attract crawlers in the way you want. Using a domain name containing a keyword from your content usually improves your site ranking.

A few more things that you should keep in mind when you're determining your domain name include:

- Keep the name as short as possible. Too many characters in a name mean increased potential for misspellings. It also means that your site address will be much harder for users to remember unless it's something really startling.

- Avoid dashes, underscores, and other meaningless characters. If the domain name that you're looking for is taken, don't just add a random piece of punctuation or numerology to the name to "get close." Close doesn't count here. Instead, try to find another word that's relevant, and possibly included in the list of keywords you'll be using. For example, instead of purchasing `www.yourwebsite2.com`, try to find something like `www.yoursitesubject.com`.

- Opt for a .com name whenever possible. There are lots of domain extensions to choose from: info, biz, us, tv, names, jobs. However, if the .com version of your chosen domain name is available, that's always the best choice. Users tend to think in terms of .com, and any other extension will be hard for them to remember. Com names also tend to receive higher rankings in search engines than web sites using other extensions. So if your competition has `www.yoursite.com` and you choose to use `www.yoursite.biz`, chances are the competition will rank higher in search results than you.

Again, it's important to realize that domain naming is only one facet of SEO strategy. It won't make or break your SEO, but it can have some effect. So take the time to think about the name you plan to register for your site. If you can use a name that not only reaches your audience but also lands you a little higher in search results, then by all means purchase it. But if no name really seems to work in the SEO strategy for your site, don't get discouraged. You can make up for any domain-naming issues by implementing solid keyword strategies, tagging strategies, and other elements of SEO.

Understanding usability

Usability. It means different things to different web site designers. It's also been at the top of every user's requirements list since the Web became part of daily life. When users click through to your web site from a search results page, they want the site to work for them. That means they want to be able to find what they're looking for, to navigate from place to place, and to be able to load pages quickly, without any difficulties.

Web-site users are impatient. They don't like to wait for pages to load, they don't want to deal with *Flash* graphics or *JavaScript*, and they don't want to be lost. These are all elements of usability — how the user navigates through and uses your web site. And yes, usability has an impact on SEO. Especially from the perspective of your site links and loading times.

When a search engine crawler comes to your site, it crawls through the site, looking at keywords, links, contextual clues, meta and HTML tags, and a whole host of other elements. The crawler will move from page to page, indexing what it finds for inclusion in search results. But if that crawler reaches the first page and can't get past the fancy Flash you've created, or if it gets into the site and finds links that don't work or that lead to unexpected locations, it will recognize this and make note of it in the indexed site data. That can damage your search engine rankings.

Navigation knowledge

When you consider web-site navigation, there are two types: *internal navigation* and *external navigation*. Internal navigation involves the links that move users from one page to another on your site. External navigation refers to links that take users away from your page. For your navigation to be SEO-friendly, you have to use both types of navigation carefully.

Look at a number of different high-ranking web sites. How is the navigation of those sites designed? In most cases, you'll find that the top sites have a left-hand navigation bar that's often text-based, and some have a button-based navigation bar across the top of the page. Few have just buttons down the left side, and all of them have text links somewhere in the landing page.

The navigation for many sites looks the same, because this plan works. Having a text-based navigation bar on the left works for SEO because it allows you to use anchor tags with the keywords you're using for the site. It also allows crawlers to move from one page to another with ease.

Buttons are harder for crawlers to navigate, and depending on the code in which those buttons are designed, they might be completely invisible to the crawler. That's why many companies that put button-based links at the top of the page also usually include a text-based navigation bar on the left. The crawler can still move from page to page, but the user is happy with the design of the site.

The other element you see on nearly every page is text-based links within the content of the page. Again, those links are usually created with anchor tags that include the keywords the site is using to build site ranking. This is an effective way to gain site ranking. The crawler comes into the site, examines the linking system, examines the content of the page, compares these items, and finds that the links are relevant to the content, which is relevant to the keywords. That's how your ranking is determined. Every element works together.

Take the time to design a navigational structure that's not only comfortable for your users, but is also crawler-friendly. If it can't always be perfect for the crawlers, make sure it's perfect for users. Again, SEO is influenced by many different things, but return visits from users are the ultimate goal. This may mean that you have to test your site structure and navigation with a user group and change it a few times before you find a method that works both for returning users and for the crawlers that help to bring you new users. Do those tests. That's the only way you'll learn what works.

Usability considerations

It's not always possible to please both your site users and the crawlers that determine your page ranking. It is possible, however, to work around problems. Of course, the needs of users come first because once you get them to your site you want them to come back. On the Internet, it's extremely easy for users to surf away from your site and never look back. And returning visits can make or break your site.

But the catch is that in order to build returning visitors, you have to build new visitors, which is the purpose of SEO. That means you need search engines to take notice of your site.

When it seems that users' preferences are contrary to crawlers' preferences, there is a solution. It's a *site map*. And there are two types of which you should be aware. A basic site map is an overview of the navigational structure of your web site. It's usually text-based, and it's nothing more than an overview that includes links to all of the pages in your web site. Crawlers love site maps. You should, too.

A site map allows you to outline the navigational structure of your web site, down to the second or third level of depth, using text-based links that should include anchors and keywords. An example of a site map for the Work.com web site is shown in Figure 3-5.

When a site map exists on your web page, a search engine crawler can locate the map and then crawl all of the pages that are linked from it. All of those pages are then included in the search engine index and will appear on search engine results pages. Where they appear on those SERPs is determined by how well the SEO is done for each individual page.

A second type of site map, the *XML site map*, is different from what you think of as a site map in both form and function. An XML site map is a file that lists all of the URLs for a web site. This file is usually not seen by site visitors, only by the crawlers that index your site. There are more specifics on XML site maps in Chapter 16.

FIGURE 3-5

A site map allows you to include links to all of your pages, two to three levels deep, that include keywords and anchor tags.

Components of an SEO-Friendly Page

Building an SEO-friendly web site doesn't happen by accident. It requires an understanding of what elements search engines examine and how those elements affect your ranking. It also requires including as many of those elements as possible on your site. It does little good to have all the right meta tags in place if you have no content and no links on your page.

It's easy to get caught up in the details of SEO and forget the simplest web-design principles — principles that play a large part in your search engine rankings. Having all the right keywords in the right places in your tags and titles won't do you much good if the content on your page is non-existent or completely unreachable by a search engine crawler.

Understanding entry and exit pages

Entry and exit pages are the first and last pages that a user sees of your web site. It's important to understand that an entry page isn't necessarily the home page on your web site. It can be any other page where a user lands, either by clicking through search engine results, by clicking a link from another web site or a piece of marketing material, or by bookmarking or typing directly into the address bar of a browser.

Entry pages are important in SEO, because they are the first page users see as they come onto the web site. The typical web site is actually several small connected sites. Your company web site might contain hubs, or central points, for several different topics. Say you're a pet store. Then you'll have hubs within your sites for dogs, cats, birds, fish, and maybe exotic animals. Each hub will have a main page — which will likely be your entry page for that section — and several additional pages leading from that central page to other pages containing relevant content, products, or information about specific topics.

Understanding which of your pages are likely entry pages helps you to optimize those pages for search engine crawlers. Using the pet-store example, if your home page and all the hub pages are properly SEO'ed, you potentially could be ranked at or near the top of five different sets of search results. When you add additional entry pages deeper in your web site structure (that is, a dog-training section to the hub for dogs), you've increased the number of times you can potentially end up at the top of search engine rankings.

Because entry pages are important in the structure of your web site, you want to monitor those pages using a web-site analytics program to ensure they are working the way you expect them to work. A good analytics program, like Google Analytics, will show you your top entry and exit pages.

Exit pages are those from which users leave your site, either by clicking through an exiting link, selecting a bookmark, or typing a different web address into their browser address bar. But why are exit pages important? They have two purposes; the first is to drive users from their entry pages to a desired exit page. This is called the *path* that users travel through your site. A typical path might look something like this:

```
SERP ➪ Home ➪ Women's Clothing ➪ Product Pages ➪ Shopping Cart ➪
Checkout ➪ Receipt
```

In this example, Home is the entry page and Receipt is the exit page. By looking at this navigational path, you can tell how users travel through your page and where they fall off the page. But there's an added benefit to understanding the navigational path of your users. When you know how users travel through your site, you can leave what's called a *bread-crumb trail* for them. That's a navigational indicator on the web site that allows them to quickly see where they are on your site, as shown in Figure 3-6. This is the navigation path shown on the Wal-Mart web site. You can quickly see where in the navigational structure of the site you're located.

The bread-crumb trail not only helps users return to a previous page in the navigational path; it also makes it easier for a web crawler to fully examine your site. Because crawlers follow every link on your page, this is an internal link structure that leads crawlers to individual pages that you want to have included in search engine results.

Choosing an Analytics Program

An important element in any SEO plan is *analytics* — the method by which you monitor the effectiveness of your web site. Analytics are the metrics that show you how pages, links, keywords, and other elements of your web site are performing. If your web host hasn't provided you with an analytics program, find one. Not having an analytics program is like walking around in the dark, hoping you won't bump into a wall.

Many web-site owners shy away from analytics packages because they appear to be complicated as well as expensive. However, they don't always have to be. You can find a good analytics program that's not only easy to use but is also inexpensive or even free. But use caution about making ease and low cost the deciding factors when selecting an analytics program.

The program will give you the power to see and control how your web site performs against your goals and expectations. You want it to show you everything you need to know, so here are some considerations when you're evaluating analytics programs:

- What reports are included in the tools you're examining, and how will you use those reports?

- How do you gather the information used to create the metrics you need?

- How often are your reports updated?

- How much training is necessary to understand your application and the reports provided?

- Do you get software installation or is the product provided strictly as a web-based service?

- What is the *total cost of ownership*?

- What types of support are available?

- What is the typical contract length?

Many analytics programs are available to you. Google Analytics, AW Stats, JayFlowers, ClickTracks, and dozens of others all offer something different at a different price tag. If "free" is what you can afford, don't assume you'll get a terrible package. Google Analytics is one of the free packages available; it's an excellent program and is based on what used to be the Urchin Analytics package (which was quite costly). Other programs cost anywhere from $30 to $300 a month, depending on the capabilities you're purchasing.

The cost is not the most important factor, however. Ultimately, your consideration should be how the analytics package can help you improve your business.

FIGURE 3-6

The navigational path can be shown on each web page in the path to help users understand where on the site they're located.

Navigation path

Using powerful titles

Page titles are one of the most important elements of site optimization. When a crawler examines your site, the first elements it looks at are the page titles. And when your site is ranked in search results, page titles are again one of the top elements considered. So when you create your web site, you need to have great page titles.

There are several considerations when coming up with your page titles. Here are some of the key factors to consider:

■ Unless you're Microsoft, don't use your company name in the page title. A better choice is to use a descriptive keyword or phrase that tells users exactly what's on the page. This helps ensure that your search engine rankings are accurate.

■ Try to keep page titles to less than 50 characters, including spaces. Some search engines will index only up to 50 characters; others might index as many as 150. However, maintaining shorter page titles forces you to be precise in the titles that you choose and ensures that your page title will never be cut off in the search results.

TIP The World Wide Web Consortium (W3C) has determined that the outside length of a page title should be no more than 64 characters. Search engines will vary in the size of title that's indexed. Using 64 characters or less is an accepted practice, however, that still leaves your page titles cut off in search engines that only index up to 40 or 50 characters. For this reason, staying at or below the 40-character length is a smarter strategy within your SEO efforts.

- Don't repeat keywords in your title tags. Repetition can occasionally come across as spam when a crawler is examining your site, so avoid repeating keywords in your title if possible, and never duplicate words just to gain a crawler's attention. It could well get your site excluded from search engine listings.

- Consider adding special characters at the beginning and end of your title to improve noticeability. Parentheses (()), arrows (<<>>), asterisks (****), and special symbols like ££££ can help draw a user's attention to your page title. These special characters and symbols don't usually add to or distract from your SEO efforts, but they do serve to call attention to your site title.

- Include a call to action in your title. There's an adage that goes something like, "You'll never sell a thing if you don't ask for the sale." That's one thing that doesn't change with the Web. Even on the Internet, if you want your users to do something you have to ask them to.

All your page titles should be indicated with the title tag when coding your web site. The title tag isn't difficult to use. Here's an example of such a tag:

```
<title>A Descriptive Web Site Title</title>
```

If your page titles aren't tagged properly, you might as well not be using those titles, so take the time to ensure that your page titles are short, descriptive, and tagged into your web-site code. By using title tags, you're increasing the possibility that your web site will be ranked high within search engine results.

Creating great content

Web-site content is another element of an SEO-friendly site that you should spend plenty of time contemplating and completing. Fortunately, there are some ways to create web-site content that will make search crawlers love you.

Great content starts with the right keywords and phrases. Select no more than three keywords or phrases to include in the content on any one of your web pages. But why only three? Wouldn't more keywords and phrases ensure that search engines take notice of your site?

When you use too many keywords in your content, you face two problems. The first is that the effectiveness of your keywords will be reduced by the number of different ones you're using. Choose two or three for each page of your site and stick with those.

The other problem you face is being delisted or ignored because a search engine sees your SEO efforts as *keyword stuffing*. It's a serious problem, and search engine crawlers will exclude your site or pages from indexes if there are too many keywords on those pages.

Once you have the two or three keywords or phrases that you plan to focus on, you need to actually use those keywords in the content of your page. Many people think the more frequently you use the words, the higher your search engine ranking will be. Again, that's not necessarily true. Just as using too many different keywords can cause a crawler to exclude you from a search engine index, overusing the same word will also cause crawlers to consider your attempts as keyword stuffing. Again, you run the risk of having your site excluded from search indexes.

The term used to describe the number of times a keyword is used on a page is *keyword density*. For most search engines, the keyword density is relatively low. Google is very strict about ranking sites that have a keyword density of 5 to 7 percent; much lower or much higher and your ranking is seriously affected or completely lost.

Yahoo!, MSN, and other search engines allow keyword densities of about 5 percent. Going over that mark could cause your site to be excluded from search results.

Keyword density is an important factor in your web-site design, and is covered in more depth in Chapter 4. But there are other content concerns, too. Did you know that the freshness and focus of your content is also important in how high your web site ranks? One reason many companies began using *blogs* on their web sites was that blogs are updated frequently and they're highly focused on a specific topic. This gives search engines new, relevant content to crawl, and crawlers love that.

Consider implementing a content strategy that includes regularly adding more focused content or expanding your content offerings. It doesn't have to be a blog, but news links on the front page of the site, regularly changing articles, or some other type of changing content will help gain the attention of a search engine crawler. Don't just set these elements up and leave them, however. You also have to carry through with regular updates and keep the links included in the content active. Broken links are another crawler pet peeve. Unfortunately, with *dynamic content* links will occasionally break. Be sure you're checking this element of your content on a regular basis and set up some kind of a user-feedback loop so broken links can be reported to your *webmaster*.

Finally, when you're creating your web-site content, consider interactive forums. If you're adding articles to your site, give users a forum in which they can respond to the article, or a comments section. This leads to more frequent updates of your content, which search crawlers love. The result? An interactive relationship with your web-site users will keep them coming back, and give an extra boost to your search engine ranking.

Maximizing graphics

Images or graphics on your web site are essential. They're also basically ignored by search engines, so what's the point of putting them on your site? There's a good reason that has nothing to do with SEO. Without images, your page is just boring text. You're not going to be happy with using plain text instead of that cool new logo you had designed for your company, and neither are your users. They want to see pictures.

If images are a must on a web site, then there should be a way to use those images to increase your web-site traffic or at least to improve your site ranking. And there is.

One technique that will help your SEO make use of graphics on your site is to tag those graphics with *alt tags* inside the *img tags*.

Alt tags are the HTML tags used to display alternative text when there is a graphic present. Your alt tags should be a short, descriptive phrase about the image that includes the keywords used on that page when possible.

Img tags are the tags used to code the images that will appear on your web site. Here's an example of what an img tag, with an included alt tag, should look like:

```
<img src="pic1.jpg" alt="alternative text"/>
```

Here's how that tag breaks down: `<img src="pic1.jpg"` is your image tag, `alt="alternative text"/>` is your alternative text tag. The alternative text tag is where your keywords should be included if at all possible.

You want to tag your images as part of your SEO strategy for two reasons. First, crawlers cannot index images for a search engine (with an exception, which is covered shortly). The crawler "sees" the image and moves on to the text on the page. Therefore, something needs to take the place of that image, so the crawler can index it. That's what the alternative text does. If this text includes your keywords, and the image is near text that also includes the keywords, then you add credibility to your site in the logic of the crawler.

The second reason you want to tag your images as part of your SEO strategy is to take advantage of image-based search engines, like Google Images. These image-based search engines are relatively new, but they shouldn't be undervalued. Just as a search engine can find and index your site for users searching the Web, image-based search engines find and index your images. Then, when users perform a search for a specific keyword or phrase, your image is also ranked, along with the text on the pages.

Image searches are gaining popularity. So crawlers like the one Google uses for its Google Images search engine will gain momentum, and image searches will add to the amount of web-site traffic that your SEO strategies help to build. But while not discounting the value of images, don't over-use them on your web pages either. As with any element of a web page, too much of a good thing is just not good.

Problem Pages and Work-Arounds

No matter how much time and consideration you put into your SEO strategy, there are going to be elements of your web site that require special consideration. Some sites — like portals — need a different approach than a standard web site might require. How you deal with these issues will impact the effectiveness of your SEO efforts.

Painful portals

The use of portals — those web sites that are designed to funnel users to other web sites and content — as a search engine placement tool is a hotly debated topic. Many experts will start throwing around the word "spam" when the subject of SEO and portals comes up. And there have been serious problems with portals that are nothing more than search engine spam. In the past, portals have certainly been used as an easy link-building tool offering nothing more than regurgitated information. Sometimes the information is vaguely reworded, but it's the still the same information.

Search engine operators have long been aware of this tactic and have made every effort to hinder its usefulness by looking for duplicate content, interlinking strategies, and other similar indicators. Using these techniques, search engines have managed to reduce the usefulness of portal web sites as SEO spam mechanisms.

However, because search engine operators need to be cautious about portals that are nothing more than SEO spam, your job in optimizing your site if it's a portal is a little harder. As with all web-site design, the best objective for your site, even for a portal, is to help your visitors achieve a desired result, whether that's purchasing a product, signing up for a newsletter, or finding the desired information. If you make using your site easy and relevant, your site visitors will stay on your site longer, view more pages, and return to your site in the future. Portals help you reach these goals by acting as excellent tools for consolidating information into smaller, more manageable sources of information that users find easier to use and digest.

Too often people optimizing web sites focus on the spiders and forget about the visitors. The sites you are developing have to appeal to the visitors and provide them with the information that they're looking for, or all you'll get at the end of the day is hosting bills and low conversion rates. Portal web sites enable you to create a series of information resources giving full information on any given topic while structuring a network of information covering a much larger scope.

Though the visitor is of significant importance when building a web site, the site itself is of primary significance, too. There's no point in creating a beautiful web site if no one's going to see it, and portals are a fantastic tool for increasing your online visibility and search engine exposure, for a wide variety of reasons.

Perhaps the most significant of these reasons is the increase in keywords that you can use in portal promotion. Rather than having one web site with which to target a broad range of keywords, portals allow you to have many web sites, each of which can have its own set of keywords. For example, instead of trying to put "deer hunting" and "salt-water fishing" on the same page, you can create a hunting portal that allows you to have separate sites for deer hunting, salt-water fishing, and any other type of hunting activity that you would like to include.

On one page it is much easier to target the two keyphrases "deer season" and "Mississippi hunting license" than it is to target two keyphrases like "deer season" and "marlin fishing." Targeting incompatible keywords or phrases — that is, keywords or phrases that aren't related to a larger topic — makes it harder to have both readable, relevant content and to reach the keywords that you need to use.

There are other advantages to creating web portals, as well. Having a portal allows you to have multiple home pages, which can give you the opportunity to create sites that consistently appear in top ranking. You also have more sites to include in your other SEO strategies, and more places to include keywords. However, there is a fine line between a useful portal and one that causes search engines to turn away without listing your portal on SERPs.

CAUTION Don't link all your sites to all of the others within your portal using some link-farm footer at the bottom of every page. You may not even want to link all of them to the others on a site map or links page. Instead, interlink them in an intelligent way. When you want to lead visitors to another site in the portal, or when you want those users to be able to choose which site is most useful to them, you can create intelligent links that have value for the site user. This value translates into better rankings for your web site.

As with most issues in web design, keep it user-friendly and attractive. If you have any doubt that the actions you're taking with your site or the design methods that you're using could lead to negative results for the SEO of your site, don't use them. If you're feeling that a strategy won't work, it probably won't, and you're wasting your time if you insist on using a design you're not comfortable with.

Fussy frames

Some web-site designs require the use of *frames*. Frames are sections of a web site, with each section a separate entity from the other portions of the page. Because the frames on a site represent separate URLs, they often create display issues for users whose browsers don't support frames, and for search crawlers, which encounter the frames and can't index the site where the frame is the navigational structure.

You have a couple of alternatives when frames are essential to the design of your web site. The first is to include an alternative to the framed site. This requires the use of the noframes tag. The tag directs the user's browser to display the site without the framed navigational system. Users may see a stripped-down version of your site, but at least they can still see it. When a search crawler encounters a site made with frames, the noframes tag allows it to index the alternative site. It's important to realize, however, that when you use the noframes tag, you should load the code for an entire web page between the *opening tag* and *closing tag*.

CAUTION When you're creating a noframes tag for a framed site, the content of the noframes tags should be exactly identical to the frame set. If it's not, a search crawler could consider it spam, and then your site would be penalized or even delisted.

Another problem with frames is that search engines often display an internal page on your site in response to a search query. If this internal page does not contain a link to your home page or some form of navigation menu, the user is stuck on that page and is unable to navigate through your site. That means the search crawler is also stuck in that same spot. As a result, the crawler might not index your site.

The solution is to place a link on the page that leads to your home page. In this link, include the attribute `TARGET = "_top"`. This prevents your site from becoming nested within your own frames, which locks the user on the page they landed on from the search results. It also makes it possible for crawlers to efficiently crawl your site without getting stuck.

That link back to your home page will probably look something like this:

```
<a href="index.html" TARGET = "_top">Return to Home Page</a>
```

Frames are difficult to get around when you're putting SEO strategies into place, but doing so is not entirely impossible. It's a good idea to avoid frames, but they won't keep you completely out of search engine rankings. You just have to use a different approach to reaching the rankings that you desire.

Cranky cookies

Cookies are one of those irritating facts of life on the Internet. Users want web sites tailored to them, and cookies are one way companies have found to do that. When users enter the site and customize some feature of it, a small piece of code — the cookie — is placed on the user's hard drive. Then, when the user returns to the site in the future, that cookie can be accessed, and the user's preferences executed.

When cookies work properly, they're an excellent tool for web designers. When they don't work as they should, the problems begin. So what constitutes a problem? The main issue with cookies is that some browsers allow users to set how cookies will be delivered to them. And some *source code* prompts the user to be asked before a cookie is accepted. When this happens, the search engine crawler is effectively stopped in its tracks, and it doesn't pick back up where it stopped once the cookies are delivered. Also, any navigation that requires cookies will cause the crawler to be unable to index the pages.

How do you overcome this issue? The only answer is to code cookies to ensure that the source code is not designed to query the user before the cookie is delivered.

Programming Languages and SEO

One aspect of web-site design you might not think of when planning your SEO strategy is the programming language used in developing the site. Programming languages all behave a little differently. For example, HTML uses one set of protocols to accomplish the visuals you see when you open a web page, whereas *PHP* uses a completely different set of protocols. And when most people think of web-site programming, they think in terms of HTML.

But the truth is that many other languages also are used for coding web pages. And those languages may require differing SEO strategies.

JavaScript

JavaScript is a programming language that allows web designers to create dynamic content. However, it's also not necessarily SEO-friendly. In fact, JavaScript often completely halts a crawler from indexing a web site, and when that happens the result is lower search engine rankings or complete exclusion from ranking.

To overcome this, many web designers *externalize* any JavaScript that's included on the web site. Externalizing the JavaScript creates a situation where it is actually run from an external location, such as a file on your web server. To externalize your JavaScript:

1. Copy the code, beginning at the starting tags, and paste it into a Notepad file.

2. Save the Notepad file as `filename.js`.

3. Upload the file to your web server.

4. Create a reference on your web page to the external JavaScript code. The reference should be placed where the JavaScript will appear and might look like this:
   `<script language="JavaScript" type="text/javascript" src="filename.js"></script>`

This is just one of the solutions you can use to prevent JavaScript from becoming a problem for your SEO efforts. There are many others, and depending on your needs you should explore some of those.

> **NOTE** Sometimes, people use JavaScript as a way to hide content or links from a search engine. However, search crawlers can read JavaScript and most can even follow the links that are in JavaScript. So if you try to hide content or links behind JavaScript, you run the risk of having your site labeled as search engine spam. There's more about search engine spam in Chapter 17.

Flash

Flash is another of those technologies that some users absolutely hate. That's because Flash, though very cool, is resource intensive. It causes pages to load slower, and users often get stuck on an opening Flash page and can't move forward until the Flash has finished executing. If the user is in a hurry, it's a frustrating thing to deal with.

Flash is also a nightmare when it comes to SEO. A Flash page can stop a web crawler in its tracks, and once stopped, the crawler won't resume indexing the site. Instead, it will simply move on to the next web site on its list.

The easiest way to overcome Flash problems is simply not use it. But despite the difficulties with search rankings, some organizations need to use Flash. If yours is one of them, the Flash can be coded in HTML and an option can be added to test for the ability to see Flash before the Flash is executed. However, there's some debate over whether or not this is an "acceptable" SEO practice, so before you implement this type of strategy in an effort to improve your SEO effectiveness, take the time to research the method.

Dynamic ASP

Most of the sites you'll encounter on the Web are *static web pages*. These sites don't change beyond the regular updates by a webmaster. On the other hand, *dynamic web pages* are web pages that are created on the fly according to preferences that users specify in a form or menu. The sites can be created using a variety of different programming technologies including *dynamic ASP*. The problem with these sites is that they don't technically exist until the user creates them. Because a web crawler can't make the selections that "build" these pages, most dynamic web pages aren't indexed in search engines.

There are ways around this, however. Dynamic URLs can be converted to static URLs with the right coding. It's also possible to use *paid inclusion services* to index dynamic pages down to a predefined number of levels (or number of selections, if you're considering the site from the user's point of view).

Dynamic ASP, like many of the other languages used to create web sites, carries with it a unique set of characteristics. But that doesn't mean SEO is impossible for those pages. It does mean that the approach used for the SEO of static pages needs to be modified. It's an easy enough task, and a quick search of the Internet will almost always provide the programming code you need to achieve SEO.

PHP

Search engine crawlers being what they are — preprogrammed applications — there's a limit to what they can index. PHP is another of those programming languages that falls outside the boundaries of normal web-site coding. Search engine crawlers see PHP as another obstacle if it's not properly executed.

Properly executed means that PHP needs to be used with search engines in mind. For example, PHP naturally stops or slows search engine crawlers. But with some attention and a solid understanding of PHP and SEO, it's possible to code pages that work, even in PHP.

One thing that works well with PHP is designing the code to look like HTML. It requires an experienced *code jockey*, but it can be done. And once the code has been disguised, the PHP site can be crawled and indexed so that it's returned in search results.

Other Design Concerns

You're likely to encounter numerous problems with SEO when designing your web site. Some are easy to overcome. Others can be quite difficult. And still others aren't problems you have to overcome; rather, you just need to beware of them or risk being ignored by search engine crawlers.

Among tactics that might seem okay to some, but really aren't, are the so-called black-hat SEO techniques. These are practices implemented with a single thought in mind — increasing search engine rankings, no matter how inappropriate those rankings might be. Some companies deliberately use such techniques when creating web sites, even if the results that show up have absolutely nothing to do with the search terms users entered.

Domain cloaking

On the surface, *domain cloaking* sounds like a great idea. The concept is to show users a pretty web site that meets their needs, while at the same time showing search engines a highly optimized page that probably would be almost useless to users. In other words, it's a slimy trick to gain search engine ranking while providing users with a nice site to look at.

It starts with *content cloaking*, which is accomplished by creating web-site code that can detect and differentiate a crawler from a site user. When the crawler enters the site, it is re-directed to another web site that has been optimized for high search engine results. The problem with trying to gain higher search results this way is that many search engines can now spot it. As soon as they find that a web page uses such a cloaking method, the page is delisted from the search index and not included in the results.

Many less-than-savory SEO administrators will use this tactic on throw-away sites. They know the site won't be around for long anyway (usually because of some illegal activity), so they use domain cloaking to garner as much web site traffic as possible before the site is taken down or delisted.

Duplicate content

When you're putting together a web site, the content for that site often presents one of the greatest challenges, especially if it's a site that includes hundreds of pages. Many people opt to purchase bits of content, or even *scrape* content from other web sites to help populate their own. These shortcuts can cause real issues with search engines.

Say your web site is about some form of marketing. It's very easy to surf around the Web and find hundreds (or even thousands) of web sites from which you can pull free, permission-granted content to include on your web site. The problem is that every other person or company creating a web site could be doing the same thing. And the result? A single article on a topic appears on hundreds of web sites — and users aren't finding anything new if they search for the topic and every site has the same article.

To help combat this type of content generation, some search engines now include as part of their search algorithm a method to measure how fresh site content is. If the crawler examines your site and finds that much of your content is also on hundreds of other web sites, you run the risk of either ranking low or being delisted from the search engine's indexing database.

Some search engines now look for four types of duplicate content:

- **Highly distributed articles.** These are the free articles that seem to appear on every single web site about a given topic. This content has usually been provided by a marketing-savvy entrepreneur as a way to gain attention for his or her project or passion. But no matter how valuable the information, if it appears on hundreds of sites, it will be deemed duplicate and that will reduce your chances of being listed high in the search result rankings.

- **Product descriptions for e-commerce stores.** The product descriptions included on nearly all web pages are not included in search engine results. Product descriptions can be very small and depending on how many products you're offering, there could be thousands of them. Crawlers are designed to skip over most product descriptions. Otherwise, a crawler might never be able to work completely through your site.

- **Duplicate web pages.** It does no good whatever for a user to click through a search result only to find that your web pages have been shared with everyone else. These duplicate pages gum up the works and reduce the level at which your pages end up in the search results.

- **Content that has been scraped from numerous other sites.** *Content scraping* is the practice of pulling content from other web sites and repackaging it so that it looks like your own content. Although scraped content may look different from the original, it is still duplicate content, and many search engines will leave you completely out of the search index and the search results.

Hidden pages

One last SEO issue concerns the damage to your SEO strategy that *hidden pages* can inflict. These are pages in your web site that are visible only to a search crawler. Hidden pages can also lead to issues like hidden keywords and hidden links. Keywords and links help to boost your search rankings, so many people try to capitalize on these requirements by hiding them within the body of a web page, sometimes in a font color that perfectly matches the site background.

There's no way around the issue of hidden pages. If you have a web site and it contains hidden pages, it's just a matter of time before the crawler figures out that the content is part of a hidden SEO strategy. Once that's determined by the crawler, your site ranking will drop drastically.

After Your Site Is Built

Building the right site to help maximize your SEO efforts is a difficult task. And when you're finished, the work doesn't end. SEO is an ongoing strategy, not a technology that you can implement and forget. Time needs to be spent reviewing your practices, examining results, and making adjustments where necessary. If this ongoing maintenance is ignored, your SEO efforts to this point will quickly become time that would have been better spent standing out on the street with a sign around your neck advertising your web site. That might be more effective than outdated SEO.

Beware of content thieves

Maintenance of your SEO strategies is also essential in helping you find problems that might be completely unrelated to SEO. For example, SEO strategies can help you locate content thieves. One such strategy is tagging your web site. Some people (including black-hat SEOs) take snippets of content from your site to use on their own. If you tag your content properly, you can use some very distinctive tags, which will help you quickly locate content that has been stolen.

Another way in which SEO helps you to locate stolen content is through tracking. Presumably, if you're executing SEO strategies, you're monitoring your site metrics with a program like Google Analytics. Watching the metrics used by one of those analytics programs can help you locate content thieves. For example, if you look at your incoming links on one of these programs, you might find that people are coming to your site from a completely unexpected location. If that's the case, you can follow the link back to that site to find out why. A site using stolen content is easy to find using this method. There are also many services available that will help you track your web-site content. Those services are covered in more depth in Chapter 12.

Tagging works well for finding content thieves, and there's another tactic you can use to thwart automatic content scrapers — domain cloaking. This is a process by which your web site appears to be located somewhere other than where it is. This is accomplished using an HTML frame set that redirects traffic from one URL to another. For example, if your web site address is www.you.somewhere.com, you can use domain cloaking to have your site appear to be www.yourbusiness.com.

The problem with using domain cloaking is that it can confuse a search engine crawler, because the same content appears to be on two pages, although it's only one page and one that redirects. And another problem is that some search engine crawlers can't read the frame set that's used to redirect the user, which means your site may end up not being ranked at all. This is a tactic that should only be used in special cases where content is truly unique and could possibly affect your SEO rankings (or that of someone who might steal it) in a dramatic way.

Dealing with updates and site changes

One last problem you may encounter after you've initially set up your SEO strategies is the updates and changes that your site will go through. Often, people feel that once the SEO is in place, then it's always in place, and they don't have to think about it again. But believing this can lead to a very unpleasant surprise.

When your site changes, especially if there are content updates or changes to the site structure, links can be broken, tags may be changed, and any number of other small details may be overlooked. When this happens, the result can be a reduced ranking for your site. Site crawlers look at everything, from your tags to your links, and based on what they see, your ranking could fluctuate from day to day. If what the crawler sees indications that your site has changed in a negative way, the site's ranking will be negatively affected.

Many things affect the way your site ranks in a search engine. You've seen an overview of a lot of them in this chapter, and you'll see them all again in more depth in future chapters. Realize that SEO is not a simple undertaking. It is a complex, time-consuming strategy for improving your business. And without attention to all of the details, you could just be wasting your time. So plan to invest the time needed to ensure that your search engine optimization efforts aren't wasted.

Chapter 4

Keywords and
Your Web Site

Keywords. That's a term you hear associated with search engine optimization all the time. In fact, it's very rare that you hear anything about SEO in which keywords aren't involved some way. So, what's so special about keywords?

Simply put, keywords are those words used to catalog, index, and find your web site. But of course, it's not nearly as simple as it sounds. There is a fine science to finding and using the right keywords on your web site to improve your site's ranking. In fact, an entire industry has been built around keywords and their usage. Consultants spend countless hours finding and applying the right keywords for their customers, and those who design web sites with SEO in mind also agonize over finding just the right ones.

Using popular — and effective — keywords on your web site will help to assure that it will be visible in the search engine results instead of being buried under thousands of other web-site results. There are keyword research tools that can help you find the exact keywords to use for your site and therefore for your search engine optimization. Understanding the use of keywords, where to find them, which ones to use, and the best ways to use them allows you to have a highly visible and successful web site.

The Importance of Keywords

Basically, keywords capture the essence of your web site. Keywords are what a potential visitor to your site puts into a search engine to find web sites related to a specific subject, and the keywords that you choose will be used throughout your optimization process. As a small-business owner, you will want your web site to be readily visible when those search engine results come back.

Using the correct keywords in your web-site content can mean the difference in whether you come back in search engine results as one of the first 20 web sites (which is optimum) or buried under other web sites several pages into the results (which means hundreds of results were returned *before* your site). Studies show that searchers rarely go past the second page of search results when looking for something online.

Take into consideration for a moment the telephone book Yellow Pages. Say you're looking for a restaurant. The first thing you're going to do is find the heading **restaurant**, which would be your keyword. Unfortunately, even in a smaller city, there might be a page or more of restaurants to look through. However, if you narrow your search to Chinese restaurants, that's going to cut in half your time searching for just the right one. Basically, that's how keywords work in search engines and search engine optimization. Choosing the appropriate keywords for your web site will improve your search engine rankings and lead more search engine users to your site.

How do you know which keywords to use? Where do you find them? How do you use them? The answer to these questions will save you a great deal of time when creating a web site. Where you rank in search engine results will be determined by what keywords are used and how they are positioned on your web site. It's critical to choose appropriate keywords, include variations of those keywords, avoid common (or "stop") words, and know where and how many times to place them throughout your web site.

Used correctly, keywords will allow you to be placed in the first page or two of the most popular search engines. This tremendously increases the traffic that visits your web site. Keep in mind, the majority of Internet users find new web sites through use of a search engine. High search engine rankings can be as effective, if not more effective, than paid ads for publicity of your business. The business you receive from search engine rankings will also be more targeted to your services than it would be with a blanket ad. By using the right keywords, your customer base will consist of people who set out to find exactly what your site has to offer, and those customers will be more likely to visit you repeatedly in the future.

To decide which keywords should be used on your web site, you can start by asking yourself the most simple, but relevant, question. Who needs the services that you offer? It's an elementary question, but one that will be most important in searching for the correct keywords and having the best search engine optimization. If you're marketing specialty soaps, you will want to use words such as soap (which really is too broad a term), specialty soap, bath products, luxury bath products, or other such words that come to mind when you think of your product. It's also important to remember to use words that real people use when talking about your products. For example, using the term "cleaning supplies" as a keyword will probably not result in a good ranking because people thinking of personal cleanliness don't search for "cleaning supplies." They search for "soap" or something even more specific, like "chamomile soap."

In addition to the terms that you think of, people also will look for web sites using variations of words and phrases — including misspellings. It might help to have friends and family members make suggestions of what wording they would use to find a similar product and include those words in your keyword research as well as misspellings of those words. An example might be "chamomile." Some people may incorrectly spell it "chammomile," so including that spelling in your keywords can increase your chance of reaching those searchers. Also remember to use capitalized and plural keywords. The more specific the words are, the better the chance will be that your web site is targeted. Just remember that words such as "a," "an," "the," "and," "or," and "but" are called *stop words*. These words are so common they are of no use as keywords.

Understanding Heuristics

If you're going to maintain a web site with the best search engine optimization possible, you will have to be familiar with "heuristics." This is simply a term for recognizing a pattern and being able to solve a problem or come to a conclusion quickly and efficiently by consulting what you already know about that particular pattern.

In other words, using heuristics is a way to solve a problem, although it's not always the most accurate way. Heuristics are important in search engine optimization because they allow for variations in the way that users search for a particular keyword or keyphrase. Because a combination of factors must come together to create a ranking for your web site, heuristics make it possible for some, but not all, of those factors to be present.

TIP The Greeks had a word for it. The root of the adjective "heuristic" comes from their term for "invent" or "discover." "Heuristics" has come to mean a way of education or computer programming that proceeds by experiment or observation, rather than theory, and sometimes employs "rules of thumb" to find solutions or answers. We all act "heuristically" every day.

An example: Let's say you run a travel-planning web site. If a web user is searching for "springtime vacations," a search engine crawler will visit many sites, with varying keywords, keyword placement, and keyword density. In effect, it will give each a score, calculated on a baseline for relevance. It may find one site with the phrase "some writers get their best ideas in springtime or while on vacation." But it won't score that site high, because it doesn't meet baseline criteria very well. The keywords are separated and the context is wrong. Also, links from that site are unlikely to support the idea of planning a springtime vacation. The search engine likes your travel-planning web site better, because it has a lot to say about "springtime vacations."

But the crawler doesn't stop with your site, and it doesn't look just at the words in your links, although it helps if those say "springtime" and "vacation," not something vague like "trips." But the crawler will actually go to your links to see if they're really helpful for the user who wants something about "springtime vacations." If your links are irrelevant to that, the crawler may decide you're running a "link farm," designed to catch its attention without really delivering. But if a high percentage of your links really are related to springtime vacationing — travel information, garden shows, trips to tulip festivals — then the crawler may score you high and put your site high on the list it compiles for the user. That user, after all, is the crawler's customer — and also, you hope, yours.

The crawler has operated "heuristically," making its best judgments at each stage of the process. Keywords apply to heuristics because they provide the pattern by which a problem (that is, the search) is solved. Why do you need to know all of this? Because understanding the pattern by which your site is ranked will help you to understand just how important it is to properly choose and place keywords that will improve your search engine ranking.

Think of it (as in the preceding Tip) as a rule of thumb. Heuristics provides a working guideline by which a search term is ranked. However, it's important to remember that rankings are achieved through a complex combination of factors, not all of which are completely predictable. So, these guidelines are just that — but they help you set a standard for how you plan to use keywords.

Heuristics for web-site usability were first established by Jacob Nielsen in 1990. At the time, he developed a list of ten items that when included in web-site design would make the site more usable for individuals. In 1994, Nielsen updated that list of heuristics so that it now includes the following items:

- **Visibility of system status:** This principle says that the user should always know what's going on through feedback from the system that's provided in a timely manner.

- **Match between the system and the real world:** According to this, the system should speak the user's language. This means that keywords, phrases, and concepts should be used in a way that is familiar to the user and not be just technical or marketing buzzwords.

- **User control and freedom:** This principle says that users often mistakenly make choices they don't really want. For that reason, it's essential to have the ability to undo or redo an action. A good example of this is having back and forward buttons in a web browser.

- **Consistency and standards:** Each time users click a button or see a word, they should not have to wonder what that action or word means. Consistency and standards apply to both languages and actions, and should be predictable across the Internet.

- **Error prevention:** Users are frustrated by errors. Therefore, you should design your site with the prevention of errors in mind. However, if there is a place where users *might* encounter an error, using a confirmation system is recommended.

- **Recognition rather than recall:** Don't make users remember things from one screen or dialog to another. Instead, create your pages with clearly visible instructions, actions, and objects. If you must create an element that requires additional instructions, make those instructions easy to access and clearly mark them as instructions.

- **Flexibility and efficiency of use:** This principle applies to both novice users and experienced users of your site. According to this rule, your site should apply to both groups of users by providing customizable actions.

- **Aesthetic and minimalist design:** Remember the adage KISS (Keep It Simple, Stupid)? Well, your users may not be stupid, but they still want you to keep your site as simple as possible. If your products, services, or information are complicated to locate, you'll lose site visitors very quickly. They'll go to a site where it's easy to find what they're looking for.

- **Help users recognize, diagnose, and recover from errors:** Users want error messages that help them navigate through and correct the error as quickly as possible. Make sure that error messages aren't cryptic, and provide clear, easy-to-follow instructions.

- **Help and documentation:** It's always best *not* to have to refer users to help and documentation files. But there are some instances when you must. If that's the case for your site, be sure your help and documentation files are easy to navigate and written in a clear, understandable language.

The Ever-Elusive Algorithm

One element of search marketing that has many people scratching their head in confusion is the algorithms that actually determine what the rank of a page should be. These algorithms are proprietary in nature, and so few people outside the search engine companies have seen them in their entirety. Even if you were to see the algorithm, you'd have to be a math wizard to understand it. And that's what makes figuring out the whole concept of optimizing for search engines so difficult.

To put it as plainly as possible, the algorithm that a search engine uses establishes a baseline to which all web pages are compared. The baseline varies from search engine to search engine. For example, more than 200 factors are used to establish a baseline in the Google algorithm. And though people have figured out some of the primary parts of the algorithm, there's just no way to know all of the parts, especially when you realize that Google makes about half a dozen changes to that algorithm each week. Some of those changes are major, others are minor. But all make the algorithm a dynamic force to be reckoned with.

Knowing that, when creating your web site (or updating it for SEO), you can keep a few design principles in mind. And the most important of those principles is to design your web site for people, not for search engines. So if you're building a site about springtime vacations, you'll want to include information and links to help users plan their springtime vacations.

Then if a crawler examines your site and it contains links to airfare sites, festival sites, garden shows, and other related sites, the crawler can follow these links, using the algorithm to determine if they are related, and your site ranks higher than if all the links lead to completely unrelated sites. (If they do, that tells the crawler you've set up a bogus link farm, and it will either rank your site very low or not at all.)

The magic number of how many links must be related and how many can be unrelated is just that, a magic number. Presumably, however, if you design a web page about springtime vacations and it's legitimate, all the links from that page (or to the page) will be related in some way or another. The exception might be advertisements, which are clearly marked as advertisements. Another exception is if all your links are advertisements that lead to someplace unrelated to the topic (represented by keywords) at hand. You probably wouldn't want to have a site that only had links from advertisements, though, because this would likely decrease your search engine ranking.

The same is true of keywords. Some search engines prefer that you use a higher keyword density than others. For all search engines, content is important, but the factors that determine whether or not the content helps or hurts your ranking differ from one search engine to another. And then there are meta tags, which are also weighted differently by search engines.

So this mysterious baseline that we're talking about will vary from search engine to search engine. Some search engines look more closely at links than others do, some look at keywords and context, some look at meta data, but most combine more than one of those elements in some magic ratio that is completely proprietary.

What that means for you is that if you design your web site for search engines, you'll always be playing a vicious game of cat and mouse. But if you design your web site for people, and make the site as useful as possible for the people who will visit the site, you'll probably always remain in all of the search engines' good graces.

Of course, most of these heuristics apply more specifically to web-site design and less specifically to keywords and SEO. However, because SEO really should be part of overall site usability, these are important principles to keep in mind when you're designing your web site and implementing your keyword strategies. As mentioned previously, don't design your web site for SEO. Instead, build it for users, with SEO as an added strategy for gaining exposure. Always keep the user in mind first, though. Because if users won't come to your site, or won't stay on your site once they're there, there's no point in all the SEO efforts you're putting into it.

Using Anchor Text

Anchor text — the linked text that is often included on web sites — is another of those keyword anomalies that you should understand. Anchor text, shown in Figure 4-1, usually appears as an underlined or alternately colored word (usually blue) on a web page that links to another page, either inside the same web site or on a different web site.

FIGURE 4-1

Anchor text helps you gain more mileage from your keywords.

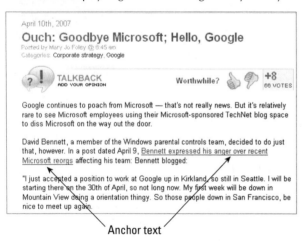

Anchor text

What's important about anchor text is that it allows you to get double mileage from your keywords. When a search engine crawler reads the anchor text on your site, it sees the links that are embedded in the text. Those links tell the crawler what your site is all about. So, if you're using your keywords in your anchor text (and you should be), you're going to be hitting both the keyword ranking and the anchor text ranking for the keywords that you've selected.

Of course, there are always exceptions to the rule. In fact, everything in SEO has these, and with anchor text the exception is that you can over-optimize your site, which might cause search engines to reduce your ranking or even block you from the search results altogether. Over-optimization occurs when all the anchor text on your web site is exactly the same as your keywords, but there is no variation or use of related terminology in the anchor text.

Sometimes, web-site owners will intentionally include only a word or a phrase in all their anchor text with the specific intent of ranking high on a Google search. It's usually an obscure word or phrase that not everyone is using, and ranking highly gives them the ability to say they rank number one for whatever topic their site covers. It's not really true, but it's also not really a lie. This is called *Google bombing*. However, Google has caught on to this practice and has introduced a new algorithm that reduces the number of false rankings that are accomplished by using anchor text in this way.

The other half of anchor text is the links that are actually embedded in the keywords and phrases used on the web page. Those links are equally as important as the text to which they are anchored. The crawler will follow the links as part of crawling your site. If they lead to related web sites, your ranking will be higher than if the links lead to completely unrelated web sites.

These links can also lead to other pages within your own web site, as you may have seen anchor text in blog entries do. The blog writer uses anchor text, containing keywords, to link back to previous posts or articles elsewhere on the site. And one other place that you may find anchor text is in your site map. This was covered in Chapter 3, but as a brief reminder, naming your pages using keywords when possible will help improve your site rankings. Then to have those page names (which are keywords) on your site map is another way to boost your rankings and thus your traffic — remember that a site map is a representation of your site with each page listed as a name, linked to that page.

Anchor text seems completely unrelated to keywords, but in truth, it's very closely related. When used properly in combination with your keywords, your anchor text can help you achieve a much higher search engine ranking.

Picking the Right Keywords

Keywords are really the cornerstone of any SEO program. Your keywords play a large part in determining where in search rankings you'll land, and they also mean the difference between a user's finding your page and not. So when you're picking keywords, you want to be sure that you've selected the right ones. The only problem is, how do you know what's right and what's not?

Selecting the right keywords for your site means the difference between being a nobody on the Web, and being the first site that users click to when they perform a search. You'll be looking at two types of keywords. The first is *brand keywords*. These are keywords associated with your brand. It seems pretty obvious that these keywords are important; however, many people don't think they need to pay attention to these keywords, because they're already tied to the site. Not true. Brand keywords are just as essential as the second type, *generic keywords*.

Generic keywords are all the other keywords that are not directly associated with your company brand. So if your web site, `TeenFashions.com`, sells teen clothing, then keywords such as clothing, tank tops, cargo pants, and bathing suits might be generic keywords that you could use on your site.

Going back to brand keywords for a moment, if you don't use the keywords contained in your business name, business description, and specific category of business, you're missing out. It seems as if it wouldn't be necessary to use these keywords, because they're already associated with your site, but if you don't own them, who will? And if someone else owns them, how will they use those keywords to direct traffic away from your site?

Before we go too much further in this description of keywords and how to choose the right one, you should know that keywords fall into two other categories: those keywords you pay a fee to use (called *pay-per-click*), and those naturally occurring keywords that just seem to work for you without the need to pay someone to ensure they appear in search results (these are called *organic keywords*).

When you think about purchasing keywords, these fall into the pay-per-click category. When you stumble upon a keyword that works, that falls into the organic category.

When you begin considering the keywords that you'll use on your site, the best place to start brainstorming is with keywords that apply to your business. Every business has its own set of buzzwords that people think about when they think about that business or the products or services related to the business. Start your brainstorming session with words and phrases that are broad in scope, but may not bring great search results. Then narrow down your selections to more specific words and phrases, which will bring highly targeted traffic. Table 4-1 shows how broad keywords compare to specific key phrases.

TABLE 4-1

Broad Keywords vs. Specific Key Phrases

Broad Keywords and Phrases	Specific Key Phrases
Knives	Hunting Knives
Indian Knives	American Indian Knives
Damascus Knives	Vintage Damascus Knives

Chapter 5 contains more specifics about choosing the right keywords and key phrases. The principal for choosing keywords is the same, whether the words you're using are in PPC programs or they occur organically, so all of the elements of keyword selection for both categories are covered there.

NOTE When you're considering the words that you'll use for keywords, also consider phrases of two to three words. Because key phrases can be much more specific than single words, it's easier to rank high with a key phrase than with a keyword. Key phrases are used in the same ways as keywords, they're just longer.

What's the Right Keyword Density?

Keyword density is hard to quantify. It's a measurement of the number of times that your keywords appear on the page, versus the number of words on a page—a ratio, in other words. So if you have a single web page that has 1,000 words of text and your keyword appears on that page 10 times (assuming a single keyword, not a keyword phrase), then your keyword density is 1 percent.

What's the right keyword density? That's a question that no one has been able to answer definitively. Some experts say that your keyword density should be around five to seven percent, and others suggest that it should be a higher or lower percentage. But no one seems to agree on exactly where it should be.

Because there's no hard and fast rule, or even a good rule of thumb, to dictate keyword density, site owners are flying on their own. What is certain is that using a keyword or set of keywords or phrases too often begins to look like *keyword stuffing* to a search engine, and that can negatively impact the ranking of your site.

See, there you are. Not enough keyword density and your site ranking suffers. Too much keyword density and your site ranking suffers. But you can at least find out what keyword density your competition is using by looking at the source code for their pages.

TIP Looking at your competition's source code is also a good way to find out *which* keywords they're using. The listed keywords should appear in the first few lines of code (indicated in Figures 4-3 and 4-5).

To view the source code of a page if you're using Internet Explorer, follow these steps:

1. Open Internet Explorer and navigate to the page for which you would like to view the source code.

2. Click **View** in the standard toolbar. (In Internet Explorer 7.0, select **Page**.) The View (or Page) menu appears, as shown in Figure 4-2.

FIGURE 4-2

Use the Page menu in Internet Explorer 7.0 to view the source code for the displayed web site.

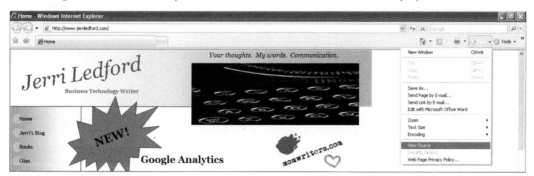

3. Select **View Source** and a separate window opens to display the source code from the web page you're viewing, as shown in Figure 4-3.

If you're using the Firefox browser, the menus are slightly different, and the source code looks a little different. These are the steps for Firefox:

1. Open Firefox and navigate to the page for which you would like to view the source code.

2. Click **View** in the standard toolbar. The **View** menu appears, as shown in Figure 4-4.

3. Select **Page Source** to open a separate window that displays the source code for the web page, as shown in Figure 4-5. Alternatively, you can use the keyboard combination **Ctrl + U** to open the source code window.

You may notice that the source code looks a little different in Internet Explorer than it does in Firefox. The differences are noticeable, but the basic information is all there. That said, it's not easy to get through this information. All the text of the page is jumbled in with the page encoding. It may take some time to decipher, but ultimately, this is the best way to find out not only what keywords the competition is using, but also how they're using them, and how often the keywords appear on their pages.

FIGURE 4-3

The source code for the displayed web page appears in a separate window.

FIGURE 4-4

The Firefox View menu is located in a different place and labeled differently than in Internet Explorer.

FIGURE 4-5

Although the source code is the same, different browsers display it differently.

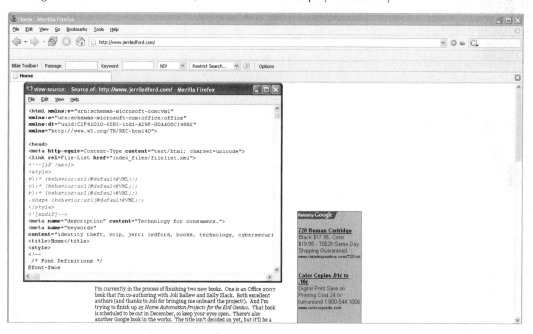

Taking Advantage of Organic Keywords

We've already covered brief information about organic keywords. As you may remember, organic keywords are those that appear naturally on your web site and contribute to the search engine ranking of the page. By taking advantage of those organic keywords, you can improve your site rankings without putting out additional budget dollars. The problem, however, is that gaining organic ranking alone can take four to six months or longer. To help speed the time it takes to achieve good rankings, many organizations (or individuals) will use organic keywords in addition to some type of PPC (pay per click) or *pay for inclusion* service.

To take advantage of organic keywords, you first need to know what those keywords are. One way to find out is to us a web-site metric application, like the one that Google provides. Some of these services track the keywords that push users to your site. When viewing the reports associated with keywords, you can quickly see how your PPC keywords draw traffic, and also what keywords in which you're not investing still draw traffic.

Another way to discover what could possibly be organic keywords is to consider the words that would be associated with your web site, product, or business name. For example, a writer might include various keywords about the area in which she specializes, but one keyword she won't necessarily want to purchase is the word "writer," which should be naturally occurring on the site.

The word won't necessarily garner high traffic for you, but when that word is combined with more specific keywords, perhaps keywords that you acquire through a PPC service, the organic words can help to push traffic to your site. Going back to our writer example, if the writer specializes in writing about AJAX, the word writer might be an organic keyword, and AJAX might be a keyword that the writer bids for in a PPC service.

Now, when potential visitors use a search engine to search for AJAX writer, the writer's site has a better chance of being listed higher in the results rankings. Of course, by using more specific terms related to AJAX in addition to "writer," the chance is pretty good that the organic keyword combined with the PPC keywords will improve search rankings. So when you consider organic keywords, think of words that you might not be willing to spend your budget on, but that could help improve your search rankings, either alone or when combined with keywords that you are willing to invest in.

Avoid Keyword Stuffing

Keyword stuffing, mentioned earlier in this chapter, is the practice of loading your web pages with keywords in an effort to artificially improve your ranking in search engine results. Depending on the page that you're trying to stuff, this could mean that you use a specific keyword or keyphrase a dozen times or hundreds of times.

Temporarily, this might improve your page ranking. However, if it does, the improvement won't last, because when the search engine crawler examines your site, it will find the multiple keyword uses. Because search engine crawlers use an algorithm to determine if a keyword is used a reasonable number of times on your site, it will discover very quickly that your site can't support the number of times you've used that keyword or keyphrase. The result will be that your site is either dropped deeper into the ranking or (and this is what happens in most cases), it will be removed completely from search engine rankings.

Keyword stuffing is one more black-hat SEO technique that you should avoid. To keep from inadvertently crossing the keyword stuffing line, you'll need to do your "due diligence" when researching your keywords. And you'll have to use caution when placing keywords on your web site or in the meta tagging of your site. Use your keywords only the number of times that it's absolutely essential. And if it's not essential, don't use the word or phrase simply as a tactic to increase your rankings. Don't be tempted. The result of that temptation could be the exact opposite of what you're trying to achieve.

More About Keyword Optimization

There is much more to learn about keywords and pay-per-click programs. In the next chapter, you learn more about how to conduct keyword research, what pay-per-click programs are, and how to select the right keywords for your web site. But remember, keywords are just tools to help you improve your search rankings. When designing your site, the site should be designed to inform, enlighten, or persuade your site visitor to reach a goal conversion.

And that's truly what SEO is all about. Keywords may be a major component to your SEO strategies, but SEO is about bringing in more visitors who reach more goal conversions. Without those conversions, all of the site visitors in the world don't really mean anything more than that people dropped by.

Chapter 5

Pay-per-Click and SEO

Pay-per-click (PPC) is one of those terms that you hear connected to keywords so often you might think they were the conjoined twins of SEO. They're not, really. Keywords and PPC do go hand in hand, but it is possible to have keywords without PPC. It's not always advisable, however.

Hundreds of PPC services are available, but they are not all created equal. Some PPC services work with actual search rankings, whereas others are more about text advertisements. Then there are the category-specific PPC programs, such as those for keywords, products, and services.

The main goal of a PPC program is to drive traffic to your site, but ideally you want more out of PPC results than just visits. What's most important is traffic that reaches some conversion goal that you've set for your web site. To achieve these goal conversions, you may have to experiment with different techniques, keywords, and even PPC services.

PPC programs have numerous advantages over traditional search engine optimization:

- No changes to a current site design are required. You don't have to change any code or add any other elements to your site. All you have to do is bid on and pay for the keywords you'd like to target.

- PPC implementation is quick and easy. After signing up for a PPC program, it might only take a few minutes to start getting targeted traffic to your web site. With SEO campaigns that don't include PPC, it could take months for you to build the traffic levels that PPC can build in hours (assuming your PPC campaign is well targeted).

- PPC implementation is also quick and easy, and it doesn't require any specialized knowledge. Your PPC campaigns will be much better targeted, however, if you understand keywords and how they work.

IN THIS CHAPTER

How pay-per-click works

Pay-per-click categories

How PPC affects SEO

Conducting your competitive research

Choosing effective keywords

Finalizing your keyword list

As with any SEO strategy, there are limitations. Bidding for keywords can be fierce, with each competitor bidding higher and higher to reach and maintain the top search results position. Many organizations have a person or team that's responsible for monitoring the company's position in search results and amending bids accordingly. Monitoring positions is crucial to maintaining good placement, however, because you do have to fight for your ranking, and PPC programs can become prohibitively expensive. The competitiveness of the keywords or phrases and the aggressiveness of the competition determine how much you'll ultimately end up spending to rank well.

NOTE One issue with PPC programs is that many search engines recognize PPC ads as just that — paid advertisements. Therefore, although your ranking with the search engine for which you're purchasing placement might be good, that doesn't mean your ranking in other search engines will be good. Sometimes, it's necessary to run multiple PPC campaigns if you want to rank high in multiple search engines.

Before you even begin to use a PPC program, you should consider some basics. A very important point to keep in mind is that just because you're paying for placement or advertising space associated with your keywords, you're not necessarily going to get the best results with all of the keywords or phrases that you choose. With PPC services you must test, test, and test some more. Begin small, with a minimum number of keywords, to see how the search engine you've selected performs in terms of the amount of traffic it delivers and how well that traffic converts into paying customers.

An essential part of your testing is having a method in place that allows you to track your return on investment. For example, if your goal is to bring new subscribers to your newsletter, you'll want to track conversions, perhaps by directing the visitors funneled to your site by your PPC link to a subscription page set up just for them. You can then monitor how many clicks actually result in a goal conversion (in this case a new subscription). This helps you to quickly track your return on investment and to determine how much you're paying for each new subscriber.

Before investing in a PPC service, you may want to review a few different services to determine which is the best one for you. When doing your preliminary research, take the time to ask the following questions:

- How many searches are conducted each month through the search engine for which you're considering a PPC program?

- Does the search engine have major partners or affiliates that could contribute to the volume of traffic you're likely to receive through the PPC program?

- How many searches are generated each month by those partners and affiliates?

- What exactly are the terms of service for search partners or affiliates?

- How does the search engine or PPC program prevent fraudulent activity?

- How difficult is it to file a report about fraudulent activity and how quickly is the issue addressed (and by whom)?

- What recourse do you have if fraudulent activity is discovered?

- Do you have control over where your listing *does* appear? For example, can you choose not to have your listing appear in search results for other countries where your site is not relevant? Or can you choose to have your listing withheld from affiliate searches?

When you're looking at different PPC programs, look for those that have strict guidelines about how sites appear in listings, how partners and affiliates calculate visits, and how fraud is handled. These are important issues, because in each case, you could be stuck paying for clicks that didn't actually happen. Be sure to monitor any service that you decide to use to ensure that your PPC advertisements are both working properly and that they seem to be targeted well.

It often takes a lot of testing, monitoring, and redirection to find the PPC program that works well for you. Don't be discouraged or surprised if you find that you must try several different programs or many different keywords before you find the right combination. But through a system of trial and error and diligent effort, you'll find that PPC programs can help build your site traffic and goal conversions faster than you could without the program.

How Pay-per-Click Works

Pay-per-click marketing is an advertising method that allows you to buy search engine placement by bidding on keywords or phrases. There are two different types of PPC marketing.

In the first, you pay a fee for an actual SERP ranking, and in some cases, you also pay a per-click fee meaning that the more you pay, the higher in the returned results your page will rank.

The second type is more along true advertising lines. This type of PPC marketing involves bidding on keywords or phrases that appear in, or are associated with, text advertisements. Google is probably the most notable provider of this service. Google's AdWords service is an excellent example of how PPC advertisements work, as is shown in Figure 5-1.

FIGURE 5-1

PPC advertisements are those advertisements that you see at the top and on the sides of search pages.

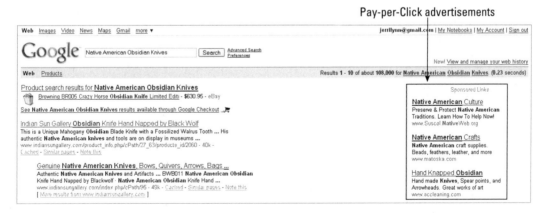

Determining visitor value

So the first thing that you need to do when you begin considering PPC strategies is to determine how much each web-site visitor is worth to you. It's important to know this number, because otherwise you could find yourself paying far too much for keyword advertising that doesn't bring the traffic or conversions that you'd expect. For example, if it costs you $25 to gain a conversion (or sale) but the value of that conversion is only $15, then you're losing a lot of money. You can't afford that kind of expenditure for very long.

To determine the value of each web-site visitor, you'll need to have some historical data about the number of visitors to your site in a given amount of time (say a month) and the actual sales numbers (or profit) for that same time period. This is where it's good to have some kind of web metrics program to keep track of your site statistics. Divide the profit by the number of visitors for the same time frame, and the result should tell you (approximately) what each visitor is worth.

Say that during December, your site cleared $2,500. (In this admittedly simplified example, we're ignoring various things you might have to figure into an actual profit and loss statement.) Let's also say that during the same month, 15,000 visitors came to your site. Note that this number is for all the visitors to your site, not just the ones who made a purchase. You divide your $2,500 profit by *all* visitors, purchasers or not, because this gives you an accurate average value of every visitor to your site. Not every visitor is going to make a purchase, but you have to go through a number of non-purchasing visitors to get to those who will purchase.

Back to the formula for the value of a visitor. Divide the site profit for December ($2,500) by the number of visitors (15,000) and the value of your visitors is approximately $.17 per visitor. Note that I've said approximately, because during any given month (or whatever time frame you choose) the number of visitors and the amount of profit will vary. The way you slice the time can change your average visitor value by a few cents to a few dollars, depending on your site traffic. (Also note that the example is based on the value of all visitors, not of conversions, which might be a more valid real-life way of calculating the value of individual visitors. But this example is simply to demonstrate the principle.)

The number you got for visitor value is a sort of breakeven point. It means you can spend up to $.17 per visitor on keywords or other promotions without losing money. But if you're spending more than that *without increasing sales and profits*, you're going in the hole. It's not good business to spend everything you make (or more) to draw visitors to the site. But note the preceding italicized words. If a $.25 keyword can raise your sales and profits dramatically, then it may be worth buying that word. In this oversimplified example, you need to decide how much you can realistically spend on keywords or other promotions. Maybe you feel a particular keyword is powerful enough that you can spend $.12 per click for it, and raise your sales and visitor value substantially. You have to decide what profit margin you want and what promotions are likely to provide it. As you can see, there are a number of variables. Real life is dynamic, and eludes static examples. But whatever you decide, you shouldn't spend everything you make on PPC programs. There are far too many other things that you need to invest in.

Popular keyword phrases can often run much more than $.12 per click. In fact, some of the most popular keywords can run as much as $50 (yes, that's Fifty Dollars) per click. To stretch your PPC budget, you can choose less popular terms that are much less expensive, but that provide good results for the investment that you do make.

Putting pay-per-click to work

Now that you have your average visitor value, you can begin to look at the different keywords on which you might bid. Before you do, however, you need to look at a few more things. One of the top mistakes made with PPC programs is that users don't take the time to clarify what it is they hope to gain from using a PPC service. It's not enough for your PPC program just to have a goal of increasing your ROI (return on investment). You need something more quantifiable than just the desire to increase profit. How *much* would you like to increase your profit? How many visitors will it take to reach the desired increase?

Let's say that right now each visit to your site is worth $.50, using our simplified example, and your average monthly profit is $5,000. That means that your site receives 10,000 visits per month. Now you need to decide how much you'd like to increase your profit. For this example, let's say that you want to increase it to $7,500. To do that, if each visitor is worth $.50, you would need to increase the number of visits to your site to 15,000 per month. So, the goal for your PPC program should be *"To increase profit $2,500 by driving an additional 5,000 visits per month."* This gives you a concrete, quantifiable measurement by which you can track your PPC campaigns.

Once you know what you want to spend, and what your goals are, you can begin to look at the different types of PPC programs that might work for you. Although keywords are the main PPC element associated with PPC marketing, there are other types of PPC programs to consider as well.

Pay-per-Click Categories

Pay-per-click programs are not all created equal. When you think of PPC programs, you probably think of keyword marketing — bidding on a keyword to determine where your site will be placed in search results. And that's an accurate description of PPC marketing programs as they apply to keywords. However, there are two other types of PPC programs, as well. And you may find that targeting a different category of PPC marketing is more effective than simply targeting keyword PPC programs.

Keyword pay-per-click programs

Keyword PPC programs are the most common type of PPC programs. They are also the type this book focuses on most often. By now, you know that keyword PPC programs are about bidding on keywords associated with your site. The amount that you're willing to bid determines the placement of your site in search engine results.

In keyword PPC, the keywords used can be any word or phrase that might apply to your site. However, remember that some of the most common keywords have the highest competition for top spot, so it's not always advisable to assume that the broadest term is the best one. If you're in a specialized type of business, a broader term might be more effective, but as a rule of thumb, the more narrowly focused your keywords are, the better results you are likely to have with them. (And PPC will cost much less if you're not using a word that requires a $50 per click bid.)

> **NOTE** Did you know that Google and Yahoo! have $100 caps on their keyword bids? They do. Imagine paying $100 per click for a keyword. Those are the kinds of keywords that will likely cost you far more money than they will generate for you. It's best if you stick with keywords and phrases that are more targeted and less expensive.

The major search engines are usually the ones you think of when you think keyword PPC programs, and that's fairly accurate. Search PPC marketing programs such as those offered by vendors like Google, Yahoo! Search Marketing, and MSN are some of the most well-known PPC programs.

Product pay-per-click programs

You can think of product pay-per-click programs as online comparison shopping engines or price comparison engines. A product PPC program focuses specifically on products, so you bid on placement for your product advertisements.

The requirements for using a product PPC program are a little different from keyword PPC programs, however. With a product PPC, you must provide a *feed* — think of it as a regularly updated pricelist for your products — to the search engine. Then, when users search for a product your links are given prominence, depending on the amount you have bid for placement. However, users can freely display those product listings returned by the search engine in the order or price from lowest to highest if that is their preference. This means that your product may get good placement initially, but if it's not the lowest-priced product in that category, it's not guaranteed that your placement results will stay in front of potential visitors.

Some of these product PPC programs include Shopping.com, NexTag, Pricegrabber, and Shopzilla.

> **NOTE** Although product PPC programs are popular for controlling the placement of your product listings, there are some services, like Google Base, that allow you to list your products in their search engine for free. These product PPC programs still require a product feed, however, to keep product listings current.

Implementing a product feed for your products isn't terribly difficult, although, depending on the number of products you have, it can be time-consuming. Most of the different product PPC programs have different requirements for the product attributes that must be included in the product feed. For example, the basic information included for all products are an item title, the direct link for the item, and a brief description of the item.

Some of the additional attributes that you may need to include in your product PPC listings include:

- title
- description

- link
- image_link
- product_type
- upc
- price
- mpn (Manufacturer's Part Number)
- isbn
- id

Some product PPC programs will require XML-formatted feeds; however, most will allow *text delimited Excel files* (simple CSV files). This means you can create your product lists in an Excel spreadsheet, and then save that spreadsheet as text delimited by selecting File ⇨ Save As and ensuring the file type selected is text delimited.

Service pay-per-click programs

When users search for a service of any type, such as travel reservations, they are likely to use search engines related specifically to that type of service. For example, a user searching for the best price for hotel reservations in Orlando, Florida, might go to TripAdvisor.com. Advertisers, in this case hotel chains, can choose to pay for their rank in the search results using a service PPC program.

Service PPC programs are similar to product PPC programs with the only difference being the type of product or service that is offered. Product PPC programs are more focused on e-commerce products, whereas service PPC programs are focused on businesses that have a specific service to offer.

Service PPC programs also require an RSS feed, and even some of the same attribute listings as product PPC programs. Some of the service PPC programs you might be familiar with are SideStep.com and TripAdvisor.com. In addition, however, many product PPC programs have expanded to include services. One such vendor is NexTag.

TIP In addition to the three categories of PPC programs discussed in this text, there is an additional one. Pay-per-call is a type of keyword advertising in which search results include a phone number. Each time a call is connected through that phone number, the company that owns the number is charged for the advertising, just as if it were paying for a traditional pay-per-click service.

Understanding How PPC Affects SEO

There's a lot of debate about how an organization should use organic keyword marketing versus the way those same organizations should use PPC marketing. And there seem to be two (and possibly three) distinct camps about what should and shouldn't happen with these different types of marketing.

The first position is that PPC programs can hurt organic keyword programs. According to subscribers to this position, PPC programs damage organic rankings because the act of paying for a listing automatically reduces the rank of your organic keyword efforts. Those who follow this theory believe that there is no place for PPC programs.

Another position in this argument is that PPC has no effect at all on SEO. It's a tough concept to swallow, because one would naturally believe that any organization *paying* for a specific rank in search returns would automatically push organic keyword returns into a lower slot (which supports the first theory). Those who follow this theory believe that there is no need to invest in PPC, because you can achieve the same results with organic keywords, though it takes much longer for those results to become apparent.

The most widely held belief, however, is that a combination of PPC and organic keywords is the best approach. This theory would seem to have a lot of validity. According to some researchers, PPC programs tend to be much more effective if an organization also has organic keywords that rank in the same area as the PPC ranks. For example, if you've bid on a keyword that's consistently placed number two or three in search engine returns, and you have organic keywords that fall in the next few slots, you're likely to find better conversion numbers than either organic keywords or PPC programs can bring on their own.

It's important to note here that all search engines make a distinction between PPC and organic SEO. PPC doesn't help your organic rankings. Only those activities like tagging your web site properly, using keyword placement properly, and including great content on your site will help you on the organic side. PPC is a search marketing strategy.

PPC Is *Not* Paid Inclusion!

One distinction that is important for you to understand is the difference between PPC and *paid-inclusion (PI) services*. Many people believe that PPC and PI services are the same type of marketing, but there can be some subtle differences. For starters, paid-inclusion services are used by some search engines to allow web-site owners to pay a one-year subscription fee to ensure that their site is indexed with that search engine all the time. This fee doesn't guarantee any specific rank in search engine results; it only guarantees that the site is indexed by the search engine.

Yahoo! is one company that uses paid inclusion to populate its search index. Not all of the listings in Yahoo! are paid listings, however. Yahoo! combines both normally spidered sites and paid sites. Many other search engines have staunchly avoided using paid-inclusion services — Ask.com and Google are two of the most notable — because most users feel that paid inclusion can skew the search results. In fact, search engines that allow only paid-inclusion listings are not likely to survive very long, because users won't use them.

There is a bit of a gray line between paid inclusion and PPC. That line begins at about the point where both services are paid for. Detractors of these types of programs claim that paying for a listing — any listing — is likely to make search returns invalid because the theory is that search engines give higher ranking to paid-inclusion services, just as they do to PPC advertisements.

NOTE Throughout this book, you'll like see the terms SEO and search marketing used interchangeably. Very strictly speaking, search marketing and SEO are quite different activities. Search marketing includes any activity that improves your search engine rankings — paid or organic. SEO, on the other hand, usually refers to strictly the free, organic methods used to improve search rankings. Very often, the two terms *are* used interchangeably by people using SEO and search engine marketing techniques. SEO and SEM experts, however, will always clearly differentiate the activities.

Keyword Competitive Research

Keyword research is the core of any SEO campaign and it is vitally important when developing PPC programs. You should choose carefully the keywords that are most effective, because the keywords selected during the research phase will be included in your web-site copy, as well as your PPC programs, and many other types of campaigns.

To begin with, you should select valid keywords from a variety of sources, which include:

- **Your own knowledge of the product or service that you're marketing.** From your own knowledge you should be able choose at least one word that characterizes that product or service. If you're unable to select that word, spend some time getting to know your products and services better.

- **Your customers.** Your customers will be able to tell you what keywords they think of or use when searching for your product or service. Customers can be your best source for valid and relevant keywords, because you're trying to reach people just like them.

- **Competitors' web sites.** Check your competitors' web sites for additional keywords that you may not have considered during your initial brainstorming session. Obviously, if your competitors are using these keywords, there will be some competition for them, but better to have the competition than to be left outside the arena while the games are taking place.

CROSS-REF Remember checking out competitors' web sites back in Chapter 4? The same method of viewing the source code for those sites is the method that you would use here to check for keywords on your competitors' sites. If you need a reminder, flip back now to review the section on keyword density.

Keyword suggestion tools

One tool that you should use when developing your keyword list is a *keyword suggestion tool*. Keyword suggestion tools are just that, tools that provide a list of suggested keywords based on a base word that you enter into the search tool. Some of the words returned may not have occurred to you when you were brainstorming keywords and talking to your customers about the words they would use. In addition, keyword suggestion tools provide some of the information that you'll need to determine how much competition there is for the keywords and phrases you're considering using.

In the past, measuring the competition for your search terms was done by performing a search for each keyword or phrase using one search engine at a time. When the SERPs were returned, you could see how many times that keyword or phrase turned up. It was a tedious and ineffective method of keyword research. Today, keyword suggestion tools speed the competitive research process.

Here's how it works: first, you input your proposed keywords into a keyword suggestion tool, and it examines a database that contains millions of instances of keyword usage. Using these tools, you can quickly learn how many users are conducting daily searches for that term, how many of those searches resulted in an actual visit, and what related search terms were used.

Many keyword suggestion tools are available on the Web. Some of the top tools, which you'll hear about most often, include:

- **Overture Keyword Selector Tool:** Overture's Keyword Selector Tool, shown in Figure 5-2, shows you how many searches have been conducted over a given month for a keyword or phrase related to the search term you entered into the Selector Tool. You can find the Overture Keyword Selector Tool at this URL: `http://inventory.overture.com/d/ searchinventory/suggestion/`

- **Wordtracker:** Wordtracker allows you to search for terms in the database of terms collected. This program tells you how often a keyword or phrase was searched for and how many competing sites use the keywords. In addition, like Overture, the list of keywords and phrases returned may include words or phrases that you haven't considered using.

  Additionally, Wordtracker offers a top 1,000 report that lists the most frequently searched-for terms and a Competition Search option that helps you determine the competitiveness of each phrase. This report is useful for figuring out how difficult it will be to reach a specific rank for any given term. You may also find keywords on this list that have low competition rates, but high relevancy. For example, Figure 5-3 shows some of the results for a Wordtracker search for the term "business technology writer." As you can see in the figure, the term "writing business plan emerging technology" has very little competition. Therefore, if you have a site that includes information about writing business plans for emerging technology business, this keyphrase might be a good choice because there is little competition, but it can be a highly effective phrase. A free version of Wordtracker is available at `http:// freekeywords.wordtracker.com/`.

- **Trellian Keyword Discovery Tool:** The Trellian tool is a subscription tool (about $50 per month) that allows users to ascertain the market share value for a given search term, see how many users search for it daily, identify common spellings and misspellings, and discover which terms are impacted by seasonal trends. Figure 5-4 shows the some of the results that are returned with a Tellian search for "Sydney Hotel." As you can see in the figure, each keyword or phrase returned includes information about the number of searches for the word in addition to having capability to analyze each word or phrase further.

FIGURE 5-2

Overture's Keyword Selector Tool is a simple to use tool to help you find keywords related to your topic word.

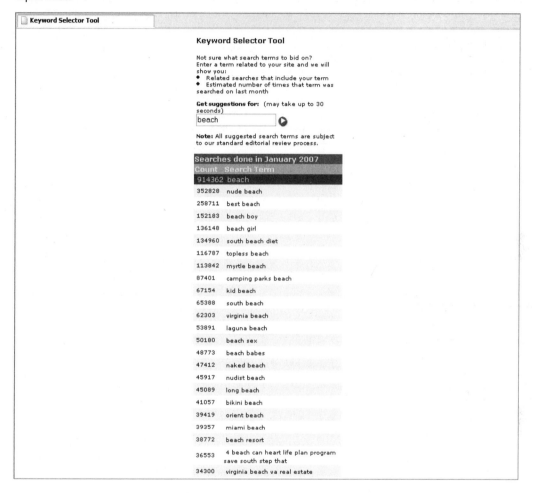

FIGURE 5-3

Wordtracker shows not only related words, but also where those words rank in searches, and how much competition there is for each word selected.

Remaining: [0] seconds...

BEST SEARCH TERMS FOR MSN

Msn gets 9.0000% of all search engine traffic (approx. 59 million a day).

What do these headings mean? Click here

0	10	Good Keyword	100	400+
Poor Keyword				Excellent Keyword

No.	Keyword Why quotes?	KEI Analysis (?)	Count (?)	24Hrs (?)	Competing (?)
1	"mla writing format"	284.484	253	40	225
2	"writing business plan emerging technology"	225.333	26	4	3
3	"articles of latest new technology"	129.086	245	39	465
4	"new technology microsoft"	37.975	364	58	3489
5	"new technology microsoft"	32.479	336	53	3476
6	"facilitation technology"	32.388	248	39	1899
7	"writing on the walls"	16.163	491	78	14916
8	"graffiti writing"	3.828	226	36	13342
9	"writing grants"	3.315	401	64	48502
10	"writing prompts"	1.040	366	58	128782
11	"writing a resume"	0.987	237	38	56933
12	"writing contests"	0.697	290	46	120625
13	"history of technology"	0.515	251	40	122348
14	"creative writing"	0.436	982	156	2214242
15	"future technology"	0.384	330	52	283229
16	"new technology"	0.165	1025	163	6365285
17	"letter writing"	0.140	319	51	726802
18	"computer technology"	0.138	529	84	2020570
19	"report writing"	0.108	244	39	550822
20	"science & technology"	0.086	683	108	5410422
21	"technology news"	0.079	484	77	2965860
22	"medical technology"	0.078	279	44	996383
23	"assistive technology"	0.061	284	45	1317353
24	"technology"	0.056	3198	508	182287997
25	"writing"	0.020	1263	200	77984521
26	"information technology"	0.018	568	90	17503152

FIGURE 5-4

Trellian provides slightly different information about each keyword or phrase, and is a subscription service.

■ **Google AdWords Keyword Tool:** Google's Keyword Tool provides suggestions for additional words that you may not have considered. In the results shown in Figure 5-5 (again using the term "business technology writer"), there are some graphs related to the number of times the words are searched for and to the competition that you might face if you select that word. However, there are no actual numbers, so your decisions about competition will include a high element of guesswork.

What you might find unique about the Google Keyword Tool is the ability to have the tool examine your web page or even your entire web site and make suggestions for keywords and phrases that might be useful in marketing your site. The results of such a search, as illustrated in Figure 5-6, may include terms that you haven't considered.

One thing that you should remember as you're using any of these keyword suggestion tools is that you're not only checking to see how competitive a keyword is, but you're also checking to see if it's popular, and you're keeping your eyes open for those unexpected keywords that are not highly competitive but are completely relevant to your site.

While you're testing potential new terms, it's also a good idea to test any keywords that your site is already using to see which ones are effective and which are not. The keywords that are effective — meaning those that result in visitors and goal conversions — are the keywords to hang on to. Any that aren't performing well should be replaced with new keywords.

What this means is that your keyword research is an ongoing chore. Because your site is likely to change over time, your keywords will also change. Therefore, it's necessary for you to conduct regular keyword research to see which keywords or phrases are working and which are not, as well as to add new keywords to your list.

FIGURE 5-5

Google's Keyword Tool offers no concrete numbers, just graphical representations for popularity and competition.

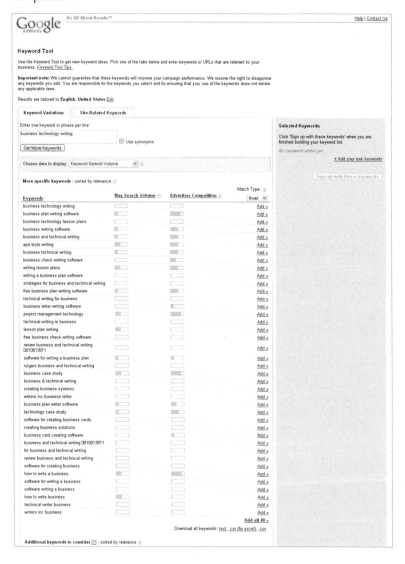

FIGURE 5-6

Google's Keyword Tool also includes the ability to examine your site and make keyword suggestions for you.

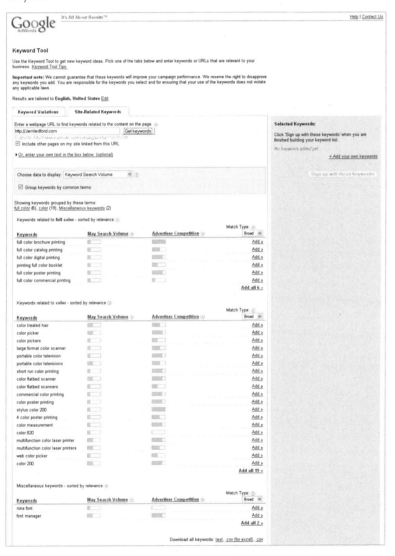

In doing your keyword research, here are some basic guidelines you can follow to ensure that you're conducting the most thorough research while being highly efficient:

- Search from the point of view of your potential customers.

- Select as many relevant keywords or phrases as possible.

- Monitor your keywords to see which attract your target audience. Keep those that perform and replace those that do not.

- Select keywords and phrases that aren't the most competitive but also not the least competitive. These medium competitive words should yield good results without eating a ridiculous amount of your budget.

Choosing Effective Keywords

When you're using keyword marketing to optimize your site, you can run into a lot of frustrating situations. Despite your best efforts, it's possible that the keywords you select are just not generating the traffic that you need. On the other hand, sometimes keywords that work well in the beginning will just stop working. You can tell when this happens because the numbers associated with your keywords (assuming you're using a metrics program to track them) drop without warning or explanation.

Many things can happen to make your keywords quit being as effective as they were in the past. And many times you didn't do anything at all to make this happen. That's why it's essential to regularly develop concepts, test, and implement new keywords for your PPC programs and for your web site.

Creating your first keyword list

The initial idea of keyword research can be daunting. Trying to come up with the perfect combination of words to drive customers to your site, improve your conversion rate, and make yourself visible to search engines could easily give you a serious tension headache. Even using some of the techniques that have been discussed in this chapter to find the right keywords and perfect your methods of research take time. It's not something that you can just jump into today and be successful at before the sun sets. It's far more successful if you start slowly and build your way to greater success.

You already know that you must first create a list of potential keywords. Brainstorming and asking customers are two ways to build that list. You can also include all of the keywords that are suggested by keyword suggestion tools, and you might even consider pulling out a thesaurus to find additional words and phrases that you haven't considered. Come up with enough words to cover all the services your site offers and avoid broad or generic terms that are so all-encompassing they apply to every site that's even remotely related to yours. These words are incredibly difficult to rank high with and won't drive quality traffic to your site. Instead, focus on words that are relevant but not overly used, and always keep your eyes open for those words that are very specific but highly targeted to your site or offerings.

When creating your first keyword list, include all of the words that you can come up with. This part of selecting your keywords and phrases is actually easy. You can include everything and don't have to worry about the quality of what you're including until later. Unfortunately, because it is so easy to create this first list, many people make the assumption that PPC marketing is easy. This first step may be, but it does get much harder as you research and qualify words and phrases and then work those words and phrases into PPC marketing programs.

Keywords and phrases will need constant revision, so you should always be creating that "first" keyword list. Keep a running list of words that will apply to your site. Each time something is changed on the site, or something changes in the field that you're in, you'll have to go through all of these steps again. If you are not constantly testing, analyzing, adding to, and removing nonperforming keywords and phrases as appropriate, you'll find that PPC programs that worked really well in the beginning lose effectiveness over time.

You'd better believe that your competition will be constantly monitoring and revising their keyword and PPC strategies. And if you're not regularly taking advantage of all your keyword resources, you might as well hand over your customer lists to your competition, because they're going to end up with all of your customers anyway.

Keywords are what draw potential customers to your web site. These potential customers are either visitors who are ready to buy now or they're browsers whom you can motivate into making a purchase or reaching a goal conversion that you've established. So remember that when you're building your initial keyword list, you're using a little educated guessing to get started in reaching highly qualified site visitors. Later, you can rely on specific keyword-related tools and analysis to replace your educated guesses with more concrete keywords and phrases that will help you reach your goals.

Forbidden search terms and poison words

When you're creating your keyword lists, it's important to keep in mind that some search terms will result not in higher quality visitors, but instead in either a low ranking or even complete removal from search listings. These aren't just ineffective keywords and phrases. These are what are called *forbidden search terms* or *poison words*. These words are known to decrease your pages' rankings if a search engine finds them in your site's title, description, or even in the URL. These words can either kill or lower your pages in rankings.

Here's the problem with the forbidden or poison terms: there's really no consistent or standard list of terms to which you can turn for guidance on the words you should not use. For example, vulgar words are usually considered to be forbidden or poison; however, you can do a search for one of these words and you'll return a fair number of results. However, using the words in your site tagging as a means to rank high in a search will result in your site being buried or even omitted from search results.

So although there are no official lists of words that search engines use for filtering inappropriate keywords, you can figure out some guidelines for yourself. Two types of words have the potential to create issues for your site if you use them as keywords within the site or for PPC marketing purposes:

- Vulgar words
- Politically incorrect words (these words are especially dangerous in countries like China and North Korea where censorship is prominent).

Despite what seems like a simple list for types of words to avoid, it's really not that simple. Many words can be excluded or even flagged by a search engine because those words are associated with search engine spam. When it becomes apparent that a word or term seems to be used strictly to rank highly, even when included on a page full of unrelated content or links, search engines will flag that word or phrase and will consider closely the relationship to other words and links on a page before making a ranking determination. The problem with that, however, is that as soon as search engines crack down on a word or phrase, another one pops up to take over.

Now, don't confuse poison words with *keyword poison*. Keyword poison is actually the use of keywords on your site far too many times. When you're including keywords on your site, you should use them only as often as necessary and not one time more than that. If you throw your keywords into the site randomly, you're poisoning the search term ranks and run the risk of having your site knocked farther down in the ranking or even having it delisted completely as spam.

Finally, forbidden search terms and poison words are different from *stop words*. Stop words are those words that are so common on the Web that they are usually ignored by search engines and are completely useless in your PPC programs and other keyword marketing efforts. Here's a brief list of some of the most common stop words, though there are dozens more that might be included:

- A
- An
- The
- But
- E-mail
- When
- Where
- How
- Free
- If
- And
- While
- Or

An example of how stop words are ignored in a search query is the search term "the sunny beach." As shown in Figure 5-7, when this search term is used on Google, the word "the" is ignored (as indicated by its solid black coloring, and lack of linking). The words "sunny beach," then, are the only words that are included in the search (as indicated by the blue lettering of the words and the fact that they are links).

FIGURE 5-7

Some common words, called stop words, are ignored when searches are performed.

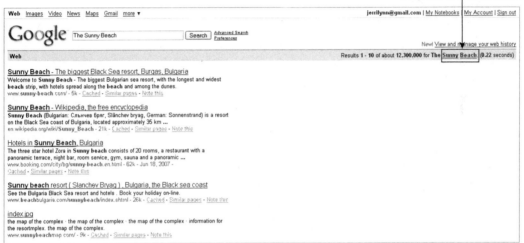

Only the linked words
are included in a search.
Stop words are not linked.

Forecasting search volumes

Once you have decided on your initial keyword list — and even after you've narrowed the list down some — you need to begin looking at the budget that you'll have for use with a PPC program. One way to determine how much mileage you'll get for the budget dollars that are allocated to your PPC program is to forecast search volumes. Forecasting allows you to control your marketing expenditures by predicting the performance of your keyword choices and desired positions. Simply put, for every amount invested, a company can predict a corresponding amount in sales.

Before you get too deeply into forecasting search volumes, however, you should make a determination about what rank will work best for you. A number one rank is not always the best strategy for everyone. You will probably need to balance the volume of your keyword costs (clicks) with the *cost per acquisition (CPA)*. So, for example, if it costs you $2 per click to reach a number one slot in search results and your budget is for $100 per month, then you can only afford about 50 clicks per month (volume). These 50 clicks per month don't equate to a great volume, therefore, you might consider a slightly lower ranking in the SERPs that will generate more volume within the budget that you have to spend.

On the other hand, there is an exponential decrease in the number of clicks that you'll receive as you decrease your ranking position. In general, there is about a 20 percent difference between the first and second ranking slots on a SERP. Each ranking slot below that increases the difference, so some experts estimate that being ranked first on a SERP might produce at least 10 times the traffic generated by a tenth-ranked site.

Using this information and your budget availability, you can decide whether it's cost effective to stay in a lower position, or if bidding for a higher spot would net greater click potential. Here's the bigger question, however. Ranking higher will result in much more traffic, but does the additional traffic result in more goal conversions? If not, then spending the extra money to reach the top ranking slot is probably a waste of money.

Carrying over our preceding example, if you're paying $2 per click for a top ranking that generates 50 clicks per month, but only 1 percent of those visitors make a purchase from your site, you don't have a good conversion rate. But if you were to change your keywords a bit to make them more specific and then reduce your cost per click to $1 for a slightly lower rank (let's say a number three ranking slot) that generates 100 clicks per month, and those 100 clicks also resulted in a 1 percent conversion, you're still reaching more conversion goals, and therefore making more money with the lower rank than you would be with the higher rank.

So how exactly do you forecast search volumes and the cost associated with those volumes?

It's best to start by researching a keyword list that includes 100 to 300 keywords and phrases. Use a varied keyword list that includes both broad and specific terms. And during your research, use both personal investigation and keyword selection tools to determine the click volume and the cost per click for each of those terms. Using this information, you can then estimate search volumes and the cost of those search volumes, but additionally you can estimate other performance metrics that will help you to determine both the cost and the value of the keywords that you've selected. Those additional metrics include:

- Projected *Impressions*
- Estimated *Click-Through Rate (CTR)*
- Estimated Clicks per Month
- Average *Cost per Click (CPC)*
- Estimated Budget Requirements

Using this information, you can increase the effectiveness of the budget that you invest in your PPC program. For instance, keywords with lower CPC rates typically have less competition than more expensive ones. If you can select some of these keywords that are more efficient for creating goal conversions, then you've invested less in your PPC program for better results.

One thing that's important to understand, as you're estimating your search volumes and the budget that you'll invest into your PPC program, is that all of these projections are based on historical data. This means that you should collect data about your keywords and use it to improve your PPC program effectiveness over time. Additionally, you should know that there are many other factors — seasonal changes, sales, competition, and even landing pages — that can affect your actual performance results. This is just another reason you should plan to constantly monitor and revise your keywords and phrases and your PPC marketing efforts.

Forecasting search volumes and budget considerations is just the first step toward creating a PPC program that both meets your needs and fits within your budget. In addition to initial forecasting, you will also need to conduct ongoing *keyword testing*.

Keyword testing is the process by which you examine keywords and how many searches they're included in, as well as what the competition for those keywords is. Once you've completed that research, you begin to implement your keywords on your site very slowly, monitoring the results of your site traffic and goal conversions after each new word or set of words is added.

It's a time-consuming activity, but keyword testing has the potential to improve your PPC program results if you take the time do it properly. Through careful testing, you can learn what your most effective keywords are; then you can use those keywords to improve your position and impressions.

One way to start the testing process is by understanding exactly what you are testing for. Are you testing to see how effective your most recent ad copy is? How do landing pages hold up in attracting and keeping site visitors? If those landing pages are experiencing a lot of *bounces*, you may need to work with them to create more stickiness. Other questions you may want to answer to ensure you understand what you're testing for include: Are visitors reaching goal conversions? Does ad placement really make a difference?

As you're considering keyword testing, you may decide that you just don't have time to efficiently forecast your PPC traffic. However, not taking the time to do the testing could result in wasted budget dollars. People add keywords to their pages, but that doesn't mean that all keywords and PPC programs will be effective. It's necessary to go through the proper testing steps to ensure that your PPC program is as efficient and effective as possible.

Finalizing your keyword list

A lot of effort has gone into creating, researching, and narrowing your keyword list so far. Now it's time to finalize that list and begin putting your keywords and your PPC programs to work for you.

Finalizing your keyword list doesn't really mean that it's completely final. As you've learned already, a keyword list (as it applies to PPC programs) is an ongoing element in your PPC program. You should constantly be changing and updating your keyword list. And this can be a very time-consuming process.

The Long Tail of Search

The Long Tail of Search is a concept created by Chris Anderson, an editor at *Wired Magazine*. It defines the non-competitive keywords — usually three- to five-word phrases that site visitors use to find web sites. The idea of non-competitive keywords and phrases relates to the more specific terms that you can use to describe your products or information. The concept of the Long Tail of Search is that you begin any search with a very broad term. For example, if you're searching for Italian dinner recipes, that term is broad enough to return far too many results to be useful.

Using the Long Tail theory, however, the more precise and less common keywords and phrases are usually the most effective. These are located at the end of the "tail" and are represented by a very small tip (as if on the end of a tail).

Normally, a product site gets visitors by several types of keywords and phrases:

- Product names and brands
- General keywords and phrases
- Long-tail keywords and phrases

The magnificence of the Long Tail of Search is that you don't know how effective it is until you have optimized your site and have some content on your site to attract it. Sure, there will be some Long Tail queries in your logs, but it will be only a fraction of what could be there.

To conquer the Long Tail of Search, you need to create a rich foundation of content. The tricky part is knowing what content to create. If your focus is on providing value to your customers, it'll be easier for you.

To capture the Long Tail, you need to create content that not only is relevant to your product or service, but is also related to your product or service, even if the relationship is remote. You do this because you need to target not only people who know about you and your product, or who know just what they need — that's pretty simple — but you need to attract people who have the same problems as your target audience and who are looking for a solution.

However, there are a few things that you can do to ensure that your final keyword list is the most effective and up-to-date list available to you:

- Remove all of the unrelated search terms from your list. An unrelated term is a term that doesn't apply to your site in any way. You may have words or phrases on your list for which you have no web-site content at all. You have two choices here: Either create new content specifically for those words, or just discard the words in favor of better-targeted and more efficient PPC marketing.

- Remove words for which the competition is too high. Unless you have an unlimited budget for your PPC program, you'll want to eliminate keywords for which the competition is fierce. You won't gain a number one slot by eliminating broad terms, but you may find that your job in optimizing your site becomes much easier.

- Remove any keywords that your potential audience is likely to overlook or not use at all. You can usually tell what types of keywords your potential visitor will use when searching for your site, service, or product. This also means that you should remove any words that are industry buzzwords, but that someone outside of the industry might not consider using.

Once you've narrowed your words to the most relevant keywords and phrases with an acceptable amount of competition, it's time to start putting those keywords to work. Placing the keywords in the right place and using them properly will go a long way toward making your PPC program successful. But that's all information that's coming up in Chapter 6.

Writing Ad Descriptions

Keywords and PPC programs are just the beginning of your PPC campaign. Once you have the keywords that you plan to use, you have to begin putting them to work, and creating PPC ads is one way to do that. Creating a PPC ad isn't usually too difficult. Each search engine or PPC company does it differently, but most have tutorials that walk you quickly through the ad process.

Creating an ad and creating a great ad are not the same thing, though. Anyone can create an ad. And in some instances, that ad will work just fine for whatever purpose it was created. But if you really want to get the most from your PPC program, you should be adept at creating great ad descriptions that quickly catch potential visitors and entice them to come to your site. It may seem like an easy task, but in truth it's pretty difficult.

With a typical search engine description, the object is to entice as much traffic to a site as possible in the hopes of converting that traffic into customers. PPC requires a little a different approach. You don't want to pay for unlikely prospects, so the description used in your PPC ads should be designed to eliminate those who are just window shopping, while attracting those who want nothing more than to buy your products, hire your services, or sign up for your newsletter. For this reason, your PPC ad description should describe exactly what your business offers. At the same time, proven marketing copy techniques should be employed to ensure that the description is enticing enough to attract ideal prospects.

Relevancy is the name of the game when it comes to copywriting for paid listings, not only for your potential customers, but increasingly to meet the stringent requirements of the search engines themselves.

Including your keyword in the title and description of your listing can increase your click-through rate and relevant listings are not only rewarded with more clicks from consumers but also with a higher position on SERPs.

Writing ad copy for search engine listings is not only about knowing the right formula for creating good ads. Following good copywriting guidelines gets you past tough search engine editors, and in front of potential consumers. Understanding that, here are some suggestions for writing great ad copy:

- **Use your keywords:** Including your keywords in your advertisements can increase the efficiency of those ads. Additionally, if you're using the keywords that you've selected, then your ads are likely to appear in conjunction with related topics, making it easier for you to entice traffic.

- **Qualify your traffic:** Creating an advertisement that people will click on is not enough. You must create an ad the *right* people will click on. Not all traffic is equal. Even people who search with the same phrase might have different needs. One purpose of your ad is to appeal to your target audience, while signaling to anyone else that your business would not be a good fit for their differing needs.

- **List features and benefits:** In your ad description, include at least one feature and benefit for the product or services that you're advertising with the PPC program. Generally, you have very little space in which to include a description, so choose the words that you plan to use very carefully.

- **Use a call to action:** Too often, advertisements are created without including a call to action. However, studies show that including a call to action will increase your conversion rates, whereas ads that do not contain a call to action tend to perform less efficiently and effectively than those that include it.

- **Stand out:** Many PPC advertisers in the same areas will have very similar PPC advertisements. If you can create ads that stand out from these other, more generic ads, you have a much better chance of having an effective PPC program. It will be worth your time to spend some planning hours creating an ad that helps you stand out from the crowd. That extra effort will be well worth the results.

Monitoring and Analyzing Results

It's been mentioned several times in passing in this chapter, but it's essential that you see this message again:

You're not finished with your PPC campaign once you have it set up. PPC is not one of those programs you can set up and then walk away from and expect it to work properly. It is crucial to the success of any PPC campaign that it be monitored regularly, because positions can and do change every day. Apart from position monitoring, it is also important to track and analyze the effectiveness of individual keyword phrases on a monthly basis. Viewing click-through rates and studying visitor habits can lend valuable insight into their motivations and habits, and help to further refine your PPC program.

These monitoring and analyzing activities must be ongoing. It's not enough to say, "I'll check on this PPC program next month." Monitoring and analyzing PPC results should become part of your daily routine. In some cases, your rank in a search engine can change very rapidly. If you're focused on your PPC program, however, you'll likely find far more success (or at least the potential for success) if you regularly monitor and analyze the program's results.

Chapter 6

Maximizing Pay-per-Click Strategies

Understanding Keyword Placement

IN THIS CHAPTER

Understanding keyword placement

Alt and other tags and attributes

URLs and file names

Writing keyword advertise-ment text

Creating great landing pages

Understanding and using A/B testing

Avoiding keyword stuffing

Having the right keywords is far more than just ownership. Once you have them, you have to use them properly to gain any value from them at all. For example, you might know what the hottest keyword on the Internet is, but if you don't use that keyword on your web site properly, it won't do you much good at all.

Once you're developed the perfect list of keywords, what are you supposed to do with them? In previous chapters, you've heard a little about the tags, text, and links where you can use your keywords. But it's not as simple as just throwing a keyword in here and there. You must know where and how to place them on your site properly so that search engines will interpret them properly and take notice of your web site.

Alt and Other Tags and Attributes

You've probably heard the term "alt tags" a time or two. It's been mentioned more than once in this book. But hearing the term and understanding how it works are two different things.

The first thing you should understand about alt tags is that they're not really "tags" at all. Rather, the proper name for these is *alt attributes*. The term "attributes" is used because these are (more accurately) different attributes that enhance the tags you use on your web site. Alt, which stands for alternative, is a specific type of attribute that refers specifically to the alternative text you may see in place of graphics.

Most people who are not professional web designers use the terms "tag" and "attributes" interchangeably. That's why you often see alt attributes referred to as alt tags.

Several different tags and attributes are used when placing keywords into the coding of your web site. This chapter covers five of them, but there are far more attributes on a typical web page. For example, although it's not covered in this chapter, `bgcolor` is an attribute that's often used on a web page to specify the background color of the page.

Title tags

Title tags are perhaps the most important SEO tags for any web site, and if you can place your keywords in the beginning of the title tag, that improves the effectiveness of those tags much more. The maximum number of characters allowed by most search engines for title length is 60 to 65 for proper display. However, a few search engines allow fewer or more characters in a title.

Search engine spiders use these title tags as the main source for determining the web-page topic. Spiders or crawlers examine the title, and the words used in it are then translated into the topic of the page. That's one reason it's always best to use your keywords in your page title, and to use them as close to the beginning of the title as possible. The text included in the title tag is also the text that will appear in SERPs as the linked title on which users will click to access your page.

For example, if you have an informational web site that provides guidelines for choosing retirement funds, and the most important keywords for your web site are "retirement funding" and "retirement income," then a page title (which is the text used in the title tag) along the lines of "Retirement Funding Options to Increase Income," is highly relevant to the topic of the site. Spiders will crawl your site, and because the title tag is the first element encountered, the spider will "read" it and then examine your site, as well as the keywords used in other places on your site (which you learn about shortly), to determine how relevant the title is to the content of the site.

That's why it's vitally important to target the most critical keywords in the title tag. You may use 20 keywords on your web page, but two or three of those keywords (or even just a single phase) are the most important keywords you've selected. These are the keywords that should be used in your title tag.

Another important factor to remember when using title tags in your web-site design is to create a unique title for every page in the site. Make the title as descriptive as possible, and again, use the most important or effective keywords you've selected for the page, because the words you use in your title tag will appear in the reverse title bar, or the tab title, of your web browser, as shown in Figure 6-1.

Now that you know why you should use a title tag, the question becomes what exactly does a title tag look like, and where do you use it?

FIGURE 6-1

The text within the title tag appears in the reverse title bar or the tab title of your web browser.

The best way to learn where you should place your title tag is to look at the source code for other web sites. As Figure 6-2 shows, the title tag is located within the head tag, along with the meta description tag and the meta keyword tag.

FIGURE 6-2

The title tag is located within the head tag, along with the meta description and meta keyword tags.

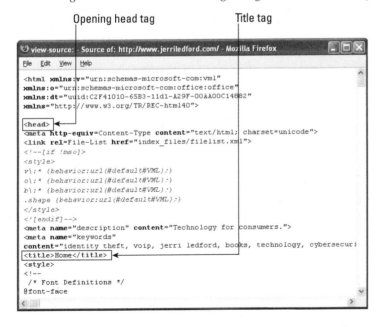

This illustration is taken from the actual source code for a real web site. However, it's difficult to see exactly how the title tag comes between the opening and closing head tags, so here's a little more simplistic view:

```
<HEAD>
<TITLE> Home </TITLE>
<META name="description" content="Technology for consumers.">
<META name="keywords" content="identity theft, voip, jerri ledford,
    books, technology, cybersecurity, spam, phishing, pharming, trojans,
    computer virus, malware, cyberstalking, cyberharrassment, security">
</HEAD>
```

If you take this code apart line by line, here's what you have:

`<HEAD>`: This is the opening head tag.

`<TITLE> Home </TITLE>`: This is the title tag, including both the opening and the closing code.

`<META name="description" content="Technology for consumers.">`: This is the meta description tag, where you place a brief description of your site, keywords included.

`<META name="keywords" content="identity theft, voip, jerri ledford, books, technology, cybersecurity, spam, phishing, pharming, trojans, computer virus, malware, cyberstalking, cyberharrassment, security">`: This tag is where you'll list the keywords that you're using to describe your site. These could be either organic or purchased keywords.

`</HEAD>`: This is the closing head tag. It indicates that the information in the header of the page has ended.

It's important that the title tag appear somewhere within the opening and closing head tags. If the title tag is located in other places in your web-site encoding, it won't render properly, and you'll be left with a web site that doesn't behave the way that you expect it to.

When creating your title tags, remember that the best title tags are those that contain targeted keywords, help develop the brand for the site, and are both concise and attention-grabbing. Usually, the text included between the opening and closing title tags also translates into the linked text that is displayed in search engine rankings. In other words, the title tag provides the first (and sometimes only) impression of your web page. It can either draw in visitors or cause searchers to choose a different search result altogether.

Meta description tags

Meta description tags are also important for every page on your web site. In some search engine results, the text beneath the linked title (shown in Figure 6-3) comes directly from the information included in the meta description tag.

FIGURE 6-3

In some search engine results, the text displayed below the title comes from the meta description tag.

Meta description text

Despite the fact that not all search engines use the description included in the meta description tags, all of them do *read* the description tag. They also use the description included there as one of the factors considered during the ranking process.

The catch with meta description tags is that they work differently for different search engines. For example, Google gives very little weight to meta descriptions. Instead, the Google search engine looks at the text on a page. And on the SERPs, Google doesn't display the meta description text either. What does show is the content surrounding the instance of the keyword on your site. Google calls this a snippet.

The Yahoo! search engine, however, does put weight on meta description text, and it uses that text directly under the web site link on SERPs.

So, what does this all mean? First, it means that your meta description tag isn't the most important piece of coding your web page. However, it also means that you don't want to skip over the meta description tag, because some search engines actually do use it.

So you should include the meta description tag on each page of your web site using the following guidelines:

- Different search engines allow different description text lengths. A good rule of thumb is to keep your descriptions to around 200–250 characters. That's about enough space for one to two descriptive sentences.

- Every page in your web site should include its own, unique meta description tag.

- Meta description tags should include keywords with high levels of importance or effectiveness.

- Meta description text should not be the same as the text included in the title tag.

Like the title tag, the meta description tag belongs inside the `<Head> </Head>` section of your web pages. Ordinarily, web-site designers include the meta description tag after the title tag and before the meta keywords tag, but that's not set in stone. As long as the meta description tag appears between the opening and closing head tags, it will be read by crawlers as it should be.

When creating your meta description tag, this is what it should look like:

```
<META name="description" content="Your description goes here.">
```

For example, the meta description tag that I might use for my personal web site would look like this:

```
<META name="description" content="Technology for consumers.">
```

It's important to note that not everyone agrees on the value of the meta description tag. However, it takes very little time to include this tag (or any of the tags included in this section of the book) in your web-site coding; therefore, including it should be a given. As with many different strategies in SEO, these tags are not a sure thing, and they are not the absolute solution to ensuring that your site ranks well. But they are one more element that could affect your ranking, so including them should be automatic.

Anchor text

Probably one of the most important elements of keyword use is in *anchor text*. Anchor text is text found on a given web site that appears to be a hyperlink. Figure 6-4 illustrates how anchor text appears on a page.

Chances are, you see anchor text every day. In fact, anchor text has become such a major inclusion on web pages that companies often use it without any thought as to how it could affect their search engine rankings.

How you use anchor text does matter, however, because anchor text is one of the most important search engine ranking factors. When a search engine looks at your web page, it automatically follows all the links that you have on the page. If those links (or even a large portion of those links) are text-based links, that's even better, because then what the search engine sees is not just the link to another page, but also your keywords. It's not enough just to make all your links text-based, however. There's a fine science to taking advantage of the power of anchor text.

The first thing you should understand is that there are two kinds of anchor texts: yours and everyone else's. I'm not being facetious here. It really is important that you consider not only how you link with other people, but also how they will link back to you. For example, if you do a Google search for the term "click," you'll find that the Apple QuickTime web site is at the very top of the list. This isn't because Apple loaded down the QuickTime site with the keyword "click." What's actually happened is that many people link to QuickTime using the word "click" in their anchor text. This isn't hard to believe, because most web sites that use the QuickTime application usually include a text link to "Click here to download" or something similar. As you can see, it's not just your own anchor text that matters. How your site is included in others' anchor text is also important.

FIGURE 6-4

Anchor text is the linked text on a web page and plays a large part in determining your search engine ranking.

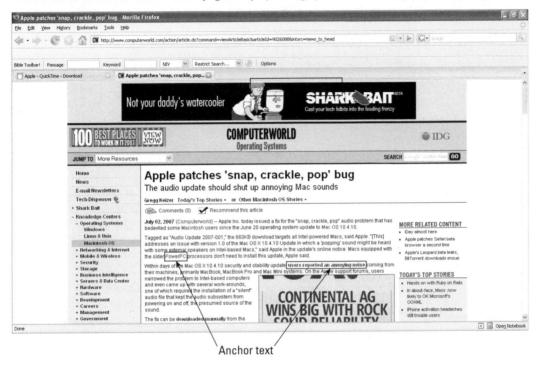

Anchor text

We'll come back to how other people link to you. For now, let's consider how you use anchor text in your web site. As we've already established, anchor text is the linked text on your web site. This text can be linked either to other pages within your own web site, or it can be linked to others' web sites that are relevant to the content of your site. And that's the real key to how anchor text can be so powerful—the relevance of the link and the words used to create the link.

When a search engine crawls your site, it's looking at several different factors—the topic of the site as indicated by the words used in the text, the links leading away from the site, and the links leading into the site. Of course, these aren't the only factors that matter, but they're among the top-ranking factors, because how these elements are handled determines how user-friendly (and authentic) your site is. So if your site caters to gourmet cooks, the information on your site might include articles about gourmet techniques, gourmet recipes, and links to web sites where site visitors can purchase gourmet ingredients or tools.

When the crawler examines your site, it's going to see that the topic of the site is gourmet cooking (which will be determined by the keywords you use in the site text). Then it's going to follow all the links on your site. If those links happen to be text-based links that use your keywords, and they lead to web sites that are relevant to the topic of your site, you're going to score well with the search engine crawler. The result is that you'll appear higher in SERPs than you would if you didn't have relevant keywords in your text and links.

You should use care when creating anchor text links, however. If you use the wrong words, you won't get nearly the mileage that you need from the links. One mistake some web-site owners make is to create web pages with the anchor text "click here." That phrase is in no way related to the content of the site, so when a crawler examines the anchor text, it doesn't see relevant keywords, even if the links are relevant to web sites that are relevant to the content of the site. Think of your anchor text as a chance to showcase the relationships you have with related companies.

What works best is to use as many of the keywords as you can from the list of relevant keywords that you developed during the planning process. Going back to our gourmet cooking example, if you use an anchor text link that reads Gourmet Ingredients and links to a web site that sells gourmet foods, a search engines sees your key phrase (Gourmet Ingredients) and it sees a link that leads to a web site that sells gourmet ingredients. So for the effort of creating that small piece of anchor text, you not only have a valid reason to use your keywords and phrases, but you also have a link that leads to a relevant web site.

So if you're adding the anchor text for Gourmet Ingredients to your web page, you must add a piece of HTML like this in each spot where you want the anchor text to appear:

```
<a href="http://www.gourmetingredientslink.com">GourmetIngredients</a>
```

Then, on your web site, what the user sees is shown in Figure 6-5.

FIGURE 6-5

Anchor text may also be called text links.

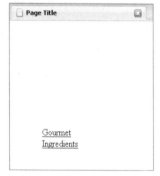

One more strategy for anchor text that you should consider is varying the anchor text. When you repeat the same anchor text over and over again on a given web page, it begins to lose its effectiveness, and in fact can cause a search engine crawler to rank your site lower in the SERPs. It's much more effective to use multiple keywords and phrases as anchor text on a web page. This allows you to vary the anchor text, but to maintain a consistency in the keywords and phrases you use.

The other type of anchor text is that which others use to link back to your site. Many times, this anchor text is overlooked as an SEO strategy; however, it's one of the most effective types of optimization that you can use. Here's an example: One savvy marketer on the Internet decided to see how quickly he could make his site rank high in the Google SERPs. So he used anchor text links on his page, and then solicited *reciprocal links*, based on highly targeted keywords and phrases that were relevant to his site. The result was that within four days, the web site had shot to the number four position in the Google SERPs.

There are two elements to consider in this story. The first is that the web-site owner sought reciprocal links. These are links to your page from another web site, in return for your site linking to them. The reciprocal links are most effective when they come from sites that are relevant to your web site. But most often, you'll have to seek the links out. Furthermore, in order to take advantage of all the value of reciprocal links, you also need to ensure that your site is linked to in a certain way. Instead of having another site just link to your main page, it's most effective to provide a potential linking site with the code that includes the anchor text you want to use.

The second element of the story, to which you should pay special attention, is that the links used by the webmaster were highly targeted keywords. In order to learn which keywords will be most effective for your site, you should refer to your keyword research. The keywords that are searched for most often, but are as narrowly related to your site as possible, are the keywords that you should consider using in your anchor text. The whole point of anchor text is to optimize your site to gain higher search engine rankings, which in turn brings visitors to your site.

So how often should you use anchor text on a web page? That's one of those magic numbers that no one really knows for sure. Different people will tell you different things. Some say no more than two or three times, others say no less than 10 or 12 times. A good rule of thumb is to use anchor text as many times as there is a solid reason to use it. Don't load your content with anchor text just to have the links, but if you have a relevant link that can be included, don't skip it just because you've used anchor text five other times on the page.

Determining what anchor text is essential and what isn't is a personal decision. However, if you're using a good analytics program that tracks the links on your web pages, you should be able to determine which anchor text links are most effective and how using them on a page affects your normal traffic flow. Anchor text is a good way to improve your search engine ranking, but as you've seen many times before in this book, your web pages should be designed with the user in mind.

One more note about anchor text before moving on. One of the most effective ways to use anchor text is in *dynamic content*. Dynamic content is content that changes regularly. Most often, that means blogs. Anchor text is well suited to blogs that change daily or weekly. This is fresh content (which is also a plus for improving your search engine rankings). It gives you an opportunity to change your anchor text regularly. Search engine crawlers get bored, too, and if you can provide them with dynamic content that contains relevant anchor text, those crawlers will look on you with favor.

CAUTION One anchor-text tactic to avoid is *Google bombing* (or *link bombing*). Google bombing refers to the methods used by black-hat SEOs to artificially inflate their web-site ranking by connecting an unrelated keyword to a specific web site. For Google bombing to work, more than one web-site designer must be willing to participate in a link exchange that will then grow exponentially because of the "apparent" popularity of the site.

For example, if in September 2006 a user searched for the phrase "miserable failure," that user was taken to the George W. Bush web site. A group of web-site designers got together and all of them used the anchor text "miserable failure" to link to Bush's web site, pushing far more traffic to the site than would otherwise have gone there.

Usually, Google bombing is politically related, though it is not exclusively political. And Google bombs aren't limited to the Google search engine. Any search engine can be affected by Google bombing, which is also sometimes called link bombing.

Header tag content

Another attribute that should be included in web-site design is the *header tag*. Header tags are the attributes that set up the different levels of headings and subheadings on your web site. There can be as many as six different levels of headings, though most web sites use only about four.

The debate about the value of header tags in SEO is a long-standing one. Some feel that header tags have zero value for impressing search engines about the importance of text on a page, whereas others feel that header tags are absolute necessities if you plan to put emphasis on certain keywords in the headings and subheadings of your web site.

The truth probably falls somewhere in between the two points of view. Looking at header tags from a strictly design point of view, you should absolutely include them in your site. Headers tell users what the topic of a page is and what the segments of body text are about. They also give readers an idea of what they should be taking away from the content they're reading. For example, if you have a web site that contains an article outlining all the medical reasons readers should purchase a new mattress, your level-one header would likely be the title of the article. The level-two headers indicate the main subheadings within the article, and the level-three headers indicate the sub-subheadings. It might look something like this:

Losing Sleep Over Poor Sleep Habits?

Your Mattress Could Keep You Awake

Too Firm?

Too Soft?

Choosing the Right Mattress

That heading hierarchy reads like this:

H1: (Page Topic) Losing Sleep Over Poor Sleep Habits?

H2: (Main Topic) Your Mattress Could Keep You Awake

H3: (Sub Topic) Too Firm?

H3: (Sub Topic) Too Soft?

H2: (Main Topic) Choosing the Right Mattress.

Headings on a web page behave the same way that headings on a page behave. They denote important information, and best of all, on a web page, they give you an opportunity to use your most important keywords in a contextually appropriate manner. Most specifically, search engine crawlers take into consideration the text within a header tag and how it fits with the body text around it (which is discussed in the next section). Again, looking at the different levels of headings, first-level headings then should contain the most important keywords on your web page, assuming they can be used naturally within the heading.

It's important to make that distinction — keywords should work in your headings. If they don't, avoid using them. It's okay to include headings that contain no keywords at all. What's most important is that the headers help readers to easily read the content in which the headings are included.

So if you're using your most important keywords in level-one headings, lower-level headings (levels two through six) should contain decreasingly important keywords.

Don't fall for the assumption that because level-one headings contain your most important keywords, you should use them all over your web pages. It doesn't work that way. Most SEOs and web-design experts will tell you that you shouldn't use a level-one heading on your web page more than one time. Using it more could cause a search crawler to decide that you're spamming the search engine, which will result in lowered rankings and might even cause your web site to be delisted from search results entirely.

The heading tags are similar in format to other tags that you've examined to this point:

```
<H1>Header 1</H1>
<H2>Header 2</H2>
<H3>Header 3</H3>
<H4>Header 4</H4>
<H5>Header 5</H5>
<H6>Header 6</H6>
```

Header tags should be included immediately before the body-text tags of your site, and the text of the header goes in between the opening and closing tags. These are automatically sized headings, though you can change the size of the headings using *Cascading Style Sheets (CSS)*. Cascading Style Sheets are a language that allows you to create your web site using a specific style. For example, in some programs you can create a web site using a preset theme. This theme usually contains all of the CSS information needed to ensure that the design of the site — from text to layout — is consistent across all pages of the site.

If you're manually coding your web site (writing the HTML yourself, instead of using predesigned sites from some application like Microsoft FrontPage or Adobe Dreamweaver), you would use CSS to ensure that your site is consistent from page to page. The nice aspect of CSS is that you can change your header sizes to suit your needs.

Unfortunately, some less-than-honest SEOs have determined that CSS can be used to artificially implant header tags into a web site in a way that doesn't actually change the size of the text included in the header tag. However, using this method to "fool" search crawlers into seeing more headings than are actually on a page could backfire, leaving you much lower in the rankings than you would prefer to be.

Body text

Body text is that text visible to readers of your site, but not included in a header. When you look at the pages of this book, for example, the text that's between headings is the body text. It's the same for web pages.

Although you've already used keywords in several places on your web site, body text is another place where you'll want to include your keywords when possible. There is no hard-and-fast rule on the number of times that your keywords should appear on a page, but a good rule of thumb is that you use them about once every paragraph or two, on the condition that they make sense in the content of the site.

What many people who are optimizing their sites don't realize is that all the strategies for SEO can be overdone, including the use of your keywords in the body text of your site. You should use these words regularly in your text, but don't use them out of context or just as a ploy to improve your search engine standings. If the keywords don't work in the normal flow of the text on the page, don't include them. Nonsense will gain you no points at all with search engine crawlers.

Body text should be placed into your web site using the body-text tags: `<body>`Insert Body Text`</body>`. These are not the only body-text tags that you'll use, however. In addition to the tags that indicate where your body text begins and ends, there are also tags that indicate special formatting in text. Those tags are:

```
<b>Bold</b>
<i>Italics</i>
<strong>Strongly Emphasized</strong>
<em>Emphasis</em>
<li>New Line in List</li>
```

Each of these tags indicates special formatting for the word or phrase within the opening and closing tags, and the special emphasis makes a search engine crawler take notice of those words. Therefore, if you can use keywords within those tags, you should try to. But the same rule applies to these formatting options for body text: Only use keywords where appropriate and avoid stuffing keywords into your site simply to improve your search engine rankings. If you use those tactics, it's likely they will fail.

Making your web site's body text visible (or readable) to search engine crawlers isn't all that complicated. Even so, many site designers still struggle with the issue, because there are certain text styles that cannot be indexed by search engines. These styles are often used on web sites in an effort to improve the appearance of the site. Some of the text visibility issues that site designers contend with include:

- Text embedded in JavaScript applications or Macromedia Flash files.
- Text contained in image files (including those with these extensions: jpg, gif, png, bmp).
- Text that is accessible only on a submission form or other portion of the page that requires some action or interaction with the user.

If search engine crawlers can't see your web-site text, they can't index that content for visitors to find. So having "seeable" content is essential to ranking well and getting properly indexed. In some cases, you must use a graphic, a special type of formatting like JavaScript or Flash, or even forms that contain text. If you must use these unreadable forms of text, try to optimize your site by using keywords in headings, title tags, URLs, and alt tags on the page. Just remember that you shouldn't go overboard with embedding keywords into headings, or other tags.

CAUTION Never try to hide text on your site in an attempt to "fool" search engine crawlers into thinking your site is something it's not. If you try to include text on your site that's the same color as the background, or if you use other types of CSS tricks, you run the risk of being detected by search engine crawlers. And even if those crawlers don't detect your trickery, it's just a matter of time before some competitor or even one of your users discovers your dishonesty and reports your actions.

Writing well for search engines is both an art and a science, and is covered in more depth in Chapter 11.

Alt tags

If you use images on your web pages, it's good practice to include *alt tags* for all those images. Alt tags are the alternative text that's displayed on your site while a graphic is loading or if it doesn't load at all. They also make your site more accessible to visually impaired people who might be using text readers. And these tags are another place where you might want to include your keywords to help boost keyword frequency and improve search engine rankings. Even if your site is already content rich and that content is tagged for optimization, alt tags allow you to reinforce your most important keywords within the context of the site content.

There is a lot of debate over how valuable alt tags actually are in search engine optimization. They have been drastically abused by some web designers who fill the alt tags with streams of keywords rather than accurate descriptions of the images they are meant to represent. But they are required for standards-based HTML web sites, and can play a small role in helping to improve your search engine rankings. What's more, alt tags should be used for every image on your site (even if they have no SEO value), because seeing what the image descriptions are helps those users who might have difficulty loading your site.

An example of an alt tag might be the description of a picture of the Mona Lisa on your web site. Your alt tag, then, should look like this:

```
Alt="Mona Lisa"
```

The alt tag usually falls at the end of the image tag. An image tag might look something like this:

```
<img width="100"
height="100"
src="monalisa.jpg"
alt="Mona Lisa">
```

The image code breaks down like this:

`<img width="100"`: The width (in pixels) of the image.

`Height="100"`: The height (in pixels) of the image.

`Src="monalisa.jpg"`: The source of the image file.

`Alt="Mona Lisa">`: The alternative text that's displayed when the image is not.

One more note about alt tags: To be really effective, these tags should be used for every single image on your web site. That could become an arduous task if your site hasn't been properly coded to start with (and depending on the number of images that you have on your site). However, the addition of these tags should be advantageous to your SEO efforts as long as you don't overstep the unspoken boundaries of alt tags.

Alt tags in graphic links

To this point, you've heard that alternative text for graphics (or graphic links) should always be included in your web pages. Now is where you find out the exceptions to that rule. Alternative text, in the form of alt tags, is very useful in circumstances where visitors to your site are using text-only browsers, when those visitors have graphic capabilities turned off on their browser, or when they use screen readers to "read" your web pages to them. And that's what makes alt tags so important.

However, if your web site features a lot of repetitive images, it might be redundant for you to use the same alt tag over and over again. What's more, when you're using graphics (like pictures and clip art) as links, visitors will quickly tire of seeing `alt="hyperlink"`. Unless the graphics used on your page and in your links contain information that is vitally important to your web site, you can usually use one instance of a descriptive alt tag, and then for each repetitive picture, use an empty alt tag: `alt=""`.

If you're using alternative tags for graphic links, you can differentiate each one by using the website address that you're linking to in the alt tag. However, don't use web addresses that string on for three or four lines. Instead, use a basic web address (`www.basicaddress.com`). For example, Figure 6-6 shows what graphic links look like without alt text, and what both graphic links and graphics look like with alt text.

You should avoid using overly long alt tags, no matter what type of graphic you're using them with. A good rule is that your alt tag should be no more than one line long, and if you can create effective, shorter tags, it's that much better.

If an image on your site is strictly text — for example, a company logo that is stylized text — one way to handle it would be to create stylized text using a style sheet to suggest some particular properties through type face, size, or color. For example, using the CSS rule `strong` the code for your text might look like this:

```
{ background: #ffc none; color: #060; font-weight: normal; font-
family: "Comic Sans MS", Western, fantasy; }
```

The problem with creating stylized text in place of a text-only graphic is that sometimes it just doesn't work as well. The company logo that was mentioned earlier *might* be acceptable in a text-only format, but only if the logo was designed that way to start with. If the logo has any graphic element to it at all, even though it is text, changing the display to a non-graphic style would cause you to lose the brand recognition that comes with the logo.

FIGURE 6-6

Alt text helps visitors who don't have or don't allow graphics displays, and also those with screen readers.

Graphic files without alt text   All text for both a graphic and a link

Another problem that you may run into when creating alt tags is bulleted lists that contain decorative (graphic) bullets. One way to handle alt text for bullet images is to write the tag using an asterisk or a dash to indicate each new bullet point like this:

```
alt="*"
```

or

```
alt="-"
```

Your other alternative is to use an alt tag that actually describes the graphic used for the bullet point:

```
Alt="black musical note"
```

Alt tags, whether you're using them in graphical links or just in place of graphics, are one way for people who can't see your images to understand your site. Many times, graphics play a large part in how your site displays. But there are times when the use of alt tags is just redundant, and in those cases, avoiding them is the best option.

URLS and File Names

The URL (Universal Resource Locator) is the literal address of your web site on the Internet. It's the address that site visitors type into their browser's address bar to reach you. Or in some cases, it's the link those users click to find you.

Ideally, your URL should be as descriptive as possible without being long and hard to remember. So, as you've learned, a URL of `www.atopkeyword.com` is much more effective than a URL of `www.partofyourcompanynameonline.com`.

But there is more to a URL than just the base name. For example, your site's structure probably has several levels of pages and files. So the base URL will then include a path to additional pages and folders. Unfortunately, if you have a site that has hundreds of pages or dynamic content, you could end up with a URL that looks like this:

```
http://www.yoursite.com/o/ASIN/B00023K9TC/ref=s9_asin_title_1-
1966_p/102-8946296-2020168?pf_rd_m=ATVPDKIKX0DER&pf_rd_s=center-
1&pf_rd_r=1A562KV3VPEPKDF3Z65D&pf_rd_t=101&pf_rd_p=291577501&pf_
rd_i=507846
```

There are a couple of problems with that URL. The first is that there's no way visitors will remember all of it. And the second is that you've lost valuable keyword real estate because the URL is an undecipherable collection of letters and numbers.

A better option with your URLs is to try to keep them as short and descriptive as possible. Say that the preceding long URL was one that leads users to a handmade red scallop shell necklace that you have for sale. Rather than creating a long URL that has no meaning at all, you could create a URL for the page featuring the necklace that reads something like this:

```
http://www.yoursite.com/products/necklace/shells/id=507846_red_scallop
```

That URL is much shorter, and it's much more memorable than the longer one. Individuals might still have difficulty remembering the URL, but it's more likely they will remember it than one that's full of random letters and numbers. This illustrates the two key bits of advice we're talking about: URLs should be descriptive without being overly long, and they should give visitors a good idea of what to expect on the page. Using this method of creating URLs for the pages in your web site, you open up the potential for including keywords in your URL, which not only helps as crawlers look at your site, but also when your URL is posted as a link on other web sites or mailing lists.

Note that you should keep URLs limited to as few *dynamic parameters* as possible (like the product ID in the example URL). A dynamic parameter is the part of the URL that provides data to a database so the proper records can be retrieved. The product ID or category ID are good examples of dynamic parameters. Another good example might be the pages of a blog. Each page will usually contain one post, or posts for a week or a month. Those pages are most often created using dynamic parameters in the URL to indicate that the information stored in a database is what should be retrieved when a user visits the site.

The URL that you select for your web site and create for your web pages is an important piece of text. Those URLs can be crawled by search engine crawlers, and they should be easy for visitors to use, to remember, and to understand. These tips, like many of the others covered in the book to this point, are all small parts of SEO. It's when all of the small parts come together that your SEO efforts bring great strides.

Chapter 7

Increasing Keyword Success

It would seem that picking out the right keywords and then employing them in keyword advertisements would be an easy enough task. But don't let the simplicity of the concept fool you. There is much to learn about how to use your keywords effectively to draw traffic to your web site.

One of the biggest mistakes web-site owners or designers make is to assume that once the site is properly tagged and *seeded* with keywords, their work is finished. It's not. There's more to do. You can't just throw your keywords into PPC advertisements and expect them to do well. There's a fine science to writing the ad.

Then, when site visitors do see your ad and they click it to go to your site, what's going to greet them? Your *landing page* is as important as the text that you place in your advertisement. And sometimes, choosing the right advertisement text, based on the right keywords, requires some comparison testing.

Keyword advertising is not a simple process. It's also not a process that you can do once and forget about. To be truly effective, you should be working with your keywords all the time. Only through regular, consistent attention can you increase your keyword success and maximize the return on your keyword investment.

Return on investment (ROI) is a term that you'll hear frequently associated with keyword advertising (and most other types of advertising and technology, but we're not interested in those right now). There is more detailed information in Chapter 9 about PPC ROI, but for now you should understand that PPC advertising is getting more and more expensive.

It is by no means as expensive as more traditional methods of advertising have been. If you have a small advertising budget and think that PPC advertising is going to be the best way to maximize it, you could be correct — if you keep up with the maintenance and ongoing efforts that are required for keyword advertising.

However, it all starts with your PPC advertisement, so that's where you must first concentrate on maximizing your return on investment.

Writing Keyword Advertisement Text

Before you can even begin to write your keyword advertisement text, you should have a finalized list — or even multiple finalized lists — of keywords selected. If you've used a keyword research worksheet (like the one included in Appendix D), you can easily use this list to group your keywords according to topic. For example, if your keywords include dayspring, spa, aromatherapy, lavender soap, relaxing herbal wrap, and mud bath, your groups will look something like those shown in Table 7-1.

It's important that you keep your keywords grouped together, especially because they associate with the different pages of your web site. It's these words that you'll be working with as you create your keyword advertisement text. According to research done by major search engine companies, using keywords in your advertisement text can increase your advertisement click-through rates by as much as 50 percent. Keywords are important to your advertisement text, and the right keywords for the advertisement are vitally important.

Another thing to consider before you begin to write your keyword advertisement text is what you hope to accomplish with the text. Do you want visitors to buy something? Do you want them to call your office for more information? Do you want them to sign up for a newsletter or some other service? It's important to know what you want users to do when they see the advertisement, because you'll use some form of this in a *call to action* in the advertisement.

It helps if you clearly write down several different sentences that express what you want the visitors to do. You don't have to worry about writing the sentences in short form right now. Just get the ideas down on paper. You can whittle away unnecessary words as you move forward with writing the text.

TABLE 7-1

Related Keyword Groups

Group 1	Group 2
Dayspring	Aromatherapy
Spa	Lavender soap
Mud bath	Relaxing herbal wrap

One last thing to consider before you begin writing your PPC ad text is what the immediate benefits of your product or service are. These, too, will be used in ad text, so take the time to write out several benefits that you might draw from as you're writing your ad text.

Once the preliminaries are done, you can begin to write your text. This job starts with your audience. Very often, when someone is writing ad text, they fail to take into consideration the audience they're trying to reach. Each generation of people communicates differently, so different tones and styles of writing will be needed to reach them.

A good example is the difference between today's teen generation and the senior generation. If you're trying to reach teens with your video editing software, you'll want to write your advertisement in a language that will catch their eye and be understood. So, if your advertisement includes the call to action, "Show the world you're an emo!" those teen users will immediately understand it means, "Show the world you're part of the emotional crowd." Senior visitors would not get that unless they happen to have grandchildren who have explained that the term emo in teen-speak is a designation for a group of people who openly share their emotions (incidentally, emo can also be a sub-designation for groups like Goths, Punks, and Metal Heads).

On the other hand, if you were trying to reach the seniors, your slogan might be something like, "Share your precious memories." To a senior, this says, "Hey, we can help you share your recollections with anyone you want." To a teen, it says **boring!**

If you know your audience, you can write ad text that is specifically targeted to the most qualified potential visitors for your site. Sometimes, you'll want to reach more than one group of people. In this case, you'll want to write different ads for each group of people. Don't try to reach everyone with one ad. You won't. Instead, you'll come closer to reaching no one at all.

Each PPC program has its own unique requirements for ad text, so take the time to learn the requirements for the PPC program that you've selected. Also, the only PPC programs that rank advertisements solely on the amount that the ad's owner bids on placement are with secondary search engines like Marchex and Kanoodle. Most PPC programs from major search engines use an algorithm that combines the amount paid for each click with the relevance of that ad and how compelling the position of the ad is to the user. Ad position is everything. For example, Google ranks ads appearing in different places either at the top or side of a page. How relevant and compelling your ad is, combined with the amount that you're willing to pay per click, will determine where in that placement scheme your ad will land.

The take-away is that if your ad text is well written and performs well, you could potentially pay less for the ranking you want, or pay the same and achieve a better ranking than you expected.

There are, however, a few ad text requirements that will apply to nearly all PPC programs:

- **Include keywords in your ad text.** As you've already seen, ads that contain keywords can perform up to 50 percent better than ads that don't include them.
- **Make your offer.** Tell potential visitors what you have and why they want it. Just be careful not to exaggerate claims about the benefits of your products and services. Keep your claims accurate and compelling.

■ **Call visitors to action.** Study after study has proven that using a call to action actually does work. Include a call to action in your ad text to motivate the potential visitor to click through the ad to your web site to accomplish whatever it is you want them to do. One word of caution, however. Many PPC programs will not allow, or strongly recommend against, using the phrase, "Click Here Now." It's a seriously overused phrase that conveys no motivation at all.

■ **Include keywords.** Keywords should be used in both the ad title and in the body of the ad text if possible. Keywords are what make PPC ads relevant and compelling. And when your ads are relevant and compelling, you get far more exposure for a smaller cost per click.

■ **Create a sense of urgency.** It's one of the oldest sales tricks in the book, but it still works amazingly well. Create a sense of urgency in your potential visitors by using words such as "limited availability," or "expires soon." Have you ever been told by a salesperson that you're looking at the last or one of the last items available, whether it's a car or television or something else? Did you feel a sense of urgency to make the purchase much more quickly than you would have if there were many of that item left? That's the purpose of creating urgency — it drives the user to take whatever action is your ultimate goal with the advertisement.

■ **Draw clicks, not views.** Write your advertisement with the intention of enticing users to click on it. Though you shouldn't use the phrase "Click Here Now," that *should* be the goal of your advertisement. The purpose in PPC advertisement is to draw potential visitors to your site. With that in mind, you should design your PPC ads to draw clicks, not simply *impressions*. It's not enough for users to see your advertisement. You won't build any brand recognition, and users won't see it now and return to your site later. They'll view it, forget it, and move on. Be sure that your ads are designed to collect clicks, not eyeballs.

■ **Write your ad long and cut it.** Writing your ad long is a copywriting trick that helps in reducing the ad to only the most relevant and enticing ad text. Begin by writing your ad in full sentences, using each of the preceding elements, and then cut those sentences down to only the strongest words that will entice potential visitors to click on them. Look at the ads that already appear in the PPC program that you've selected. This will tell you how long your ad should be and what works for others. You can then build on that to create ads that work for you.

■ **Use strong, powerful words.** Because you'll have a very limited amount of space in which to write your ad, be sure that you're using the most powerful words that you can conjure up. For example, instead of using the word "skilled," use the word "professional." And instead of "markdown," use "discount." Strong, powerful words convey more meaning and emphasis, and they do it in less space than other words or phrases.

■ **Experiment tirelessly. Experiment endlessly.** If your PPC ad is perfect right out of the gate, it will truly be an anomaly. What's more likely to happen is that you write a PPC ad, it performs okay, and then you try something a little different. That's how it should be with PPC ads. It takes constant attention and testing to find the right combinations of words, punctuation, keywords, and placement to hit the "sweet spot" in PPC advertising. And even once you do, you'll likely find yourself having to readjust the ad frequently because of changes in your products or services. Plan a little time (an hour or two) to put into your PPC ad campaign. Only through experimentation and testing can you achieve PPC success.

PPC advertising has plenty of appeal. It's quick, it's effective, and it's nowhere near as expensive as other types of advertising. But don't be fooled. PPC advertising isn't all sunshine and light. It requires work and commitment to find the methods and combinations that work for you. Once you've done that, you have to make the click worth the visitor's time. And you do that by creating great *landing pages*.

Create Great Landing Pages

Landing pages are those pages that potential site visitors reach when they click your PPC (or other) advertisement. These pages are usually not connected to your web site in any way. They are not linked through the site map, nor are they linked through the body of your web site. And to ensure that they're fully disconnected from all other methods of discovery, landing pages should also not be spidered (which is accomplished using Robots.txt, but that's covered in Chapter 16).

It sounds like a disaster in the making right? It would seem that it would be. But the truth is, these landing pages are designed for two things: first, a landing page is designed specifically to reach a goal conversion when someone clicks your link; second, landing pages are designed as a way for you to keep track of how well your PPC ads draw not just qualified traffic, but converting traffic.

If the goal of SEO is to draw more qualified traffic that converts more often than organic traffic, landing pages are your way to monitor whether or not that's happening. A landing page also gives you an opportunity to create a relationship with a new site visitor who has clicked your link for one specific purpose. You meet that person's needs, and then you can funnel the user into the remainder of your site to see what else you have available.

There is some debate as to the value of landing pages that don't link to any other source on the web site. Some experts think that once you've pulled visitors to the landing page, then the more you engage them, and the more likely they are to return to your site and eventually reach a goal conversion. That may be true.

Using that assumption, there would seem to only be one kind of landing page: the landing page (like the one shown in Figure 7-1) associated with a PPC campaign. However, there is a second type of landing page — organic — that's primarily for users within your own web site who click through a link or advertisement you have created. These pages are designed a little differently than the landing pages used for PPC ads. Essentially, however, these pages require the same efforts during creation and testing that landing pages for PPC ads require.

FIGURE 7-1

The landing page for an FTD PPC ad looks just like every other page on the FTD site.

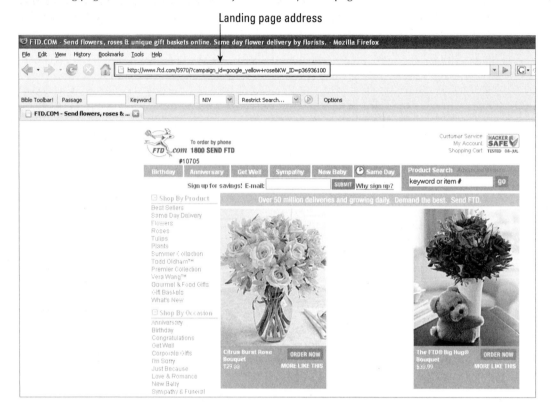

The landing page shown in Figure 7-1 actually does have live links that allow visitors to interact further with the site. However, notice that the URL for the landing page:

```
http://www.ftd.com/5970/?campaign_id=google_yellow+rose&KW_ID=p36936100
```

is different than the URL that appears when the user clicks to another page in the site:

```
http://www.ftd.com/5970/catalog/category.epl?index_id=occasion_birthday
```

This is your indication that the page is actually the landing page for a PPC ad. It would appear, then, that FTD has another way of tracking conversions from that page rather than from other pages on the site.

One more tidbit about landing pages before going through the list of elements that should be included in such pages. It's usually a wise idea to create several different landing pages and test them to determine what type of page works best for your PPC ads. It's even possible you'll learn that your PPC landing page should be a dynamic one that changes with each visitor who clicks through the link in the PPC ad. This is a determination that you make only through testing.

When you're creating your landing pages, you want them to be an extension of the PPC ad for which they are designed. For example, if you're advertising Navajo turquoise jewelry, your landing page should first be targeted to the correct market. It will only confuse visitors if they're expecting Navajo turquoise jewelry for people and they find turquoise jewelry for (or on) dolls. To further extend the concept of understanding your audience, your landing page should also provide what's promised. If your ad promises Navajo turquoise jewelry and your visitors find anything else, they're not going to stick around to learn about what is there. Finally, just as you would use a call to action with your PPC advertisement, you'll want to also use such a call on your landing page. The purpose of the landing page is to create conversions, and you have to ask for the sale (or other interaction) to receive it.

Keep in mind that your call to action might actually be for the user to sign up for a newsletter, or to participate in a survey. Whatever that call to action is, present it to your visitor on the landing page.

Here are some additional tips to help you design landing pages that convert visitors who click through your PPC ads:

- Create specific landing pages for each PPC ad. Individual landing pages allow you to tailor the pages to specific audiences, which can increase your chance of conversion.

- Quickly orient the visitor with the purpose of the landing page by using direct and concise headlines. When users click through an ad to your landing page, they must immediately see that the page will help them reach whatever goal they have in mind. If they don't see this, they'll just click back to their search results.

- Don't overcrowd your landing pages. Too much information, too many graphics, and too many multimedia elements can make it difficult for users to load your landing page. Even if they do load it, they're likely to become sidetracked by overstimulation. Keep pages clean and include plenty of white space.

- Include everything that visitors need to complete a conversion. That means users should be able to sign up for your newsletter, make a purchase, or fill out a form, all on the landing page. If users have to click much deeper into your site, you may lose them.

- Test, test, test. You'll hear that mantra over and over again associated with many different SEO strategies. For landing pages, you may have to test several versions before you find one that works for the ad you're currently running. Then, when you change the ad, the landing page will need to change, too. It's an ongoing process that's never quite finished.

Understanding and Using A/B Testing

You've heard it so many times by now that you're probably sick of it, but testing is your best friend during any SEO efforts that you put forth, and specifically with your PPC efforts. The most common and easiest-to-use form of testing is *A/B Testing*. A/B Testing in its simplest form is to test one ad version against another.

For a PPC advertisement effort, that means testing two or more ads at the same time. You should follow some guidelines when testing different ads, however.

The first of these guidelines is to understand what you hope to achieve with the testing. Are you trying to increase traffic? Are you trying to increase conversions? Or do you want to increase or change some other element of your PPC performance? Ask yourself these questions and then use that as a guideline for making changes to test.

When you know what you're trying to accomplish, you must start your testing with an ad that serves as your baseline. In order for this to happen, you have to first create at least one PPC ad and then allow it to perform long enough to have a good baseline of data against which you can compare future ad designs.

Once you have your baseline established, you can begin comparing that ad against new ads that you've created to test different elements of the PPC ad. Some of the elements you can test include:

- The headline
- Keywords
- Call to action
- Ad text
- Different landing pages

The key to successful A/B Testing is to change only **one** element in the test ads. And once that element has been changed, you have to give the ads time to develop performance data so that you can tell which of the ads is performing better. If you try to change more than one element at a time, you'll find yourself in the position of having to decide what ad changes affected the traffic and conversion. Stick to one change at a time to make it easier to be certain what changes cause what results.

When you're A/B Testing your PPC ads, you should have a control ad — that will be the one you used to create your baseline — and also a test ad. If you don't have a control ad, you don't have anything to compare your results to. Just remember that you must run both the control ad and the test ad at the same time in order for your testing results to be accurate and meaningful.

Using A/B Testing, you can learn what works and what doesn't in your PPC advertisements. It's not the most sophisticated testing method that you can use, but it's the easiest, and it's highly accurate. Testing your ads will help you tweak and fine-tune them until they are as successful as you can make them.

Avoiding Keyword Stuffing

As you're maximizing the value and return of the keywords that you've selected, you should be aware of one danger: *keyword stuffing*. This is the practice of overloading your web pages with keywords. The problem is, it's hard to know exactly how many times to use a word on a web page.

Search engines don't publish the maximum allowable number of keywords or keyword appearances on a page, so you're left to determine how many times you should include keywords in your tags, titles, text, links, and headings.

Keyword stuffing, purposely or not, occurs in several ways on web pages. The first is when the writer includes on the web page (usually at the bottom, but it can be anywhere) a block of text that is nothing more than a repetition of the chosen keyword, like this:

AKC Breeding AKC Breeding AKC Breeding

AKC Breeding AKC Breeding AKC Breeding

AKC Breeding AKC Breeding AKC Breeding

AKC Breeding AKC Breeding AKC Breeding

Sometimes, this block of text is shown in the same font that other text on the page is shown; however, it's not at all unusual for a block of text like this to be colored the same color as the page background so that it's invisible to visitors, but perfectly readable by search engine crawlers. When it's invisible to visitors, it's called *invisible keyword stuffing*.

You also run the risk of accidently falling victim to keyword stuffing on your page. This can happen when you're placing too many keywords into tags, text, and other elements of your web page. As a general rule, you'll want to keep the occurrence of keywords (called *keyword density*) at seven to 10 percent of the words on your web page.

Keep in mind that seven to 10 percent keyword density isn't a hard and fast rule. It's more a guideline that you should try to stay close to. Some search engines will allow a little higher keyword density before flagging your site as a spam site, whereas others might allow less than 10 percent. It's a game that you'll have to experiment with to learn what works and what doesn't.

One way to ensure that you're not overdoing it with your keywords is to use several on each page that are unique to that page. These keywords should come from the keyword groups that you learned about back in the beginning of this chapter.

Keywords are still one of the least expensive methods of advertising your web site. However, they're not a simple select-and-forget-it solution. You'll have to put plenty of effort and experimentation into learning what works and what doesn't with your PPC ad and keyword placement. Keep the efforts consistent and regular, though, and you'll eventually find the right combination that will not only provide the increased traffic and conversions you're looking for, but will also do it within the confines of your budget.

Chapter 8

Understanding and Using
Behavioral Targeting

Mass marketing techniques that were used in the twentieth century, like many other techniques from that era, are pretty much out of date. Reaching potential customers using television and newspaper ads still works, but it's not the most efficient way to advertise.

Traditional methods of advertising target a large group of people. Generally, that means large sections of the audience that see an ad won't be interested in it at all. As a result of that "blanket" type of advertising, companies spend a (relatively) large amount of money to reach a small segment of the population.

One way that advertisers have found to improve the success rates of their advertisements is through *contextual targeting*. Contextual targeting is basically the practice of placing ads in a specific medium based on the elements surrounding the ad.

Here's an example: Open up any women's magazine (or men's, or even children's) and look at the advertisements. Maybe one of the articles in the magazine is about weight loss. Along with the text in the pages of the article and at the end, you might find advertisements for online dieting services, diet pills, or even gym memberships.

These advertisements are placed in context based on the content of articles with the assumption that someone reading an article on weight loss might be interested in dieting services, diet pills, or gym memberships. This is contextual advertising—the act of placing ads in the context of the content that will surround those ads.

Contextual advertising is a big step toward reaching specific groups of people, but it's not nearly enough. With today's technology, a much more targeted advertising method should be possible, one that works within the confines of the medium that potential customers are using. In many cases, that medium ends up being the Internet. And of all the places where advertisers can reach highly qualified potential customers, the Internet is the best, as long as the targeting methods are appropriate for the audience.

What Is Behavioral Targeting?

In addition to contextual targeting, another method of reaching a narrower, but more qualified, group of potential customers is *demographic targeting*.

For example, if you're trying to sell a music sharing service, your main target age group might be the 18- to 25-year-old crowd. But if you're advertising a drug used to treat sickle cell anemia, you can further target your advertising to 22- to 35-year-old African Americans.

As effective as demographic targeting can be, however, it's still not the best way to reach highly qualified leads on the Internet. What works much better is *behavioral targeting*. Behavioral targeting is a relative newcomer to advertising targeting. It's the practice of serving ads to users based on their past search behaviors and web-surfing habits. And even though behavioral targeting is fairly new, it's getting a lot of attention from web marketers.

Behavioral targeting is so effective because search marketing has expanded so much. In the past, search marketing was only about search. Today, search marketing can target demographics, *dayparting* (addressed in Chapter 9), and behavior. And because today's audiences are more fragmented than they have ever been, the more specific marketing efforts can be, the more effective they'll be.

Behavioral marketing has many other benefits, too. For example, although behavioral targeting results in fewer impressions, it also results in a higher conversion rate, because the ad is more targeted than a contextual ad might be. Additional benefits of behavioral targeting include:

- **More click-throughs.** Click-throughs are those times when potential customers or site visitors click *through* your PPC (or other) ad and land on your site.

- **More conversions.** As you've seen already, behavioral targeting tends to reach fewer people, but it results in more goal conversions. Because your goal conversions should be designed to result in either a sale or the collection of data to help you reach a sale, the conversion rate for ads placed using behavioral targeting is much higher.

- **Improved return on investment.** Return on investment is the metric that seems to drive everything these days. Behavioral targeting helps to improve the ROI of your PPC and other advertising programs, because ads placed using behavioral targeting are more pinpointed to the type of audience that is most likely to make a purchase, provide data, or sign up for a newsletter or other service.

Taking Advantage of Behavioral Targeting

Another element that makes behavioral targeting more attractive is the growing ability of companies to capture and record behavior. This is accomplished through the use of *cookies*, which are small pieces of code that make it possible for companies to track how people behave on the Web without capturing any specific personal information about those people.

The concept is this: a company places a cookie on a user's hard drive, and then using that cookie tracks what the user searches for online and then where the user travels within those search results. Say that you're contemplating buying a hybrid car. The first thing that you're likely to do is research hybrid cars on the Internet. If a search company (or some other organization) is tracking your search movements, they'll learn that you're researching hybrid cars.

At this point in the purchasing process, you're not ready to commit to buying a car, so an advertiser may hold its ads back, not wanting to pay for exposure that results in no conversions. However, the company that placed the cookie on your hard drive can continue to monitor your searches and movements on the Web. Then when you begin to search for the phrase "buying a hybrid car," or something similar, the search company can alert the advertiser who will then place an ad in front of you. This ensures that you're in the right frame of mind to see the ad, which means that you're more likely to click through the ad and reach a conversion goal than other surfers might be.

The truly useful element of behavioral targeting is not that you're tracking users' behaviors, but that you're meeting these potential customers in the place where they are most likely to make a purchase, sign up for your newsletter, fill out a form for more information, or accomplish whatever conversion goal you've established.

This *search profiling* also has the added benefit of allowing you to target your ads much more effectively in the buying process. It's the part of behavioral targeting that seems to draw the most attention. But it allows more than just pre-purchase (or pre-conversion) advertisements. You can also use search profiling as part of behavioral targeting to develop appropriate *post-search ads*.

Post-search ads appear on the landing pages that you or others have created. These ads are highly targeted to the people who are most likely to click through a PPC ad to reach the landing page. Once there, the ads offer additional, related products and services. These post-search ads are popular because they tend to get more traffic than some other types of advertising, leading to more goal conversions than with other types of advertising.

When behavioral targeting is used, there are several methods by which behavior is evaluated. Those methods include:

- **Expected behavior:** Expected behavior is just that — what you would expect users to do on a given type of site. For example, if you operate a site that requires users to log in to use the site, even if it's a free site, you would expect users (who are also qualified sales leads) to fill out the form necessary to sign up for your web-site service. This behavior can sometimes allow you to see patterns that you would not have otherwise seen in the behavior of your customers or potential customers.

- **Repetitive behavior:** This the same type of behavior from potential customers over and over again. This could include everything from users accessing your pages in a certain order, to users repeatedly jumping to your site on a specific page or at a specific time. This repetitive behavior makes it much more possible for you to define patterns of behavior that lead to purchasing decisions or to other decisions that lead to the targeted goal conversion.

- **Sequential behavior:** This occurs when users sign on to your site and then visit pages or perform actions in a sequential manner. Monitoring sequential behavior helps you to discover established routines that lead to goal conversions. When you know what users are likely to do, because their habits are always the same, you're more likely to stay one step ahead of your competition.

In addition to these broad categories of behavior evaluation, there are many categories of behavior that are much more specific. Here's a short list of some of the categories that can be monitored using behavioral targeting:

- Mobile users
- Internet power users (those who are always on it)
- Gamers
- Auto buyers
- Home buyers
- Personal investors
- Credit card shoppers
- New/expecting moms
- Hotel seekers
- Vacationers
- Luxury car researchers
- Sports car researchers
- SUV researchers
- Pick-up truck researchers
- Passenger car researchers
- Movie watchers

Using these methods of behavior monitoring, it's much easier to target your ads to just the right people at the right time. If you've discovered that many people buy from your site, but they first click through some of the articles on your site and you see this in the sequential behavior of several users, you can begin to infer that if you place additional relevant content (that's not too sales-y) on your site, then at a certain point in the process users will be more likely to click through your advertisements.

The problem with behavioral targeting is that the companies that conduct professional behavioral targeting activities can't monitor all the different behaviors. The preceding list includes some of the behaviors that the MSN search engine monitors. However, other search engines might monitor some of these behaviors and not others. And those other search engines might monitor some behavior that is not included in that list.

It's possible to create a system by which you monitor a specific behavior that's important to you. Maybe you're selling a product like plasma screen televisions. And maybe the behaviors that you want to monitor are the research phase of the buying cycle and the buying phase of the buying cycle. You can monitor both behaviors if you have a clear understanding of what you're looking for. All it takes is the creation of a cookie or set of cookies that will monitor those behaviors.

The key here is determining the searches or page views that are going to lead to the conversion that you are trying to accomplish — in this case, selling a plasma screen television. There is no hard science to tell you what behaviors will definitely lead to a sale; however, there are some indications as to what point searchers must reach before they are willing to buy.

For this example, let's just say that the ideal time to place your ad in front of them is when they have returned to the Internet for a second time to research plasma screen televisions. At this point, you can place your ad in front of these searchers, and the ad is more likely to result in a goal conversion. To track these movements, you would need cookies to track the specific behavior that you've determined leads to goal conversion, as well as the pages that the potential customers are viewing. You may even want to include a cookie that helps you to exclude site visitors who have already reached the goal conversion that you've established.

Additionally, your web site will need the capability to read these cookies and then to serve up the right content to the user, based on the contents of those cookies. It's a complicated process, but with the right web designer, it's a very doable one. And it really shouldn't be all that expensive.

Additional Behavioral Targeting Tips

Behavioral targeting may sound like the solution to all your advertising worries, but it does have a few problems. By its nature, it cuts the number of potential customers who will see your advertisement. This could mean that you'll miss some segments of the market (like those who don't know yet that they are interested in what you're offering, but would be if you presented an ad to them).

For this reason, behavioral targeting shouldn't be the only method you use to target your potential customers. Sure, it's a method that will make your PPC campaigns more effective, and that alone may be all that you need to be sure that behavioral targeting is right for you. But it may not be in all cases. Take the time to research behavioral targeting abilities with whatever vendor you choose, but don't put all of your hope in it. For most people it works great, but not as a stand-alone targeting method. To be truly effective, you should use programs that leverage contextual targeting and demographic targeting as well.

You may also want to use other targeting methods because some households have one computer with multiple users. This can cause the wrong person to be served with the wrong ad. If you're considering the average family, for example, you have two parents and maybe a teenager who are all using the same computer. Mom spends a lot of time online looking at recipes and household tips to make the job of taking care of her family easier. Dad spends a lot of time looking at sports scores. And the teenager spends a lot of time downloading music.

When Dad goes to the computer to look up scores, he may find an ad for cookware, because Mom was the last person to use the computer. Or the teen may be served an ad about a specific type of gourmet ingredients. The behavioral targeting is working properly, but because there are multiple users on the same computer, the user ends up seeing the wrong ad.

To some extent, the different profiles enabled by the Windows operating system will help with this. Cookies are stored according to user profile. But that's making the assumption that each member of a family or each different computer user actually does use the profile. It's not a foolproof system. And because it's not, you should consider the possibility that this could skew your behavioral targeting effectiveness.

One more problem, and perhaps the most bothersome issue about behavioral targeting, is the privacy issue. In today's market, everyone is screaming about privacy. With the drastic rise in the number of identity thefts, people are guarding their personal information more closely than in the past. And those people may take offense at having their online activities monitored in an attempt to provide the best possible advertisements.

NOTE To some, behavioral targeting sounds a bit like adware or spyware, both of which are methods of collecting information from users without their permission. And adware is used with the express intent of pushing unwanted advertisements out to users. Behavioral targeting is designed to better target your advertisements; however, users are aware that their movements are being tracked, and they agree to that tracking. Behavioral targeting also enables more than just pushing relevant advertisements. It also allows an organization to see how it can serve users better according to their activities while they are on the organization's web site.

Legislation can also make it more difficult to monitor people's behaviors closely without their consent. To ensure that potential customers are not offended before the relationship even begins, many companies are including opt-in (or out) methods for being included in your marketing efforts (or not).

Study after study has found that your potential customers may be willing to let you track their movements on a couple of conditions. The first is that they know you're tracking them. This requires putting out some kind of privacy notice that allows those potential users to decide not to allow you to track their movements. In the case of those who have no interest in being monitored, you'll have to find some other way to serve them the right advertisements at the right time.

The second condition is that your potential customers want to see some kind of value from allowing you to access their personal information. This value could be that you provide higher quality information, better quality services, or lower prices (among other things). Whatever the value to your potential customers, the higher it is the more likely your potential customers will be to participate in your efforts, and to let you use information about their movements on the Internet to serve them more targeted advertisements.

One of the most fortunate aspects of behavioral targeting is that you don't need personal information for the targeting to be effective. Because all the tracking done with behavioral targeting is monitored by cookies, the only information that's collected is movement behavior. What you're doing is persuading potential customers to participate in the collection of their web movements by offering them value for doing so.

Chapter 9

Managing Keyword and PPC Campaigns

Keywords and PPC campaigns, like any type of advertising campaign, need to be monitored carefully to ensure that they are as effective as possible. Of course, you'll also want to be sure that you're spending only as much of your advertising budget as you need. But determining those factors requires monitoring activities, spending, and conversions, and managing the strategies that you use to improve those factors.

One factor that will influence your PPC campaigns the most is money. Be it in the form of your PPC budget, the amount of money that you need to save, or determining your ROI, you'll be constantly justifying your PPC campaign with financial values. Tracking those values isn't difficult, but it can be time-consuming.

What's more, the competition for keywords and PPC advertisements is quickly becoming more and more rigorous. If you're not constantly tweaking your PPC campaigns to make them as effective as possible, you'll be throwing your budget away like empty candy wrappers.

Keyword Budgeting

Part of the allure of PPC advertising is that it appears to be a low-cost alternative to other types of advertising. The attraction is that you can reach more people using less of your advertising budget. The reality could be much different, however.

PPC programs are designed to create competition between bidders. You find the perfect keyword, and then you get caught up in a bidding war. Before you know it, you've upped your maximum bid-per-click. And to accommodate this, you've upped your daily maximum budget. It doesn't take long for this addiction to lead to one of two possibilities: either your entire advertising budget is completely consumed by your PPC campaign, or, worse, your PPC costs have skyrocketed to the point that your advertising budget is gone and then some.

When the PPC campaign takes over the budget, eventually the campaign will fail. It's impossible to realize any return on investment when the bids on a keyword skyrocket. And because there is no ROI, your company is likely to cut your PPC campaign completely from its advertising budget, or if you're an individual, you could end up deep in debt chasing the best keywords.

That's why it's essential to start with the budget when designing your PPC campaign. Only with a well-thought-out and strategically planned budget can your PPC campaign be both effective and profitable.

Before you can begin to determine your PPC budget, you must first determine what a goal conversion is worth to you. Determining the value of a conversion can be a bit tricky. Note, too, that the value of a conversion is different from the *cost per conversion*. The value of a conversion is how much you stand to make when one of your PPC ads leads to a conversion.

If you have an e-commerce business, it should be easy for you to determine the value of a conversion. It's equal to the average profit per order. So, if your average profit per order is $5, you can assume that the value of a goal conversion associated with your PPC campaign is $5.

If you're not running an e-commerce business, determining the value of a conversion might be a little more difficult. For example, if you're operating a content site your targeted goal conversion might be a newsletter sign-up. What's the value of that newsletter sign-up to you? It varies from company to company, but if your newsletter draws advertisers, your advertising income might be what your conversion value is based on. So, as an example, if your monthly newsletter has 10,000 subscribers and your advertising income is $10,000 a month, then a subscriber is worth $1. Therefore, a good value to assign to your goal conversion (which in this case is for a site visitor to sign up for your newsletter) is $1.

With your conversion value determined, you can begin to determine your PPC budget, and it starts with determining how much you want to spend on PPC overall. This amount (whether it's $50 or $5,000) is your firm limit. Very often, PPC costs can increase over time, so it's important that you pay particular attention to your maximum spend.

Now, to budget for your different keywords, you need a few additional metrics for each keyword:

- Average conversion rate
- Goals for number of conversions desired
- Cost per keyword

To find the average number of conversions, you need to multiply the number of clicks per day by the percentage of conversions associated with that keyword. And finally, to determine your daily budget for a keyword, multiply the average value of a conversion by the average number of conversions in a given day. To find the monthly budget, multiply the daily budget by the number of days in the month. The whole equation should look something like this: (The numbers used here are for example purposes and have no corresponding metrics.)

Average Number of Conversions = 15 (clicks per day) × .08 (% conversion rate) = 1.2 (conversions per day)

Daily Keyword Budget = $5 (average conversion value) × 1.2 (conversions per day) = $6 (daily budget)

Monthly Keyword Budget = $6 (daily budget) × 30 (days in the month) = $180 (monthly budget)

One more thing about these equations: The budget illustrated would be your absolute maximum budget because spending that amount would equate to spending all of the profits that you're making with your PPC campaign. Obviously, you won't want to do that. Breaking even is not the point of PPC advertising. Making a profit is. Therefore, it would be more realistic to expect to spend about $3–$5 a day on that one keyword. That would make your keyword budget in a 30-day month $90–$150 each month.

A Different Kind of Auction

As we talk about auctions and bidding on keywords, you may be tempted to think of that end table you bought down at the Auction Barn last Tuesday. But there are big differences. Although you say you're bidding on the keyword, what you're actually bidding on is the placement of an advertisement containing the keyword. And there are numerous placements, numerous times per day, and probably millions of searches in which the ad could theoretically be displayed.

So, let's say your maximum bid is $1 on a keyword of your choice. This means that every time your advertisement is shown, you can be charged up to $1. Now if someone else comes along and bids higher than you, that person's ad will be shown in a more optimal place than yours.

Because it's possible that you're being charged $1 every time your ad is shown, your advertising budget could be inflated to a sizable bill within 24 hours if your ad were shown every time the keyword you're bidding on was shown. So to keep the advertising budget manageable, you can put a cap on your budget for each keyword.

If your budget for that keyword is $25 a month, and the word stays at the $1 level (it can drop below that at any time, depending on what your competition's highest bid is), your ad can be shown 25 times a month. But the price of words (or the ads in which they appear) is dynamic, going up and down as other ad owners increase or decrease their bids. If the price drops below $1, this increases the number of times your ad can be shown, and any amount over that $1 bid decreases the times it will be shown.

We'll get into this in a little more detail as we discuss bid management and such practices as bid jamming.

That's for a single keyword, however. So if you're bidding on 20 keywords, and you choose to pay the same amount for all those keywords, your overall monthly PPC spend would be $1,800–$3,000 per month. Most small and medium-sized business can't afford to sink that much money into a PPC program, so you've got to find a way to reduce that amount. That's usually accomplished by beginning with a few of the keywords that you've defined and then replacing the ones that don't work with others from the list that you've defined.

It's important to remember, however, that PPC shouldn't be the only element within your SEO budget. In fact, PPC should equate to only 20 or 30 percent of your total SEO budget. Other SEO efforts should also be ongoing, so that over time your organic keywords and other SEO efforts become as effective as your PPC and other paid marketing campaigns.

Understanding Bid Management

According to some experts, online marketers will spend more than $7 billion on PPC campaigns by the year 2010. This means that PPC campaigns are going to become more competitive and more expensive in the very near future. To help you compete, you'll need to monitor and manage your keywords very closely. *Bid management* is the method by which you control the amount spent on keywords. There are two methods for bid management: *manual bid management* and *automated bid management*.

Manual bid management

Manual bid management is bid management that you conduct on your own. To manually manage your PPC bids, you must keep up with what your competition is doing, track your conversions, test and monitor the performance of existing and new keywords, watch your PPC campaigns for fraud, and make changes to all campaigns when necessary. And if you happen to be running PPC campaigns with more than one PPC provider, you must do all that for every group of PPC ads you're running. It's a very time-consuming process.

That fact is enough to make some people opt for using automated bid management software or services. But even with automated bid management, there are a few strategies that you'll need to manage on your own:

- **Don't obsess over the number one slot.** It's contradictory to what you would expect, but you don't really need to be number one. Nor can you afford to be number one in most cases. The number one slots are usually snatched up by large companies that are using PPC to boost their sales. And they often have seemingly unlimited budgets to spend on their PPC efforts. That means if you're fighting for the number one slot, you're likely to spend so much on that spot that your PPC campaign will be pointless.

  Another reason to avoid the number one slot is that most people don't trust the first ad or search result on which they click. Many people will click through several ads before they make a purchase, provide information that generates a lead, sign up for a newsletter, or whatever else it is that you're hoping to entice them to do. Having your ad or search result a little further down than number one — say number three or four — will result in great savings and will probably be just as effective, if not more so, than if you were paying for the number one slot.

- **Select keywords for the stages in the buying process that you're targeting.** Manual bid management is often about choosing the right keywords. If you can define various steps in the purchase process then you can target each step in a different way, investing less in the research stage and more in the final purchasing stage. If you're not selling products, there may still be stages in which you can invest, and determining which of those stages is most valuable to you will help you decide how to best spend your PPC budget.

- **Delete duplicate words from your keyword lists.** Many organizations have several different keyword lists for different departments or different stages. And often a keyword will apply on several of those lists. But you shouldn't include a keyword on more than one list for your organization. If you do, you'll be bidding against yourself for placement.

- **Set aside time each day to monitor your keywords and PPC campaigns.** Even if you're using a bid management application or software, hands-on management will still be required. You'll need to monitor and make decisions for the application or software. Usually an hour or two a day is enough.

Manual bid management isn't nearly as effective or as realistic as having an automated bid management solution, unless you only have a few keywords to monitor. If you're like most companies, though, you have dozens and even hundreds of keywords to stay on top of, and handling all of those keywords and PPC campaigns manually could be so time-consuming that it's all you would ever do.

Automated bid management

Automated bid management can take one of three forms: as part of a solution provided by your analytics or PPC program provider, as desktop software, or as a hosted service. Many analytics providers (like Google Analytics) and PPC program providers include some form of keyword management reports and capabilities with their products. These reports are great for basic keyword and PPC campaign management, but they often lack the functionality that desktop software and hosted services provide. However, if you're only managing a handful of keywords, the capabilities provided by your analytics provider should be all that you need.

If you're managing more than a handful of keywords, you'll need something much more powerful to help you stay on top of your keywords and PPC campaigns. Desktop software is one option. This is software that you install on your computer. You maintain the software, and it helps you to manage your PPC campaigns and keyword bids. Most desktop software is sufficient for your needs, but because it requires that you maintain the resources to operate the software, manage the software updates and upgrades, and in general manage and monitor it, you may decide that a hosted bid management application is the better choice.

Hosted bid management applications are those provided by third-party vendors. The vendor manages the software, the resources required to maintain the software, and all of the maintenance for both software and resources. An added benefit of using a hosted application is that often the application is much richer and more robust than one you could manage and maintain on your own.

There are dozens of companies offering bid management services. Just a few among them are WebSideStoryBid, Searchignite, PPCPro, KeywordROI, and BidRank. Each vendor offers some similar and some different features for the applications that they provide, and the cost of hosted bid management software can be from $125 per month to more than $1,200 per month. The cost depends on the number of keywords you're tracking and the different features that are available to you. Some management application providers will also allow you to create custom management applications that also fall into the same cost range.

When you're considering an automated bid management product, you should look for several features. The most basic of these include:

- **A single interface for multiple PPC campaigns.** You will most likely be running PPC campaigns from several different providers, so you need a solution that allows you to manage all of those campaigns, regardless of provider, from a single control panel.

- **Conversion tracking**, including conversion rates and cost per sale for each keyword that you're tracking.

- **Global change capabilities.** When you make a change to your PPC campaign, whether it's changing a word, changing your strategy, or changing your bids, you may need to have those changes reflected in multiple places. Good bid management software offers the ability to make global changes — you make the change one time, and all of the campaigns you specify are updated automatically.

- **Keyword monitoring capabilities.** Bid management software should let you see where your keywords are performing at any given time.

- **Automatic bid-management capabilities.** One trick some companies use to keep the competition at bay is called *bid jamming*. Because keyword bids, unlike those in a traditional auction, are dynamic and can go both up and down, the auction isn't over when you've paid a lot and won your word. You'd like to rebid it at a lower price. And here's where the keyword jammer, by offering only a penny less than your inflated bid, tries to keep you at that level and drain your SEO budget. (Of course, you can play the same game by letting the jammer have the word and then becoming a bid jammer yourself.) Automatic bid management can keep you from going crazy by ensuring that you're bidding at the most efficient level all the time.

- **Fraud monitoring and documentation.** *Click fraud* can be very costly. A good bid management software will monitor your PPC campaigns for signs of click fraud.

- **Reporting capabilities.** Nearly every bid management application includes the ability to generate and share reports. What those reports contain varies from vendor to vendor. Be sure to check the types of reports that are available with the solution you choose.

Costly Click Fraud

One of the most onerous problems with PPC campaigns is click fraud. Click fraud happens when a person, group of people, or automated script "clicks" on PPC advertisements. Because the concept of PPC is that advertisers pay each time someone clicks on their ads, this drives the cost of ads higher and higher without resulting in any conversions.

Click fraud happens for many reasons, the most common being that a competitor is trying to drive competition out of the market. By arranging for a competitor's ads to be clicked on repeatedly without any intention of making a purchase or completing whatever goal conversion the competitor has established, the overall cost of the advertisement can be inflated, while the average conversions and the value per visit are deflated.

Some advertisers also believe that PPC providers commit (or encourage) click fraud because they benefit from the additional clicks. In fact, there have been several court cases that resulted in settlements when PPC providers like Google and Yahoo! were sued for contributing to or allowing click fraud to happen.

One of the most frustrating aspects of click fraud is that unless all the clicks come from the same IP address, it's hard to prove that click fraud is actually happening. Some criminals have created programs, called *click bots*, that can create clicks from what appear to be different IP addresses. In other cases, people are paid to read and click advertisements. In some cases, there are indicators of click fraud: an inflated number of clicks without conversions, clicks that all occur from the same computer or even the same city, and a large number of clicks within a short period of time, especially if the pattern of clicks is unusual.

If you suspect that you're being targeted by click fraud, immediately contact the fraud department of your PPC provider. And if you don't receive satisfactory results from reporting the activity, you should consider pursuing legal action. Click fraud can cost your company thousands, even tens of thousands of dollars. Worse, click fraud can destroy your PPC advertising campaign. Monitor your stats closely for any signs that you may be falling victim to click fraud.

In addition to the basic features that you should look for in bid management software, you may want to consider some additional features. These are not essential features, but they offer additional value and make monitoring your PPC campaigns and keyword bids a much easier process.

- **Rank Management:** Most bid-management software is based solely on the bidding guidelines you define. However, some software includes the ability to have your bids automatically adjusted according to the rank of a given keyword. This can be helpful if what matters to you is the rank that your ad reaches, rather than the cost of the click.

- **Balancing Strategies:** These are capabilities within bid management software that maintain a steady conversion rate, by adjusting bids according to the number of conversions. This also helps to ensure that your ROI remains steady, rather than fluctuating according to the cost of your bids.

■ **Gap Management:** In PPC bidding there's a phenomenon called a gap that appears between bids. For example, the cost per click, according to ranking, might look like this: $.56, $.53, $.49, $.28, $.27, $.26. The large drop from $.49 to $.28 is called a gap. These gaps are caused when large companies bid the same amount for each of their keywords, regardless of the average bid or the bid necessary to reach a specific rank.

When you're looking at a gap in bidding, it's often possible to "fill the gap" and still reach a great ranking. Using the preceding example, if you were to bid $.30, you could jump to the fourth position. But to make it to the third position you would need to increase your cost-per-click a full 21 cents. For the difference between the number four and the number three spot, the additional expenditure doesn't make sense.

Some bid management software offers gap management, and will alert you when there is a gap of which you can take advantage. And taking advantage of these gaps can result in lower PPC costs with the same or better results.

■ **Keyword Suggestion Tools:** Keyword suggestion tools aren't necessarily part of the bidding process, but they can still be useful and should be considered when you're considering bid management software. Keyword suggestion tools can provide additional resources or options for your PPC keywords, which can result in finding lower-cost keywords that perform as well as those that cost considerably more.

Bid management is a time-consuming process. But you can take advantage of bid management applications and software to help you reduce the time spent managing your PPC campaigns and to increase the effectiveness of those campaigns.

Tracking Keywords and Conversions

One of the keys to a successful PPC campaign is tracking the performance of those campaigns — both the performance of the keywords and the number of conversions that result from a campaign — and adjusting your campaign according to those tracking results. This tracking helps you achieve the best possible performance level for the least cost. In short, conversion tracking is the most important part of any PPC campaign.

Conversion tracking can be accomplished in one of several ways:

■ **Tracking tools integrated with your PPC program.** Some PPC providers (most notably Yahoo! Search Marketing and Google AdWords) provide tracking tools built into their PPC control panels. These tools should allow you to track traffic, conversions, and possibly even value per visit.

■ **Third-party tracking tools.** These tools tend to be more powerful than those offered by PPC providers. The most important area of increased functionality is the capability to track PPC campaigns across companies. Because most web-site owners have PPC campaigns running from more than one PPC provider, the ability to manage and control all those campaigns from a single location can be valuable.

- **In-house tracking tools.** Because some companies are unable to find tracking tools that provide the information they need, they create their own tracking tools in-house. If you have the capabilities to create in-house tracking tools, you can have tools that provide only the specific information you need.

- **Tracking using a spreadsheet.** Before there were PPC campaigns and the tracking tools that go along with them, web-site owners would track their online advertising using a spreadsheet, developed to include all of the different categories that needed to be tracked. Today, there are still some web-site owners who prefer to track their PPC campaigns (and their other online advertising campaigns) using the "old-fashioned" spreadsheet. It's one of the least expensive ways to track your PPC campaigns, but it's also one of the most time-consuming. Should you decide that a tracking spreadsheet is the way to go, you may want to consider include columns for:

  - Keywords
  - Headlines
  - Ad Copy
  - Click Through Ratio (CTR)
  - Keyword Cost
  - Sales Indicators (to show which keywords resulted in sales)
  - Information Requests Harvested
  - Information Requests Resulting in Sales

No matter what method you decide to use to track your PPC campaigns, you'll need a way to differentiate one keyword ad from another. Some PPC providers require that this be done by inserting a snippet of tracking code on your web site. This code then catalyzes the tracking process so that when someone clicks through your PPC ad, you can track whether the click-through results in a conversion.

Following is an example of what the tracking code for your PPC campaign might look like if you're running a Google AdWords campaign. This specific code is intended as an example only. If you try to use this code to track your web site, you'll find that it won't work because this code was designed only as an example by the Google AdWords team.

```
<!-- Google Code for Purchase Conversion Page -->
<script language="JavaScript" type="text/javascript">
<!--
var google_conversion_id = 1234567890;
var google_conversion_language = "en_US";
var google_conversion_format = "1";
var google_conversion_color = "666666";
if (1) {
var google_conversion_value = 1;
}
var google_conversion_label = "Purchase";
```

```
//-->
</script>
<script language="JavaScript"
src="http://www.googleadservices.com/pagead/conversion.js">
</script>
<noscript>
<img height=1 width=1 border=0
src="http://www.googleadservices.com/pagead/conversion/1234567890/
?value=1&label=Purchas
e&script=0">
</noscript>
```

The code is placed in the HTML of your web site, according to directions provided by the PPC provider.

Another way to track your PPC campaigns is by URL. Using this method, each PPC ad is given a separate URL, which is used only by that keyword. Then, when a visitor clicks through a PPC ad and is taken to your web site, you will know which ad is working best according to the amount of traffic on the specific site.

This method does require that you have a way to track your web-site traffic, but you should be doing that anyway. If you're not tracking it, how will you know what kind of traffic your web site gets?

Before you get too far into tracking your keywords and conversions, it helps to have a plan for what you want to gain from your PPC campaign. The first things that you'll need to know are the long- and short-term goals for your PPC campaign. You need to track both long- and short-term goals because without both you could find yourself throwing money into a PPC campaign that doesn't provide the results you need.

Far too often, web-site owners find that they've instituted a PPC campaign that does really well in the beginning but then over time becomes more costly and less effective. If you're conducting all the elements of SEO for your site properly, it isn't worrisome to find that the effectiveness of your PPC campaign drops after a while — as long as the overall traffic to your site and the number of conversions on your site continue to rise.

This means that your organic SEO efforts are working. When this happens, it's time to consider other keywords for your PPC campaign. Instead of pouring more money into improving your ranking, which will decrease the return on investment from your PPC campaign, you might change the campaign by using different keywords.

CAUTION As you're monitoring your PPC campaigns, pay close attention that your organic SEO efforts don't suffer because of your PPC efforts. Organic keywords are your true ticket to a high ROI. The more search engines rank you for free, the more effective you can make your investment in PPC. However, if you're not careful about the keywords that you use in PPC, the ads that you write for PPC, and the frequency with which you change your PPC campaigns, you could end up cannibalizing your organic rankings. And when PPC replaces your organic rankings, you have to spend more money for lower results.

As you're tracking your PPC campaign, you should also have a set of *key performance indicators (KPIs)* that you compare your results to. KPIs are performance indicators that you develop based on the long- and short-term goals you have in place for your PPC campaigns. These indicators are of value for deciding when it's time to change some element of your PPC campaign.

Reducing Pay-per-Click Costs

The one phrase associated with PPC campaigns that you're likely to hear more often than "conversion rate" is "reducing costs." In today's world, every penny invested in advertising and marketing needs to be well spent, and PPC campaigns are no exception. Budgets must be monitored and maintained, and that means finding a way to reduce the costs associated with your PPC campaigns.

During the early years of PPC advertising, you could pretty much figure a bid for a keyword or phrase and then assume that you didn't need to monitor it too closely. But that was before PPC advertising became one of the most effective advertising methods used on the Internet. Today, the competition for PPC keywords and phrases is very high, which means you're likely to spend way more money to achieve the same rank than you needed to in the past.

If you're not careful about your budgeting habits in the context of a PPC campaign, you could spend tons of money without getting better results. Management strategies, however, will help you reduce the cost of your PPC campaigns while maintaining or even improving your click-through and conversion rates.

Managing PPC campaigns

When you consider management of your PPC campaign in the context of reducing the budget, there's a lot you can do to reduce your costs without decreasing the effectiveness of your campaign. Your first step should be to replace any poorly performing ads. Monitoring your ads should already be a key part of your PPC campaign, so determining those that aren't performing well should be easy.

Another way to reduce your PPC costs is to reduce the amount of your bid per keyword. As noted earlier, it's not necessary to strive for the top advertising slot. And reducing your keyword bid by a few cents per click can make a huge difference in the cost of the campaign.

Just remember that reducing your bid shouldn't necessarily mean reducing your budget. Instead, use your existing budget more effectively. If you cut your budget too much, you'll lower the number of times that your keyword ad is shown each day, which in turn lowers your conversion rate.

In addition to reducing the amount you're bidding on keywords, you should also examine the keywords you've selected to see if you can remove any that are general in nature or high demand. "General" and "high demand" can be the same, but there can be a subtle difference. General keywords are good for branding purposes (and branding purposes only), so they are automatically high demand and high cost. Competition for them is keen. But less general keywords can also be high demand. As an example, if you're in the tissue business, "tissue" is a coveted branding keyword and will cost you a lot. "Facial tissue" is less general, but it's still going to be in high demand and thus expensive. Unless it's essential that your brand be associated with one of these high-demand keywords, it's better to avoid them and not pay a lot for keywords that won't increase your number of qualified clicks all that much.

High-demand keywords are also very expensive. The more popular a keyword is, the more you'll pay for it. And with many high-demand keywords, the resulting traffic may not be as well targeted as it could be. This means a reduced number of conversions, resulting in a lower ROI. It's far better to choose keywords and phrases that are not in as much demand but are more targeted. You'll pay less for these keywords and will likely end up with much more qualified traffic from them, which will translate into more conversions and a better ROI.

Match types can also help you control your PPC budget. A match type is the condition under which you prefer that your PPC ad is shown. So, if you've selected a keyword or phrase — let's say "SEO consultant" — for your PPC advertisement, you can specify if you would like to have that ad shown only under certain condition.

When you set up your PPC campaign, most PPC providers offer the option to choose a match type, though it might not be immediately obvious. By default, your match type will be the broadest match possible (because that means more money for the search engine). But there are several general match types that you could use:

- **Broad Match:** A broad match occurs when your ad is shown to the broadest possible segment of searchers. What that means is that anytime someone searches for "SEO consultant" your ad will be shown, no matter whether those two words appear together or if there are other words included with the term.

- **Phrase Match:** A phrase match occurs when your ad is shown for searches that contain the key phrase you've selected, in the correct word order, but also including other words. So instead of showing your ad only for searches containing "SEO consultant," your ad might also be shown for searches like "free SEO consultant," or "SEO web-design consultant."

- **Exact Match:** An exact match takes place when your PPC ad is shown only for searches that contain the exact words that you've selected, in the exact order in which you've selected them, with no other words included in the phrase. In other words, if you choose an exact match for "SEO consultant," the only time the ad will be shown is when a user searches for "SEO consultant."

Match types offer an excellent method for reducing the cost of your ads while increasing the effectiveness of the ads. You should use caution when narrowing your match types too much, however, because you could miss possible clicks from people who aren't exactly sure what they're looking for.

One more method for decreasing your PPC budget is to modify your PPC strategy. This, actually, should be an ongoing strategy for any PPC campaign, even if you're not trying to reduce your budget. Monitor and review the amount of PPC spending versus the number of conversions you achieve. Then use this information to make changes to your keywords and ad copy to increase the effectiveness of your PPC campaigns.

Negative keywords

Negative keywords are words that cause a PPC ad *not* to be shown. These are words that can be associated with the topic that you're targeting, but not with the specific product or service that you're advertising. For example, if your web site sells traditional Christian music, it's not likely that you'll want your ad to show for people who are looking for rock, pop, blues, or rap music. You can use those words as negative keywords to reduce the number of times that your PPC ad is shown.

Some PPC providers actually have a *negative keyword tool* that makes it easy for you to add negative keywords to your PPC campaigns. If your PPC provider doesn't have such a tool, you can add negative keywords to your keyword lists by placing a negative (-) sign in front of them. Using the music example, then, your negative keyword list might look something like this:

> -rock
> -pop
> -blues
> -rap

Negative keywords should result in better qualified traffic from your PPC ads. But some people are concerned that negative keywords can have an adverse effect on their PPC campaigns because they do reduce traffic from the ads. If your main purpose for having a PPC campaign is to gain exposure for your web site, then yes, negative keywords could have an adverse effect. If, however, the purpose of your keyword advertisements is to increase the amount of qualified traffic and conversions, then negative keywords are a great strategy to help reduce the cost of your PPC campaign while improving the quality of your clicks.

Finding negative keywords adds another dimension to creating your keyword lists. You must be careful when using negative keywords in keyword groups. You want to choose negative keywords that won't affect other PPC ads within the keyword groups that you're using.

The most obvious place to begin looking for negative keywords is within your keyword list. If you're brainstorming keywords, you're likely to come up with some that don't apply to your products and services, but that *could* trigger your ad being shown. You can also use a keyword suggestion tool to suggest the different keywords and phrases associated with your products and services. Negative keywords will usually appear all over the lists that are suggested by these tools.

It's possible to go overboard with negative keywords. Don't include so many negative keywords that your ads are never shown. Just use them when the keywords that could trigger your ad truly are unrelated to your products and services.

Dayparting

One of the most effective methods of reducing the cost of your PPC campaign is to target your campaign to the most effective times of day or days of the week. Called *dayparting*, this strategy requires that you monitor your PPC campaigns to know what days and hours of the day your campaigns perform the best.

Not all PPC companies offer dayparting capabilities, but many do, and some even allow you to set up automatic bid adjustments according to your dayparting schedules. This helps to reduce the cost of your ads while showing them during the most effective times of the day or days of the week.

There are other reasons you might want to use dayparting aside from the savings. Some companies use dayparting to improve the demographics to which their ads are shown. Different demographic groups use the Internet at different times of the day. If you're targeting teens, you might find they are most active online between the hours of 3 p.m. and 10 p.m. If you know that, you can schedule your ads to be shown more often during those times, and the result should be that more teens see those ads.

The best way to determine the most active times for your ads is to look first at the average time on your site metric. The average time it takes visitors to click through your ad indicates their level of interest. For example, if you find that people who click through your ads between 8 a.m. and 5 p.m. spend twice as much time on your site than those who click through at other times, you can assume that those who come during the daytime hours are more interested in what you have to offer. As a general rule, those who are more interested will contribute more goal conversions.

Once you've determined during what hours your site visitors spend the most time, you can look at the number of visitors who come during that time and the number who result in goal conversions. These numbers should give you a pretty clear idea of what your dayparting schedule should look like. An example of a dayparting schedule is shown in Table 9-1.

TABLE 9-1

Typical Dayparting Schedule

Hours	Monday	Tuesday	Wednesday	Thursday	Friday	Saturday	Sunday
8–9	Closed	Closed	Closed	Closed	Closed	Closed	Closed
9–10	32.7	33.5	31.6	33.4	33.3	Short Staff	Closed
10–11	31.1	38.2	35.6	39.2	36.9	Short Staff	Closed
11–12	21.0	21.6	20.5	18.5	22.0	Short Staff	Closed
12–1	18.6	17.2	19.4	18.4	16.5	Short Staff	Closed
1–2	18.3	18.1	18.9	19.1	17.7	Short Staff	Closed
2–3	45.9	39.2	41.7	49.9	43.6	Short Staff	Closed
3–4	56.7	57.9	51.0	60.3	51.1	Short Staff	Closed
4–5	59.9	56.7	55.3	59.7	60.4	Short Staff	Closed
5–6	60.4	61.7	55.8	59.0	59.3	Short Staff	Closed
6–7	18.7	23.5	19.1	18.0	17.9	Short Staff	Closed

Looking at the schedule, it's easy to see the pattern in the average number of seconds that visitors spend on your site. During the hours of 9 a.m. to 11 a.m. visitors spend slightly more time than they do during the lunch hours. However, the most time that users spend on the site (by seconds) is between 2 p.m. and 6 p.m. It's these hours in which you should invest the most.

Additionally, if you're looking at the schedule, you see the company is closed all day on Sunday and before 9 a.m. during the week, and is short-staffed all day on Saturday. These are times when you'll want to keep your ad exposure low or non-existent.

 NOTE Dayparting also has an additional benefit that many people don't think about. It can help you reduce the instances of click fraud that you may face. Because your ad is shown only at specific times, it is less available for your competition or other malicious souls to use it to drive up your PPC advertising costs.

Dayparting also works for days of the week and is especially useful if your products and services are seasonal in nature. For example, if you find that your ads gather the most traffic on weekends, you may decide that exposure during the week isn't as important as exposure on the weekend. In that case, you can keep your exposure during the week to a minimum and increase it dramatically over the weekend. This should result in your budget being lower, or at the very least your budget should stay the same while the effectiveness of your PPC campaign should increase noticeably.

CROSS-REF Another strategy that can help you reduce your PPC costs is geo-targeting. You'll find more information about geo-targeting in Chapter 14.

Improving Click-Through Rates

Some of the efforts you take to reduce the cost of your PPC campaigns can also lead to improved click-through rates. It's essential that you work toward increasing these rates. Even though more clicks drive up the cost of your PPC campaign, they also lead to more sales or conversions.

Aside from the efforts that you've already seen (like dayparting and better targeting) you can also improve your click-through rates by improving the ad copy in your PPC campaigns. Ad copy is covered in more depth in Chapter 12, but for now you should know that there are a few strategies for beefing up that copy.

- **Include special offers or incentives in ad text.** If you have coupons to offer, discounts available, or even free gifts with purchase or other special offers and incentives, be sure those are included in your PPC ad text. People are drawn to specials, and advertising them should draw more people to your site.

- **Consider including price in ads for products and services.** Many people shy away from advertising their prices, but those prices (especially if they're real bargains) can entice customers. If you have great prices, tell the world. Just make sure you check out the competition before you decide you have the best prices on the Internet.

More about Click Fraud

As noted earlier, *click fraud* is becoming an increasingly difficult problem with PPC advertising. Don't fall victim to the lure of participating in some click fraud scheme to increase your click-through rates. The results will be disastrous.

Click fraud is a crime. Just as you should avoid being victimized, you should avoid taking part in falsely inflating the number of click-throughs on PPC ads either for personal gain or simply as a way to harm competition.

Click fraud can be conducted in several ways. Competitors may click through your ads repeatedly to increase the number of click-throughs for which you are charged. Some advertisers have been billed for more than $100,000 in PPC costs because a competitor has arranged to have their PPC ads clicked repeatedly.

In an effort to insulate themselves from criminal charges, and to create as much havoc as possible, some advertisers will employ *clickbots*, or programs that search for and click on PPC links to drive up prices. These clickbots are usually automated and very often can't be traced back to their "owners."

Click fraud is also conducted by a program called Paid-to-Read (PTR). Underhanded businesses hire readers to read and click through PPC ads. Again, this can be costly, but even more worrisome is the fact that PTR schemes are difficult to track because multiple people using valid IP addresses are clicking through the ads. It's much harder to track multiple individuals than to track a single individual using some repetitive activity or clickbots to commit click fraud.

Click fraud is monitored by watching the sources of PPC traffic. If a large number of clicks come from the same IP address, it's obvious that fraud is being committed. Often, though, this isn't the way it happens. Criminals use IP alternating software programs to click on ads. These clicks appear to come from legitimate site users.

Another indication of click fraud is if a number of ad clicks also seem to come from the same time frame (for example, 100 clicks over the course of 10 minutes). Monitoring traffic patterns is one way that anyone committing PPC may be caught.

In the past, anyone caught conducting click fraud schemes would receive what equaled a slap on the wrist. Today, however, many search engines are being made to answer for click fraud and the costs that PPC users are having to pay because of it, so those search engines are cracking down. If you get caught conducting a click-fraud scheme, you could face stout fines, and possibly even a criminal prosecution that could result in jail time.

Click fraud is a serious crime. Don't be victimized — and don't be tempted to do it yourself.

- **Highlight a key feature of your product or service.** Key features can be used to draw additional clicks, and they should be better qualified clicks than if you just include the name of a product or other more general information.

- **Create a sense of urgency.** People are motivated by time. If you have a limited-time offer, make sure your PPC ad makes it clear that there's a special going on, but only for that time. You can also create a deadline, which will motivate potential customers to click through your ad.

- **Use a call to action.** People won't take action all on their own. Your PPC ads will be much more effective if you include a call to action that gives people a reason to click through your ad. Buyers need directions, and they want you to make as many decisions for them as possible, so if you can definitively tell customers they should take some action (like "click here," "act now," or "hurry") they're more likely to click through your ad.

When you're creating PPC ads, you also want to use the most active language possible. The following two ads are for the same product, but the first is written in a weak style, using language that's not strong enough. The second ad improves on those factors, making the ad more effective for your PPC campaigns.

Not great ad:

Learn about government grants. E-book provides details about grants available to you.

Better ad:

Free money from Uncle Sam! Learn how to land federal grants and free money!

The hook and the active language in the second ad make it much stronger (and therefore more effective) than the first ad, even though they both say almost the same thing.

Don't be afraid to play with your ad copy a little if you find your PPC ads aren't performing as well as you would like them to. You'll find that changing the copy just a little can make a huge difference

The ROI of PPC

Return on Investment (ROI) is the final word on the success of many PPC campaigns. However, sometimes organizations look at ROI differently than they should. Most people associate ROI with strictly a monetary value. In truth, however, there's much more to it than just money.

If you're interested in learning just the monetary value of your PPC ROI, it's easy enough to figure. Some PPC companies or the tracking companies that you use will provide the metrics for you. However, if you need to figure it yourself, the equation is simple:

```
Profit = Sales - Ad Spend - Expenses
ROI = Profit/Ad Spend
```

That's all there is to figuring what your monetary ROI is. And with PPC campaigns that are properly managed, the ROI on your PPC campaigns should be impressive. But there is much more to PPC ROI than this.

Other aspects of ROI that should be considered are not money-oriented, though they should always be coupled with monetary valuations. For example, if the goal of your PPC campaign is to gather information about your customers, then one of your ROI measurements should be how successful your PPC campaign is at gathering that information.

Another ROI measurement could be brand loyalty or even satisfaction. What your additional ROI measurements will be should be based on your PPC campaign and the goals of that campaign. But don't weigh your whole campaign only on the monetary ROI, even if it turns out that monetarily your PPC campaign is very successful. Monitoring all your ROI measurements will help you keep your PPC campaign on track.

Chapter 10

Keyword Tools and Services

With so many keyword and PPC tools and services, it's hard to know which one to choose. You'll find, though, that only a few companies are major players in this space. The top three are Google AdWords, Yahoo! Search Marketing, and Microsoft adCenter. Others exist, of course, but these three are the most well known.

They also represent both directories and search engines, which gives you a good idea of how the different types of PPC services work. The basics from the advertising end are about the same. It's the setup and some of the more advanced features that are different.

When you're looking for a PPC program, remember that you'll probably use more than one, and some companies use several to reach both broader and narrower markets. Which company you choose and whether you choose to work with more than one company should be determined by your needs. But when you're considering PPC agencies, here are some qualifications to keep in mind:

- **Length of Service:** How long has this company been around? If you're considering a new agency, use caution. New companies aren't necessarily stable and you might find that you get your campaign started only to have the company gobbled up by another — or could just fall off the face of the Internet.

- **Industry Participation:** The PPC industry has been around a while, but as with anything on the Internet, it changes often. Find out how invested your target company is in the industry. Industry investment usually means long-term plans and goals within an industry. It also means that the company is more likely to stay in good standing with customers.

IN THIS CHAPTER

Google AdWords

Yahoo! Search Marketing

Microsoft adCenter

Position-checking and tracking tools

151

- **Features and Feature Combinations:** Your company might have different requirements from other companies. Look at the different features and feature combinations that are offered by your target PPC provider. Some of the services that should be available are bid management, education, reporting, link submission, copywriting, and even some elements of research. Determine what features you must have and then find the vendor that can provide them.

- **Number of Campaigns:** Some PPC providers have restrictions on the number of PPC campaigns you can run at any one time. Others have restrictions on the types of campaigns you can run (that is, global versus local). Be sure to ask about limitations in this area, because you'll find later on that it's an important issue to address up front.

- **Average Spend:** Can your prospective PPC company give you an estimate of the average spend for companies that use their services? This average helps you to quickly determine if your budget is sufficient.

- **Client Referrals:** Client referrals are an often overlooked aspect of PPC company research. What are other clients saying about the service? You can look for these comments online or ask the company specifically for referrals. However, if you're asking the company to provide referrals, keep in mind they will point you *only* in the direction of good referrals.

Google AdWords

Google AdWords is the PPC company you've probably heard the most about. AdWords is one of the top search engine marketing programs, and Google is one of the biggest providers of search, and many other services as well.

Being biggest doesn't always mean being the best, though. When you're evaluating the PPC companies you may use, be sure to check not only the traffic rate, but also the conversion rate if possible. It's great if your ads receive lots of impressions, but if those impressions don't turn to clicks, you'll find your PPC campaign is not at all effective.

Google AdWords. You may have heard the name so often that you think there's nothing else — and certainly it's one of the most diverse PPC companies out there. It not only offers search engine marketing, but also includes marketing by radio and even a telephone service that potential customers can use to call you. Google will soon begin offering purchase of TV, newspaper, and embedded video advertising. Even the radio and phone models of AdWords are charged on a bid-per-keyword basis. Additionally, AdWords is linked to Google's AdSense program, which is an advertisement publishing program in which web-site owners place ads on their web sites; when users click through those ads and make purchases, the web-site owner gets paid a small amount. Many web-site owners use this service to help offset the cost of having a site.

AdWords ads are shown when someone searches on Google, AOL Search, Ask.com, and Netscape. This gives Google AdWords one of the largest markets for keyword advertisements. However, a larger market doesn't guarantee a higher quality lead, so when using AdWords, it's essential that you pay attention to the details that help your ads place when they're most effective.

Signing up for Google AdWords is quick and easy. When you begin the registration process, you must choose between the basic and standard editions of AdWords. The basic edition is great if you've never used a PPC program before. It includes one set of keywords, basic reporting capabilities, and basic targeting. The standard edition includes multiple sets of keywords and more advanced targeting and reporting in addition to a few other tools.

If you begin with the starter edition, you can graduate to the standard edition when you're ready to. When you do, your starter campaign will be moved to your standard AdWords account, so you don't lose any of your existing advertisements. No matter which option you choose, you'll walk through the process of setting up your first AdWords PPC ad when you sign up for the account. Even though you've created an account, however, the ad won't be active until you fund the account.

Funding just means that you provide a credit card number to which Google will charge your monthly advertising costs. Once you fund the account, your ads will begin showing immediately, based on the budget that you created when you set up the account.

Google lets you change your budget, or even your ads and keywords, without too much trouble. When you sign into your AdWords account, you should see four tabs across the top of the page, as shown in Figure 10-1. These tabs lead to different segments of the AdWords web site that allow you to manage your ad campaigns and your AdWords account.

FIGURE 10-1

Use the navigation tabs in Google AdWords to manage your campaigns and your account.

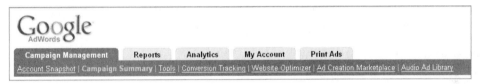

Campaign management

The Campaign Management tab is where you'll perform most of the tasks to manage your account. This tab contains an overview of the ads that you have running as well as links to an account snapshot, tools for managing your accounts, conversion tracking tools, a web-site optimizer, an ad creation marketplace, and an ad audio library.

The account snapshot, as shown in Figure 10-2, shows a quick overview of your campaign performance as well as any alerts that you might need to see.

The Tools link is where you're most likely to find the tools that you need to edit, change, or delete your ad campaign. When you click this link, you're taken to another page with links to applications such as the Keyword Tool, the Traffic Estimator, and the Ad Creation Marketplace, which is a fee-based service that makes it easy for you to hire someone to help you create your PPC ads.

FIGURE 10-2

The account snapshot is a brief overview of your AdWords campaign.

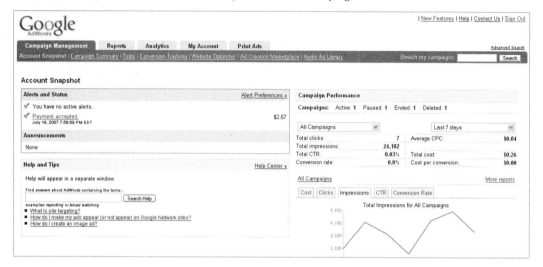

The conversion tracking provided by Google AdWords will give you a basic understanding of how your ads are converting customers. The actual conversion metrics are on the Campaign Summary page of the Campaign Management tab, but on this page you can find educational information about conversion tracking and *cross-channel tracking*. Cross-channel tracking is a method for tracking all of your ads through all of the media available on AdWords—PPC ads, radio ads, newspaper ads, and so on.

The web-site optimization link takes you to a page that shows you results from different campaigns that you might be testing. The first time you come to this page, you'll be prompted to go through a tutorial, create a plan for the testing that you'll be doing, and view a sample report. Once you've clicked through these elements, you can click the **Get Started** button to begin using the web-site optimizer. You'll be taken to a page like the one shown in Figure 10-3 that you can use to create a new experiment or testing session.

CAUTION As of this writing, the Website Optimizer is in the beta edition. If the program works well, Google will finish designing it and working the kinks out. Then it will no longer be a beta program. This could take as much as a year or longer. However, your participation and feedback in the beta edition will help ensure that it's as fully functional as possible.

The Ad Creation Marketplace is a service that allows you to hire someone to create your PPC ads. Ad specialists are available, and using a service like this will help you ensure that you're getting the most effective copy possible.

The Ad Audio Library is one of the newest features of AdWords. This feature allows you to create audio ads for use with the audio capabilities that Google AdWords has recently put into place.

FIGURE 10-3

Use the Website Optimizer to test different configurations for your PPC ads.

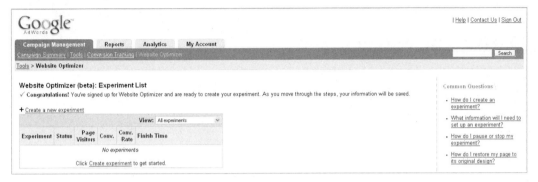

Each time you open one of these links, you're taken to a page that displays further information, capabilities, and training materials about that feature.

Reports

The Reports tab is where you'll find all your reporting capabilities. Figure 10-4 shows the opening page of the tab, where you can see existing reports and the links to create new reports. The reports that are available here include:

- Statistical Reports
- Financial Reports
- Conversion Reports

In addition to these reports, you can also create your own report, building from a foundation of available reports. Those reports include:

- Keyword Performance
- Ad Performance
- URL Performance
- Ad-Group Performance
- Campaign Performance
- Account Performance
- Search-Query Performance
- Placement Performance

FIGURE 10-4

An overview of reports allows you to see current reports and what reports are set to run automatically.

These reports can be customized to include specialized dates or date ranges, level of detail viewed, and several other options. Filters let you further customize the reports, so that the information you receive is the information you need.

Finally, you can download and print reports and even have reports run automatically on a specific day of the week or month and sent directly to your e-mail inbox. This ensures that the report you need is there on the same day, even if you're too busy to stop and think about it.

Analytics

Analytics reports measure different aspects of your PPC campaigns, such as keywords used to find your site, entry path, exit path, conversions, and even the amount of time spent on the site. Instead of just supplying the basic analytics with AdWords, Google takes it one step further and allows you to connect your AdWords campaigns with your metrics in Google Analytics. The result is a much clearer picture of how your campaigns are running in the context of how other SEO efforts are affecting your site.

If you don't have Google Analytics, it's no problem and it is free. AdWords will walk you through the process of setting up your Analytics account; then within a few days you should begin seeing metrics from your web-site traffic. You will, of course, need to tag your PPC campaigns so that you can differentiate one from another in your Google Analytics reports, but the help files on the Google Analytics web site (`www.google.com/analytics`) can help you have your campaigns tagged in just a short while.

My account

Keeping track of your invoices, billing information, account access, and account preferences can be a nightmare if all that information is located in different places. But with AdWords, it's all on the My Account tab.

When you first open the tab, a billing summary is displayed, as shown in Figure 10-5. This summary just shows basic information about your last couple of billing cycles. For more information or to change your billing methods, click the **Billing Information** link near the top of the page.

On this tab, there's also a link that allows you to manage who has access to your account. This is an especially handy feature when there are others in your organization who you would like to have access to your AdWords account. Just be cautious when allowing others to access your account, because once you've added them to your account, they have the ability to change and delete reports, and even to delete other users, including you. Be sure that you trust anyone you plan to add to your account.

FIGURE 10-5

My Account opens to a billing summary that lets you quickly see some details of your last two invoices.

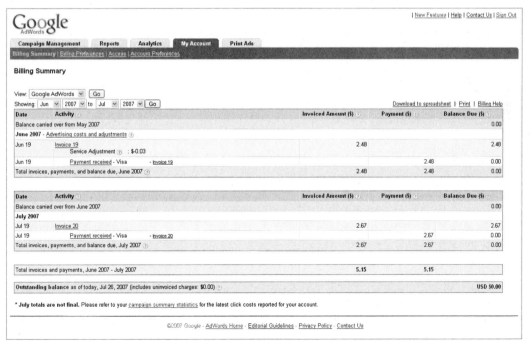

Print ads

The last tab on the AdWords page is the Print Ads tab. This is a newer feature of AdWords that allows you to create your own print-newspaper ad, decide in what newspapers you'd like to have it appear, and in which sections your ad should be shown. Once you've selected these options and created your ad, you can bid for placement, just as you would bid for keyword placement.

Although the Print Ads feature of AdWords has little to do with your PPC campaigns, it is an interesting way in which you can increase the effectiveness of your advertising without necessarily increasing your total advertising budget. And if the print ads are bringing traffic to your web site, you still need to maintain your SEO efforts, including PPC advertising.

Yahoo! Search Marketing

Another type of search engine is the directory search engine. Directories don't display search results based on keywords; instead they display results by category and subcategory. Web sites are usually categorized by the site, not by pages on the site. What this means is that your overall listing in directory search results will depend largely on either paid placement or on correctly categorizing your site as tightly as possible.

Yahoo! Search Marketing is a PPC program that's similar to AdWords, but there's one big difference. Yahoo! is a very commercial search engine, which means that many of the search results are paid placement ads or are web sites that have been added by the web-site owner. Editors usually review and approve submitted listings before they are shown in search results.

Yahoo! is also a portal that contains many different services, such as instant messaging, e-mail, maps, and much more (Google is structured in a similar manner). Being a portal means that Yahoo! has many loyal users who are likely to see your ads once you begin a PPC campaign with Yahoo! Search Marketing.

When you sign up with Yahoo! Search Marketing, you have two options for the type of account you'd like to have. These options are different from Google, because you can have a free PPC plan that you use, create, and maintain on your own, or you can choose to have a Yahoo! specialist help you create your campaign. If you decide to use a Yahoo! specialist, there's a one-time $199 set-up fee.

As with Google, there's no reason you should pay to begin your PPC advertising with Yahoo! Search Marketing. You can begin with the basic, free PPC service, and if you find that your ads don't perform well or that you need help managing your campaigns, you can always upgrade to the paid service. You even have the option of creating your first ad, but not providing billing information to activate the ad. As with Google, the ad won't begin showing in search results until you have activated it with billing information.

After you complete the sign-up process and log in to your account, the set-up is similar to AdWords. The tabs are a little different, but it all works about the same. The tabs that you have available in Yahoo! are the dashboard tab, a campaigns tab, a reports tab, and an administration tab. In addition, there are links on the pages that will take you to additional features and capabilities.

Dashboard

The Dashboard in Yahoo! Search Marketing is shown in Figure 10-6. It gives you a brief overview of some of the metrics related to your PPC campaigns. For example, one of the report snapshots that you'll see is for account performance. This is just a fast and dirty look at the number of clicks, the number of impressions, and the cost of your PPC campaign.

One feature that doesn't exist on the dashboard (it would be nice to have) is the ability to add or remove metrics based on your specific needs. Perhaps Yahoo! will include it in future versions of the program. But for now, what you see is what you get. And it's enough to get you started.

FIGURE 10-6

The account dashboard provides an overview of some of the most important PPC metrics.

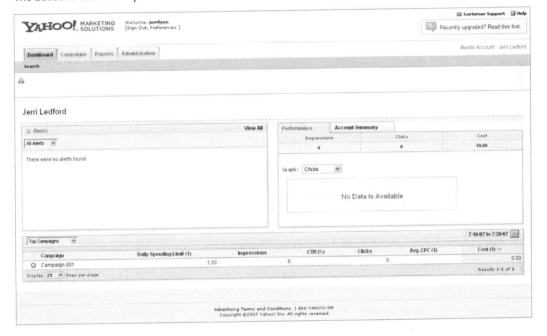

Campaigns

The Campaigns tab is where you'll manage and monitor your PPC campaigns. When you click the Campaigns tab, you're taken to a Campaigns Summary page. This page shows you all the campaigns that you're running at any given time, the status of those campaigns, and basic metrics such as click-through rate, cost per click, and daily spending limit.

Each campaign that's listed is linked to another page, the campaign detail page shown in Figure 10-7. The information on this page is related strictly to that campaign. But you can dig deeper into the information by clicking one of the *ad groups* listed in the **Ad Group** column. When you click an ad group, you're taken to a page that lists the keywords you have chosen for that ad group along with basic metrics like maximum bid per click, average position, impressions, clicks, and more. There's also an editorial column that allows you to see at a glance if your keyword has been approved or disapproved.

NOTE   Circumstances may prevent your keywords from being approved. For example, if you have duplicate keywords, you'll receive notice of it as soon as you try to set up your campaign, or if you have keywords that are trademarked, they may be disapproved for legal reasons. If a keyword that you want to use is not approved, try selecting a similar phrase.

Each of the keywords in the list shown on the Ad Group page is actually a link to one more level in detail. If you click a keyword, you're taken to a keyword detail page. This page shows information such as your maximum bid for the keyword, a forecast for position or number of times the ad will be shown based on your budget, and a prediction for how much higher you will rank if you increase your daily bid. Editing features, like keyword replacement and changing your destination URL, are also available.

FIGURE 10-7

The campaign detail page shows high-level data about your entire PPC campaign.

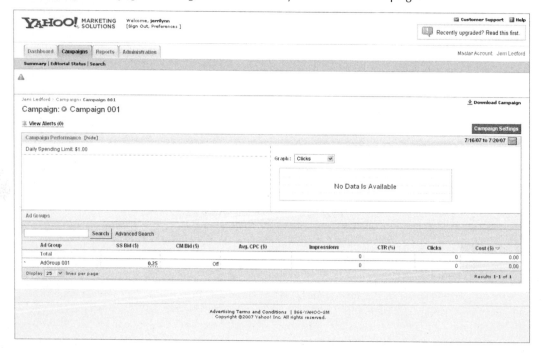

Now let's go back to the top-level Campaigns page. When you're ready to create a new campaign, you can click the **Create Campaign** button to start a wizard that will walk you through the creation process. If you have not yet funded your account by providing billing information to Yahoo! this button will not appear and you can't create additional campaigns.

The Campaigns Summary page is one of three pages available on the Campaigns tab. The other two are the **Editorial Status** page, which details the editorial status of any new campaigns and keywords, and the **Search** page, which allows you to search your campaigns by keyword. This is a useful tool if you're running more than a handful of campaigns.

Reports

The third tab in the lineup is the Reports tab. From this tab, you can view the available reports that Yahoo! provides (shown in Figure 10-8), but you cannot create custom reports. The extent of the customization that you can achieve is changing the date ranges to something other than the default.

FIGURE 10-8

The Reports tab allows you to view reports from the summary level to more detailed reports such as Ad Performance.

Even though you can't customize Yahoo!'s reports, there's a good selection of reports available to you. The main report on the Reports tab is a summary. It's another of those at-a-glance reports that provides the most commonly accessed basic metrics. In addition to the summary report, there are also eight other reports:

- Ad Performance
- Daily Performance
- Keyword Performance
- Performance by Geographical Location
- Daily Spend Performance
- URL Performance
- Monthly Financial Reports
- Billing Transaction Detail

Administration

The last tab, Administration, is where you'll handle all of the "housekeeping" issues associated with your Yahoo! Search Marketing campaign. When this page opens, you're taken to an administrative summary that details information about several different aspects of your Yahoo! Search Marketing account. The information available to you includes:

- Account General Information
- Account Daily Spending Limits
- User Administration
- Billing and Payment Information
- Tactic Settings

User Administration is where you'll handle adding users from other accounts to your account, deleting users from your account, and creating new user accounts. You'll also have access to the **Master Account User** profile, which allows you to change passwords and assign the level of administration that master users and account users can have.

The Tactic Settings area has another set of useful capabilities. Tactic Settings are those that guide how your PPC ad is distributed. With Yahoo! Search Marketing you have the option of allowing sponsored searches, different types of content matching, and excluded words. These settings help you to further target your PPC campaign for the best results possible.

There are some differences in the capabilities between Google and Yahoo! but those differences should be easy to get used to once you begin using either of the programs. Both are designed in a way that makes it easy to quickly orient yourself and begin using the programs. One advantage of Yahoo! over Google, however, is that Yahoo!'s help files are less circular and much easier to understand. A major difference between the two engines is that Yahoo requires a minimum bid of $.10 for each keyword, whereas Google's minimum bid on keywords can be as low as $.01.

Microsoft adCenter

Microsoft adCenter used to be known as MSN AdCenter. Microsoft has rebranded the advertising program to draw it closer to the Microsoft family of products. But it's essentially the same adCenter that has always ranked among the top PPC programs available.

PPC ads through Microsoft adCenter are distributed on the MSN web portal and on the Live Search network. And setting up your Microsoft adCenter account is a little different from setting up a Google or Yahoo! account. Microsoft requires you to provide your billing information up front, even before you create your first ad. There is also a one-time setup fee of $5 that is charged to the credit card you add for payment. This setup fee is charged immediately to your account.

Once you've provided billing information, you can begin to set up your first adCenter ad. When you sign into adCenter, you're taken to a general page first. On that page are four tabs, which you can use to manage your adCenter ads. These tabs are Campaign, Accounts & Billing, Research, and Reports.

Campaign

The Campaign tab in adCenter is like the Campaign tab in both the Google and Yahoo! programs. When you click the Campaign tab, you're taken to an overview page (shown in Figure 10-9) where you can create or import PPC campaigns. To create campaigns, click the **Create Campaign** link to start the creation process.

You'll be asked to provide all the same information that you've had to enter in both Yahoo! and Google campaigns, including a name for the campaign and the information necessary to target your customers. Once you've completed this step, you'll move on to creating your ad and developing your budget.

FIGURE 10-9

The Campaign overview page is where you begin creating your first campaign.

One thing you'll notice that's a little different in the adCenter campaign creation process is the ability to target even your first ad to specific times or days of the week. Other PPC providers may have this service, but Microsoft's adCenter is the only one that allows you to set up a schedule when you create the first campaign. As you may remember from the section on dayparting in Chapter 9, this strategy can help you better target your ads to the time periods when your click-throughs and conversions are likely to be the highest.

The importing capability is also unique to adCenter. Using this capability, you can import PPC ads that you've created in Excel or another spreadsheet program. If the ads were not created in Excel, you should save the file as a .csv file for importing.

Accounts & Billing

The Accounts & Billing tab is where you'll find controls for your PPC accounts and billing information. When you click the Accounts & Billing tab, you're taken to an Account List page, like the one shown in Figure 10-10. From this page you have access to three additional tabs: Company Information, Payment Methods, and Billing.

The tabs make it obvious that you can access different information about your accounts from this page, but there's a much easier way to access that information. Instead of having to click a tab to read specific information, you can simply click the account number to access all the basic information on one page. From there you can make whatever changes need to be made, including changing billing information and canceling campaigns.

There are additional features on some of the tabs, however. For example, on the Billing tab, you can pull up billing statements, which can't be accessed by clicking the account number on the Account List page.

FIGURE 10-10

The Account List page is where you can access company and billing information about your adCenter campaigns.

Research

Maintaining a PPC campaign means constantly researching new keywords. The Research tab in adCenter gives you the option to generate new keyword lists based on a single keyword, a key phrase, or a web site. Simply enter the keyword, phrase, or web site that you would like to use as a basis for your keywords and click **Submit**. A keyword list like the one shown in Figure 10-11 is generated.

FIGURE 10-11

Use the Research tab to generate new keywords to add to your PPC campaigns.

If there are keywords on the list that you would like to add to your existing list, place a check-mark next to the box beside the keyword in the column on the left. It will be transferred to the column on the right. When you're finished, you can copy and import the desired keywords into your keyword list.

One feature of the keyword research tool provided by adCenter is the metrics that are provided with each keyword. Each keyword in the list generated by the research tool has two numbers next to it. The first is the number of searches for that word or phrase during the previous month. The second is the number of searches that have been done using those keywords in the current month. These numbers help you to see quickly how popular your selected keywords are.

Reports

The final tab in the adCenter dashboard is the Reports tab. Like Yahoo! and Google, this tab contains reporting capabilities to help you monitor and maintain your PPC ads. When you click the Reports tab, you're taken to the **Create New Report** page, where you can create new reports. Once you've created a first report it will appear on the Recent Reports tab with any other reports that you may have run in the past. You can choose to leave the report there or delete it if you no longer need it.

Also within the Reports tab is the Report Templates tab. This is where you'll find any templates that you've created for reports. Storing a template here makes the process of generating more specialized reports much faster. You don't need to create a new report type each time you need to generate it. Simply save the report as a template; then the next time you want to run a report, select the template during the report creation process.

Overall, Microsoft adCenter is a little different than either Yahoo! or Google, but the same basic concepts and capabilities apply. One big difference between the three PPC programs, however, is traffic. According to studies done by industry analysts, Google tends to have very high traffic but it's one of the least expensive PPC programs. It would seem that Google, then, would be the logical choice for a PPC campaign. However, it's possible that under the right circumstances, Microsoft's adCenter might have a much better conversion rate. It's one of the most expensive PPC programs you'll find, but the audience is smaller, so the traffic is better targeted and the conversion rate can be much better for some ads.

Yahoo! has the highest traffic of any of the three, but the conversions at Yahoo! are not as high as at either Google or adCenter. Some experts believe that it all comes out in the wash. For example, because Google has high traffic, medium conversions, and low cost, it can be as effective as adCenter with its higher costs, lower traffic, and higher conversions.

It makes it difficult to decide where you should invest your PPC budget, and that's the reason many organizations use more than one PPC campaign provider. Using multiple PPC vendors means better coverage with your PPC ad, which can lead to better conversions.

Chapter 11

Tagging Your Web Site

Y ou may remember that back in Chapters 3 and 6 we covered some of the HTML tags most commonly used in SEO. These included title tags, heading tags, body tags, meta tags, and the alt tag. No web site should be without those tags in the HTML that makes up the site. However, those tags aren't the only ones that you should know.

In addition, there are several others you might find useful. In fact, a basic understanding of HTML is nearly essential for achieving the best SEO possible for your web site. Sure, you can build a web site using some kind of web design software like Microsoft FrontPage or Adobe Dreamweaver. However, those programs won't necessarily ensure that all the essential HTML tags are included in your site. It's far better if you know enough HTML to understand where your HTML tags go, and how to put them there without trashing the design of the site.

There's also another aspect to tagging your web site, and that's using the right strategies to ensure the tags are as effective as possible. For example, some HTML tags are strictly for formatting (like the `<bold>` tag), but formatting a word with `<bold>` doesn't tell the search engine that the word is important. Using a more appropriate HTML tag (like `<strong>`) works much better.

These are all elements of site tagging that you should know. And if you haven't taken steps to ensure that your site is tagged properly, do it now. Search engine crawlers don't read web sites or web pages. They read the text on those pages, and HTML is a form of text. With the right HTML tags, you can tell a search engine far more about your site than the content alone will tell it.

What's So Important About Site Tagging?

You must be thinking that for site tagging to be addressed in this book three times it must be very important to SEO. And you would be correct. Even beyond the keywords and the PPC campaigns, site tagging is one of the most effective ways to ensure that your web site shows up on search engine results pages.

The HTML tags that you include on your web site tell search engine crawlers much more about your site than your content alone will tell them. Don't misunderstand. Content is an essential element for web-site design. But it's a more customer-facing portion of the design, whereas HTML is a crawler-facing portion. And before customers will see your content, crawlers must see your HTML.

So when you ask the question, "What's so important about site tagging?" there's only one possible answer: Everything. Your SEO ranking will depend in large part on the tagging that controls your page behind the scenes. Customers never see it, but without it, they never see you.

How Does Site Tagging Work?

Site tagging, as you already know, is about putting the right HTML commands in the right place. The difficulties come in knowing what types of tags to use and what to include in those tags. The basic tags—title, heading, body, and meta tags—should be included in every page that you want a search engine to find.

But to make these tags readable to the search engine crawlers, they should be formatted properly. For example, with *container tags*, you should have both an opening and a closing tag. The opening tag is usually bracketed with two sharp brackets (`<tag>`). The closing tag is also bracketed, but it includes a slash before the tag to indicate that the container is closing (`</tag>`). Notice that the tag name is repeated in both the opening and closing tags. This just tells the crawler or web browser where a specific type of formatting or attribute should begin and end. So, when you use the `<b>Bold</b>` tag, only the words between the opening and closing tags will be formatted with a bold-faced font, instead of the entire page being bold.

There's another element of web-site design that you should know and use. It's called *cascading style sheets (CSS)* and it's not a tagging method, but rather a formatting method. You should use CSS so that formatting tags are effective strictly in formatting, while the other tags actually do the work needed to get your site listed naturally by a search crawler.

Think of cascading style sheets as boxes, one stacked on top of another. Each box contains something different, with the most important elements being in the top box and decreasing to the least important element in the bottom box. With cascading style sheets, you can set one attribute or format to override another under the right circumstances.

We won't go into creating cascading style sheets in this book. There's enough to learn about that to fill at least two additional books, and in fact dozens have been written about them.

When you're using an attribute from a CSS, however, it's easy enough to incorporate it into your web page. The following is a snippet of HTML that uses a cascading style sheet to define the heading colors for a web page:

```
<HTML>
  <TITLE>Your Web Page Title</TITLE>
  <STYLE>
    H1, H2 { color: green }
  </STYLE>
  <BODY>
    <H1>First Heading</H1>
    <P>Enter any text that you would
        like to have appear here.
    <UL>
      <LI>List item one.
      <LI>List item two.
      <LI>List item three.
    </UL>
    <H2>First subheading</H2>
    <P>Another paragraph of text can go
        here. Add whatever you like.
  </BODY>
</HTML>
```

Looking at this bit of code more closely, you see:

`<HTML>` This tag indicates that HTML is the language used to create this web page (were this part of an entire web page).

`<TITLE>Your Web Page Title</TITLE>` indicates the title of the page.

`<STYLE>` This is the beginning of a CSS indicator for the style of the web page. In this case the style applies only to the headings.

`H1, H2 { color: green }` is the indicator that heading styles one and two should be colored in purple.

`</STYLE>` is the closing CSS indicator.

`<BODY>` indicates the beginning of the body text.

`<H1>First Heading</H1>` is the first header. In the live view of this page on the web, this heading would be purple.

`<P>Enter any text that you would like to have appear here.` This is your first paragraph of text.

`<UL>` is the opening tag for an unordered list.

`<LI>List item one` is the first item in your list.

`<LI>List item two` is the next item in your list.

`<LI>List item three` is the last item in your list.

`</UL>` is the closing tag for the unordered list.

`<H2>First subheading</H2>` This is the first subheading. In the live view of this page on the Web, this heading would be purple.

`<P>Another paragraph of text can go here. Add whatever you like.` Again, another paragraph of text.

`</BODY>` is the closing body tag. This indicates that the body text of the web page is complete.

`</HTML>` is the closing HTML tag, which indicates the end of the web page.

It's not difficult to use CSS for the stylistic aspects of your web site. It does take a little time to get used to using it, but once you do it's easy. And, when you're using CSS to control the style of your site, you don't need to use HTML tags, which means those tags will be much more efficient.

Additional HTML Tags

You've already seen the most important HTML tags for SEO. But there are literally dozens of such tags that you could use on your site. Some of them are more important than others. That doesn't mean they will be the deciding factor on your search engine ranking. What it does mean is that if you can include them, they'll help.

Nofollow

One of the first tags you should consider using, as long as you can use it appropriately is the *nofollow tag.* This tag, which is represented by `<rel="nofollow">` is an attribute that tells a search engine crawler not to follow a certain link on your web site. For example, if you want to include an example of a bad site (like a hacker's site or an SEO spam site) you may want to show that link on your web site. However, that link could reduce your search engine ranking because it's a known bad site, and when you include the link to it the crawler thinks you're endorsing the site.

To save face and still have a link to your example, you can use the `<nofollow>` tag in the URL. The coded URL without the tag will look like this:

```
<a href="http://www.examplesite.com/">Bad Site</a>
```

But when you add the tag it looks something like this:

```
<a href="http://www.examplesite.com" rel="nofollow">Bad Site</a>
```

Your URL with the <nofollow> tag could also look like this because it doesn't matter where in the link tag that you put the <nofollow> attribute:

```
<a rel="nofollow" href="http://www.examplesite.com">Bad Site</a>
```

Again, the <nofollow> tag isn't essential in your SEO efforts. However, it could help prevent your site ranking from being reduced, and maybe even increase its ranking a little. At any rate, anything that keeps your ranking from falling is a good measure to take.

Strong and emphasis

When you're formatting the text on your web site, how do you format the bold and italic words? Do you use the <b>bold</b> and <i>italics</i> tags? If you do, you should consider using CSS formatting as discussed earlier. When you format a word with <bold>, the actual site visitor can see and understand why the word is bold. A search engine crawler, and a screen reader, cannot. All the crawler or screen reader sees is the <bold> tag. There's no "emotion" associated with it.

A much better use of your HTML is to use the <strong>strong</strong> and <em>emphasis</em> tags. The <strong> tag translates into bold formatting and the <emphasis> tag translates into italics formatting. And the difference is that when a search engine crawler or screen reader encounters these tags, it knows to pay attention to the word or words that are included in the container.

Those words within the container will also be given more weight. So, if you simply boldface or italicize your keywords, they will look just like any other words on the page when the crawler or screen reader comes through. But using the <strong> and <emphasis> tags around your keywords tells those bots to notice that the following words have importance and are more than simply additional words in the text of a page.

Noframes

Another tag that we touched on briefly in Chapter 3 is the <noframes> tag. This tag is supposed to make your framed web site appear to search engine crawlers as if it has no frames. Crawlers can't read multiple frames on a page, and if you're using frames it's going to be much harder to get your site ranked in the search engine results.

The <noframes> tag will help, but it's not entirely foolproof. Even using the tag, you can still run into problems with browsers and crawlers. Some crawlers won't crawl a site even if it has <noframes> tags. So if you can avoid using frames, that's always your best option. However, if you have to use frames, be sure to include the <noframes> tag. Table 11-1 shows the difference between the HTML construction of a normal page, a frames page, and a frame page with the <noframes> tag.

As you can see in Table 11.1, the <noframes> tag goes after the <frameset> tags. However, it's still read by the crawler and in most cases, the <frameset> tags are ignored. The result is that your page, without the frames, is what is indexed by the crawler.

TABLE 11.1

Normal, Frames, <noframes> Comparison

Normal Page	Frame Page	Frame Page with `<noframes>` Tag
`<HTML>`	`<HTML>`	`<HTML>`
`<Head>`	`<Head>`	`<Head>`
`<Title>Page Title</Title>`	`<Title>Page Title</Title>`	`<Title>Page Title</Title>`
`</Head>`	`</Head>`	`</Head>`
`<Body>`	`<Frameset>`	`<Frameset>`
`Body Text goes here`	`Frame Code goes here`	`<Frameset cols="25%,*">`
`</Body>`	`</Frameset>`	`<Frame SRC="nav.html">`
`</HTML>`	`</HTML>`	`<Frame SRC="display.html">`
		`</Frameset>`
		`<Noframes>`
		`Alternative HTML goes here`
		`</noframes>`
		`</HTML>`

CAUTION   *Deprecated tags* are ones that are no longer useful. They have either been replaced by better tags or are not used enough now to be considered good form. An example of a deprecated tag (as of HTML 4.0) is `<Center>Center a Block of Text</Center>`. Because the use of CSS is becoming so widespread, some tags are being replaced by the style sheet. Be careful not to use deprecated tags in your web-site design. Using them could cause your search engine ranking to drop, because it makes the site appear to be poorly maintained.

Table summary tag

Remember back in Chapter 3 when we discussed alt tags? Those are the tags that are used to present alternative text when images are essential to understanding the content of your page. Well, just as you need alt tags for your graphics, you also need *table summary tags* for your tables.

The table summary provides web crawlers and screen readers with alternative text for the table. For web crawlers, this means that instead of seeing a graphic, the crawler sees your description, in which you can include keywords if they are appropriate.

To use a table summary tag it should be inserted in your table code before the table caption tag. It should look something like this:

```
<TABLE border="1"
        summary="This table provides information about average 12
                 year old girls: average height, weight, and
                 percentage with brown eyes.">
<CAPTION><EM>Characteristics of Average Girls</EM></CAPTION>
<TR><TH rowspan="2"><TH colspan="2">Average
    <TH rowspan="2">Brown<BR>eyes
<TR><TH>height<TH>weight
<TR><TH>Females<TD>1.7<TD>0.002<TD>43%
</TABLE>
```

Acronym and abbreviation tags

One last tag that you should consider using on you web pages is the `<acronym>` or `<abbr>` (abbreviation) tag. These tags simply tell a web crawler or text reader that an acronym or abbreviation is being used, and what the full text for that acronym or abbreviation is.

The advantage to having your abbreviations and acronyms included in HTML tags is that if those words happen to be keywords for your page, the full text can be read by the crawler, rather than just the letters in the abbreviation or acronym.

When you're using the acronym tags in your HTML this is how they should look:

```
<acronym title="Search Engine Optimization">SEO</acronym>
```

And abbreviation tags should look like this:

```
<abbr title="United States of America">USA</abbr>
```

These two tags, although named differently, do exactly the same thing. Thus, many web designers have gone to using the abbreviation tag rather than the acronym tag. No matter which you choose to use, it at least offers an additional way for you to include your keywords on your page if they happen to have an associated abbreviation or acronym.

Virtual includes

A *virtual include* is a tag that allows you to use information just once if it's repeated often on the web site. For example, if you have a navigation bar on the left side of your first page that will appear exactly the same way on every other page, you can use a virtual include to repeat that navigation bar without the need to code the bar repeatedly throughout your site.

Tagging: Social Bookmarking

Tagging used to refer just to the tags that you placed in your web site's HTML to indicate certain types of formatting or commands. Tagging today often refers to something entirely different. When you hear the terms "tagged" or "tagging" in conversation today, it could very well refer to a phenomenon called *social bookmarking*.

Social bookmarking is a way for Internet users to store, share, classify, and search Internet bookmarks. There is some debate over how important social bookmarking is in SEO, but the consensus seems to be leaning toward the idea that social bookmarking, along with many other *social media optimization (SMO)* strategies, is quickly becoming a serious consideration for SEO. SMO is covered in more detail in Chapter 18, but let's look at social bookmarking here.

Social bookmarking is provided by services such as de.icio.us, Digg, Technorati, and Furl.net, which are taking the Internet by storm. They're often referred to as *Web 2.0* services, because they involve a high level of social interaction, which is the fastest growing element of the Internet today.

In social bookmarking, people create their own topics and lists for places on the Internet that they like or dislike. Those people can then give the places they choose a category (or tag) and a rank. Once they've ranked a site, they have the option to send that ranking out to anyone who is subscribed to their RSS feed.

The implications this can have on SEO are dramatic. For example, let's say that one person visits your site during a web search and finds that it's easy to use, and contains all the information they were looking for. That person could very well tag your site. The tag is then distributed to the people who are subscribed to his or her RSS feed. It's word-of-mouth marketing—called viral marketing in today's world—at its best.

One person tells 25, who then visit your site. Then maybe 15 of those people (60 percent) tell another 25 people each. The list keeps growing and growing.

So, the question, "Should you pay any attention to social bookmarking?" becomes "How do I take advantage of social bookmarking?" And the answer is, make your site worthy of bookmarking. Bookmarks appear to web crawlers as links to your page, and that makes them very valuable SEO tools. For some search engines, the more bookmarks that lead back to your site, the more "votes" you have on their popularity scale.

So, visit some of the social bookmarking sites on the Internet. Learn how they work. And set up your own account. Then, create your own list of links that includes your web sites, as well as other web sites that users might find relevant or useful.

On the web-site side, be sure to include the code snippets provided by social bookmarking organizations that allow users to tag your site easily. Then, maintain it all. Don't just forget your account completely. If you do, eventually it will disappear and all the advantage of having one will go as well. Instead, continue using social bookmarking. Over time, the rewards will be increased traffic to your web site.

Virtual includes can be used with ASP and PHP applications, but we'll only look at the straight HTML version here. If you desire more information about writing includes for another application, try using Google to find that information. There are many good (free) tutorials on the Internet.

One more thing you should know about virtual includes is that they only work with servers that allow *server side includes* (*SSI*). This means that users coming from a server that does not allow SSI will not be able to see your virtual includes. That will leave large holes in your site for them, and in the case of navigation bars, it could make it difficult for them to navigate around your site.

Even though this is a possibility, you may still decide to use virtual includes. If you do use them, here's how a navigation bar and a copyright notice might look on your page:

```
<HTML>
<head>
Page Heading
</head>
<body>
<!--#include virtual="navbar.inc"-->
 The text of your web page goes here.
Remember that you want the text to be no
less than 250 words.
<!--#include virtual="copyright notice.inc"-->
</body>
</HTML>
```

If you do decide that virtual includes are the right choice for your site, use caution with them. Virtual includes make a server work harder to serve information to site visitors, so make sure your server isn't overextended. If it is, the server will crash, bringing your site and everything else down with it.

Using Redirect Pages

One more item you should be aware of is the effect of redirect pages on your search engine rankings. The type of redirect that you use can affect how your site is treated by a search engine. One type of redirect page is permanent, and another is temporary. The one you decide to use has serious implications for your site ranking.

Three types of redirect pages are the most common ones used in designing web pages:

- **301 Redirect:** The 301 redirect is a permanent redirect page. The page appears to users as they are redirected from one web site to another or from one web page to another. The original page that is no longer available will be removed within a few weeks when 301 redirects are used.

- **302 Redirect:** The 302 redirect is a temporary redirect page. This page displays to users as they are redirected from one web site to another. The original page is temporarily unavailable, so when the 302 redirect is removed, the user goes back to the original site instead of the site used for redirection.

- **404 Error Pages:** A 404 error page redirects users to a page that displays an error message, usually one that says something like "This page is no longer available, please check the URL and try again or use the refresh button on your browser."

It's important that you understand that a search engine crawler reads a redirect according to the number that it is given. For example, although 301 and 302 redirects do the same thing, the codes are different, which tells the search engine crawler that one means the page no longer exists and the other means the page is only temporarily not being used.

Each redirect number should be used under different circumstances. For example, a 301 redirect should be used when you migrate all your web pages from one URL to another. A 302 redirect should be used when you have a temporary web site that you would rather have users see — if you have a different look for your site during a holiday, for instance, you may choose to use the 302 redirect. And the 404 redirect is an error indicator. This is used when the web site that a user is trying to access errors out for some reason; either it no longer exists and there is no 301 redirect, or there is an error in the coding for the site or the way the user typed the site address into the address bar.

The confusion with the redirect numbers comes in when web-site owners try to use the wrong code for the wrong reasons. Here's another example: Say you move your web site from one URL to another, and you want to redirect your traffic to the new site. Using the 301 redirect is the correct choice in this case, because it tells the search engines that your site has moved, and that the search equity built at the previous URL should be moved to the new URL.

With a 302 redirect, the search engines will never update their indexes to reflect the change in destination URL, because you have indicated that the move is temporary.

Some savvy web-site designers have decided that creating custom redirect pages is a good way to improve the SEO on their site, but unfortunately this doesn't always work the way it should. What happens is that the custom redirect page doesn't provide the proper redirect number to the search engine crawler, so it reads the site differently than a redirect page. This could affect your search engine rankings negatively, because the page will appear to be unrelated to the other pages in your web site.

So how to handle redirect pages? The best way for SEO purposes is to use redirect pages in the manner in which they are meant to be used. Using them in any other way is risky in terms of your search engine results rankings.

Chapter 12

The Content Piece
of the Puzzle

"Content is king!" You've heard that phrase so many times that it probably just rolls off your mind. It shouldn't, though, because content really is one of the most important aspects of your web site, both from the design and SEO aspects.

Studies show that the number-one reason people visit a web site is in search of information. Even the buying process isn't often accomplished in one visit. Instead, it sometimes takes visitors four or five visits to decide to make a purchase on your site. But it's your content that brings them back to your site those four or five times until they make the purchasing decision.

The loyalty factor is what content is all about. It's easy on the Internet for users to click to a site only to find it's not what they're looking for and then to click away. But if you can target your site properly and serve up the right content, you can create a site that draws users back time and again. And that's when content becomes king.

When content contributes dramatically to your customer loyalty, it's like royalty — to be respected, babied, and even accorded some awe. Because if your content is terrible, there will be no return traffic on your site. Period. You might still succeed with so-so content, but it won't be at all easy. You need and want the best.

How Does Web-Site Content Affect SEO?

The catch with web-site content is that is must be fresh and original to be most effective. If it's not, the content can do more harm than good. As you've already seen, content is the one element that can keep customers coming back to your site time and again. When customers return often, your site ranking improves, because the traffic registers the site with search crawlers as a valid and in-demand site.

When your content stinks, though, your site is headed in the opposite direction. If you have content on your site that's not professional, the search engine crawler will register this, and your ranking may drop lower and lower and you could possibly be delisted altogether.

How do you know if your content stinks or not? It's mostly a game of finding the right combination of content types and consistent updates. But before you can even get to determining the right type of content, you need to create a content strategy.

Your content strategy is the plan by which you'll infuse your site with the right types of content at the right times. It starts with determining how to reach your target audience. By now your target audience should be engraved on your forehead, but how you reach that audience is something entirely different. If your audience is teens, the language and method with which you'll reach them will be different than if your audience is senior adults or stay-at-home moms, or even full-time professionals.

So what words and phrases will your target audience use to find your web site? Those are some of the keywords that you'll be using in your content. Additional keywords may be discovered using some of the methods that have been covered in previous chapters.

Next, determine what users will benefit from visiting your site. Visitors click through a link looking for something. If you don't provide some benefit, the users will click away nearly as fast as they found you. When determining what value you have to offer, don't think in terms of your desire to bring users to your site, think in terms of what those users are seeking. What do *they* want?

Along with determining users' reasons for coming to your site, you should also be considering why they might want to return to your site. Do you have regular sales? Is there some form of *dynamic content*, like a blog or news page, that would draw them back? What other types of media might you include on your site, and what value would that be to your visitors (for example, using videos or podcasting to present training materials)?

Only when you've figured out what you can give your site visitors should you determine what you want from them. If you want them to sign up for a newsletter or make a purchase, include a call to action on your site and provide the tools they'll need to complete the task that you want them to complete. Every page on your web site should have a purpose. You have to determine, on every page of your site, what it is you want from visitors.

One more consideration as you're planning your content strategy: what do you do that's different from your competition? You should already have a good idea of what your competition does, and how it seems to work for them. But what can you do differently? What sets you apart from all of the other web sites out there that come up when a user searches for widgets?

Next you need to determine what type of content you plan to include on your site to meet all the needs that have been defined by the preceding questions. There are several different types of content, and each type has its own implications:

- **Licensed Content:** Licensed content is what you might buy from a content broker. For example, if you're looking for a quick way to populate your site with articles, you might turn to a company like FreeSticky.com that offers many different articles you can use. The problem with this type of content is that it's often repeated all over the Internet. You're not the only one who will need to populate your site, and others will likely use some of the same services you do. Being used often doesn't make the content less valuable, but it's not going to rank as well with search engines because of the duplication.

- **Original Content:** There are several types of original content. There's the content you write and share with others for free. This is a good way to get links back to your site. You can use the content for a limited amount of time exclusively on your own site and then allow others to use it for nothing more than a link back to your site. This incoming link adds credibility to your site.

  Another type of original content is that which is distributed freely by visitors to your site. This original content can take the form of comments on your site or forum message boards. This type of original content is an excellent addition to your SEO efforts, because it tends to be focused on a specific subject.

  Some original content is exclusive to your site. This is content that you create, and the only place it appears is your web site. This is the most valuable type of content for your site, and it's the type search engine crawlers like the best. Think of it as giving the crawler some variety in its diet. It gets tired of the same thing day in and day out, just like we do. The more original and exclusive content you can provide for a crawler, the better you'll rank in search results. It also doesn't hurt if that content has an appropriate number of keywords in it.

- **Dynamic Content:** Dynamic content can be licensed or original. Blogs are the perfect example of dynamic content.

Once you have all these elements decided upon, you can begin to create your content. It sounds easy enough, but there's more to it than meets the eye. Not only does your copy need to be compelling to people, but it also needs to be focused to help increase search engine rankings.

Elements of Competitive Content

When you begin to create your web-site content, your audience is your customer or potential customer. Every word written for your web site should be written for the customer. Consider what type of information you have that would be of value to the customer, and those are the topics that you should be addressing.

Once you've determined what is most interesting to your target audience, it's time to get down to the task of actually writing the content. You can either write the content yourself, or hire someone to write it for you. And of course, there are the services that provide content to you, as noted earlier in this chapter. Assuming you're writing your own copy, you should be aware that some elements of web-site content are more effective than others.

First, certain types of copy both draw more return visitors and please search engines. The most important of those types is the content that updates and changes frequently. It's one of the reasons blogs have become such an overwhelming phenomenon. People like content that changes. We get caught in the daily stories of people's lives, of business operations, and of useful information. And if your content changes daily, we're more likely to visit your web site.

Update your content as often as is appropriate. It's always a bad idea just to create content for content's sake. Keep an eye to adding at least one page of new content each week. You *could* go to a monthly schedule, but doing so would make it very difficult for people to remember you except for that one time per month when they're notified that your content has changed (assuming you have a notification system). And if they receive no notification, the chance of their remembering your site is even smaller.

As a general rule, people today are so busy they can't keep things in their minds for more than a few hours. If you have a site that updates monthly, and tell customers or subscribers that you'll have a sale the next month, it's unlikely that many of them will remember. Some will, but most won't. You lose the effectiveness of regularly updated content when you update only once a month or less.

When you're writing your content, there are some rules about how the content is best written for the Web. Words on a screen are viewed much differently from words on a page. Where possible, your customers should be able to interact with your words. So include links and other interactive features in your text.

Here are some additional guidelines to follow when creating your web-site content:

- Make sure any content that you include on your site is contextually relevant. People and search engine crawlers will be looking at the relevance of content to your site and to any advertisements that led them to the site. Make sure everything you include is relevant in some way. It also helps if the content addresses a need the customer might have.

- Use original content whenever possible. Original content is much more valuable than articles that have been distributed to you and all of your competitors. Why should visitors come to your site if they can find the same information somewhere else?

- Be sure that all of your content uses proper spelling and grammar. Nothing looks more unprofessional than web-site content that looks as though the writer flunked English 101. And it does happen, so if you're not an editor, find someone who is and ask that person to check your content before it's posted to your web site.

- Use mostly short sentences, with 10 words or less. If you must use a medium-length sentence, try to incorporate it with shorter sentences around it. Users don't have a lot of patience for long, rambling sentences in print publications and even less patience for them on the Web. (But there is value to varying a succession of short sentences with one a little longer — it keeps your writing from sounding like a kindergarten primer.)

- Use short paragraphs with lots of white space in between. In the print world, white space is your enemy. Too much white space means wasted space. But on the Internet, where real estate isn't quite as expensive, white space is essential to the flow of the content. Reading on the screen is much more difficult for most people, so the extra white space helps them to keep up with their place in the content. A good rule of thumb is to keep your paragraphs to no more than four or five short sentences.

- Use bulleted and numbered lists as often as possible without interrupting the flow of the article or the other content on your site. Such lists are easy to read. They provide the at-a-glance content that readers love. It's easy for them to find quickly the information they need.

- Break up your content with interesting titles, headings, and subheadings. Again, this is one of those elements of web-site content that make it more at-a-glance in nature. The variety helps your readers quickly skim through to find the exact information they need. Titles, headings, and subheadings are much more important on the Web than they ever were in print.

- Use keywords where possible, but don't overdo it. You've heard this so many times by now that is should be branded into your brain. Use keywords only where they make sense. Period.

- Use a call to action. Users will not take action if you don't invite them to. So invite them. When you need a form filled out, when you want them to join a mailing list, or when you want them to make a purchase, ask them. The old adage "ask and ye shall receive" is just as valuable online as it is in real life.

To Use or Not? Duplicate Content

Duplicate content is a hotly debated issue when it comes to how it affects your web-site ranking. And it's become an even bigger issue over time as spammers and other malicious Internet users have taken to the practice of *content scraping*, or scraping the content from a web site to use on their own with only minor changes to the appearance, not to the content itself.

Content scraping has become such a problem that search engines now look for duplicate copy, even when it's hidden behind a link like the **Similar Pages** that Google uses for related content (see Figure 12-1). If they find it, your site may be lowered in the rankings or even delisted completely.

Still, the duplicate-copy issue isn't as simple as it may seem. Some people think there's too much worry about it, whereas others insist the problem needs to be addressed. And both are right to some degree. Let me explain.

FIGURE 12-1

Google uses a Similar Pages link to group web sites with related content.

Google groups pages with similar content.

First, you need to understand that not all duplicate content is the same kind. You need to appreciate some differences.

- **Reprints:** This is duplicate content published on multiple sites with the permission of the copyright holder. These are the articles that you or others create and then distribute to create links back to your site or to sites that are relevant to the content of yours. Reprints are not bad duplicate content, but they can get your site thrown into the realm of **Similar Pages**, which means they'll be buried behind other results.

- **Site Mirroring:** This is the kind of duplication that can cause one or more of your sites to be delisted from a search engine. *Site mirroring* is literally keeping exact copies of your web site in two different places on the Internet. Web sites used to practice site mirroring all the time as a way to avoid downtime when one site crashed. These days, server capabilities are such that site mirroring isn't as necessary as it once was, and search engines now "dis-include" mirrored content because of the spamming implications it can have. Spammers have been known to mirror sites to create a *false Internet* for the purpose of stealing user names, passwords, account numbers, and other personal information.

- **Content Scraping:** Content scraping is taking the content from one site and reusing it on another site with nothing more than cosmetic changes. This is another tactic used by spammers, and it's also often a source of *copyright infringement*.

- **Same Site Duplication:** If you duplicate content across your own web site, you could also be penalized for duplicate content. This becomes especially troublesome with blogs, because there is often a full blog post on the main page and then an archived blog post on another page of your site. This type of duplication can be managed by simply using a partial post, called a *snippet*, that links to the full post in a single place on your web site.

Of these types of duplicate content, two are especially harmful to your site: site mirroring and content scraping. If you're using site mirroring, you should consider using a different backup method for your web site. If you're using content scraping you could be facing legal action for copyright infringement. Content scraping is a practice that's best avoided completely.

Stopping Copyright Infringement

Copyright infringement can happen to you, too. If you include original content on your site, it's very likely that someone will come along and copy that content without your permission for use on their site.

It's important that you spend a little time each week checking for copyright infringement on your original articles. One way to do this is to pull a unique phrase from your article or other content and search for it on the Internet. If others are using your copy, it's likely that your unique phrase will pop up in the search results.

The problem with manually searching for unauthorized copies of your web-site content is that it's very time consuming, especially if you have hundreds of pages of content. But there's good news. Some services and software applications can help you quickly find duplicate copies of your content.

One web-based service is provided by Copyscape (www.copyscape.com). You can use its free service to search the Web for content found at a specific URL. The results are usually accompanied by links to search other pages on your site.

Copyscape checks the Internet for copies of the content on your web pages.

continued

continued

One disappointment I noticed with the free version of Copyscape is that the pages that returned in the search results were old pages. Some of the pages shown in the preceding illustration for my web site no longer exist. It seems that to receive the most benefit from Copyscape you need to pay for the premium version of the application.

Copyscape isn't expensive. Copyscape Premium is just $.05 per search, and Copysentry, an application that automatically monitors the Web for your content, is just $4.95 per month.

Another service you can use to monitor or search the Web for copyright infringement is CyberAlert (http://www.cyberalert.com). There are also several other services, so you have some choice of protection should you decide that you need it.

Even though reprints and same-site duplication are not entirely harmful, they are also not helpful. And in fact they can be harmful if they're handled in the wrong way. You won't win any points with a search engine crawler if your site is full of content that's used elsewhere on the Web. Reprints, especially those that are repeated often on the Web, will eventually make a search engine crawler begin to take notice.

Once it takes notice, the crawler will try to find the original location of the reprint. It does this by looking at where the content appeared first. It also looks at which copy of an article the most links point to and what versions of the article are the result of content scraping. Through a process of elimination, the crawler narrows the field until a determination can be made. Or if it's still too difficult to tell where the content originated, the crawler will select from trusted domains.

Once the crawler has determined what content is the original, all of the other reprints fall into order beneath it or are eliminated from the index.

If you must use content that's not original, or if you must have multiple copies of content on your web site, there is a way to keep those duplications from adversely affecting your search rankings. By using the <robots.txt> or <noindex> tags, you can prevent duplicated pages from being indexed by the search engine.

The <noindex> tag should be placed in the page header for the page that you don't want to be indexed. It's also a good idea to allow the crawler that finds the tag to follow links that might be on the page. To do that, your code (which is a meta tag) should look like this:

```
<meta name="robots" content="noindex,follow">
```

That small tag of code tells the search engine *not* to index the page, but to follow the links on the page. This small snippet of code can help you quickly solve the problem of search engines reading your duplicate content.

CAUTION Don't make the mistake of using the `<noidex>` tag as a sneaky method of covering up duplicate content intentionally included to increase your search engine ranking. The process will most likely backfire on you. The search engine crawler will eventually realize that your site doesn't rank well on all of the criteria the engine uses to rank sites, and you'll find that your search engine rankings begin to fall.

The `<robots.txt>` tag can be used for a similar effect, but it won't be covered here. Look for information about robots.txt in Chapter 16.

Stay Away from Search Engine Spam

Search engine spam is one of the most difficult problems that search engine crawlers encounter. And it can be a real problem for web-site owners, too, because those who use search engine spam in an attempt to improve their site rankings make it even more difficult for legitimate web sites to achieve good rankings.

So, what exactly is search engine spam? Yahoo! defines it like this:

Pages created deliberately to trick the search engine into offering inappropriate, redundant, or poor-quality search results.

Other search engines have a similar definition for search engine spam. Ultimately, what your concern with search engine spam should be is to avoid it at all costs. There's a fine line between optimizing your web site and creating search engine spam. And you can cross that line unexpectedly. The problem is that search engines will penalize your site if they perceive any element of the site as being search engine spam. And in some cases, that penalty can be delisting your site from search rankings entirely.

There are more than a dozen types of search engine spam. Some types, like content scraping, we've already covered. But many more exist and in order to avoid them, you should know what they are.

Doorway pages

Doorway pages are often confused with landing pages, but they are not even close in their functions. Landing pages are designed to be rich in content, and visitors usually come to these pages through PPC ads. Doorway pages, on the other hand, are created specifically for search engines with the intent of increasing search engine results rankings.

Doorway pages usually use some form of redirection so that when visitors click through the link in the search engine results and land on the page, they are immediately taken to another page. This is either accomplished with a fast *Meta refresh*, JavaScript, or *server side redirection*. The Meta refresh is a technique that is used less often now than in the past, because many search engines penalize web sites that use such tactics.

In place of the Meta refresh, some web sites have found clever ways to trick visitors into clicking a link that leads them forward to the web site they're being drawn to. There are also some web sites that have designed *content-rich doorways*, which are doorway pages that have some element of content included as well as a basic navigational structure that's consistent with the rest of the web site. These pages, like other doorway pages, are still designed to draw high quantities of visitors.

Hidden and tiny text

If you plan to use hidden or tiny text on your page to draw search engine rankings, you should probably change your plans. The practice of using hidden and tiny text was used a lot in the past. It's accomplished by including keyword-rich text that is the same color as the background of your site. This text can't be seen by the visitors that come to your site, but it can be read by search engine crawlers.

The problem with using this technique is that search engines have caught on, so they are looking for this trick and if they find it, you'll be penalized or possibly even delisted. The offense is further compounded if you happen to use *keyword stuffing* in addition to hiding your text within your web site. Keyword stuffing is using a nonsensical stream of keywords, or using keywords out of place on your site. When you combine this method with hiding your text, it's just a matter of time before search engines refuse to include your site in their search rankings.

SEO oversubmission

Submitting your sites to search engines and directories is one tactic that some web-site owners use to ensure their sites are detected by search engines (and it is covered more in Chapter 14). But most of the larger engines, while providing a way to submit a URL, actually suggest that the best way to be included in their index is to get a link to the URL.

Don't use automated submission services if you decide to submit your URL. Submit everything by hand, taking care to read the instructions completely.

Page jacking

Page jacking is a method of search engine spam that's similar in nature to scraping. The difference is that with page jacking, whole pages — and even whole web sites — are copied for the purpose of increasing search ranking and traffic for another site.

In one example of page jacking, a person might copy a whole site like Microsoft. They then *cloak* that site, but it still appears in search listings. Then, when unsuspecting users click through the listing for Microsoft they're taken not to the Microsoft page, but to another page that the hijacker funnels them to.

Not only is page jacking a good way to get your web site delisted from search engine results, but it's also a crime that can result in a stiff fine and possibly jail time. There are also trademark and copyright infringement issues associated with page jacking.

Bait and switch

Remember the old bait-and-switch cons that used to be so popular? Someone would offer a product as a great deal, and then, when users showed up to purchase it, the seller would try to switch them to more expensive products or ones with less quality. This bait and switch still happens today, and it's come to the Internet.

Bait and switch in SEO is the practice of creating an optimized web page specifically for search engines with the intent of obtaining good rankings. When those rankings are obtained, the company replaces the optimized site with one that's less optimized and more normal. The result is nearly instant traffic when the site has been switched.

Bait and switch does have one downfall. Most search engine crawlers revisit a site several times a month. And when the crawler revisits a bait-and-switch site, it will see that the content of the site has changed, and will adjust search rankings accordingly. In other words, the person who set up the bait and switch put a lot of time into a temporary optimization solution.

It makes much more sense to do your optimization the right way the first time out. Then, when the crawler comes back through looking at your site, it sees a consistent picture of the site, and the ranking of the site will remain consistent.

Cloaking

Cloaking is another sleight-of-hand SEO technique. For SEO purposes, cloaking a site is a method of delivering a page based on who is requesting the page. For example, if a web site is using cloaking, when a regular visitor comes to the site, that visitor will see one page. But when a search crawler comes to the site, it sees a much more relevant, better optimized site.

Search engines frown on cloaking, and if you're caught using cloaking techniques, your site will be penalized or even delisted completely.

There is another reason that people use cloaking on their web sites. Instead of trying to trick search engines, some web-site owners use cloaking to protect the source code of their web site. Because it's possible for anyone to choose **Show Source** or **Display Source Code** from their browser's tool menu, it's sometimes frustrating for organizations that want to keep their source code proprietary.

Instead of putting it out for the whole world to see, these companies use page cloaking. But this is not an advisable way to protect your code. Search engine crawlers don't like cloaked sites and your site will be penalized if you choose to use cloaking for any reason.

Hidden links

Hidden links are created using the same methods used to create hidden text. The difference between hidden links and hidden text is that, with hidden links, the search crawler can follow the links to other sites or to other pages within the same site.

Because many search engines now pay close attention to the links that lead into and off of a web site, hidden links have become more popular. However, they should not be used under any circumstances, because the ultimate result when your hidden links are discovered is that your site will be penalized by the search engine. And anything that reduces your site ranking or has the potential to affect the ranking in a negative way should be avoided.

Spamming a search engine for any reason is never a good idea. And you can be penalized even for inadvertently spamming, so take the time to learn what techniques could lead a search engine to believe that you're intentionally spamming it. Then, avoid those techniques no matter what might lead you to believe that spamming a search engine might be a good idea.

Considerations for Multi-Lingual Sites

Creating SEO-optimized content for a multi-lingual web site presents a whole new challenge for SEO. Needing a multi-lingual site is a good problem to have. It usually means that you have customers in multiple countries. However, it also means you have to double or triple your SEO efforts.

The good news is that optimizing your foreign-language web site is very much the same as optimizing your English one. You just do it in a different language. Here are some guidelines that should serve as reminders of what you should plan to do during the SEO process:

- **Translate keywords into the new language.** In some cases, you won't be able to translate your keywords into a matching word in another language. In that case, you'll need to choose new keywords.

- **Translate existing web content.** Again, translations can sometimes be squirrelly. Unless you're an expert in the language to which you're translating, hire someone to do it for you. A bad translation could cost you more in lost traffic than the services of a good translator.

- **Apply all of the same SEO rules** to your foreign content that you've learned for your English content. Just because the language is different doesn't mean that the search engine or the search engine crawler is any different.

- **Include the proper links** both to and from your English site to your foreign-language site, but also include the appropriate links to English on the foreign-language site.

- **Make language options clearly available** on your web site. If these options are not clearly marked, your foreign visitors could miss them, and then you'll lose visitors before they're fully engaged in your site.

SEO is really no different in any other language than it is in English. The biggest concern when translating your site to another language is the actual translation. The SEO efforts are essentially the same, but getting the language wrong could cost you just as much as not having a foreign-language site at all.

Content Management Systems

Content is one of the most important elements of your web site, because it can organically improve your search engine rankings. But that only applies if the content is well written, interesting, and focused. If you have a web site that's hundreds of pages in size and those pages change regularly because of your content strategy, managing all of that content can be a nightmare.

That's where content management systems (CMS) become very useful. A content management system is a tool used to create, update, publish, discover, and distribute content for your web site. This piece of software is usually very easy to use, and it quickly becomes one of the most useful tools you'll find for developing your web site.

When should you use CMS?

Content management systems are hugely helpful for web sites that have hundreds of pages of content to manage. If your web site is smaller than that, should you use it? The answer to that question is "It depends."

What it depends on is how much content you actually have that *needs* to be managed, how much time you have to manage it, and how much of your budget you want to invest in managing it. For the last point, there is good news. Some content management systems are completely free. Drupal (http://drupal.org) is probably one of the best-known free systems. It's open source, which means that the software is both free and can be tweaked by you to meet your specific needs. It's through this collaborative development that open-source software applications are improved for everyone involved.

If you feel you need a CMS that's a little more expensive than free, you can find those out there, too. The cost of the most basic CMS software starts at around $1,500 and increases to more than $7,000 for the initial license. More complex versions can cost as much as $500,000 for the initial licensing. Fees for additional licenses, extra features, or monthly maintenance fees may also apply.

But price should not be the main reason you choose a content management system. Instead, your CMS decisions should be based on your corporate need. And that will vary from one organization to another.

Choosing the right CMS

If you decide that a content management system is a tool you need for managing your web-site content, you should take some time to investigate the different options that are available to you. Like any other software, not all CMS systems are created equal.

When you begin to look for the right CMS, the first thing you should do is consider what budget you have for the system. Your budget will narrow your field some. Then you can begin considering different factors about each company that will help you narrow the field even more:

- **Look first at the history of the company.** Companies that are new to the market are risky, especially if they are drastically different from existing companies. The length of time that a company has been in business is a good indicator of its strength. This is not foolproof, but you can generally have more trust in companies that have been in business longer.

- **Look at workflow and collaboration features.** You know what you need to accomplish with a content management system. Whether it is plugging in content from vendors outside your company, or allowing for collaboration within your organization, make sure that the services that you are considering can meet all of your needs now and as your organization grows. It's difficult to migrate from one content management system to another, so think long-term as you're making your decision.

- **Consider how the software will integrate** with your organization. Do you need software that you install and manage from your own machines or will a web-based program serve your needs better? Also, how will the system you choose work with the technology that you already have in place? If you have to invest in additional technology to support the CMS, the actual cost of the system will be higher than originally thought.

- **Consider elements of personalization, too.** How much personalization do you need? Will multiple people need different capabilities? And what about dealing with archived content? Personalization reaches to more than just defining how many users will use the CMS for different jobs. It also means looking deeper into all the situations in which a different element of CMS may be needed.

As with any technology, there are many other factors to consider. But these questions will get you started. Then, as you narrow the field you can request references from organizations that currently use the CMS software you're considering. Remember, though, that a vendor isn't going to supply a customer reference that will speak badly of them, so also check Internet forums and software reviews to round out your picture of the company that you're considering. A great resource to compare CMS software is http://www.cmsmatrix.org/.

How CMS affects SEO

One real concern many web-site designers have is how a content management system will affect their SEO efforts. In the past, CMS applications often published content with long, complex URLs or created multiple copies, which search engine crawlers were likely to look down on. Today, however, CMS applications are much more SEO-friendly.

SEO has become a large part of owning any kind of web site. Even individuals now consider how they're going to get their sites to rank well in search engines, and small or even micro-businesses need more and more technological assistance, including SEO assistance. So CMS companies have listened when customers demanded a management system that plays well with search engines.

Today, most CMS applications are designed to improve your SEO rather than to hinder it. Still, it's a factor that you should consider as you're looking for a CMS. Ask very specific questions, like "How does your software or application help with my SEO efforts?" and "What specific elements of your application or software will help to improve my SEO efforts?"

In looking at CMS applications, you should also consider the structure with which it will help you develop your content. Because a CMS is designed to maintain your content in an orderly manner, it can help to solidify your content strategy and your web-site structure.

Understand and Use Viral Content

If you've ever heard of *viral marketing*, you know that it involves marketing materials that are spread via social networking. For example, you may have an article that's largely a piece of marketing and that you post to a blog. The article then gets tagged in a social network, and begins to spread like a virus. Each time someone tags the article, more people see it. And then more people tag it and more people see it and so on. It's like the snowball effect applied to marketing.

Viral marketing or any other kind, however, begins with good content — *viral content*. The content that's spread virally by social networking doesn't have to be your only marketing. And in fact it will be much more effective if the content isn't "market-y" at all. Users are much more interested in content that provides what they need at the time — real information — than in content that tries to sell them something.

And that's where viral content comes in. Social networking and social media optimization are covered in depth in Chapter 18, but for now you should know that viral content should be written with the medium of distribution in mind. If you plan to use blog tagging to distribute your content, then the proper format for that content should be a blog post, written short and to the point, but including useful information (that's more than just a link to another blogger's web site).

You can also include articles and news stories in viral content as long as you use the appropriate social networking systems to distribute them. If you've ever seen an article with a button at the bottom that says **Digg This**, you've seen the seed of viral content. Digg is a social networking site that visitors can use to share information of interest.

The methods of SEO covered to this point are mostly based on SEO that has worked in the past. The Internet, in true Internet fashion, is changing all the time. And the most recent shift has been toward socially networked content systems. SEO for these types of content systems will require different strategies than the content systems of the past. It's something that you should start considering now. Taking advantage of these social networking systems sooner, rather than later, will help you at least keep up with the pack if not take the lead.

Chapter 13

Understanding the Role of Links and Linking

Back during the early days of the Internet, before it began to interest the general public, there were two ways to get around in it. You either had to have the URL of the page that you wanted to reach, or someone had to send you a link to it. There were no search engines to help you find what you wanted.

Even though we have powerful search engines today to help us find information on the Web, linking from one page to another is still a powerful tool for helping your site get found. And links can group together sites that are relevant, giving you more leverage with search engines than a site without links might have.

There is a fine science to creating a linking strategy, however. It's not enough just to sprinkle a few links here and there within the pages of your site. There are different types of links that register differently with search engines and it's even possible to get your web site completely delisted from search results if you handle your links improperly.

When you really begin to consider links and how they affect web sites, you see that links are interconnected in such a way as to be the main route by which traffic moves around the Internet. If you search for a specific term, when you click through the search engine results, you're taken to another web page. As you navigate through that web page, you may find a link that leads you to another site, and that process continues until you're tired of surfing the Internet and close your browser. And even if the process starts differently — with you typing a URL directly into your web browser — it still ends the same way.

How Links Affect SEO

If keyword is the word you hear most often with SEO, then links or linking is the word you hear second-most often. Links are the foundation of topical communities, and as such they have as much, if not more, weight with search engine crawlers than keywords do.

A web page without links is like a desert island. It's sitting there, right in the middle of the ocean, but no one really knows it's there. The island could be littered with diamonds. The plants that grow on the island might heal every disease known to man. But if man doesn't know the island is there, none of that matters.

It's the same with your web site. It doesn't matter how great the information or the products on the site might be. If people can't find it, it's as good as a desert island.

The purpose of links, then, is to first link your web site to others that are relevant to the information included on your site. In addition, links provide a method by which traffic to your site is increased. And isn't that the reason you're playing the SEO game? Your desire is to increase the traffic to your site, which in turn increases the number of products that you sell, the number of sales leads you collect, or the number of appointments that you set with highly qualified clients. In short, links lead to increased profit and growth. So of course you'd want to use them on your site.

Another reason links are so important is that links into your site from other web sites serve as "votes" for the value of your site. The more links that lead to your site, the more weight a search engine crawler will give the site, which in turn equates to a better search engine ranking, especially for search engines like Google that use a quality ranking factor, like *PageRank*.

Understanding Google's PageRank

PageRank is a family of algorithms that assigns a numerical value to pages on the Web in an effort to determine the relevance or importance of that page. PageRank, which was developed by Google founders Larry Page and Sergey Brin, is proprietary to Google, but there are other search engines that use a ranking system to help determine the order of search engine results. It's interesting to note that PageRank is named for Larry Page and doesn't refer to the rank of the page.

The exact algorithms that make up PageRank are not available to the general public. A version of the algorithms that you'll find here was filed with the patent for PageRank, but only Google knows every variable that's taken into account. It will help, however, if you understand how PageRank is calculated, so the following example (from Wikipedia.org) should help clarify those calculations.

Simplified PageRank Algorithm

Assume a small universe of four web pages: A, B, C, and D. The initial approximation of PageRank would be evenly divided between these four documents. Hence, each document would begin with an estimated PageRank of 0.25.

If pages B, C, and D each link only to A, they would each confer a 0.25 PageRank to A. All PageRank PR( ) in this simplistic system would thus gather to A because all links would be pointing to A.

$PR(A) = PR(B) + PR(C) + PR(D).$

But then suppose page B also has a link to page C, and page D has links to all three pages. The value of the link-votes is divided among all the outbound links on a page. Thus, page B gives a vote worth 0.125 to page A and a vote worth 0.125 to page C. Only one third of D's PageRank is counted for A's PageRank (approximately 0.083).

$$PR(A) = \frac{PR(B)}{2} + \frac{PR(C)}{1} + \frac{PR(D)}{3} \; .$$

In other words, the PageRank conferred by an outbound link L( ) is equal to the document's own PageRank score divided by the normalized number of outbound links (it is assumed that links to specific URLs only count once per document).

$$PR(A) = \frac{PR(B)}{L(B)} + \frac{PR(C)}{L(C)} + \frac{PR(D)}{L(D)} \; .$$

In the general case, the PageRank value for any page u can be expressed as:

$$PR(u) = \sum_{v \in Bu} \frac{PR(v)}{L(v)}$$

That is, the PageRank value for a page u is dependent on the PageRank values for each page v out of the set Bu (this set contains all pages linking to page u), divided by the number of links from page v (this is Nv).

PageRank Algorithm Including Damping Factor

The PageRank theory holds that even an imaginary surfer who is randomly clicking on links will eventually stop clicking. The probability, at any step, that the person will continue is a damping factor d. Various studies have tested different damping factors, but it is generally assumed that the damping factor will be set around 0.85.

The damping factor is subtracted from 1 (and in some variations of the algorithm, the result is divided by the number of documents in the collection) and this term is then added to the product of (the damping factor and the sum of the incoming PageRank scores).

That is,

$$PR(A) = 1 - d + d \left(\frac{PR(B)}{L(B)} + \frac{PR(C)}{L(C)} + \frac{PR(D)}{L(D)} + \cdots \right).$$

or (N = the number of documents in collection)

$$PR(A) = \frac{1 - d}{N} + d \left(\frac{PR(B)}{L(B)} + \frac{PR(C)}{L(C)} + \frac{PR(D)}{L(D)} + \cdots \right).$$

continued

continued

So any page's PageRank is derived in large part from the PageRanks of other pages. The damping factor adjusts the derived value downward. The second formula supports the original statement in Page and Brin's paper that "the sum of all PageRanks is one." Unfortunately, however, Page and Brin gave the first formula, which has led to some confusion.

Google recalculates PageRank scores each time it crawls the Web and rebuilds its index. As Google increases the number of documents in its collection, the initial approximation of PageRank decreases for all documents.

The formula uses a model of a random surfer who gets bored after several clicks and switches to a random page. The PageRank value of a page reflects the chance that the random surfer will land on that page by clicking on a link. It can be understood as a Markov chain in which the states are pages, and the transitions are all equally probable and are the links between pages.

If a page has no links to other pages, it becomes a sink and therefore terminates the random surfing process. However, the solution is quite simple. If the random surfer arrives at a sink page, it picks another URL at random and continues surfing again.

When calculating PageRank, pages with no outbound links are assumed to link out to all other pages in the collection. Their PageRank scores are therefore divided evenly among all other pages. In other words, to be fair with pages that are not sinks, these random transitions are added to all nodes in the Web, with a residual probability of usually $d = 0.85$, estimated from the frequency that an average surfer uses his or her browser's bookmark feature.

So, the equation is as follows:

$$PR(p_i) = \frac{1-d}{N} + d \sum_{p_j \in M(p_i)} \frac{PR(p_j)}{L(p_j)}$$

where $p1, p2, ..., pN$ are the pages under consideration, M(pi) is the set of pages that link to pi, L(pj) is the number of outbound links on page pj, and N is the total number of pages.

The PageRank values are the entries of the dominant eigenvector of the modified adjacency matrix. This makes PageRank a particularly elegant metric: the eigenvector is

$$R = \begin{bmatrix} PR(p_1) \\ PR(p_2) \\ \vdots \\ PR(p_N) \end{bmatrix}$$

where R is the solution of the equation

$$R = \begin{bmatrix} (1-d)/N \\ (1-d)/N \\ \vdots \\ (1-d)/N \end{bmatrix} + d \begin{bmatrix} \ell(p_1, p_1) & \ell(p_1, p_2) & \cdots & \ell(p_1, p_N) \\ \ell(p_2, p_1) & \ddots & & \vdots \\ \vdots & & \ell(p_i, p_j) & \\ \ell(p_N, p_1) & \cdots & & \ell(p_N, p_N) \end{bmatrix} R$$

where the adjacency function

$$l(p_i, p_j)$$

is 0 if page pj does not link to pi, and normalized such that, for each j, the equation is:

$$\sum_{i=1}^{N} l(p_i, p_j) = 1,$$

That is, the elements of each column sum up to 1.

This is a variant of the eigenvector centrality measure used commonly in network analysis.

The values of the PageRank eigenvector are fast to approximate (only a few iterations are needed), and in practice it gives good results.

As a result of Markov theory, it can be shown that the PageRank of a page is the probability of being at that page after lots of clicks. This happens to equal t ? 1 where t is the expectation of the number of clicks (or random jumps) required to get from the page back to itself.

The main disadvantage is that it favors older pages, because a new page, even a very good one, will not have many links unless it is part of an existing site (a site being a densely connected set of pages, such as Wikipedia). The Google Directory (itself a derivative of the Open Directory Project) allows users to see results sorted by PageRank within categories. The Google Directory is the only service offered by Google where PageRank directly determines display order. In Google's other search services (such as its primary Web search) PageRank is used to weight the relevance scores of pages shown in search results.

Several strategies have been proposed to accelerate the computation of PageRank.

Various strategies to manipulate PageRank have been employed in concerted efforts to improve search results rankings and monetize advertising links. These strategies have severely impacted the reliability of the PageRank concept, which seeks to determine which documents are actually highly valued by the Web community.

Google is known to actively penalize link farms and other schemes designed to artificially inflate PageRank. How Google identifies link farms and other PageRank manipulation tools are among Google's trade secrets.

To say that links are an important part of SEO for your web site is probably an understatement. If you want your site to be found, you must have links in from other sites. Without those links, you may as well be an island sitting in the middle of an ocean full of other web sites.

How Links and Linking Work

You've seen how important links are to your SEO strategy, and you've seen how links affect your Google PageRank, but how, really, do links work for improving your SEO? As you've already seen, a link *to* your site is a vote for the relevance of your site. So, if you're linking *out* to other sites, then you're voting for them. And internal links ensure that a search engine crawler can find the various pages in your site. A *dangling link* is a link that leads into a page that has no links leading out of it.

Each of these different types of links affects site ranking differently for engines that take linking architectures into consideration. For example, a dangling link could be ignored entirely by a search engine, or the page to which the link points could score lower on the linking metrics because all the links are coming into the page, but there are none going out. And that's what makes linking such a fine science. You need to know how the links on your site will affect the amount of traffic the site has. You also need to know how to have links without going overboard, so that the crawler labels your site as a *link farm*.

Snagging inbound links

Nearly every web site has links that lead out to other web sites. It's rare to find a site that doesn't link to another site somewhere on the Web. That's how communities are built around specific industries and topics. And the links that leave your site are important, but they're not nearly as important as those links that lead to your site. These *inbound links*, as you've already discovered, are seen by search engines as votes for your site within a particular community of sites.

Anytime you're being voted for, you want to have as many votes as possible. Inbound links are no different. You want to have a large number of links that lead to your site. You can achieve those links in a variety of ways, some more effective than others:

- **Requesting Links:** The oldest method of gaining inbound links is to request them. This requires that you study your market to find out who the players involved in the market are. Then, you contact each one of the sites that you discover and ask them to link to your site. In most cases, the person you contact receives your request, but providing links to other sites is the least of their worries, so you may not even hear from them. If you do, it can sometimes be months later. So, you put a lot of time into requesting links from other sites for a relatively small return on your efforts.

- **Writing Articles:** One of the most effective methods of gaining inbound links is to offer an article for other companies to use as long as they include a paragraph of information at the bottom that includes credits for you as well as a link back to your site. This method of gaining inbound links works well, because web sites are always looking for good content to include on their pages. The catch here is that the article you write should be well-written, accurate, and useful to other sites in your industry. Once you've produced an article that meets these requirements, you can begin to let others know that you have content available for them to use for free. Just remember to require a link back to your site in return for the freedom to use your article on their sites.

- **Blogs:** Another way to get links back to your site is from bloggers. What started as a strange phenomenon that was mostly personal has now become a powerful business tool, and many businesses rely on links back to their sites from the various industry bloggers out there. In most cases, though, bloggers aren't just going to stumble onto your web site. It's far better for you to contact the blogger with information about your organization, some product that you offer, or with news that would interest them. This information then gives the blogger something to use in his or her regular posts. Keep in mind, however, that you can't control what a blogger might say, so it's possible that the review you get from the blogger won't be favorable.

■ **Press Releases:** Press releases are one of the mainstays of any marketing program. It can be so effective that many organizations hire companies to do nothing but distribute their press releases as widely as possible. What's so powerful about a press release? It's just the facts, including benefits, and it's sent out to publications and organizations that might publish all or part of the press release. Use press releases to send out new items of all types, and send them as widely as you can. New organizations, publications, newsletters, even some forums will post press releases. When you write it, make sure a link back to your site is included in the press release. Then, when someone posts it, the link you provide leads back to your site.

■ **Affiliate Programs:** *Affiliate programs* are a type of paid advertising. Amazon.com's affiliate program is one of the best-known affiliate programs. You provide a link to people who want to link back to your web site. They place the link on their site and then when someone clicks through that link to your site and makes a purchase (or converts any other goal you have arranged), the affiliate — the person who placed your link on their site — gets paid a small percentage. Usually the payment for affiliate programs is very low ($.01 to $.05 per click or a small percentage of the sale). But some people make a good living being affiliates, and many organizations receive additional traffic because of their affiliate programs.

There are some ethical considerations with affiliate programs. Many believe that because you're paying for the link back to your site it's less valid than if you were to land organic links. However, most search engines see affiliate programs as an acceptable business practice and they don't reduce your rankings because you use affiliate programs. The trick with affiliate programs is to not allow them to be your sole source of incoming links. In addition, most affiliate programs utilize some click-tracking software, which by definition negates the value of the link, because the link on the affiliate's page is going from that page, to the ad server, to your site. So the link is from the ad server rather than the affiliate site.

■ **PPC and Paid Links:** Pay-per-click advertisements (which were covered in Chapters 5–10) are an acceptable business practice. There is no problem with using PPC advertisements to achieve inbound links to your site. Remember that, like affiliate links, PPC links are not direct links to your site. Paid links, on the other hand, are different from affiliate links — you pay to have a direct, or *flat* link, placed on a page. Some search engines frown on the practice of using these types of links. Using paid links (especially those that land on *link farms*) is a practice that carries some business risk.

■ **Link to Yourself:** Linking to yourself is a technique that sits right on the line between ethical and unethical. Linking to yourself from other sites that you might own is an acceptable practice. But if you set up other sites simply to be able to link back to your own site and create the illusion of popularity, you're going to do more damage than it's probably worth to you. If you are linking to yourself and you suspect that you might be doing something that would adversely affect your search engine ranking, then you shouldn't do it. There are plenty of links to be had without linking back to your own web sites; you just have to work a little harder for the higher quality links.

Inbound links are such an important part of a linking strategy that some organizations find themselves caught up in the process of learning who is linking back to them. It's not a bad thing to want to know where your links are coming from. And one of the places you can gather that information is from your web-analytics application. Some analytics programs will show you at least the top-performing links to your site. These reports are usually part of the marketing element of the application.

You can also perform a search at Google for the term `link:yourwebsite.com`. This returns search results for all the web sites that Google considers relevant links to your web site. A similar search on Yahoo! will result in a more complete list of incoming links. This is a good way to figure out who's linking to you unless there are hundreds of links. If there are more than a dozen or so, you could find yourself surfing the results of this search for far more time than you have to spend examining your inbound links.

That's why there's also link management software that will track your links for you. LinkMachine is one link management software (`http://www.linkmachine.net`). Link management software allows you to track and manage your links and linking strategies. It takes away some of the time-consuming manual tracking tasks.

Creating outbound links

If controversy were an SEO strategy, everyone would be at the top of their SEO game. Unfortunately, it's not. All controversy does is muddy the waters. And that's exactly what the controversy over whether or not you should have outbound links on your site is good for — making life difficult.

The subject of outbound links has often been debated. There are some who worry about *leaking PageRank* — what (supposedly) happens when you link out to other sites. The fear behind leaking is two-fold: when you lead people away from your site they may not come back (hence your visitors "leak" away), and when you link out to other pages, you're reducing the value of each "vote" because the value of an outbound link is divided by the total number of outbound links.

No one knows for sure exactly what mix of elements is considered when your page is ranked by a search engine. However, it's safe to say that if you have only inbound links and no outbound links, it can't look good for your site. And especially these days when social marketing is becoming more and more of a factor for search engine results. The best plan of action is to have a balanced mix of inbound and outbound links. Your site visitors will expect to see some links leading to other sites on the Web, whether those links are simple resources to help them find what they need or something else.

Outbound links also help to establish your expertise in a particular area. Yes, inbound links help with that as well, but it's not enough just to have people pointing to you. You should also have some favorites out there that you find helpful and that you think others will find helpful. When your visitors click through these links and find that you do know what they're looking for, the loyalty points will be awarded to you.

This is how you build relationships with your visitors. And relationships are the ultimate reason to create a web site at all, part of making sure your web site appears in front of as many people as possible. As long as relationships are your main priority, all of the other elements of link building should fall right into place.

When you're creating your outbound links, you should keep some guidelines in mind to appease search engine crawlers, because even though the main target for your links should be your site visitors, search engines will pay attention to your links and your search ranking could be affected by them.

- **Keep your links relevant.** That doesn't mean that you can only link to pages that are in the same industry as your own, but if you do link outside your industry, make sure there is some logical reason for sending your visitors in that direction.

- **Don't overuse links.** There's nothing more frustrating for site users than to find that every other word in an article is linked. A good rule of thumb is no more than two or three links per article or blog post on your site. Other links, like ads for other services, can be added in addition to these text links, but again, keep them to a minimum.

- **Use keyword anchor text as often as possible** when creating your links. Using the phrase "click here" won't gain you any leverage with a search engine crawler. Using a link that reads "gourmet ingredients," when that phrase is one of your key phrases, will help improve your search engine ranking as long as the link leads to a page that truly is about gourmet ingredients.

- **Be careful whom you link to.** You may have heard the phrase "Don't link to bad neighborhoods." What it means is that you don't want to link to low-quality sites, because some search engines will penalize you for that. For example, if you link to a spam site or a link farm, search engines are not going to look favorably on that link. If, however, you link to high-ranking sites, you'll gain even more traction with search engines. Remember, though you may not be penalized for sites that link to you, the outbound links on your site are under your control.

- **Don't create pages that contain only links.** This common practice from the early days of the Internet is no longer useful. Search engines see pages that contain nothing but links and read them as spam pages. If you must use a resources page, be sure to include descriptions of each link that you include on the page. Better yet, avoid this practice altogether if there's any way you can.

- **Monitor links and update broken ones.** A broken link is worse than not having a link at all. When you link to a page and don't check back on the links periodically, things could change — companies go out of business, web sites change and disappear altogether. Then, when the search engine crawler follows the links on your page and finds a broken link, this reflects badly on your site. If the broken link is there for a long time, the search engine could reduce your ranking because it appears that you're not maintaining your site properly.

Outbound links aren't the beginning and end of your search engine linking strategy, but there's also no reason to avoid them completely. Use outbound links where these are relevant and useful to your site visitors and not one time more. And when you do use them, take the time to ensure that your links are accurate and connect to the page that you intend them to connect to.

Taking advantage of cross-linking

Like many other topics we've covered in link strategies, *cross-linking* is one of those practices that isn't black or white but more accurately has dozens of subtle shades of gray. Cross-linking is the practice of linking several sites together, usually sites that are owned by the same company or individual. A group of six sites connected by a cross-linking scheme might look something like the diagram shown in Figure 13-1.

Notice how the cross-linked sites are connected and that every site has the same number of links coming into and leaving the page. This is a pattern that search engines look for to determine if web sites are using linking schemes simply to increase their search engine results rankings — a practice that search engines frown upon. Additionally, cross-linking happens most often with people or companies who own multiple web sites, and that also gives the search engine reason to doubt the validity of the links.

FIGURE 13-1

Cross-linked sites create a circular linking scheme that can be read by search engines as a trick to increase rankings.

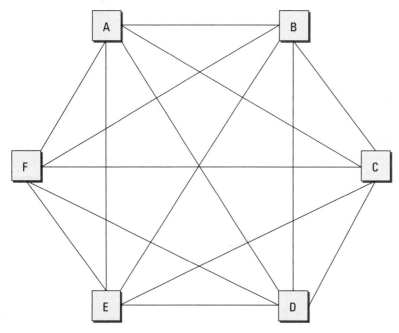

So, how do search engines know if one person owns all of the sites that are cross-linked? The structure of a set of cross-linked sites is the first clue. A group of sites that have naturally occurring links might look more like the diagram shown in Figure 13-2.

Other factors that may help a search engine decide that all the sites are owned by the same person are the IP address of the site and the *WHOIS information*. The IP address is unique to each different web site. Two sites that are owned by the same company are usually hosted on the same server, and so the IP address of those sites would be the same. And WHOIS information is the record of domain ownership. You're required to provide this information when you purchase a web site.

When sites owned by the same company or individual are cross-linked, search engines look very closely to ensure that the sites are relevant to each other. If they are, then there are no issues with the cross-linking. For sites that are not related, however, search engines look down upon the practice of cross-linking and your site (or sites) could be penalized for search engine spamming.

FIGURE 13-2

Natural linking between web sites is not as circular or organized as cross-linking schemes are.

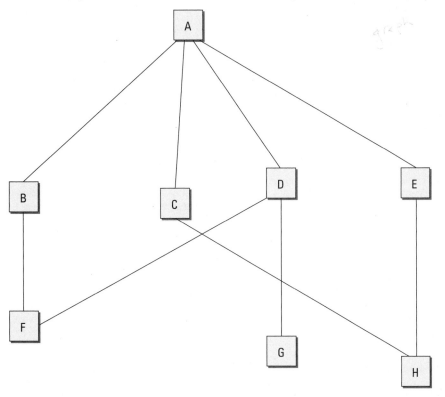

It's also likely to throw up a red flag when you're cross-linking hundreds or even thousands of sites. When this occurs, the only real configuration that makes sense is a *link farm* or set of link farms. And search engines don't like link farms at all. If you want to get your sites completely delisted from the search engine, then set up and take part in a link farm. It will just be a matter of time before your sites are bounced into oblivion.

So, cross-linking isn't always a bad thing. There are times when it works nicely. And the main requirement is that sites have something in common so that the links would have occurred naturally anyway. Another thing that helps to keep cross-linking a legitimate linking strategy is for every site to have unique content. If you've created a handful of different sites with exactly the same content on all of them, search engines are going to take notice and your sites will be penalized.

As long as you're using cross-linking in a legitimate way, there's no reason you should avoid it completely. But like all the other linking strategies, use it wrong and you'll pay the price.

The skinny on link farms

Have you ever seen a large farm from the air? From a few thousand feet up, farms look like orderly divisions of land. Each little square looks perfectly proportioned and perfectly laid out.

That's exactly how link farms look. If you've ever landed on a page with links ordered neatly around the page, and with little or no text explaining all of the various links, then you've landed on a link farm. That's all they are, too — collections of links that lead to other web sites, or sometimes off to other link farms.

You'll hear this term often in SEO because link farms are not a good strategy for improving your search engine rankings. Search engines don't like link farms, because they offer no information that's of any value to the people who perform searches. And for that reason, link farms are usually delisted as soon as they're discovered.

It's easy for you to get pulled into a link farm, thinking it's a legitimate link to your site. You'll usually receive some type of solicitation for you to place a link to one of these sites in return for a link to your site; it's even possible that you'll hear of an SEO firm that uses link farms in an attempt to artificially produce results that help them to charge you more.

That's why it's wise to check closely the places where your links will be placed. If you receive a request for a *reciprocal* link, be sure you check to make sure that the page that will be displaying your link actually is a relevant web page that has some association with the topic of your page. If you check it out and find that what you're just being added to a collection of links on a page, many of which are unrelated, don't allow your link to be displayed there.

You may not be the person who created the link farm, but your site can be delisted just as fast as the page for the link farm can if you provide a link back to the link farm. All they care is that someone is spamming the crawler, trying to make it believe something that's not true.

Knowing what constitutes a link farm is easy. In addition to the site characteristics that have already been mentioned, there are some other indicators that a site might not be legitimate. And it's your responsibility to ensure that the pages with which your site is linked are real pages, designed for site visitors, not for crawlers.

- Link farms have no connection at all to your site, either in topic or in actual relation to the content that's on your site.

- Link farms have long, complex URLs and links are often stored in deep directories so that it's harder for search engine crawlers to find them.

- Link farms will usually accept any link that is sent to them, so it's not unusual for links to be unrelated. If someone wants to add your link to a site that isn't even close to yours, don't accept.

- Link farm owners will sometimes send you an e-mail stating they have linked to you and would like a link to their page in return. Again, be cautious of whom you link to or whom you allow to link back to you.

The Basics of Link Building

Building a great linking structure for your web site is not something that happens in the time it takes to throw a web page together. Building a successful link structure takes months, and sometimes longer.

When you begin creating your link structure, you'll probably have mostly outgoing links. Those are links that lead to other pages — popular pages if you can manage it — that will help to bring traffic back to your site. But over time, you should be building your links to include not only links back into your site, but other useful links that aren't damaging to your search engine results rankings.

One of the most important things to remember as you're building your link structure is that quantity isn't nearly as important as quality. Your linking strategy will be far more successful if you create links (both inbound and outbound) that are high quality. Link to great sites that are more popular than your own and try to gain links from those sites to your own, as well.

Of course, getting those inbound links won't be nearly as easy as creating links out to other web sites. Gaining links to your site is a business process. It takes time, and lots of consistent effort on your part. As mentioned earlier, one strategy for gaining inbound links is to send letters to prospective sites, requesting a link. But don't just send out 10,000 letters, generated by some mail-merge program that doesn't customize the letters to the particular site that you're targeting.

Your link request will be most effective if you can give potential linking partners a good reason for them to support you. Perhaps you can show their customers why they should purchase more of that site's products. Whatever the reason, try to give the site you're requesting a link from some motivation to take the time to add your site to their linking system.

Also keep in mind that link building is time-consuming. You're not going to populate the Web with links to your site in one week or even one month. Once your site is built and ready for customers, link building will be an ongoing process that you'll work at for the lifetime of the web sites.

Using Internal Links

One linking strategy that's often overlooked is *internal linking*. Internal links are those that lead people from one page to another within your web site. This is different from the navigational structure. Internal links are more natural links that occur in the text on your web pages.

Without a good internal linking strategy, you run the risk of not having your site properly spidered. It's not enough simply to have a navigational structure or a site map (though site maps help considerably). You should also have links that lead from one element (like a blog post) to other important elements (like an archived article or news clipping on your site), so site visitors find that moving through the information they're examining on your site is a natural process that takes place without too much difficulty or thought.

The most effective methods of internal linking are text links, links within the footers of your pages, and inline text links. Text links are those with which you can use anchor tags and keywords. These links most often appear in the text of a page, though they can also appear in other places within your page, so long as the text links are relevant to the content of the page.

Links within the footers of pages are a common practice now. Figure 13-3 shows how some web pages use links within the footers of pages.

Finally, inline links are those links most often contained within the body of some element of your site content, such as articles and blogs. These links can either be proper names or descriptors that are relevant to the pages being linked to.

FIGURE 13-3

Footer links are common among linking strategies and they usually take visitors to some element of the administrative functions of the site.

```
Beanstalk Search Engine Positioning: SEO Services | Privacy Policy | From Canada | At SES | SEO Sitemap
Search Engine Optimization Services:Business Services | Extreme Services | SEO Training | SEO Consulting Services |
Paid Review | SEO Copywriting |Press Release Writing | Link Popularity Services | Maintenance
SEO Articles Archives: Link Building Articles | Pay-Per-Click | SEO Articles | SE-Friendly Web Design | Past Newsletters |
Dave Davies | Mary Davies | Daryl Quenet
High Ranking Tactics: White Hat | Grey Hat | Black Hat | Report SEO & Search Engine Spam
SEO Resources: Free SEO Tools | Directories | Major Search Engines | PPC Engines |
Secondary Search Engines & Directories | White Papers | Glossary
```

Internal linking is a practice that most companies use to help ease the navigational structure of their sites, and also to create links based on important or keyword text. Plan to use internal linking on your site, but don't allow it to have so much power over your SEO strategy that you don't include other elements of SEO.

Judging the Effectiveness of Your Links

After all of the time that you'll put into creating a link strategy and a link structure that you hope will increase the traffic flow to your site, you should still take some actions to ensure that you have the most effective links possible.

Don't ignore the importance of monitoring your links for successful linking. Remember to avoid broken links, and maintain the ability to change links when your content changes. Manual monitoring can be a pain and very time-consuming. That's why it's so important to keep up with your links. This is usually done through a *link analysis* program. You can use link analysis software, like NetMap (`http://www.netmap.com`). Link analysis programs, once set up properly, can handle everything from placing new links to monitoring the links that you already have in place. It simply requires that you set the software and then allow time to work on your links in the ways covered by this chapter.

Part III

Optimizing Search Strategies

Y ou can use more than one search strategy to optimize your site for search engines. You've seen how keywords and PPC programs work, but there are many other ways to get your site in front of potential site visitors and customers.

Part III explains the different types of search strategies you should be considering as you're developing the SEO for your site. In addition to search engines, there are indexes and directories to keep in mind. You can also use pay-for-inclusion services, which are different than the PPC services that you've already explored.

You should understand robots, spiders, and crawlers in order to target these different types of search strategies. And of course, you don't want to harm your rankings, so there's also a chapter about SEO spam in this section. And finally, we've added information about "social-media" and automated optimization.

All of these elements come together to make your SEO strategies a richer, more effective method of drawing site visitors, and converting those visitors to paying customers.

Chapter 14

Adding Your Site to Directories

Very often search engines and search *directories* are all piled into the same category. After all, you type in a search term and click a button and the results for that search are returned to you, right? That's right. It's just that the data collected by directories and search engines, and the way those search results are returned, is very different. In fact, the fundamental differences between directories and search engines lie in how they collect data, the search results, and how those search results are ranked.

Yahoo! is one of the most well-known search directories on the Internet. It was one of the first names in search, and it still remains one of the stronger players in the search market. But there are dozens of other directories available on the Internet, and, like search engines, these search directories can be very specialized, so that entries cover a single topic or a related group of topics. Search directories can also be implemented within an organization, so that you can list and find all the important documentation your company owns.

The advantage of these highly targeted search directories is not traffic volume like what you would receive from a search engine or a general search directory; what's important here is the quality of traffic you receive. Specific search directories attract specific users who are searching for specific items. This means that their chances of reaching a goal conversion on your site (assuming your site is targeted correctly) are much higher than those of visitors who come from search engines.

What Are Directories?

Search directories offer a way of collecting and categorizing links to other web sites. They are *not* search engines, and behave nothing like search engines. For example, where a search engine collects entries using a search crawler or a robot, search directories are populated by people. You or someone else enters your web site into a directory. And in some cases, once you've entered it, the entry is reviewed by a real person before the site is included in directory listings.

The way that your site is added to a search directory is not the only difference between search engines and search directories. Several additional differences are illustrated in Table 14-1.

Categorization is also likely to be more accurate with a monitored directory, because someone actually checks the site to ensure proper listing. There can be fees associated with monitored directories.

The most closely monitored directories are edited ones. These have a very strict structure, and to get your web site included in the listings, you must accurately provide all requested information. Additionally, edited directories reserve the right to edit or change your entry in any manner that they believe is more suitable to the directory with which you're registering. The fees associated with these types of directories can be very steep, because a person or group of people must always be monitoring the directory.

TABLE 14-1

Directory vs. Search Engine Comparison

Feature	Directories	Search Engines
Entries are collected using what method?	Manually. Usually individuals or groups of individuals add the web sites that are included in directories	Search engine crawlers, spiders, and robots collect entries, and people never review those indexes until a site is returned in search results.
How are web sites categorized?	Whole web sites are categorized as single entities.	Each page in a web site is categorized according to the keywords included on that page.
How are results sorted?	By categories and subcategories.	By keywords and in some cases, web-site popularity.
Are there inclusion limits?	In some cases, yes. Some directories allow sites to be entered into only one or two search categories.	No. Web sites can be included in as many keyword categories as the sites are optimized for.
One differentiator?	Directories are browsable by subject or categories and subcategories.	Search engines search the full text of a web page, making the results much more comprehensive.

There is also a fourth kind of directory: a *hybrid directory*. A hybrid directory is actually a combination of a directory and a search engine. Yahoo! and AOL both operate hybrid directories.

The more directories your site is listed in, the better you'll perform in search results. Most search engines crawl directories, and some even use directory listings to supplement their search results. Just be aware that directories can be outdated, so make time to check your directory listing to ensure it stays fresh. If you notice that the directory doesn't seem to be updated regularly, you may want to remove your listing, because being included on the directory could reflect poorly on your site.

Submitting to directories

By now you've figured out that directories work differently from search engines. You must complete the submission process to have your site included in most directories. But even when you're submitting information about your site, there's an art to doing it.

How you list your site can mean the difference between the site being included in the directory or not. Before you even begin to create your listing, it's usually a good idea to navigate through the directory that you're submitting to. Look at other listings and make note of what works in them.

Keywords are of little importance when you're creating your directory listing. Instead, what will make the difference is the content on your web site. So if you're faced with listing in a directory that's strict about reviewing sites before they are listed, make sure you have fresh content on your site. And it's also a good practice to keep that content fresh by updating it regularly.

Links can also be important when your site is being reviewed for inclusion in a directory, so be sure you keep your links updated. Broken links can be detrimental to your site, and links that lead to unrelated pages won't reflect well either.

Other elements of your listing that editors evaluate for include:

- Appropriate categorization
- Accurate titles and descriptions
- Title and descriptions relevant to the subject of the web site
- Domain names that match site titles
- Secure ordering capabilities on e-commerce sites
- Contact information that's easily accessible
- Links to privacy policies, return policies, and product or service guarantees
- Working and appropriate links to other sites and resources
- Images that display properly in the most common browser formats
- JavaScript that's free of errors

In addition to these requirements, most directories have a long list of criteria that are reviewed before a site is actually added to the directory. That's why it can sometimes take weeks or months for your site to be listed. Depending on the volume of submissions to the directory, it can be a slow process for editors to review each web site.

When you're ready to submit your web site to a directory, take the time to read completely the directions provided by the directory. If you don't follow these directions closely, it's far more likely that your site will be rejected from the listings. One other submission guideline to remember is to submit only your site's main page. Because directories include sites that have been reviewed, they usually list the whole site as a single entity, rather than listing each page separately, as search engines do.

One of the most well-known directories on the Internet is the *Open Directory Project (ODP)* that's managed by dmoz.org. This general directory is edited by a team of volunteers, and it's representative of the various types of directories that are available for you to list your site with. So although there might be some slight differences, the directions for listing your site with ODP are very similar to those you would find when listing with other directories.

To list your web site in the ODP directory, take these steps:

1. Open the Open Directory Project web site (http://www.dmoz.org).

2. Navigate to the category and subcategory where it would be appropriate for your site to appear. Then in the top-right corner of the page click Suggest URL.

3. You are taken to the submission site. Remember to read all the instructions carefully and fill in the submission form completely.

4. When you're finished filling out the form, click the Submit button. You're taken to a Thank-You page, and your submission process is complete.

5. Now you just have to wait for the editorial committee to complete its review. When the review is complete, you should receive notification of whether or not the site has been accepted and listed.

It seems like a simple enough process to suggest your site for inclusion in a directory, and for the most part it is. What's difficult is adding your site to all the directories that are appropriate for it. This can be time-consuming, so plan to spend consistent time at it each day until you've submitted to all of the sites you've selected.

Once the submission process is finished, that time can be used to ensure that your sites are updated to reflect any changes you've made. Changes for which you may want to send an update to a directory include:

■ Changes to the site's URL

■ Correction of grammatical or spelling errors in the title or description of your site

■ Changes to the title or description of your site if the scope of the site changes

■ Suggestions for a new category if the scope of your site changes

Major online directories

Like search engines, there are hundreds of different directories online. Some are general directories, whereas others are very specific and associated with only one industry or organization. When you're selecting the directories to which you'd like to submit your site, be choosy. Don't try to list your site in a directory that's inappropriate. You'll just be wasting time and collecting rejection slips.

Some of the most well-known directories on the Web are:

- Yahoo! Directory (`dir.yahoo.com`): The Yahoo! directory is one of the oldest directories on the Internet, but when you go to `Yahoo.com` you actually won't be taken to it. Instead, you'll be taken to a search engine, because Yahoo! changed its format not too long ago. However, you can still access the directory, by going to the web site just listed. Yahoo! directory is a general directory.

- GoGuides.Org (`www.goguides.org`): This directory's purpose is to be completely spam-free. It's a comprehensive search directory that even has image-searching capabilities.

- Open Directory Project (`www.dmoz.org`): The Open Directory Project is one of the most widely accessed directories on the Web. Users submit sites, and volunteer editors review them. ODP is also an open-source technology, so many other directories use this technology as a basis for their own offerings.

- Google Directory (`directory.google.com`): The Google directory is one of those directories built on the ODP platform. Google is most well-known for its search capabilities, but adding a directory takes advantage of the desire of Internet users to dig deeper into very specific search results.

- SearchSight (`www.searchsight.com`): Another general directory, SearchSight is one of the lesser-known directories, but it's quickly gaining traction in the search market.

One reason search directories are still hanging on in an age of search engines is the social nature of those directories. Internet users like to participate in organizing the Web (and you learn more about that in Chapter 18). Socially monitored sites also seem to have more viability with Internet users. People trust others who have the same needs and desires they do much more than they trust robots, crawlers, and spiders.

Paid vs. free directories

The free versus paid debate is one that's hit every aspect of the Internet and Internet technologies at one time or another. There was worry about free web-site hosting versus paid web hosting, and fret over free e-mail versus paid. And in both cases, whether free or paid is better for you, turns out to depend on what your specific needs are.

The same is true of the debate over free versus paid directory listings. Many experts will try to say that free directory listings have nothing of value listed in them. This is simply not true. Some free directories are actually very strict about the listings that are included in their results. On the other hand, most users believe that paid directories automatically equate to better quality sites. Again, not true. Paid directories can be just as lax about the review process as any other directory.

The Skinny on Meta Search Engines

Search engines, search directories, and hybrids of the two are not the only search game on the Internet. Another search tool that many people like to use are meta search engines. Meta search engines are search engines that search other search engines.

One of the better known meta search engines on the Web is DogPile (http://www.dogpile.com). If you conduct a search on DogPile, you'll receive results for that search from more than half a dozen different search engines. Nifty, right? But how do you apply that to your SEO efforts?

One of the criteria that meta search engines use when searching other search engines is the meta data that's included in your site. Keywords and many other aspects that you'll optimize for are also criteria that meta search engines use. So, if you're optimizing for search engines, you should automatically be optimizing for meta search engines.

Meta search engines also do not behave like regular search engines. These search engines do not include a database of possible results; rather, a meta search engine pulls the results together from other search engines — effectively aggregating them — and then returns only the top search results. The concept is that collecting the top results from many different search engines will help users to find the results they're looking for much faster.

Don't discount the impact that meta search engines can have on your site traffic. Although meta search engines are not as popular as some search engines, many people use them, and they have the potential to drive significant amounts of traffic to your web site.

So whether you use paid or free directory listings shouldn't depend on cost alone. What matters when you're selecting a directory in which to list your site is how relevant the directory is to your site. After relevance, the next consideration is the quality of the sites that are listed in the directory. If a directory you've selected is full of outdated sites, spam sites, or mis-categorized sites, it's probably not the best choice of places to list your web site.

One more element to consider when choosing directories is the audience that's most likely to use the directory. The company should be able to provide a typical audience profile for you if you can't tell by looking at the types of sites listed in the directory. Going back to a principle you've heard often in this book, your site should be created with the user in mind. The same is true for listing your site. It will do you absolutely no good to list your site in a directory of law-based web sites if your site is about home and family topics and products. Audience first. After that, everything will fall into place.

Geo-Targeting SEO Strategies

Creating an SEO strategy for your web site requires more than just choosing what search engines and directories it should appear in. Another consideration is where your site should be listed geographically. *Geo-targeting* is a method of targeting specific traffic for your web site, based on the geographical location of your business.

As more and more Internet users take advantage of the Internet as a purchasing and research tool, those same users are integrating local searches into their behaviors and habits. For example, if a person is in the market to buy a plasma television, he may spend time on the Internet searching for facts and information about plasma TVs. In the beginning, this information can be generic in nature. It doesn't matter where it comes from, so long as it answers the customer's questions.

The next phase of the buying process will then be pricing the television. And this will also take place on the Internet. Geography now is becoming more important, but it's not until the actual sale takes place that geography becomes essential. Because many users choose to research on the Internet and purchase in the store (or purchase on the Internet and pick up in the store), that customer might take the time to find a local store (using the Internet) that offers the brand and price he is looking for. If your site isn't listed in some kind of local directory or categorized on at least one level by location, you'll miss out on those sales.

Geo-targeting is the practice of catering to site users based on their location. And it's smart SEO. Many search engines and directories offer some type of geo-targeting capabilities. Usually, these either require that your physical location be included on your web site, or that you list your site in the right section of a directory.

You've heard it said, "location, location, location." Well, location is just as important on the Internet as it in the real world, so don't skip the geo-targeting aspect of optimizing your web site. Give search engines and directories the extra information they need to ensure that your site shows up in local searches.

Using Submission Tools

You may have already figured out that getting your site included in search engines and directories is no easy task. It can take a lot of time, and if you don't follow all the directions to the letter, you risk the chance of being refused for listing. To help ease the process, a class of software tools, called *submission tools*, has emerged for the SEO market.

Submission tools are automated software programs and applications that remember the repetitive information that must be provided to get your web site listed in a search engine or directory. And they sound like a great deal. Some can be, but not all of them.

One of the problems with many submission tools is that they try to scam web-site owners by promising to submit their site to thousands of search engines and directories for one low fee. The problem with that claim is that most of those search engines are either nonexistent or mostly worthless to your site.

So, when considering web-site submission tools, look closely at the claims the programs make. And then apply that golden rule, "If it sounds too good to be true, it probably is." You can ask for a list of the search engines and directories the tool will submit your site to. Request this list and then take the time to research the sites before you invest in the program.

Submission tools can take two forms: *deep submission tools* and *multi-submission tools*. Most web sites are dozens and even hundreds of pages deep. "Deep" means those pages are several levels down in the structure of the site. And often those sites are missed by search engine crawlers, or they're not considered important. But that's not always the case.

Deep submission tools will submit those deep pages to search engines and directories. The process is automated, and the submission tools can be more successful at submitting the deep pages than you might be, just because it takes time to submit pages and the deeper you go, the longer the process.

Multi-submission tools submit your site to multiple different search engines and directories. These tools also help ease the burden of getting your site listed. Rather than having to go repeatedly through the discovery, research, and submission process, multi-submission tools do the work for you.

Unfortunately, it's hard to know if the submission tool you select will be the right one. Because of this, it is always the best practice to manually submit your site and URLs to directories. Take the time to consult with other program users. And if the company that's providing the submission tools refuses to provide a list of references, move on. There are more submission tool providers out there. The right one will meet your expectations and provide the references you need to be comfortable using the application.

Chapter 15

Pay-for-Inclusion Services

S earch Engine Marketing is composed of two very different elements. Search engine optimization (SEO), strictly speaking, is about improving your *natural* search engine rankings through tweaking your web site. Pay-per-click (PPC) programs on the other hand are based on the ability to pay for placement. Even Google has separated the two on its search results, with natural search results appearing on the left side, and paid search results appearing on the right.

When you're fighting today's competition to improve your web-site ranking, you need to use every tool in your arsenal. One of those tools is *paid inclusion*. But there's a lot of confusion around paid inclusion and when it should be used. Very often, paid inclusion is confused with *paid placement*. They're very different strategies.

When you hear about paid inclusion, you may well hear it called Pay for Inclusion (PFI) or Pay per Inclusion (PPI). Even when you're looking at those two terms, you're looking at differences in meaning. Pay for Inclusion is a strategy whereby you pay a fee simply to be included in a search index. This fee doesn't guarantee your rank in the index. It's a simple flat fee that's usually paid annually.

Pay per Inclusion is also a strategy in which you pay a fee to be included in a search index, but the fee that you pay in PPI is based on the number of clicks you receive as a result of that inclusion. Like PFI, PPI still doesn't guarantee your rank in the search engine. Your only guarantee is that you will be included. And that per-click fee can often be comparatively high, in the range of $.30 per click.

The service that guarantees your rank in a search index is paid placement, which is also called Pay for Placement (PFP). When you pay for placement, you are guaranteed that your site will not only be listed, but that it will place in a specific rank consistently as long as you're willing to pay the fee for that rank.

There are some other "pay-for" strategies that you might consider. *Paid directory review (PDR)* services will guarantee that a review for a directory will take place in a guaranteed length of time (usually much faster than it would otherwise), but again, this is no guarantee of inclusion or placement. *XML inclusion* is another story. This is a strategy to ensure that the dynamic content on your site is included in search results. Because some sites have constantly changing content, XML inclusion may be a requirement for them.

The different types of inclusion and what your payments will buy you can be confusing. Table 15-1 recaps some of the differences among the types of inclusion.

TABLE 15-1

Fee-Based Inclusion Services

Strategy	Description	Companies	Cost
Paid Inclusion, Pay for Inclusion (PFI)	A strategy that requires you to pay a search engine to include your site in its index rankings. Where in those rankingsis not guaranteed.	AskJeeves, AlltheWeb, Yahoo!, EntireWeb	$25–$50 per year and up, depending on the service.
Pay-per-Inclusion (PPI), Pay for Inclusion per Click	A strategy that requires you to pay a search engine to include your site in its index and rankings. Your placement in those rankings is not guaranteed.	LookSmart, Yahoo!	Flat rate set-up fee, and then $.20–$.50 per click.
Paid Directory Review	Paying a directory to review your web site listing faster than it would ordinarily be reviewed. The review usually happens in 2–4 days, but does not guarantee your inclusion or placement.	Yahoo!, AlltheWeb	Flat fee, usually $30–$75 but can be higher depending on the directory.
Pay for Placement, Paid Placement, Pay per Click (PPC)	This strategy requires that you pay for the placement of your web page in search results. This guarantees that you appear at a certain spot in the results.	AltaVista, Yahoo!, AOL Search, Windows Live Search, Google, FindWhat	Some search engines charge a flat fee for setup. After the set-up fee, there is usually a per-click fee ranging from $.05 per click to $.50 or more per click, depending on the topic and position.
XML Inclusion, Trusted Feed	Used for large sites (usually with 500 pages or more), this strategy allows RSS content feeds to search engines so that regularly changing content is indexed	AltaVista, AlltheWeb, Kanoodle, Google, Yahoo!	Usually requires a flat fee for setup and then a per-click fee of $.25 to $.50. Google doesn't charge a fee.

NOTE Over time, Yahoo! has gobbled up a number of other search properties, so you may still see their names, but those properties — including Inktomi, AlltheWeb, AltaVista, and FastSearch — actually all come back to Yahoo!. When you're weighing factors for the search engines to select, keep in mind that all of these actually are just one.

When to Use Pay-for-Inclusion Services

Pay for inclusion, pay per click, and all other types of fee-based services are widely debated in SEO circles. But of those, pay-for-inclusion services are probably the most controversial. Pay for inclusion is considered by some to be just this side of unethical, and it's only just this side because it's such a widely practiced strategy. However, there is a time for paid-inclusion services.

The thing to remember with paid inclusion is that unless you're using it properly, you're just wasting money. Because paid-inclusion services don't guarantee your rank in search results, it's not a strategy that you'll want to use for all your search engine optimization. In truth, using paid inclusion for even *most* of your pages will result mostly in a loss of budget that would be better spent on more effective (or at least better guaranteed) SEO efforts.

The exception to this is when you're using paid inclusion as a method of testing the placement of a web page based on your SEO efforts. For example, if you have a page on your web site for which you would like to improve the traffic, and you need to do it quickly, you could register for a paid-inclusion service. This would get your site listed very quickly in search results. And you can use this capability to view the effectiveness of your SEO efforts. Then, if you find that your SEO efforts aren't effective, you can tweak the page you're paying to include until it reaches the level of search result rankings that you need. Once you're at that level, you'll know how to optimize other pages on your site for the same results.

Paid-inclusion services are generally inexpensive in relative terms. That makes them ideal services to help you develop a winning SEO strategy through testing. But to use paid inclusion for multiple pages on your site, you'll probably have to spend a lot of money that would be better spent on more effective strategies (such as pay-per-click advertising).

Understanding the Business Model

Another reason many paid services have a bad name in SEO is the number of scams that exist to take advantage of webmasters who use the services. It's not at all unusual to see an advertisement that claims your site will be added to "thousands" of search engines for one "low" fee (that's usually well over $300).

The problem with such a claim is that, first, there aren't thousands of search engines to which a site can be added. A few dozen would likely be the limit for most organizations, and that's if you include all the highly specialized search engines that a site could be added to.

What happens, then, is that the organization signs a contract with you, you pay their fee, and then you may or may not ever be submitted to any sites, much less to the sites that are appropriate for your web pages. In most cases, your own SEO efforts will achieve some search results rankings for you before these services will.

That's not to say there are not legitimate companies out there that will help you gain better placement for your web site. And those other services may actually submit your site to search engines and directories using paid-placement or paid-submission capabilities. But unless these services are coupled with other SEO services, you could probably do much better without spending the extra money. The one consideration that can cut the other way, though, is the time factor. It will take many hours to research and submit to search engines on your own.

If you do find one of these services that looks like it offers the features you need — reporting capabilities, URL monitoring capabilities, web metrics, and so on — and you have the budget to invest in it, there's a preliminary step or two. Before you hire a company, take the time to learn about what is has to offer. Is it realistic? If a company promises that it can make your site rank number one in all the different search engines the company works with, you can bet this won't happen. The number one spot is very tough to achieve. And if that company offers the same guarantee to all its customers, well . . . there is just no way everyone can be number one.

Take the time to check on a company's claims to ensure it has a legitimate business model. If it says it will submit your site to 1,000 search engines (or even 100), ask for a list of those search engines. Look up each search engine and ensure that your site is appropriate for those engines. Most of the time, the company's claim is that it will "submit" your site to that huge number of search engines and directories. But submission is *not* inclusion or even paid placement. There's no guarantee that the company can make your site appear in the index, much less in the search results.

Finally, if you're considering hiring a company to submit your site to a variety of search engines, look very closely at the company's business model, and ask for customer referrals. Of course, the company is only going to provide names of customers who have demonstrated a willingness to speak well of the company, but you can still call those references and ask very specific questions.

Ultimately, hiring a company to submit your site to search engines should be a decision based on your specific needs. If you have time, you can do all the search engine submissions that are needed by yourself. It may take longer for you to submit to all those sites, but the positive side of doing it yourself is the budget savings that you can apply to other, more efficient marketing and SEO tactics.

Managing Paid Services

When you choose to use paid services, like PFI or PPC, you may find that managing the different services quickly becomes as difficult a task as working without them. You need strategies to manage all of them as efficiently as possible.

One huge help when trying to manage your SEO, paid services, and everything that goes along with them is to find a software solution that will let you manage as many facets of your SEO strategy as possible from one location. You won't find a single service or software that will manage everything, but it's possible to find one that allows you to manage your PPC, PFI, and some of your other marketing efforts all at the same time.

When selecting a software management program, look for something that has a trial period so you can try it out before you sink a lot of your budget into it. User interfaces, the capabilities of the program, and several other factors can work against you and leave you hating the solution that you've selected.

Another strategy for managing your paid services effectively is to devote a block of time each day to staying on top of the management process. That might be as little as 20 minutes or as much as two hours, depending on how much you need to monitor. But scheduling that into your day assures that it will happen. And that's essential, because when you fall behind on your management tasks, it can seriously affect your SEO campaigns (not to mention making it much harder to catch up).

Finally, when you're managing your paid services, stay within your budget. If your strategies require more than is available in your budget, two things can happen. Your SEO strategies can lose effectiveness because they're not funded, and eventually they can fail altogether, because the funds that make the strategies possible won't be forthcoming.

Hiring the Right Professionals

One thing is absolutely certain about SEO, whether or not you're using paid services: it's going to be a time-consuming process. Cutting corners is not an option, because the wrong SEO practices are far more detrimental to your site than doing nothing at all. When time isn't on your side, hiring an SEO professional is an option to consider.

It's not at all unusual to hear about a company or web-site owner that's been scammed by a supposed SEO consultant who guaranteed them top placement in hundreds of search engines. It's just not possible that anyone, even an SEO expert, could guarantee they can put your site at the top of search engine rankings. Yet, there are many people claiming to be SEO experts who will tell you they can do just that. Don't believe them.

Only a few accreditation programs exist for people who claim to be SEO experts. In most cases what happens is this: a web-site designer or owner who has had to create a site for SEO decides he or she can implement SEO for others for a profit. But just because these people have done SEO on their own sites doesn't mean they can plan SEO on your site in the most effective manner possible.

Two accreditation programs *are* offered, by SEMPO (www.sempo.org) and Bruce Clay, Inc (www.bruceclay.com). So if the individual or firm that you're looking at to help with your SEO efforts claims to be an expert, ask if they have been accredited. In most cases, the answer will be no. You can contact both SEMPO and Bruce Clay and request a reference for an accredited SEO consultant.

In most cases, it will take a team of people to perform proper SEO techniques for your site. That team might include someone to submit your site to directories and search engines, someone to create and submit articles to other sources that will link back to your site, someone to design or supplement the design of your site to make it attractive to search engines, and someone to manage the whole SEO program from beginning to end, including reporting to you, the web-site owner.

Contract Considerations

If you want someone to help with SEO on your web site, here are some requirements to consider:

- Ask for references and look at those references for previous customers who rank well in searches in their industry. The most successful SEO firms can provide references and case studies that prove those companies are worth your SEO budget investment.

- Ask about the practices that the firm under consideration considers unethical. Many unethical SEO tactics can get your site removed from search rankings entirely, so you could find yourself with a big bill and a site that doesn't appear in search results at all. If possible, have a list of unethical practices, labeled as such, included in the contract, along with penalties for use of those tactics.

- No SEO professional or firm will guarantee results. If the professional or firm you are considering is guaranteeing specific results, move on. A good SEO firm will not guarantee anything that's not completely in its control (search engine rankings are not in its control, because no one knows the specifics around any search engine's ranking algorithm).

When you find an SEO firm that offers the services that you need, you can expect to receive certain specific services from them. The services will vary from firm to firm, but here's a list that you can use as a good rule of thumb:

- A professional SEO audit. The audit should thoroughly examine your site and your existing SEO efforts to determine what works and what needs to be improved or started.

- Keyword and competitor research.

- On-page SEO. On-page SEO tells how each page of your web site is optimized. On-page SEO includes elements like HTML tags, keywords, and content.

- Optimization of internal site navigation. Your internal navigation can have a serious effect on how your site performs in search results, so a good SEO will examine and optimize that navigation structure.

- Link building.

- Progress monitoring.

- Staff training. SEO requires ongoing efforts. Your staff will need to be trained in the most successful methods for maintaining optimization.

Professional SEO firms can offer a lot of benefits to your web site. The good ones specialize mainly in SEO and can properly optimize your site, and your services, in less time than you can. Your core business is likely not SEO. But an SEO firm's is. That reason alone should be enough to make you consider hiring an SEO firm, whether or not you end up doing so.

When the Relationship Isn't Working

Despite all of your best efforts, factors can combine to make a relationship between your organization and an SEO firm not work. The problem can be in the relationship, in the SEO strategies, or even in some other aspect of the situation. The question is, what do you do if you find that your SEO firm (or an individual SEO professional) is just not what you expected?

There's no easy answer to that question, unless you address it at the very beginning of the relationship. If you address it early, you can include a clause in your contract that outlines the situations under which either side can terminate the relationship.

If you don't address the possibility early, however, you may find yourself stuck with an SEO firm or professional that's doing nothing for you except running up a big bill. Do whatever you can to protect yourself. Know your contact at the SEO firm, and how to reach that contact when you need to ask questions or find out why something is (or isn't) happening.

Your relationship with your SEO firm should take the same structure that a relationship with any other provider takes. Don't think that, because SEO is different from using a hosted technology or dealing with a service vendor, it should be governed by less stringent requirements. SEO is a service for you, and the relationship is like that with any other vendor. Just as much attention should be given to it.

Chapter 16

Robots, Spiders, and Crawlers

You're nearing the end of the book, so you should have a pretty good handle on what exactly robots, spiders, and crawlers are, right? No doubt you do, but did you know that there is much more to these Internet creatures than just the fact that they crawl from one web site to another?

Spiders, robots, crawlers, or whatever else you choose to call them can determine how well you rank in search engines, so it's best to make friends with them as quickly as possible. Certain strategies will help you find favor with these crawlers (which is the name we'll use to lump them all together), and others, unfortunately, will help you find your way right out of search engine rankings.

A sad fact of crawlers is that sometimes you'll be treated unfairly when you've done absolutely nothing wrong. Some of the strategies that you may want to use to improve the optimization of your site can look suspicious to crawlers. They'll see those strategies and automatically penalize you for trying to spam the search engine, even when you're not.

That's what makes it so important for you to understand not only the intimate details about how crawlers work, but also about what makes them happy and what makes them move on without looking back.

What Are Robots, Spiders, and Crawlers?

You should already have a general understanding that a robot, spider, or crawler is a piece of software that is programmed to "crawl" from one web page to another based on the links on those pages. As this crawler makes it way around the Internet, it collects content (such as text and links) from web sites and saves those in a database that is indexed and ranked according to the search engine algorithm.

When a crawler is first released on the Web, it's usually *seeded* with a few web sites and it begins on one of those sites. The first thing it does on that first site is to take note of the links on the page. Then it "reads" the text and begins to follow the links that it collected previously. This network of links is called the *crawl frontier*; it's the territory that the crawler is exploring in a very systematic way.

The links in a crawl frontier will sometimes take the crawler to other pages on the same web site, and sometimes they will take it away from the site completely. The crawler will follow the links until it hits a dead end and then backtrack and begin the process again until every link on a page has been followed. Figure 16-1 illustrates the path that a crawler might take.

FIGURE 16-1

The crawler starts with a seed URL and works it way outward on the Web.

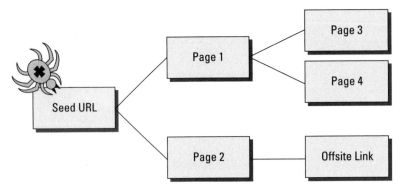

As to what actually happens when a crawler begins reviewing a site, it's a little more complicated than simply saying that it "reads" the site. The crawler sends a request to the web server where the web site resides, requesting pages to be delivered to it in the same manner that your web browser requests pages that you review. The difference between what your browser sees and what the crawler sees is that the crawler is viewing the pages in a completely text interface. No graphics or other types of media files are displayed. It's all text, and it's encoded in HTML. So to you it might look like gibberish.

The crawler can request as many or as few pages as it's programmed to request at any given time. This can sometimes cause problems with web sites that aren't prepared to serve up dozens of pages of content at a time. The requests will overload the site and cause it to crash, or it can slow down traffic to a web site considerably, and it's even possible that the requests will just be fulfilled too slowly and the crawler will give up and go away.

If the crawler does go away, it will eventually return to try the task again. And it might try several times before it gives up entirely. But if the site doesn't eventually begin to cooperate with the crawler, it's penalized for the failures and your site's search engine ranking will fall.

In addition, there are a few reasons you may not want a crawler indexing a page on your site:

- Your page is under construction. If you can avoid it, you don't want a crawler to index your site while this is happening. If you can't avoid it, however, be sure that any pages that are being changed or worked on are excluded from the crawler's territory. Later, when your page is ready, you can allow the page to be indexed again.

- Pages of links. Having links leading to and away from your site is an essential way to ensure that crawlers find you. However, having pages of links seems suspicious to a search crawler, and it may classify your site as a spam site. Instead of having pages that are all links, break links up with descriptions and text. If that's not possible, block the link pages from being indexed by crawlers.

- Pages of old content. Old content, like blog archives, doesn't necessarily harm your search engine rankings, but it also doesn't help them much. One worrisome issue with archives, however, is the number of times that archived content appears on your page. With a blog, for example, you may have the blog appear on the page where it was originally displayed, and also have it displayed in archives, and possibly have it linked from some other area of your site. Although this is all legitimate, crawlers might mistake multiple instances of the same content for spam. Instead of risking it, place your archives off limits to crawlers.

- Private information. It really makes better sense not to have private information (or proprietary information) on a web site. But if there is some reason that you *must* have it on your site, then definitely block crawlers from access to it. Better yet, password-protect the information so that no one can stumble on it accidently

There's a whole host of reasons you may not want to allow a crawler to visit some of your web pages. It's just like allowing visitors into your home. You don't mind if they see the living room, dining room, den, and maybe the kitchen, but you don't want them in your bedroom without good reason. Crawlers are the guests in your Internet house. Be sure they understand the guidelines under which they are welcome.

What's the Robot Exclusion Standard?

Because they do have the potential to wreak havoc on a web site, there has to be some kind of guidelines to keep crawlers in line. Those guidelines are called the *Robot Exclusion Standard, Robots Exclusion Protocol,* or robots.txt.

The file robots.txt is the actual element that you'll work with. It's a text-based document that should be included in the root of your domain, and it essentially contains instructions to any crawler that comes to your site about what they are and are not allowed to index.

To communicate with the crawler, you need a specific syntax that it can understand. In its most basic form, the text might look something like this:

```
User-agent: *
Disallow: /
```

These two parts of the text are essential. The first part, `User-agent:`, tells a crawler what *user agent*, or crawler, you're commanding. The asterisk (*) indicates that all crawlers are covered, but you can specify a single crawler or even multiple crawlers.

The second part, `Disallow:`, tells the crawler what it is not allowed to access. The slash (/) indicates "all directories." So in the preceding code example, the robots.txt file is essentially saying that "all crawlers are to ignore all directories."

When you're writing robots.txt, remember to include the colon (:) after the `User-agent` indicator and after the `Disallow` indicator. The colon indicates that important information follows to which the crawler should pay attention.

You won't usually want to tell all crawlers to ignore all directories. Instead, you can tell all crawlers to ignore your temporary directories by writing the text like this:

```
User-agent: *
Disallow: /tmp/
```

Or you can take it one step further and tell all crawlers to ignore multiple directories:

```
User-agent: *
Disallow: /tmp/
Disallow: /private/
Disallow: /links/listing.html
```

That piece of text tells the crawler to ignore temporary directories, private directories, and the web page (title Listing) that contains links — the crawler won't be able to follow those links.

One thing to keep in mind about crawlers is that they read the robots.txt file from top to bottom and as soon as they find a guideline that applies to them, they stop reading and begin crawling your site. So if you're commanding multiple crawlers with your robots.txt file, you want to be careful how you write it.

This is the wrong way:

```
User-agent: *
Disallow: /tmp/
```

```
User-agent: CrawlerName
Disallow: /tmp/
Disallow: /links/listing.html
```

This bit of text tells crawlers first that *all* crawlers should ignore the temporary directories. So every crawler reading that file will automatically ignore the temporary files. But you've also told a specific crawler (indicated by CrawlerName) to disallow both temporary directories and the links on the Listing page. The problem is, the specified crawler will never get that message because it has already read that all crawlers should ignore the temporary directories.

If you want to command multiple crawlers, you need to first begin by naming the crawlers you want to control. Only after they've been named should you leave your instructions for all crawlers. Written properly, the text from the preceding code should look like this:

```
User-agent: CrawlerName
Disallow: /tmp/
Disallow: /links/listing.html

User-agent: *
Disallow: /tmp/
```

NOTE If you have certain pages or links that you want the crawler to ignore, you can accomplish this without causing the crawler to ignore a whole site or a whole directory or having to put a specific meta tag on each page.

Each search engine crawler goes by a different name, and if you look at your web server log, you'll probably see that name. Here's a quick list of some of the crawler names that you're likely to see in that web server log:

- Google: Googlebot
- MSN: MSNbot
- Yahoo! Web Search: Yahoo SLURP or just SLURP
- Ask: Teoma
- AltaVista: Scooter
- LookSmart: MantraAgent
- WebCrawler: WebCrawler
- SearchHippo: Fluffy the Spider

These are just a few of the search engine crawlers that might crawl across your site. You can find a complete list along with the text of the Robots Exclusion Standard document on the Web Robots Pages (www.robotstxt.org). Take the time to read the Robots Exclusion Standard document. It's not terribly long, and reading it will help you understand how search crawlers interact with your web site. That understanding can also help you learn how to control crawlers better when they come to visit.

It pays to know which crawler belongs to what search engine, because there are some *spambots* and other malicious crawlers out there that are interested in crawling your site for less than ethical reasons. If you know the names of these crawlers, you can keep them off of your site and keep your users' information safe. Spambots in particular are troublesome, because they crawl along the Web searching out and collecting anything that appears to be an e-mail address. These addresses are then collected and sold to marketers or even people who are not interested in legitimate business opportunities. Most spambots will ignore your robots.txt file.

> **TIP** You can view the robots.txt file for any web site that has one by adding the `robots .txt` extension to the base URL of the site. For example, `www.sampleaddress.com/ robots.txt` will display a page that shows you the text file guiding robots for that site. If you use that extension on a URL and it doesn't pull up the robots.txt file, then the web site does not have one.

If you don't have a robots.txt file, you can create one in any text editor. And keep in mind that not everyone wants or needs to use the robots.txt file. If you don't care who is crawling your site, then don't even create the file. Whatever you do, though, don't use a blank robots.txt file. Crawlers automatically assume an empty file means you don't want your site to be crawled. So using the blank file is a good way to keep yourself out of search engine results.

Robots Meta Tag

Not everyone has access to their web server, but they still want to have control over how crawlers behave on their web site. If you're one of those, you can still control the crawlers that come to your site. Instead of using the robots.txt file, you use a *robots meta tag* to make your preferences known to the crawlers.

The robots meta tag is a small piece of HTML code that is inserted into the `<HEAD>` tag of your web site and it works generally in the same manner that the robots.txt file does. You include your instructions for crawlers inside the tags. The following example shows you how your robots meta tag might look:

```
<html>
<head>
<meta name="robots" content="noindex, nofollow">
<meta name="description" content="page description.">
<title>
Web Site Title
</title>
</head>
<body>
```

This bit of HTML tells crawlers not to index the content on the site and not to follow the links on the site. Of course, that might not be exactly what you had in mind. You can also use several other robots meta tags for combinations of following, not following, indexing, and not indexing:

```
<meta name="robots" content="index,follow">
<meta name="robots" content="noindex,follow">
```

```
<meta name="robots" content="index,nofollow">
<meta name="robots" content="noindex,nofollow">
```

The major difference between robots.txt and robots meta tags is that with the meta tags you cannot specify which crawlers you're targeting. It's an all or nothing tag, so you either command all of the crawlers to behave in a certain way, or you command none of them. It's not as precise as robots.txt, but if you don't have access to your web server, it's a good alternative.

NOTE Unfortunately, not all search engines recognize the robots.txt file or the robots meta tags. So in some cases, you have no control at all over what the crawler examines on your site. However, more search engines seem to be allowing these commands to help classify the Web more efficiently.

Search engine crawlers can help your site get indexed so that it appears in search results. But they can also cause problems with your site if they don't follow the guidelines outlined in the Robot Exclusion Standard or if your site is not stable enough to support the way the crawler examines it.

Knowing how to control the way that search engines crawl your site can help to assure that your site is always at its shiny best (or at least appears to the search crawler to be). It won't necessarily give you complete control of all the crawlers on the Web, but it will help with some of them.

Inclusion with XML Site Mapping

You may remember that back in Chapter 3 there was a brief mention of XML site mapping. It's time to revisit XML site mapping so that you understand how it can help your web site.

XML site mapping is actually the companion to the Robots Exclusion Protocol. It's an *inclusion protocol* — a method by which you can tell crawlers what is available for them to index. In its most basic form, an XML site map is a file that lists all the URLs for a web site. This file allows webmasters to include additional information about each URL such as the date the URL was last updated, how often the URL changes, and how important the URL is in relation to the other pages on the site.

The XML site map is used to ensure that crawlers can find certain pages on your web site, like dynamic pages. The site-map file can be placed in the robots.txt file or you can submit it directly to a search engine. Doing either of these, however, is not guaranteed to get your site indexed by the search engine, nor will it get the search engine to index your site any sooner.

An XML site map also does not guarantee that all of the pages on your site will be indexed. It's simply a guide which the crawler can use to find pages that it might otherwise miss.

Creating an XML site map is the first step to including it in your robots.txt file or to submitting it to a search engine. There are many sites on the Internet offering applications that will help you create your site map. For example, Google offers a site-map generator that will help you create your site map, once you've downloaded and installed the required software. But Google isn't the only game in town. There are dozens of other site-map generators that work just as well.

Creating your own XML site map

The alternative is to write your own XML site map. The site-map protocol extends requirements for writing a site map that's fully functional. The top two requirements of that protocol are that your site map must consist of XML tags and that is should be *UTF-8 encoded*. UTF-8 encoding stands for *8 bit UCS/Unicode Transformation Format* and is a type of code that's consistent with ASCII.

Another requirement for your XML site map is that data values within the site map must be *entity escaped*, which means that special characters indicating alternative interpretations must be used. Entity escape codes you can use in your XML site map include those listed in Table 16-1.

TABLE 16-1

Entity Escape Characters

Character		Escape Code
Ampersand	&	&
Single Quote	'	'
Double Quote	"	"
Greater Than	>	>
Less Than	<	<

These escape characters are used in URLs to replace the characters indicated. So the following URL

```
http://www.example.com/product.html&q=name
```

would look like this after the escape codes are included:

```
http://www.example.com/product.html&amp;q=name
```

In addition to entity escaping, you must also use a set of XML tags. The ones you'll use most frequently are shown in Table 16-2.

NOTE The code snippets used in this chapter are examples of how site maps should be written specifically for Google. For the most part, these snippets will be the same across the various search engines, but before you begin writing your site map code, review the guidelines set forth by the search engine you're targeting. Luckily Google, Yahoo!, and MSN have all agreed to follow the same site-map standard.

TABLE 16-2

XML Tags Used for Site Mapping

Tag	When Used	Description
`<urlset>`	Required all the time	This tag encapsulates the file and references the current protocol standard.
`<url>`	Required all the time	This is the parent tag for each URL entry. The remaining tags are children of this tag.
`<loc>`	Required all the time	This is the URL of the page. This URL must begin with the http protocol (`http://`) and end with a trailing slash, if your web server requires it. The length of the URL must be less than 2,048 characters.
`<lastmod>`	Optional, only when needed	The date of last modification of the file. This date should be in W3C Datetime format (see: `http://www.w3.org/TR/NOTE-datetime`). This format allows you to omit the time portion, if desired, and use YYYY-MM-DD.
`<changefreq>`	Optional, only when needed	This tag indicates how frequently the page is likely to change. This value provides general information to search engines and may not correlate exactly to how often they crawl the page. Valid values are: Always Hourly Daily Weekly Monthly Yearly Never The value "always" should be used to describe documents that change each time they are accessed. The value "never" should be used to describe archived URLs. Please note that the value of this tag is considered a hint and not a command. Even though search engine crawlers consider this information when making decisions, they may crawl pages marked "hourly" less frequently than that, and they may crawl pages marked "yearly" more frequently. It is also likely that crawlers will periodically crawl pages marked "never" so that they can handle unexpected changes to those pages.
`<priority>`	Optional, only when needed	This tag indicates the priority of this URL relative to other URLs on your site. Valid values range from 0.0 to 1.0. This value has no effect on your pages compared to pages on other sites, and only lets the search engines know which of your pages you deem most important, so they can order the crawl of your pages in the way you would most like.

continued

TABLE 16-2	(continued)	
Tag	**When Used**	**Description**
`<priority>` (continued)		The default priority of a page is 0.5. Please note that the priority you assign to a page has no influence on the position of your URLs in a search engine's result pages. Search engines use this information when selecting between URLs on the same site, so you can use this tag to increase the likelihood that your more important pages are present in a search index. Also, please note that assigning a high priority to all of the URLs on your site will not help you. Because the priority is relative, it is used only to select between URLs on your site; the priority of your pages will not be compared to the priority of pages on other sites.

If you're using all of these tags in Table 16-2 in your XML site map, it might look something like the following site map. This sitemap includes only a few URLs, each with a different set of optional parameters. Also notice that the escape characters are used in the URLs, too.

```
<?xml version="1.0" encoding="UTF-8"?>
<urlset xmlns="http://www.sitemaps.org/schemas/sitemap/0.9">

   <url>
      <loc>http://www.example.com/</loc>
      <lastmod>2005-01-01</lastmod>
      <changefreq>monthly</changefreq>
      <priority>0.8</priority>
   </url>
   <url>
      <loc>http://www.example.com/catalog?item=12&amp;desc=vacation_
hawaii</loc>
      <changefreq>weekly</changefreq>
   </url>
   <url>
      <loc>http://www.example.com/catalog?item=73&amp;desc=vacation_
new_zealand</loc>
      <lastmod>2004-12-23</lastmod>
      <changefreq>weekly</changefreq>
   </url>
   <url>
      <loc>http://www.example.com/catalog?item=74&amp;desc=vacation_
newfoundland</loc>
      <lastmod>2004-12-23T18:00:15+00:00</lastmod>
      <priority>0.3</priority>
   </url>
```

```
<url>
    <loc>http://www.example.com/catalog?item=83&amp;desc=vacation_
usa</loc>
    <lastmod>2004-11-23</lastmod>
</url>
</urlset>
```

The URLs that you can include in your XML site map are determined by where you site map is. For example, if you place your site map on the page `http://www.example.com/catalog/sitemap` `.xml`, any URLS that begin with `http://www.example.com/catalog` can be included in the site map. However, if you have a URL that's `http://www.example.com/images/` it won't be included in the site map, because it doesn't fall into the catalog category. You can solve this problem by creating another site map or by using only the base URL for your site (`http://www.example.com/`).

Once you've created your site map (or had one generated by a site-map generator), you need to insert it into your robots.txt file. The site-map directive is independent of the user-agent directive, so it's not important where in the robots.txt file you place it. All that's important is that you use the site-map directive, `<sitemap_location>`, and replace "location" with the URL where your site is located. For example, a site-map directive might look like this:

```
Sitemap: <sitemap_http://www.example.com/sitemap.xml>
```

You can have more than one site map for your site, too. But if you do, you need to create a site-map index for crawlers to read to learn where your site maps are. The site-map index looks similar to the site map, but includes a few different directives. Those directives include:

- `<sitemap>`: This tag encapsulates information about the individual site map.
- `<sitemapindex>`: This tag encapsulates information about all of the site maps in a file.

In addition to these tags, you'll also see the `<loc>` and `<lastmod>` tags in the site-map index. Following is an example of what that index file should look like:

```
<?xml version="1.0" encoding="UTF-8"?>
    <sitemapindex xmlns="http://www.sitemaps.org/schemas/sitemap/0.9">
    <sitemap>
        <loc>http://www.example.com/sitemap1.xml.gz</loc>
        <lastmod>2004-10-01T18:23:17+00:00</lastmod>
    </sitemap>
    <sitemap>
        <loc>http://www.example.com/sitemap2.xml.gz</loc>
        <lastmod>2005-01-01</lastmod>
    </sitemap>
    </sitemapindex>
```

The index file contains a list of locations for your XML site maps. It's not uncommon to have multiple site maps, and in some cases it's advisable to have multiples. For example, if your site is broken down into several different categories, you may want to have a separate site map for each category.

237

This allows you to separate and differentiate the links within a category, giving a different weight to each, according to its function on your site.

There is one limitation to site maps of which you should be aware. Site maps are limited to no more than 50,000 URLs and 10 MB per map. And if you're using multiple maps listed in a site-map index, there can be no more than 1,000 site maps. This is a pretty large allowance, so you may not ever have to worry about the limits, but you should still know what they are.

Submitting your site map

After you've created your site map, you have two alternatives. You can leave the directive for the site map in your robots.txt file and wait until a crawler comes along and finds it, or you can go ahead and submit it to the search engines that you're targeting.

How you submit your site map to search engines may differ widely. For example, if you want to submit your site map to Google, you need to create a Google Account and link it to the Webmaster Tools section of Google. Once you've created an account, you can submit your site map from that interface. With Yahoo!, you'll have to go through a similar process. And with other search engines the process will also be similar, though some of the details may differ.

Submitting your site map to one of the search engines won't guarantee that all the pages on your site will be crawled, or that they will be included in SERPs. However, the site map gives the crawler some direction, so it will help improve the crawling that your site receives. This is no guarantee of where your site will rank, but at least you'll know that it has been reviewed as thoroughly as it can be, given the control that the crawler has on the situation.

Chapter 17

The Truth About SEO Spam

S pam is the Internet's version of the telemarketers who call you during dinner and won't take no for an answer. It pops up where it's least wanted, it's more prolific than pine trees in Mississippi, and the only purpose that spam really serves is to generate money for the spammers. And they keep at it, because they assume that the law of averages is on their side — send out enough spam and someone will respond.

Spam in SEO operates under the same principle, except SEO spam fills the search engine results pages with results that have little to no value to the searcher. If you do something that a search engine sees as spamming it, your search rankings will be penalized. It's even likely that you'll be removed from search rankings entirely.

In SEO, there are clear-cut cases of spam, which is usually classified as "black-hat SEO." But there are also cases of spam that aren't necessarily as obvious. These fall into a gray area in which the practices used may or may not be considered spam, depending on how you handle them.

To make spam even more difficult to define, search engines change their definitions of spam regularly. What works and is acceptable today may well be classified as spam tomorrow. And if you don't know the change has been made or is coming, you may look at your rankings one day and find that you're above the fold on the first page, but look at the same rankings the next day to find you've been relegated to page 10 of the results.

Only the search engines know what constitutes spam from one day to the next. And that makes it very difficult for you to stay off the spammers list if you're doing any SEO activities that are borderline spam. Sure, you can monitor the search engine algorithms and try to keep up with the changes that are made, but that's no guarantee that you won't get caught up in the changes. It's also a reactive way to manage your SEO campaign.

What Constitutes SEO Spam?

So, if SEO spam is so hard to define, how do you know whether what you're doing is right or wrong?

Good question. And the answer is that you don't always know, but there are some guidelines that you can follow that will help you stay out of the spam category. Basic, good web-design practices are your best defense. If you're handling your web-site search marketing using the guidelines provided by the various search engines you'll target, you should be in a position not to worry about being classified as a spammer.

- **Don't do anything that makes you worry that you're doing wrong.** It sounds like simple advice, but when you think about it, if you're doing something on your web site that you have to worry is going to get you banned from a search engine, you probably shouldn't do it. This includes strategies like using hidden text on your web pages, using doorway pages or cloaking your pages, and creating false link structures. Even if you don't know that these strategies are banned by search engines, when you consider the sneakiness of the strategy, you'll be able to tell that it's not likely a strategy that you should use.

- **Don't make your web site appear to be something that it's not.** It's easy to "put a spin" on something to make it appear more attractive than it really is. People do it all the time where products and services are concerned. But using that same strategy on your web site may get you banned. Creating false link structures is one way you might make your site appear more popular than it really is. The problem with using that strategy is that it won't take a crawler long to figure out that all of those sites are interconnected.

- **Don't trust someone who says that a certain practice is acceptable, if you even suspect that it's not.** Some unethical SEO people will tell you that it's okay if you use certain obvious spam techniques as long as you use them correctly. Wrong. Spam is spam. It doesn't matter how you use it, the search crawler will still see it as spam and you'll still pay the consequences, while the unethical SEO consultant will take the money and leave you in the crawler's bad graces.

SEO spam is also called *spamdexing* (because you're spamming indexes) and can come in all kinds of shapes and sizes. There are some spam techniques that are obviously spam. But then there are some that aren't clearly spam, but that you should avoid. The list of spamming techniques is huge. But there are a dozen or so items on that list that are constant.

- **Transparent links:** These are links that are included in the page, but that users can't see because they're the same color as the background.

- **Hidden links:** These links are on the page but are hidden behind elements like graphics. They don't turn the graphic into a hyperlink, but a search engine can find them and follow them, even when people can't.

- **Misleading links:** Misleading links are those that appear to lead to one place but actually lead to another. An example of a misleading link is one that reads www.onewebsite.com but actually takes you to www.differentwebsite.com.

- **Inconspicuous links:** These links appear on a page, but they're usually unnoticeable because they're represented as graphics that are 1 x 1 pixels in size.

- **Keyword stuffing:** Loading the content or the meta tags of a web site with keywords that are repeated over and over.

- **Meta tag stuffing:** Stuffing meta tags with keywords that are repeated over and over.

- **Doorway pages (or gateway pages):** These pages are designed specifically to draw search crawlers but are essentially useless to visitors. Often, a doorway page will have only the visible text, "click here to enter."

- **Scraper sites:** These are web sites that "scrape," or copy their content from other pages on the Web. Search engines don't like scraper sites because they're not original and because they usually direct visitors to another site that's less relevant to their search terms.

- **Machine-generated pages:** These are web pages put together by a program that grabs the content from other web sites. The content that's grabbed could be from within the current site or from sites belonging to other people. Usually these pages are considered spam because they are of no value to web-site users.

- **Links in punctuation:** This is a clever scheme. Some unethical SEOs create a hyperlink that's contained in a piece of punctuation. It's done by using the following tag:

```
<a href=link> </a>Include real words here</a> <a href=link>.</a>
```

That little snippet of code will leave the words in the link (and you can replace link with the web-site address of your choice) in plain text, but the period at the end of the link will contain the link. It's small, so most people won't notice it, but the link is there, so search engines will notice it.

- **Cloaking:** This technique is used to make a highly optimized version of your page appear to search engines, but a more user-friendly page appear to site visitors.

- **Excessive cross-linking:** Excessive cross-linking can be a sign that a company has created multiple domains strictly for the purpose of building a false linking structure with a single web site.

- **Hidden text:** This text is the same color as the background of a web page so that users can't see it. Search engines can, and the text is usually an incomprehensible collection of keywords and phrases.

- **Duplicate content:** Duplicate content on a web site is construed as being a ploy to trick a search crawler into thinking the site is more relevant than it actually is.

- **Link-only pages:** These pages contain only links and should be avoided. The one exception to this rule is the site map that you make available to visitors so they can quickly find their way around your site.

- **Redirect pages:** Redirect pages are usually coded for SEO, but again, they're useless to site visitors. When site visitors land on this page, they're asked to wait while they are redirected to another web site. Search engines look down on this practice because very often, the web page that is redirecting is optimized for SEO but not for people.

Use Caution with Link-Trading Strategies

If content is one of the most important elements of a web site, links are probably the next. Most search engines now look at links to a web site — both those that lead to the site and those that lead away from the site.

In an effort to take advantage of the authority that links give a web site, many web-site owners have banded together to take create link-trading or reciprocal linking strategies. These are "You link to me and I'll link to you" strategies.

For a long time, those strategies worked pretty well. You could send out an e-mail to a company and suggest that the two sites create links, each to the other's site. By doing that both sites gained a link into their site and a link out of their site.

Then some people began taking advantage of the strategy and rather than exchanging links with other, relevant web sites, they began to exchange links with anyone who would allow it. Then those same unethical people began building dozens, hundreds, and in some cases even thousands of web sites with the specific intent of cross-linking with the one page for which they were trying to artificially raise the ranking.

And that's when search engines began to take note. They noticed that people were manipulating link trading schemes to boost their search ranking, and some added to their guidelines that reciprocal linking and link-trading strategies were unacceptable. The result? If you use these strategies, you could be banned from the search results.

So does that mean that you can never link to a page that's going to link back to you? No. What it means is that search engines are now paying more attention to the *places* that you link to. They're looking at the sites to which you're linking to make sure they're relevant and have something of value to offer to users who might click through the links.

If your links do meet those requirements, you won't be penalized for them. If they appear to be links just for the sake of linking, though, your site will be penalized and in some cases even delisted from a search engine. So if you plan to exchange links with other web sites, make sure those sites are relevant to the topic of your web site or the web page on which the link appears.

- **Link farms:** Link farms are simply pages of links that are only created to artificially boost a linking strategy in an effort to speed the appearance of the web site in the top search ranking positions.

- **Spamblogs:** These are machine-generated blogs and their only purpose is to draw search engine rankings.

- **Page hijacking:** Page hijacking is accomplished by copying a very popular page on the Web and using it to represent your site to search engines. When users see your page in search results, they click through the link only to be taken to your actual page.

- **Sybil attacks:** Sybil attacks are created when a spammer creates multiple web sites that are all interlinked for the purpose of creating a false link structure.

- **Wiki spam:** Using the open editability of Wiki sites to add links to a spam site in the Wiki listing. Because this practice became so frequently used, especially on Wikipedia, the nofollow tag has been added to most Wiki additions to prevent spamming search engines.

The list is long. And there are many other items that could be included. And as soon as the search engine algorithms change a little, there will be even more to add to the list.

Why Is SEO Spam a Bad Idea?

Any of the SEO techniques that are considered spam can get your site penalized at the very least or even completely banned. But there are other reasons to avoid SEO spam.

People — site visitors, your customers — don't like spam. They don't like spam in their e-mail boxes, and they don't want to be directed to web pages that are spam. So, though there is one benefit to spam — that your site will, at least, temporarily rank high in search engine results — the pitfall to that is that customers will click on to your site, but they'll leave almost immediately.

Spam on the Internet just doesn't make sense. When it's so easy for a person to move from one web site to another; one company to another, why would you want to run them off as fast as they land on your site? A much more logical approach is to build your web site with the intent of drawing, *and keeping*, the user on your site. That means providing useful information in a user-friendly format.

If visitors come to your site and see that you've tricked them to get them on your site, they're going to be annoyed. They'll click right back off your page, and they're more likely to remember your web site negatively. If you're trying to build a business, showing your potential customers your dark side isn't the way to do it.

Another reason for avoiding SEO spam is that it can give you a black eye professionally. Again, SEO spam can temporarily get your site listed well in search results, but just as site visitors will see what you've done, so will your competition. And they'll be secure in the knowledge that your rise to the top will be short-lived. Then your site will be delisted from the search results, and your competitors will be back in the positions from which you bumped them. What's the point? The only company that suffers is your own.

So if you've considered SEO spam techniques, maybe you should think again. If you've talked to SEO consultants who tell you SEO spam techniques are okay, or that you won't get caught because search engines don't pay attention to this or that detail, ignore them. SEO spam can be costly both in terms of the money that you lose implementing SEO only to be delisted from the search results, and also in terms of the sales and loyalty that you'll lose from your customers.

Avoiding SEO Spam

So spamming a search engine isn't the best idea in the world. When you are caught spamming one, the penalties will differ according to the search engine, but most will delist you from search results. Being delisted isn't the worst thing in the world that could happen to your site. In most cases, you can get your site reincluded.

It may take an explanation to the search engine of the tactic you employed, why you employed it, and how you corrected it, followed by resubmission to the index. Then it could take a couple of months (or longer) to get reincluded. Then you have to work your way back to the top of the results. The whole process could take six months to a year or longer.

Time is a valuable commodity when you're talking about the Internet and the possibilities that it brings to your revenues. Time lost on the Internet is easily as expensive as if you had a bricks-and-mortar store that you just didn't open on one of the busiest days of the week.

What's at stake makes it especially worrisome that you could possibly spam a search engine and not know it. It wouldn't be intentional, but the results would be the same. So, how do you avoid this? How do you rank well without falling into the black hole that leads to search engine spam?

That's an easy question to answer, really. There's only one way to avoid accidently (or purposely) ending up labeled as a spammer. Build your web site for your audience and not for a search engine. Really, it's that simple.

Here's why: The purpose of a search engine is to find, index, and serve content to people who use the search engine to find something. The search engine's target audience is those people. And in an effort to do the best job possible for those people, it's going to look at every page it indexes in the scope of what's best for the searcher.

So, if you approach creating your web site in the same manner that a search engine approaches serving content to its users, your goals will automatically align. And that natural alignment will keep you out of trouble with search engines.

You should already know how to design your web site with the user in mind. But you can keep a few guidelines in mind to make search engines see that your site is exactly what searchers are looking for:

- **Provide users with unique relevant content.** The most important element of your site is probably the content that you put on it. Provide the information that users need to help them understand, compare, or make decisions. Make it useful, and users (and crawlers) will love you.

- **Use links appropriately.** You want a good balance of links into and out of your site. You can't necessarily control all of the links that come into your site, but you can influence them by participating in your industry. And when you build links that lead away from your page, make sure they take users to other sites that are relevant and useful.

- **Keep your site user-friendly.** Think in terms of the design elements that users like and don't like. And if you don't know what those are, do some research, because plenty of studies have been done. Among design elements that aren't likely to gain you any love from your users are Flash pages, frames, and difficult or changing navigational structures. Crawlers don't like these any more than users do. When you're designing your site, consider using a focus group to help you design the site in a way that users will be comfortable with. And if users are comfortable with it, crawlers probably will be, too.

- **Don't obsess over where your page ranks in search results.** Yes, you want to have your web site featured as high in search engine rankings as possible, but not at the expense of everything else you should do to get your site in front of the right customers. Obsessing over your rank leads to pouring too much time and money into making a search engine happy. It's a much better practice to obsess over giving your users what they need and building loyal users.

Spam of any kind is bad. And no one wants to be labeled a spammer. But being labeled as SEO spam is probably one of the most detrimental blows that your web site can suffer. So instead of focusing on how you can make search engines like your site, focus on how you can make users like your site, and search engines will naturally follow the users.

Chapter 18

Adding Social-Media Optimization

Ask any child over the age of 10 what MySpace is, and you'll get a pretty good description. During the conversation, you'll also probably hear about other places like Flickr, FaceBook, ShoutLife, YouTube, Twitter, and Jaiku. These are all examples of the different *social networks* that have become an Internet phenomenon over the past few years.

Social networks are groups of people who are linked by some type of connection. MySpace is a social network where friends — people who know each other — connect. New friends come into the mix. Friends' friends come into the mix, and eventually you have a network of people (shown in Figure 18-1) who may not know each other in the real world but are connected on the Internet.

The phenomenon part of the social network is how quickly people have adopted it. And using the connections made available by social networking, the category of *social media* has grown nearly as quickly.

Social media are contents generated by social networking. The publishing mode for social media is many-to-many publishing. What this means is that a group of people publish a work or works that are distributed to another group, or several groups, of people.

Literally defined, social media are the technologies and practices that people use to share content, opinions, insights, experiences, perspectives, and multimedia. These technologies and practices can be translated into all different kinds of social networking. Table 18-1 is a short list of some of the types of social media and social networking available.

IN THIS CHAPTER

What is social-media optimization?

The value of social media

Social-media strategies

Measuring social-media optimization

FIGURE 18-1

A social network is a group of people connected by a common interest.

 Individual

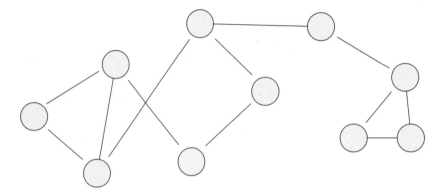

TABLE 18-1

Types of Social Media and Networks

Type of Social Media/Networks	Description	Examples
Wikis	These are collaborative web sites. The concept behind wikis is that anyone who has access to the site is able to add to or change any page on the site.	Wikipedia
Social networks	A group of people tied together by some common interest. Interests can range from reading to education to food to news or any other subject imaginable.	MySpace, FaceBook, Villij
Presence applications	Presence applications are like miniature blogs. These sites allow users to communicate back and forth using their services. Conversations run from important to completely mundane on these web sites.	Twitter, Jaiku, Pownce
Video sharing	Have a great vacation video you want to share? YouTube takes "America's Funniest Home Videos" to a whole new level. If you have a digital video camera and some time, you can create and share any kind of video that you would like.	YouTube
Virtual reality	This interesting social networking category is like living in a fantasy world. You make up your looks, personality, your life, and all of your surroundings. But don't think this is just a game. Living a virtual life can be more than just fun; it can also be a way to make a good income for some people.	Second Life

TABLE 18-1	*(continued)*	
Type of Social Media/Networks	**Description**	**Examples**
Events	Events networks connect people according to the events that they are attending or want to attend. If you want to know who's going to be at that TobyMac concert on Thursday night, check out on of the social-events networks.	Upcoming
News aggregation	These social networks are connected by current and past news. If you find a news story that you think is good enough to be shared with people whose interests are the same as yours, you can add it to your network for them to view.	Digg, Reddit
Photo sharing	Everyone wants to share pictures. Photo-sharing networks let you share your pictures with anyone that you want to. Most of these services also allow online photo storage.	Flickr, PhotoBucket, Zooomr
Livecasting	Livecasting is literally live webcasting. A community is built around the webcasts, including everything from blogs to chatrooms.	Justin.tv
Episodic online videos	These social networking sites are built around online videos, but the difference here is that each person tells a specific story in a series of episodes. The social network is built around your favorite episodes.	YourTruman-Show
Media sharing	If you want to create a network of people with whom you can share all kinds of media files, these services are the ones to use. Connect to as many or as few friends as you like when sending e-mails, videos, audio files, and more.	Izimi, Twango
Music sharing	Not music file sharing, but creating community around music. Most of these sites allow for integration with iTunes or other media players to keep track of the music you listen to, and make recommendations based on your tastes and the tastes of your network.	last.fm, pocketfuzz
Social bookmarking	Social bookmarking is one of the most widely used social-media techniques. These services allow you to tag news stories, blogs, videos, audio files, web sites, and other Internet-based services to share with friends. Tagged sites are then ranked (and searchable) according to the number of tags received.	del.icio.us, ma.gnolia.com, blinklist
Social network aggregators	Social networks have gotten so pervasive that much like metasearch engines, social network aggregators have begun to arise. The concept is to log in to one place and see all your updates from various social networks, photo sharing, and presence applications.	socialthing!, socialstream, profilactic

Social media, then, are services that allow you to publish or distribute content to a core group of people who are connected according to some central interest. If you've ever heard the term Web 2.0, then you've heard someone talking about technologies such as social media.

The concept of Web 2.0 is that the next generation of web-based services will be structured differently than those in the past. It's not about new technologies, really. Instead, Web 2.0 is about the way that people will interact with the Web.

In the past, it was pretty straightforward. You went to a web site, saw what there was to see, and then if you liked it you talked to your friends or sent them an e-mail that included a link. Web 2.0 is about streamlining that process and taking advantage of the connections that the Internet enables. Specifically, Web 2.0 is about using the Web as an application. This means that many social-media sites are considered Web 2.0 sites, but not all Web 2.0 sites are social networks.

Now, when you find something you like online, sure, you can send your friends an e-mail — or you can distribute it using one of the social-networking services. This allows you to stay connected with your friends, streamlines the connection to those friends, adds new friends to the network, and makes it possible for you to receive items of interest from them as well.

In short, social networking and social media are all about one thing: communicating with your friends about common interests. People want to classify the Web. These technologies allow them to do just that rather than depending on someone else's classification who doesn't see the world the way they do.

What Is Social-Media Optimization?

When you understand what social media are, it's not a far step from there to *social-media optimization*. It's about using social media to spread the news about your web site. And instead of tweaking the elements of your web site, when you're practicing social-media optimization you're participating in social networks and tweaking the content that you share within those networks.

It's through that participation and optimization that your site is distributed, and that's what brings traffic to your web site. There are also a couple of added benefits to social-media optimization. First, it's free in terms of monetary investment. There is no cost to participate in these networks except your time. But make no mistake about it, you will have to invest a chunk of front-end time into this type of optimization. You must become familiar with the communities and participate to establish a name for yourself before anyone will take serious notice of you.

The other benefit of social-media optimization is that it's really a *viral marketing* strategy. Nearly everyone is familiar with a virus. It's that nasty little bug that multiplies exponentially and makes you believe death would be an improvement. Viral marketing is neat, not nasty, but it works in a somewhat similar way.

When you can tap viral marketing for your online presence, word of your brand spreads like a virus — it moves faster and faster as the *buzz* increases, and there doesn't seem to be any way to stop it. And that's good. If your marketing message has become viral, you can expect to see some serious growth in the number of visitors to your site and by extension to the number of goal conversions that you see.

Viral marketing is a good thing. And when you've optimized your social-media participating, you can almost guarantee that your marketing will soon have that viral quality that you're looking for.

What's different about social-media optimization?

In short, everything. Social-media optimization is not at all like web-site optimization, though it should be part of your overall optimization strategy. Instead of adding keywords in the right places, tweaking your meta tags, and digging up the right balance of links, you're doing something different — creating relationships, generating content, and tagging the Web. Don't sell it short. The value of social media has already been proven by many organizations on the Web.

One thing to keep in mind as you're considering social-media optimization is that it's not as simple as throwing a few crumbs at a social network and waiting for people to come along and share those crumbs with their friends. They won't.

If you approach social media in that manner, you'll end up wasting your time, and then when you do get smart, the people who populate the social networking communities you tried it on won't be as easy to win over to your side. People don't forget when a faker tries to jump in their midst for purely marketing purposes. It's the fastest way to send you right to the bottom of the social-media pond.

Social-media optimization is first about joining communities and creating relationships. And it's only by going through the process of becoming part of the community that your brand will begin to be recognized by other community members. And that's when your efforts will begin to pay off.

When you're optimizing for social media, you won't be focused on adding keywords to your content or tweaking your meta tags. Instead, you'll be focused on providing something that the members of your chosen social network need. It may be an article, it may be tagging news stories that are especially relevant to your industry, it may even be adding your expertise to a forum related to your expertise. However you participate in the community, participating will be your best optimization tool.

The Value of Social Media

It's obvious that social-media optimization has value. Look around at sites like MySpace, YouTube, and FaceBook. These are all sites that no one thought would amount to anything. But they did. People love the idea of being part of an online community. The generation of kids that have just entered the work force and are growing up right now are Internet pros, and their parents are pretty proficient with it, too.

These people are involved in all kinds of activities online, from shopping and downloading music to participating in social networks. The kids are networking socially for different reasons than parents are, but both are getting involved.

The question then is not whether social media has value, but how much value it has. If you look at an experiment done by *Marketing Experiments Journal* (http://www.marketingexperiments.com), you quickly begin to believe that social media might be more valuable than you thought.

The experiment compared the cost and effectiveness of social-media marketing against pay-per-click advertising over the span of one year. And the results? Social-media marketing cost the company $3,600 — the salary ($10 an hour) for an employee to become a part of and market to social networks. That investment drew 93,207 visitors to the site over the course of the year (which works out to be just under $.04 per visitor).

The PPC application was a little faster. Instead of having to wait weeks or months to get involved in a community, the PPC ads could be started almost immediately. The company spent $1,250 on PPC ads over the course of the year, and those ads drew 2,057 visitors to the site for a total cost of almost $.61 per visitor.

Social media had much more impact, and ultimately cost the company less money on a per-visit basis. In fact, the social-media optimization yielded a 1,578 percent better return on investment than the PPC ads did.

The value of social media is there. But so are the difficulties that you may face as you try to implement a social-media optimization effort. For example, you can't rush headlong into a new social network and expect to be able to post your ads anywhere you want. That will get you banned from the community fairly quickly. It will also create animosity between you and the very people you're trying to reach.

You also have to participate in the communities. You can't fake your participation, either. Social networkers will recognize your efforts as being fake and will treat you accordingly. So the only way to be effective with social-media optimization is to become a *real* part of the social network. But if you can accomplish that, the rewards are better than any marketing plan you've used to date.

Social-Media Strategies

We've established that using social media as a marketing technique requires a different approach than some of the more traditional marketing that you've probably done to this point. It's also very different than the tasks that you'll complete as part of your SEO efforts.

Social-media optimization is a term coined by Rohit Bhargava. When he came up with it, he also came up with five strategies to help you accomplish optimization of your social-media efforts. Over the next few months, several other industry experts added to the list and there are now 16 guidelines that will help you optimize your social-media efforts:

- **Increase your linkability:** The linkability of your site is determined by the amount of content that you have available to users who might come from social networks. Old, stale, and rarely changing content will not help with your social-media optimization, so begin by updating your content and your content strategy to ensure that it is interesting for visitors who might come from your social network.

■ **Make tagging and bookmarking easy:** Don't make users try to figure out how to add your blog or site to their content feed. Instead, make it easy by a function that generates the necessary URL or code for visitors to add you to their important links. There are tools available to help with this, including the RSS Button Maker: `http://www.toprankblog` `.com/tools/rss-buttons/`.

■ **Reward inbound links:** People who link to you want something in return. If you can provide a link to them in your blog, *blogroll*, or some other area of your web site, people and companies will be much more likely to link to you. Just remember to keep the links into and out of your site directly related to the topic of the site.

■ **Help your content travel:** Having traveling content means having content that can be accessed from another site easily. If you have content that many people will be interested in, consider making that content available in PDF format or as an audio or video file. Then when users want to spread your content, it will be easy for them to do.

■ **Encourage the *mashup*:** A mashup is a web application that combines data from more than one source into an integrated experience for your site users. For example, if you make it possible for others to embed your content in their blog or web site in exchange for a link back to you, you'll find that your popularity climbs faster than if you won't let them move your content from one place to another.

■ **Be a user resource, even if it doesn't help you:** Today's Internet users, and most especially those users who participate in social media and social networking, will expect you to provide information that is useful to them. If you're not providing that information, they'll go to someone who is. So, call it being a Good Resource Ambassador, but try to help people without expecting anything in return. Your returns will come just because your actions proved your site's worth.

■ **Reward helpful and valuable users:** Helpful and valuable users will be the best help you can have as you're working with your social-media optimization. Find a way to reward those users so they'll continue to be helpful.

■ **Participate:** If you don't participate, your thoughts and opinions will not be welcomed in a social-media network for long. If you're going to leverage the power of social media, you have to be willing to participate.

■ **Know how to target your audience:** Audiences can be tough. If you approach the wrong audience with the wrong message, you'll be slaughtered in the court of opinion. Before you make that kind of mistake, take the time to learn who you'll be in the community with.

■ **Create content:** Content is one key to social-media marketing. If you make it a point to create fresh, unique content regularly, visitors will come to you because they know they can find the information they need.

■ **Be real:** Social networkers can spot a fake nearly as quickly as they could spot a three-dollar bill. Don't try to con your audiences. Eventually, they'll catch on and annihilate you. Be who you are. That will get you much further than being what you think others want you to be.

■ **Don't forget your roots, be humble:** When you participate regularly in social media, you may find yourself in the position of being considered an expert. Many people will let this distinction go straight to their ego. Just remember, someone one else was on top yester-day and will be tomorrow, so treat the people around you as you would like to be treated when you're not the talking head of the moment.

- **Don't be afraid to try new things, stay fresh:** One of the greatest benefits of social media is the ability to use your creativity to do something different. And in social-media optimization, creativity is often rewarded with better traffic and higher interest.

- **Develop a social-media optimization strategy:** As in SEO, you don't want to be wandering in circles as you're trying to optimize your social-media presence. Develop a strategy that keeps you on track and helps you target the social networks that are most closely related to your topic.

- **Choose your social-media optimization tactics wisely:** As great a marketing tool as social media can be, it can also be the most detrimental practice you institute. If you use the wrong tactics in a social-media forum, you can expect to find your efforts worthless. You can also expect that it will be very hard to rebuild the trust that you destroy.

- **Make social media optimization part of your processes and best practices:** Social-media networks require constant participation. And as with SEO, that means ongoing efforts — daily. Integrate your social-media optimization strategies into your daily SEO workflow.

Bhargava and the other social-media experts who put this list together are people in the front line of SEO and SMO (social-media optimization) every day. These guidelines will help you begin your optimization process. And if you follow them, you'll be well on your way to gaining all the value available from social networks and social media.

But there are also other guidelines that might be helpful as you try to follow the guidelines just listed. Some are technical in nature, and others are simply a matter of etiquette:

- Spend some time listening to your audience before you join the conversation. This time allows you to gain an understanding of the language, the tone, and the expectations of conversations.

- As you begin to participate in social networks, monitor what effect your participation is having. Watch closely at how you're received, and track your site metrics at the same time. Sudden jumps or dips in your metrics can point to participation that works, or doesn't.

- Use what you learn to craft your social-media optimization strategy. You have to have one. Use the information that you gather as you're watching and listening on a social network to ensure that your strategy is targeted properly.

- Deliver content that will add to the conversation. If it doesn't add anything, the other participants will roast you faster than you can burn a marshmallow at a bonfire.

- Use RSS feeds to enable your content. RSS feeds will instantly update anyone who is watching your content and that's good for you. It means that your links will spread faster than anything else you could have done to share them.

- Social media is all about relationships. Engage and encourage participation. Build relationships. And think of it from the aspect of "what can I give?" instead of "what can I get?".

- Choose a theme related to your core content that is actively being discussed online. And stay within that theme. Include articles, webcasts, videos, or whatever else works well with your theme. And try to look at the theme from different angles. That's the key to opening discussion, dialogue, back links, and all the things that go into making someone want to pass on what you've got to offer. If you choose something no one is talking about, you won't have any results.

- Approach social-media optimization as an individual. You can't approach others in a social network as a corporation. Corporations automatically garner suspicion (as in, "I know you're here only because you want to sell me something").

- Develop content that will appeal to the networks in which you participate, both from an audience perspective and from an information perspective. If you are trying to market to a 30-something soccer mom, having the 50-year-old male CEO trying to get her attention isn't going to work. But you can hire a 30-something soccer mom who will have the right perspective.

- Consider hiring bloggers or other social-media participants. If it makes sense to use social-media marketing for your organization, you may have to devote a large chunk of time to it each week. If you don't have the time to commit to that, consider hiring someone to do it for you. At ComputerWorld (http://www.computerworld.com) a whole staff of freelance bloggers helps to keep news current and related to the industries in which it appears. If they can do it, you can, too. Hiring a blogger isn't usually as expensive as you might think. You can usually pay them anywhere from $10 to $50 per post, depending on the industry.

Measuring Social-Media Optimization

If you're participating in social media, you're going to want to know how it's working. But before you even begin to measure your success, you need to know what you're measuring it against. Define concrete goals for your efforts. Those might be to increase your web-site traffic by a certain amount each month, to increase conversion values, or some other goal. Whatever those goals are, use them as a guide as you're planning your social-media optimization efforts.

Once you've decided what you want from social-media optimization, you can measure the results that you're gaining from your efforts. The most obvious indicator is web-site traffic. If your traffic begins to climb, it's a pretty good bet that your social-media efforts are working.

But if you don't want to rely solely on site traffic as in indication of your success, there are several other elements you can look to in the effort to determine how successful your social-media optimization efforts are.

You should first have a blog, and then track who is reading it. There are many good web analytics packages that will track what the most popular content on your site is. You can probably also see where those site visitors are coming from and how long they're spending on your page. This information will help you determine what blog entries are most successful and who is sending the most traffic to your blog, so that you can capitalize on that.

Next, you can monitor the number of visitors who are actually interacting with your content by checking your guest book, forums, or comment capabilities. Guest books aren't nearly as popular as they once were, but if you're participating in a social network and you don't have forums or comment capabilities on your blog, you're missing a large part of the value of social media.

Also pay attention to how often you're added to social booking sites. Sites like del.icio.us and StumbledUpon are a couple of the social bookmarking sites that can help boost your site traffic. The easiest way to monitor your site in social bookmarking networks is to create an account with them and then use the account to search for your URLs. In other words, who is actually adding your site/article/blog posts to sites.

Measure how many readers are actually subscribing to your RSS feeds. The number of subscribers you have on your RSS feeds will be a good indicator of how well you're doing in your SMO efforts. The more subscribers you have, the more popular your site is.

Another way to measure your success with social bookmarking is to watch who is linking to you. If you have a good analytics program, it will probably provide you with a report that shows where incoming links originated. If your analytics program doesn't provide this information, you can figure out who's linking to you using that old standby, a web search. To find out who is linking to your site use the following search string, replacing *yourwebsite* with the actual URL of the pages you want to track: `link:http://www.yourwebsite.com`.

One last way to monitor your success in the social-media space is to monitor how many people are connected to you. In MySpace and FaceBook, that might mean how many friends you have. In LinkedIn, it would be how many colleagues you are connected to, and on Digg the measurement you're looking for is the number of times your content is tagged.

All of these are indications that you're being followed by someone. And the more people with whom you can build a relationship, obviously the better your success will be. And that's probably the most important rule of all to remember about social-media networking and social-media optimization: build the relationship first and the rest falls into place.

Chapter 19

Automated Optimization

Pay attention in just about any technology industry, and eventually you're going to hear the term "automation." That's because so much technology consists of repetitive actions that are best suited to automation.

So when you hear the term automation associated with SEO, you may be thinking, "Wow, optimization automation! How cool is that?" It would be super cool. After all, there are a lot of repetitive tasks in search engine optimization.

Using keywords on your pages is one area where you might be able to automate the optimization. A good content-generation system would make it easy for you to quickly generate keyword-optimized content that you could change out on your site regularly. Even tagging your site might be an option for automation. It would seem like an easy task to create a piece of software that would add your chosen keywords to the correct tags.

The problem is, not all automation is created equal. And when you're working on your SEO strategies, there are some things that software programs just can't do.

Being creative is one of those things. You can tell a piece of software what to do, but the software can't look at a problem and find a creative way to solve it. If the solution isn't provided by an algorithm in the program, you'll be stuck without an answer.

Automation has its good and bad points. Some elements of SEO lend themselves to optimization. Others just don't.

Should You Automate?

Automation is a concept born of the industrial age. There was a time when people were responsible for every step in manufacturing a product of any type. Then someone realized that it would be much faster if you could have a machine do some of the menial, repetitive tasks. And that's when automation began.

Since those first glimmers of inspiration, automation has been applied to a lot of different products, strategies, and processes. Even on the Internet. Nearly as soon as computer and web applications were developed, someone started trying to automate them.

The problem with automation is that it doesn't work for everything. Customer service is a good example. You simply cannot automate customer service entirely. Sure, you can automate some aspects, but when it gets down to dealing with real people, you have to have real people do the job. Machines just don't understand how people operate.

SEO is one of those technologies that fall into the category of "you can automate some aspects, but there has to be human interaction, too." The thing about automation is that a computer program can carry out a predefined set of activities based on guidelines that are also predefined. But when you have dynamic (changing) parameters, as you do in SEO, there are limits to what you can automate.

Automating keyword research is an example. There are plenty of programs available on the Web that will help you with some aspects of keyword research. You can find programs that generate keywords for you, or that look at your competition's site to see how it's using keywords and what keywords it's using. A piece of software can also monitor keywords that you're using in PPC programs to help you know when your bid is too low. But a program can't use the human logic and understanding that goes into determining which of those keywords will work for the nuances of your web site.

Creativity is one reason not to automate. A second reason is that many search engines look down on automated SEO strategies. There are bits of SEO that you can automate without being penalized. We've talked about keywords, but you can also automate some of your management functions such as analytics and rank monitoring.

The tasks you never want to automate are site generation, automatic link programs, and content generation. It will be obvious to search engines that you've automated the tasks, and the result of that automation won't be better rankings, as you might hope. The result more likely will be having your site delisted from search engine results, at least temporarily.

When you're considering taking the automation route, stick with automation of functions that aren't critical to providing customers and site visitors with the information and capabilities that they need. Don't automate content or linking and certainly don't automate the creation of your web site. Use your creativity to make those elements of your site as appealing to site visitors as possible, and leave the automation for the administrative functions that have no impact on your customers.

It's Not Always a Penalty

If you read the information on the Internet, you'll find that many people disagree as to whether or not search engines should penalize companies that don't follow their guidelines. You'll also find that the search engines won't admit publicly to penalties that reduce your ranking; only to penalties that get you delisted from the search engine. But both things can happen, just not always for the same reason.

There are many reasons a search engine might delist you from its index. Cloaking, keyword stuffing, linking schemes, even overoptimization — these are all general spamdexing tactics that will cause a search engine to delist your site.

Once you're delisted, you can get re-listed. All you have to do is correct the problem, and then give the search engine time to recrawl your site. When the offending strategies have been removed, you'll be added back to the index — but it could take as much as six months!

What you might find happening, however, is that you're not delisted, your rank just falls suddenly. This is probably not the result of a penalty from the search engine. Instead, it's more likely that your site ranking drops because there's a problem with your site or your web server. Some of the reasons that you may find your rank falling include:

- **A search engine algorithm change.** Search engine designers are constantly tweaking their algorithms, so it's not at all unusual to find that your site position drops because of a subtle change to the way the crawler indexes your site. This is why it's always good to stay abreast of changes at the various search engines.

- **Server issues and hosting issues.** If your server is down, or if it's running slow, a crawler might have a difficult time crawling the site. If it does, it's likely to give up and move on to another site. And in some cases, your web host might ban a search engine from crawling your site because other clients have complained or because the crawler is creating problems with the hosting services provided. Any of these problems will cause your site ranking to drop.

- **A poorly written robots.txt file.** A robots.txt file is a useful tool to have on your site. But if the file is written incorrectly, it may cause crawlers to not crawl your site completely, or even at all. Make sure that file is written properly so your ranks don't drop dramatically.

- **Broken or spammy links.** Your links don't have to be actual spam. If they appear to be spammy, a crawler might abandon the indexing of your site. And broken links will stop a crawler in its forward motion. Crawlers don't like anything that makes them have to back up and start over again.

- **Another site is redesigned** and so becomes more relevant than yours. It happens. There is no such thing as perfection in SEO. Other sites will be working on improving their site rankings as much as you are, and there will be times when their efforts are just more successful than yours. All you can do is try to stay on top of the SEO game, creating new content and keeping your site as useful as possible for site visitors.

So, if you find that your site ranking drops for seemingly no reason, start investigating. Find the problem, and if you can fix it, do so immediately. If not, stay on top of the people who can. And if you're delisted? Well, again, fix the problem as soon as possible, and don't make the same mistake again. It's an expensive lesson to have to learn, but after a month or so of having no search ranking at all, you should learn how important it is to always stay on a search engine's good side.

Automation Tools

Automating certain SEO tasks is one way to make the best use of your time. Of course, you want to avoid those automation strategies that put you on a search engine's black list, but there are plenty of places you can use automation. And there are many different kinds of automation tools.

One thing you won't find is an all-in-one solution. There are some great SEO tools out there that will help with many aspects of SEO, but will leave one or two areas untouched. For example, Web Optimization Easy 4.2 (`http://www.websitepromotionsoft.com/search-engine-optimization.html`) will help with 45 ranking factors, but it doesn't cover them all. And though it will also help you to understand why the top 10 web sites in your area rank well, it won't help you manage keyword bids.

When you can find a program that does most of the automation you need, and you're comfortable with the tool's interface, then by all means try it and use other tools to supplement the areas the single tool doesn't help with.

It would be nice if there were standards in place that made it easy to monitor all your SEO efforts from a single dashboard. There are not. But you can piece together the tool solution that reduces the amount of time you put into repetitive SEO work, so you can focus your energies better on those activities that will truly improve your search rankings.

You have to be careful about choosing solutions, though. Some of the automation tools that you find available on the Web are not worth the time it takes to install them. These tools are buggy, they don't perform as they should, and they can cause your system to crash — or worse, can create problems with your web site.

When you're looking for automation tools for your SEO efforts, begin by looking at the areas that you need to automate. Are you spending hours and hours on keyword research when what you should be doing is generating unique copy for your web site? If so, then a keyword research automation tool, like WordTracker (`http://www.wordtracker.com/`), will help free up the time you need to work on your content.

Are you obsessed with your rank and how your competition measures up? You shouldn't be. Let an automated monitoring tool, like SERP Tracker (`http://sitening.com/seo-tools/serp-tracker/`), be obsessive while you spend that time doing something about your current rank.

What tools you'll need are determined on an individual organizational basis. Evaluate your needs and then look for tools that meet those needs. Also look for tools that might grow as you grow. Your automation needs will change over time as your site matures, as your SEO efforts mature, and as SEO as a strategy changes. Try to find something that's scalable and will grow as your SEO strategies grow and change.

Also remember that price isn't always the best indication of what tools are better than others. Some free tools on the Web are excellent. Those that aren't free can cost anywhere from under $100 to well over $1,000, but can also be as excellent or as lousy as some of the free tools. To make sure that you're getting a tool that will provide what you need within your budget, try finding tools that have a free trial period. These tools usually allow you to try their software for 30 days for free. The full functionality of the tool may not be available to you, but you should be able to tell from the trial if the interface is comfortable and if the tool provides the metrics and solutions that you need.

One more way to find a good tool is to ask around. Chances are, you know other people who are in SEO or who own a web site and have done their own SEO. These people may have already been through the trial process with various tools, and they may be able to reduce the amount of time it takes you to find just the right tool.

Automation works when you're automating the right aspects of your SEO campaign. Keep your automation related to administrative functions and use tools that suit your needs, and you'll find that this frees up time you can devote to far more important activities, like providing your customers exactly what they're looking for on their terms.

Part IV

Maintaining SEO

O ne of the grievous mistakes that many web designers (or whoever is in charge of SEO) make is to assume that SEO is a one-time activity. In point of fact, it is an ongoing process that must be monitored and maintained to be the most effective.

In the first of two chapters in Part IV, Chapter 20 explains some of the most important elements of monitoring and maintaining your SEO efforts. In addition, Chapter 21 helps you understand how to analyze your SEO strategies and the techniques, conversions, and even other types of logs that are associated with SEO. These techniques will help you maintain SEO and continue to gain value from your SEO efforts.

Chapter 20

SEO Beyond the Launch

I t's done. You've spent weeks or months optimizing your web site, integrating yourself into social networks as an expert, testing the right keywords, and digging for all the right links. Now you're number one for your keywords and the traffic that comes to your site surpasses anything that you've had in the past. It's time to sit back and put your feet up on the desk. A nice nap, a long lunch. Now that you're not working on SEO all the time, you're free to do some of the more interesting things that are allowed (or not) during working hours.

Stop. That's a nice dream, but it's not the way SEO works. So you've achieved a top rank? So what. Tomorrow you could be buried three pages deep in search engine results or worse, because a search engine changed its algorithm and you weren't on top of it. Or maybe you just got knocked down below the fold of the first page because other web sites added some features that made them more popular than yours. Below the fold is not terrible, but it's also not above the fold, right there where a user can see your listing without having to scroll. And it's not the top position that you held yesterday.

It's Not Over

In order to maintain that great rank that you've finally reached, you have to stay on top of your SEO efforts. You've read it more than once in this book already — SEO is a never-ending process. Once you're where you want to be, there's a lot of work that must be done to keep you there. Even taking a short time away from your efforts could lead to a drop in your position.

A good practice is to include an outline in your original SEO plan for the actions you need to take and the amount of time you'll need for them. On average, you'll need to devote at least a couple of hours a day to your ongoing SEO efforts, and at times, more than that will be required.

In the time that you allot for ongoing SEO efforts, there are plenty of things to do. But it should all start with some form of position monitoring and web-site analytics. Position monitoring can usually be accomplished by a software application. But be careful, Google specifically calls the use of automated rank checkers a violation of its terms of service, and may disable your ability to connect to and do searches on Google.com. Moderate use of such software probably won't be a problem. Many people use these tools to track their positions. So if you can't take time out of your schedule every day to look up the rank of your web site by keyword in every search engine you're targeting, an application to handle it could provide the position information you need.

Monitoring your web analytics is also an important part of your ongoing SEO, because this is where you'll find information about where your site visitors are coming from, how long they're staying on your site, and what pages they visit while they're there. An analytics program should also tell you how many people *bounce* — come to your site and leave immediately. A bounce is an indication that your site is not optimized properly. Visitors who bounce from your site are not finding what they thought they would find, based on the search engine results they clicked through.

You may also want to monitor other portions of your SEO strategy. For example, monitoring keywords and links is always a good idea. Keywords can change. The popular term for something in your industry could be one thing today and something completely different tomorrow. You have to stay on top of trends in order to take advantage of them.

Monitoring your links is a matter of making sure they lead exactly where you expect them to lead. You may also want to keep an eye on where links are coming to your site *from*. Incoming links could be damaging to you if they're coming from unrelated web sites, or if the sites they're coming from have been determined by search engines to be "bad neighborhoods." A bad neighborhood is an unethical site or group of sites.

As with monitoring your search rankings, monitoring links and keywords is also a task that lends itself to automation. A good software application can keep track of these elements of your SEO plan and let you know when you need to pay attention and improve your SEO efforts in one area or another.

In addition to monitoring your links, you'll also want to add to links, and to content, over time. If you add hundreds of links to your site overnight, search engine crawlers will likely not be impressed. Instead, they'll look at those links with suspicion and might even make the assumption that you're spamming the search engine. If that happens, you'll be delisted from search rankings until you fix what you've done wrong.

It's far better to add links to your site a few at a time. You can add a few every day or every week, depending on how many people want to link to your site. However, if you try to add all your links on a single day, it's not going to look good for you.

Content is also an element of SEO that needs to be maintained over time. Your content should change regularly. In some cases, that means every day; in others it means once a week or once a month. Even more important than the schedule with which you change your content is the content itself. Over time you should be adding to your collection of relevant, useful content. If what you have on the site isn't relevant or useful, then replace it. And don't put any piece of content on your site that doesn't give your visitors something useful.

In the same category as content is adding new pages to your web site. If you have an active site, over time it should grow. And search engines will take note of the number of pages included in your site each time you're crawled. Landing pages, articles, blogs, newsletter archives, and site maps are types of pages that will cause your site to grow, so if you're maintaining your SEO, site growth will be a natural extension of that.

If you're adding new pages, you should also be adding internal page links. Link every page on your web site. And use a comfortable linking structure. The main links for your site — to pages like your home page, the contact page, or category overview pages — should appear both on the top or side of your page in your main navigational structure, and they should be repeated at the bottom of every page.

Also remember that if you are using PPC ads that lead to landing pages, the landing pages should be added to your navigational structure as well. People don't like to be dropped in the center of a jungle and left to figure out how to get where they want to go. Instead, provide a clear path for the next direction your visitors would like to take.

Finally, if you haven't already done it, now is the time to rename pages and images that don't include keywords. Using the default titles created by your web-site design software won't win you any points with search engines. Instead, change those page names to reflect the keywords that you've chosen. Ideally, the page name will be the same as the page title. And if possible, it will also contain relevant keywords.

Your images may also need to be re-tagged. There are image-specific search engines that index your images for display. So, if you run a custom stationery company, having pictures of your stationery that are labeled with keyword-rich names may help you rank better in image searches as well as in general searches. Keep your image alt tags updated, too.

If you change your relevant keywords, don't forget to also replace meta tag keywords or update meta descriptions as your page changes. It won't do you any good at all to have one set of keywords in your meta tags and another one used on the customer-facing portion of your web pages.

In short, the basic elements that helped you reach the top spot through your SEO efforts need to be ongoing. Even the competitive research that you did back in the beginning needs to be updated regularly. Your competition will change. If you don't stay on top of those changes, you'll find that you fall behind the competition and will have to fight your way back to the top again.

Using Content Management Systems

Not very long ago, if you said content management system (CMS) and SEO in the same sentence, you'd probably draw an audible gasp from the SEO experts in the audience. That's because, in the past, content management systems had a way of demolishing all of the advantages of SEO.

Most of the problem was that content management systems created pages that contained long URLs with multiple variables that blocked search crawlers from crawling the pages. That's not the case today. CMS providers have fixed that problem and increased the usability of those systems for the express purpose of improving or maintaining SEO.

Content is the backbone of the Internet. The Internet was created as a way to share information, so it only makes sense that content is an integral part of the structure of the Web. Using a content management system can help you remain an active part of the Web, because it will help you to generate the content that you need to attract the customers you would like to have.

Content management systems are usually used in a situation where your content is coming from many different sources. For example, if you run a web site that contains a blog to which several people contribute, then adding a content management system can help you maintain control over that group of content providers. It can also help strengthen your web-site structure by automatically structuring your links and providing the templates on which your content will appear.

One more redefined capability of CMS is the application's ability to improve your content in terms of SEO. The latest CMS systems can create keyword-rich content and include SEO-appropriate titles, meta tags, and anchor text.

Including a CMS system in your SEO efforts is not a bad idea these days. If you have a site that generates a lot of content by a lot of people, a CMS system might be the application that helps make the content side of your SEO efforts successful.

SEO Problems and Solutions

There is no doubt that no matter how smoothly your SEO implementation goes, eventually you'll run into problems. Most of them won't be major. They'll be problems like having out-of-date keywords or meta tags. But you can also have a few major problems with your SEO implementation.

You've been banned!

Probably the most worrisome of issues you could encounter is being banned from a search engine, Google specifically. If you depend on your search ranking to keep you in customers and sales, being banned from a search engine is a frightening prospect. Even a single day without search engine visibility can cost your company big, not only monetarily but also in terms of customer loyalty.

There's good news. Despite the fact that you hear a lot about being banned from search engines, it's really not all that likely to happen. You have to carry out some pretty offensive tactics (like page hijacking, keyword stuffing, or other decidedly black-hat SEO techniques). Of course, there are exceptions to every rule, and even search engines have a bad day now and again.

So what do you do if you're in a top ranking slot one day and the next your site is nowhere to be found in search rankings? Before you assume you've been banned from a search engine, make sure. You can search for your site on Google using the search string `site:www.yoursitename.com`. If your site is included in Google's index, the pages that are included in the search rankings should appear in the search results. If they do, you haven't been banned, but you may have been penalized for something. Try to figure out what and make it better.

If you don't see any pages listed for your site, it's still possible that you haven't been banned. But the best way to find out is to e-mail the search engine. Be professional when you send the e-mail — you don't want to make matters worse by being rude, especially if you have done something to be banned.

Content scraping

Another of the major problems that you might encounter in your SEO efforts is having your site content stolen. This is usually accomplished by a *scraper site* that uses a *scraper bot* to copy the content on your site. This can be an SEO problem because the scraper bot will look for an XML site map. If it finds that map, that makes it far easier for the bot to gather content.

Even without an XML site map, a bot can scrape content from your site, but it's much harder. So if you worry that your content is in danger, one thing you can do is not use an XML site map at all. In some cases, this is a viable option. In other cases, an XML site map is essential to having some pages within your site indexed.

If not using an XML site map is out of the question, you could place an XML site map on your site, but remove it once the site has been crawled. The best way to know when your web site has been indexed by a crawler is to look at the server logs. Usually you'll see a request for the robots.txt file in the file log. Around that request you should see the name of the crawler that requested the site map. Once the one that you want to have access to your site map has crawled it, you can delete the file. But remember, this only makes it harder for hackers to exploit your site map, not impossible.

Click fraud

Click fraud has been addressed a couple of times already, but it bears mentioning here — briefly. Click fraud is the most troublesome of SEO problems. And what makes it more troublesome is that it's very hard to control. If you suspect your PPC ads are being targeted for click fraud, report it immediately to your PPC provider.

Any number of problems, not just click fraud, can arise with your SEO campaign. Everything from inadvertent SEO spam to the issues listed here can happen at any time. But even though the possibility exists, such things don't happen all the time, in fact probably not as often as all the warnings might make you think.

The best thing you can do to protect yourself from the problems that you can encounter with SEO is to follow the guidelines laid out by the search engine or directory that you're targeting. Avoid black-hat SEO techniques, and in general be professional about how you conduct your SEO efforts.

Chapter 21

Analyzing Success

If you want to maintain successful SEO efforts, you need to analyze what works and what doesn't, and try to extrapolate why, based on the information that you have. That information can vary, depending on how you gather it.

There are many methods for measuring the success of your SEO efforts. Some people are just happy to see their site traffic and sales rising. But if your SEO strategy is to work toward achieving a more complicated goal, you might need more ways to measure the success or failure of your efforts.

As an example, if you've implemented SEO strategies in an effort to build visitors to your site as a way of creating or improving brand recognition, you might not be as interested in the sales achieved by your SEO efforts as you are in the creation of returning visitors.

It doesn't matter if your SEO goals are monetarily based. You can create goals, and conversion values, for non-monetary activities like newsletter sign-ups, filling out a form, or even requesting additional information. Whatever your goals are, learning which SEO efforts work and which don't is vitally important to ensuring that you're always putting forth your best effort to reach those conversions.

Analyzing SEO Successes

You know that search engine ranking for your web site can change from week to week. Those changes can be caused by competition, modifications to search algorithms, and changes to your web site. To maintain your top ranking, you must constantly monitor and make changes to your web site.

It's through this monitoring that you'll also be able to see how successful your SEO efforts are. And measuring the success of those efforts is essential to keeping you on the right track.

Managing SEO expectations

Before you can begin to analyze what you're doing right and wrong in SEO, you first need to know what to expect. Realistic expectations will keep your view of your SEO results realistic as well. SEO is not the only answer for your web site, but it can help improve your site traffic and conversions if you are patient and understand how to leverage your SEO expectations.

SEO timeline

The first expectation that you'll probably have to rein in is the SEO timeline. Many people implement some aspect of SEO and expect to see results overnight. Obviously, paid results are going to be profitable faster than true SEO efforts, but either way, SEO can still be a long process. It can take anywhere from a few months to more than a year to start seeing solid rankings and targeted traffic. You'll have to be patient to be rewarded for your SEO efforts. And of course the actual time frame to see the full results will vary according to the keywords you're using and the state of your web site when you begin your optimization process.

Being hands-on

Whether you've hired an SEO consulting firm or are doing it in-house, you have to be involved in your SEO efforts from start to finish — and because the end never arrives that means you have to be involved always. Become a champion of SEO and help the others in your organization to understand and value the results that SEO efforts provide.

This applies even if you've hired a company to do the majority of the tasks needed for successful site optimization. You have responsibilities in the client/customer relationship. Your most important responsibility is to communicate what you need from the SEO company and what your goals for site optimization are. You also have a responsibility to stay involved in the SEO process, so that you know where your optimization efforts are, and where they are going, what works, and what needs to be changed, tweaked, or abandoned altogether. Your participation in your SEO program will ensure that you know what's going on, where you are, and what your SEO company is doing for you. This is also the easiest way to hold an SEO company accountable for its responsibilities to you.

With your expectations in line, you can begin to really analyze the success or failure of your SEO efforts. There are several methods for analyzing where you stand, and any of these efforts is valid. What makes one more useful than another is, first, your needs — you should understand exactly what you're trying to achieve and what indicators you're looking for to know if you're actually achieving those goals. And the second reason you might select a specific way of tracking and analyzing your success is your budget. Some organizations can afford automated tracking tools that tell them basically everything they need to know about the success or failure of their SEO campaigns. Other organizations don't have that kind of budget. Fortunately, there are some methods of analysis that won't consume your entire SEO budget.

Find yourself

If all you really need to know is where your web site appears in search rankings, you can use the search engines and directories that you're targeting to do a keyword search. That keyword search should show you where your site is ranking. It won't show you much more than that, but it does help you to monitor your position so you know if your efforts are working or not. Just don't base your decision on a single search. Search for your keywords daily over a period of time to make sure your rank on any given day isn't just an anomaly.

If you're using this method of analyzing your success, you'll need a historical view of where your site appeared in search rankings before you began your SEO efforts. With this measurement, you can compare your current rankings to see if your listing is climbing or falling. Without historical data, you should, at the very least, take stock of where your site appears in rankings on the first day of your SEO campaign. This won't tell you the average ranking for your site, but it will give you a good idea of where you should start.

Analyzing web stats

Most web-site hosting companies now provide some form of web statistics program. But this may be limited to basic measurements like the number of hits, number of unique visitors, search terms used to find your site, IP address accessing your site, and locations of people accessing your site. Even this basic information will help you to learn where your visitors are coming from, but you might want to add to those metrics by expanding your web-stats package.

If you're looking for a web-stats package that's more comprehensive, there are a few available online for free. Most notably, Google Analytics will provide most of the measurements you'll need, including keyword tracking for AdWords and for other PPC applications. There are also numerous paid versions of web statistics software, some hosted online and some that are hosted on your own computer. Find the package that's right for your needs, and you'll have all of the measurements you need to analyze how successful your SEO efforts are in terms of driving targeted, converting traffic to your site.

When you're analyzing your web statistics, there are a few principles you should keep in mind. These principles will help you understand your metrics and how they correlate with your SEO efforts.

Baseline statistics

Baseline statistics are the measurements that you collect *before* you begin to implement changes to your site, like the changes you'll make as you're optimizing your web site. Record statistics such as the average number of visitors to your site each day. You can later compare this number to statistics that you collect after your SEO strategies have been implemented, to see the results of your efforts. If your numbers aren't improving as you would expect them to, given the changes you've made, then you may not have done something right, or there may be some factor that needs to be adjusted. Your baseline measurements will help you to see (over time) where you stand.

Referring web sites

Referring web sites are those sites from which your site visitors come. If you have PPC ads on Google's AdWords network, the referring web site might be one of the search engines those ads are distributed across. If you've written articles and newsletters that have been distributed across the Web, the sites that host those might be the referring web sites.

Most analytics packages will track your referring sites. They're then provided in a report that quickly lets you see where your site visitors are coming from. This information allows you to quickly understand if your SEO efforts are paying off. If you know that you have several types of campaigns that should be leading from one site or another, but you don't find one of those sites listed, you know those efforts are not working. All that's left then is to figure out why.

Referring keywords (paid and organic)

Another useful measurement you'll find in most web statistics packages is keyword tracking. Most web statistics packages will track both paid and organic keywords. Which paid keywords are tracked will depend on the stats package you use, but nearly all of them will track organic keywords.

The value of organic keyword tracking is that you can learn how your site is being discovered. The words and phrases that visitors use to find you gives you a good look into the way they think of your business. For example, people won't usually search for "financial services." It's more likely that they'll search for "money market," or "savings account," or even "free checking account." A stats package that tracks these words will help you monitor and analyze the keywords that work for your site, and will help you stay on top of cultural shifts that change the way people think.

Additional statistics

There are a few other statistics you may want to track. These stats will help give you a clearer picture of the traffic to your site, the behaviors of your site visitors, and how those can be correlated by aspects such as location and technical capabilities. Some of the additional stats that you might want to track include:

- Page views
- Unique visitors
- Keywords used by search engine
- Pages viewed
- Location information
- Technological capabilities (web browsers, operating systems, and so on)

Knowing how you can track your SEO results will help you to use all the resources available to you to analyze your results and make changes that can improve your rankings and the accessibility of your web site so that you can increase your sales conversions and profits.

Competitive Analysis

Competitive analysis is a step you should take in the very beginning of your SEO efforts. It should be right at the top of your to-do list, along with keyword analysis and tagging your web site. In fact, you should probably do a competitive analysis even before you begin tagging your site.

But did you know that your competitive analysis doesn't end there? Like analyzing your web statistics, conversions, and other elements of your web site, your competitive analysis should be ongoing. Your competitors will change. They'll learn how to reach a search engine better. They may even change their customer approach just enough to always stay ahead of you. They'll keep you guessing, and the only way to figure out what they're doing that you're not is to spend the time it takes to analyze what they're doing.

As you're going through this analysis process, the first thing to keep in mind is that you're not checking out only your direct competitors. You need to look at those competitors who are ahead of you in search rankings, even if their offerings are different from yours.

Plan to spend a few hours a week on this analysis. You should look at all the sites that are ahead of you, but specifically those sites that rank in the top five to ten position in the SERPs.

You already know what you should be looking for. Look for the same indications that you examined during your original competitive analysis. These include:

- **Site rankings:** Where in the SERPs is the site ranked? Make note, especially, of the top three to five sites.

- **Page saturation:** How many of the competition's pages are indexed? Not every page on a site will be indexed, but if your competition has more or fewer pages ranked, there may be a factor you haven't taken into consideration about how to include or exclude your site pages.

- **Page titles:** Are page titles consistent? And what keywords do they contain, if any at all? How your competition uses titles can give you an indication of what you're doing right or wrong with your own.

- **Meta data:** What meta data is your competition including? How is it worded? And how does it differ from your own? Remember that you can access the source code of a web site by selecting **Source** from the **View** menu of your web browser.

- **Site design:** How is the competition's web site designed? Site architecture and the technology that is used to design and present the site are factors in how your site ranks. Learn what the competition is doing and how that differs from what you're doing.

- **A robots.txt file:** The robots.txt file is accessible to you, and looking at it could give you some valuable insight to how your competition values and works with search engines.

- **Content quality and quantity:** How much quality is included on your competitor's site and is it all original, or is it re-used from some other forum? If a site is ahead of you in search rankings, its content is probably performing better than yours. Analyze it and find out why.

- **Link quality and quantity:** Your competitors' linking strategies could hold a clue about why they rank well. Look at the link structure. If they're using legitimate linking strategies, what are they? If they're not, don't try to follow suit. Their actions will catch up with them soon enough.

CAUTION One thing you should use caution about is copying your competition too closely. Instead use their success as a way to jump start creative ideas for improving your own web site. Some web-site owners will fill the internal workings of their site with bogus keywords, tags, or other elements in an effort to keep the competition from catching up to them. If you follow their practices too closely, you could end up doing more damage than good to your own site.

Maintain your competitive analysis over time. It should be an ongoing activity that helps you stay abreast of how those companies that rank better than you reach those rankings. Examine them closely, and then spend some time finding creative ways to improve your rankings based on what works for the competition.

Conversion Analysis

If you're driving your customers to your site simply to have them visit you, you're wasting your time and efforts. Site traffic alone will not build brand recognition today. There must be other elements of supplying your customers or potential customers with what they need. Of course, what you should be supplying them with will depend on your industry. But even with the differing needs of audiences, there's still a way to measure or value your site visitors.

Your conversions are your ultimate measure of how well your site optimization and design work. And you should constantly be focusing on the conversions that your site drives. Without conversions, you're not making any money. That doesn't mean that conversions all have to be monetarily based, just that they have to fulfill some goal that you have designed for your web site.

There are two types of conversions: revenue conversions and pre-revenue conversions. Revenue conversions are actual sales. A sale is a conversion goal. If you sell anything from your web site, you should have a conversion goal for reaching the end of a sale. That might mean the goal is achieved when a user clicks through to the "Thank You" page or when the order confirmation is displayed. These conversions require the exchange of money for goods or services.

Another type of conversion is the pre-revenue conversion. Pre-revenue conversions are all the other steps in the selling cycle — activities that lead up to the final sale. So, a pre-revenue conversion might be something like having the visitor request additional information about a product or service or sign up for a newsletter that's offered on your site. These are valid conversions that should also be tracked.

The types of conversions remain the same across the life cycle of your web site, but the actual conversions may not. And that's the reason you need to conduct regular conversion analysis. In your conversion analysis, you're looking for a number of things including an increase or decrease in the number or pattern of conversions. Increases and decreases in these trends will help you to know when something is working or when something needs changing.

When you see a changing trend in your conversion rate, you know it's time to begin trying something different. It may be that your products need to be changed, it may be that your newsletter is no longer appealing, or it could simply be that your competition is funneling your audience away from you.

One way to see these trends in your web analytics is to look at your sales cycle. Ideally, you should know your sales cycle even before you put your web site online. The sales cycle is the steps that a user takes to complete a sale. It's usually divided according to the natural progress that visitors make from entering your site to the completed sale.

This natural progression should be trackable with your web metrics program. One report that will be extremely helpful will be a funnel report or sales funnel report. This type of report allows you to set up a sales funnel on your web site and then track the effectiveness. It also shows where your site visitors might fall off in the process of making a purchase. You can then use that information to change and improve elements of your SEO and your web site that might be causing that fall-off.

Conversions are the ultimate goal in all your search marketing efforts. Yes, you want to drive customers to your site, but more than that, you want those customers to *do something*. That something is your conversion and if you analyze the conversion process, you'll be able to track patterns of what works and what doesn't.

Analyzing Server Logs

Web server logs are the records that servers keep of who accesses files (in this case, web sites) that are stored on the server. A server log is a long, ugly, and complicated document in which lots of very usable information is buried. But if you don't know what you're doing, it could take a very long time to figure out what's usable and what's not in that server log.

That's not a huge problem, though. There are all kinds of server log analyzers that you can use to help you decipher the log and find the information that you're looking for. One of the most well-known is AWStats (http://awstats.sourceforge.net/). An example of the Robots/Spider Visitors report is shown in Figure 21-1.

One thing you'll notice about AWStats is that it looks a lot like the web analytics software that you've looked at. That's because it is essentially the same thing. Web analytics software does the same thing that a server log analyzer does. The difference is that server log analyzers sometimes provide more information than basic web analytics applications.

FIGURE 21-1

AWStats reads your server log and provides a graphic representation of the information found there.

Robots/Spiders visitors (Top 10) - Full list - Last visit			
29 different robots*	Hits	Bandwidth	Last visit
MSNBot	4640+865	150.99 MB	21 Aug 2007 - 13:12
Unknown robot (identified by 'bot/' or 'bot-')	2144+4	14.44 MB	06 Aug 2007 - 22:13
Yahoo Slurp	238+122	1.20 MB	21 Aug 2007 - 10:49
Googlebot	172+31	1.51 MB	21 Aug 2007 - 11:55
Speedy Spider	90+25	1.64 MB	20 Aug 2007 - 12:24
MSNBot-media	43+28	867.95 KB	19 Aug 2007 - 18:32
Yahoo! Slurp China	28+28	167.01 KB	20 Aug 2007 - 23:20
Alexa (IA Archiver)	0+51	39.00 KB	18 Aug 2007 - 20:42
Unknown robot (identified by hit on 'robots.txt')	0+31	21.24 KB	21 Aug 2007 - 10:26
Unknown robot (identified by 'crawl')	17+14	621.34 KB	18 Aug 2007 - 01:50
Others	63+97	1.59 MB	

* Robots shown here gave hits or traffic "not viewed" by visitors, so they are not included in other charts. Numbers after + are successful hits on "robots.txt" files.

No matter which solution you choose to use, it's a good idea to use the program to analyze your web site traffic regularly. The reports generated by both types of software will give you insight into what works and what does not on your web site.

Maintaining the analysis of your site, your competition, traffic, conversions, and server logs is one way you can stay on top of your SEO strategy. What you learn from these metrics is how your SEO and search marketing campaigns are performing. And when you know that, you can keep up with any changes that are happening and prepare for future shifts as necessary. In other words, if you're analyzing your successes, you're not left in the dark wondering what happened to your ratings.

Appendices

Appendix A

Optimization for Major Search Engines

I n general, search engine optimization basics are all the same. Each search engine differs in what it's looking for, however. So what makes you rank well with Google might not make you rank well with Yahoo! or MSN.

This is the conundrum with search engines. Each is based on its own proprietary algorithm, and even if all of the major search engines had the same requirements for ranking (and they don't), those requirements could still be ranked differently.

What you must do then is, first, include all the basics of SEO — keyword optimization, meta-tag optimization, link optimization, and content optimization. Then, after the basics are complete, you can begin to worry about individual search engines and what it takes to be ranked in each one.

IN THIS APPENDIX

Optimization for Google

Optimization for MSN

Optimization for Yahoo!

NOTE Remember, a search engine is not your customer. It will lead you to potential customers, so you do need search engine rankings, but you should think first of your own customers and then about your SEO. Be sure your site is what potential or existing customers need, and then you can begin to think about how you can tweak the inner workings of the site to improve your search engine ranking.

Optimization for Google

By this point in the book, you should have a pretty good idea of how Google works, including how your sites are indexed and what you should avoid doing. But there are a few more things to understand about Google and how your site is ranked. These additional tips will help you to improve your rankings.

The first thing you need to understand about Google is that, given time, if your site is on the Web and has at least one link to it, you will eventually be crawled. As an example, I have never done anything with my personal web site by way of SEO. I haven't checked the code to ensure that it's written with search engines in mind. I haven't used or invested in keywords, and I haven't submitted my site to a search engine.

Yet, if you type my name into the Google search engine, my personal web site will be the first result returned. I'm ranked number one for my name, because (presumably) there is only one of me. If someone searches for my name, I'm at the top of the list. And that's good.

But your site is probably going to be much more diverse than mine, so how do you get Google to take notice? Again, be patient. Google will crawl your site in a short period of time (sometimes it takes less than a week). And once your site has been crawled, you can begin the slow climb through the search results.

On my personal site, it took nearly a year to reach the top ranking slot for my site. But I never did anything to boost that rank. It's my personal web site, so I don't put a lot of effort into it. In short, it is what it is, without any type of SEO strategy at all.

If your site is topically related to other sites, however, you probably won't be able to throw your site on the Web and wait for it to be indexed at number one. And although you will be indexed automatically, you'll have to compete for top placement.

Google doesn't sell placement, either. There are ads above and to the right side of the search results, but ads are the only placement that's available for purchase. That means that where your site places is based on your SEO and search marketing efforts.

Understanding Google PageRank

Google's proprietary ranking algorithm is what makes it different from the other search engines. An element of that algorithm is Google PageRank.

Google explains PageRank like this:

"PageRank relies on the uniquely democratic nature of the Web by using its vast link structure as an indicator of an individual page's value. In essence, Google interprets a link from page A to page B as a vote, by page A, for page B. But, Google looks at considerably more than the sheer volume of votes, or links a page receives; for example, it also analyzes the page that casts the vote. Votes cast by pages that are themselves "important" weigh more heavily and help to make other pages "important." Using these and other factors, Google provides its views on pages' relative importance.

Of course, important pages mean nothing to you if they don't match your query. So, Google combines PageRank with sophisticated text-matching techniques to find pages that are both important and relevant to your search.

Google goes far beyond the number of times a term appears on a page and examines dozens of aspects of the page's content (and the content of the pages linking to it) to determine if it's a good match for your query."

In other words, a PageRank is based on a ballot system that compares your site to all the other pages on the Web that are related. The comparison allows the algorithm to determine which pages are most relevant to a search query based on numerous elements of the page. A hyperlink to a page counts as a vote of support. The PageRank of a page is defined recursively, or in comparison to the other pages that Google is also ranking, and depends on the number and PageRank metric of all pages that link to it. A page that is linked to by many pages with high PageRank receives a high rank itself. If there are no links to a web page, there is no support for that page.

Google assigns a numeric weighting for each web page on the Internet; this PageRank denotes your site's importance according to the PageRank algorithm.

CROSS-REF For more information on Google's PageRank algorithm, see the sidebar in Chapter 13 titled, "Understanding Google's PageRank."

So if you want to successfully rank on the Google search engine, you should follow the guidelines that are laid out in Google's Webmaster Central (`http://www.google.com/intl/en/webmasters/`). There is also a set of tools available in Webmaster Central that allows you to analyze and add to your site to help make it more Google-friendly. Those tools include the following:.

- **Site Status Wizard:** Determines if your site is currently being indexed by Google.

- **Webmaster Tools:** This is a set of tools designed to help you improve the indexing and ranking of your site. You can also find the Google Sitemap Generator here.

- **Content Submission Tools:** Use these to submit your site to Google, or to add products to Google Base or content to Google Book Search.

- **Google's Webmaster Blog:** Find tips and strategies for ranking well in Google on this blog. You'll also find changes to the Google algorithm and other information that you'll need to stay on top of your site rankings.

- **Webmaster Discussion Groups:** Talk to others about what they're doing to improve their Google rankings.

- **Webmaster Help Center:** If you don't understand something about Webmaster Central, here's where you'll find an explanation.

Ultimately, if you follow the guidelines laid out in the early parts of this book, and design your pages for people, not search engines, you'll rank well in Google. You may need to tweak some of the inner workings of your site — keywords, links, meta tags — and you'll need to be patient. But given time, your ranking with Google will occur naturally. Then all you have to do is continue improving your offerings for customers and stay on top of maintaining your site, and you should see your ranking climb gradually.

Optimization for MSN

MSN is now powered by Microsoft Live, and although you can go to the MSN.com web page and still access MSN search capabilities, the underlying technology has been rebranded as Microsoft Live. But it's still one of the top three search engines, and it's definitely not one that you should ignore. Studies have shown that searchers who enter your site from MSN searches may be fewer in number than those from other search engines, but they routinely have higher conversion rates.

As with other search engines, the basic optimization techniques that you've learned are the best way to get listed with MSN search. MSN also does not allow paid ranking, so your organic efforts will be the deciding factor for your rankings.

The one difference with MSN is that this search engine puts more emphasis on the freshness of content than other search engines. Specifically, sites that update high-quality, relative content on a regular basis have a better chance of ranking high with MSN. So if you have not yet implemented a content strategy, and if you want to rank well with MSN, you should plan and implement that strategy.

MSN, like Google, indexes pages according to a proprietary algorithm. And like Google, MSN (or more accurately, Microsoft Live) has a set of guidelines that you should follow if you would like your site to rank well. Those guidelines can be found by going to MSN or Microsoft Live and using the search string: Site Owner Help. The guidelines that you're seeking should return as the top search result.

MSN also looks at your meta description tags, and the title tags on your pages. So pay close attention to creating the most useful and relevant tags you can. Also include keywords and important information as near the top of each of your pages as possible.

Over time it's certain that the MSN brand will be folded into and eventually replaced by Microsoft Live Search. Branding is likely to be the only thing that changes when this happens. MSN had long used Microsoft technology (MSN, after all, *does* stand for Microsoft Network). This means that your SEO efforts will remain viable even as the MSN/Microsoft Live rebranding takes place.

Optimization for Yahoo!

Every search engine differs a little bit from the others, and Yahoo! is no exception. Where Google focuses on elements like relevance of content and links, and MSN focuses on freshness of content and the tags on your site, Yahoo! is more focused on keyword density and keywords in the URL and title tags.

So if you've used basic SEO techniques, you'll likely be listed with Yahoo! in a matter of time. Your rank on Yahoo! will depend on competition, of course. So you'll need to focus carefully on the keywords that you select if your industry is a highly competitive one. Just be careful, because using a higher density of keywords so you'll rank well in Yahoo! could cause you problems with MSN and Google. It could look to those search engines as if you're stuffing your site with keywords.

The Yahoo! Search Crawler

The Yahoo! search crawler is called SLURP, and it will rank your page based first on your keyword density. The optimum keywords density according to Yahoo! is:

- **Title tag — 15 percent to 20 percent:** Yahoo displays the title tag content in its result page. Therefore, write the title as a readable sentence. A catchy title will attract the reader to your web site.

- **Body text — 3 percent:** Boldfacing the keywords sometimes boosts the page's ranking. But be careful not to overdo it. Too much boldfaced content irritates readers.

- **Meta tags — 3 percent:** The meta description and keyword tags provide important keywords at the beginning of your web page. Just be careful not to use the keywords repeatedly in the keyword tag, because Yahoo! may consider that practice spam. Write the description tag as a readable sentence.

Yahoo! also looks at the inbound links to your site. And of course, there are other factors SLURP looks at while it's crawling your site.

Even when you're optimizing for three (or 15) different search engines, there are a few basic optimization strategies that are essential and relevant for all of them. Rather than focusing on all of the differences and stressing yourself out, focus on all of the actions that are similar for each search engine, and then think of how you could change or improve your site so that it will be the most relevant, and the most locatable, for your potential visitors.

Put customers and visitors first, and your search engine rankings should follow naturally.

Appendix B

Industry Interviews

The SEO industry, like any other technology arena, is full of people who have differing views on what works and what doesn't. There are always a few things that everyone agrees on, though.

The folks actually working in the field are the ones who know where theory and application diverge to create a workable solution. They can tell you what strategies are sure to be successful and which ones are sure to flop.

If you're working in SEO or search marketing of any form, you probably have questions you'd love to pose to someone who's been working in the industry for a while. The interviews in this section give you that opportunity — with me, Jerri Ledford, acting as your rep.

Here you'll find 16 interviews with people across the SEO industry. These are the people in the trenches, who are faced each day with implementing SEO either for themselves or for other organizations.

They understand your challenges — from budget to manpower — and they've faced the same decisions about SEO that you have. In these interviews, they share their advice with you. They offer their best tips, and their opinions about what works, what doesn't, and what's coming.

Eric Bloomfield, Vice President of Client Service & Technology, SendTraffic

Eric Bloomfield has been with SendTraffic for more than three years. During that time, Bloomfield has managed all the technological capabilities surrounding SendTraffic's SEO and SEM offerings.

SendTraffic was founded in 1999. It's an online marketing firm specializing in Search Engine Marketing and Optimization, Lead Generation, and Targeted Vertical Marketing. In addition to SEM and SEO offerings, SendTraffic also provides Paid Inclusion and Feed Management, Website Analytics, and Phone Sales Analytics.

Jerri: What do you see as the current state of SEO?

Bloomfield: It's always changing. And it requires that you just stay on the top of your game all the time. With the ever-changing algorithms that Google and Yahoo! use, they can change it on a dime. You have to stay on top of it. We hear stories all the time about Google changing their algorithm and then companies lose 80 percent of their business. We try to stay current. You have to stay ahead of the changes and that's accomplished through best practices.

Jerri: How valuable is vertical SEO?

Bloomfield: I think vertical search is just the way everything needs to go. One of the most effective SEO strategies that you can employ is knowing your vertical and knowing where it's going. For example, we deal with insurance so I know everything there is to know about insurance. I research the trends and pay attention to the news. But if I knew nothing about these things, then there are SEO strategies that I would do differently. Knowing your vertical very well and knowing what works in the vertical makes it possible for you to do better with your SEO efforts.

It really all starts with the keywords and knowing what keywords work for your industry. Then try to beef up the content and make sure you're included in the right directories in the industry. Then those keywords will pull more weight in a vertical search engine than with other general search engines. Your site is going to get weighed more heavily than if you're in general.

If you're just doing general linking and not doing things within your vertical, then you're not doing as well as you could be doing. We also stay on top of it, so we have content that's right for that vertical. And we often make sure that we're pushing the content out to them. But we need to generate it. There are other companies that have the content and just need for us to tell them what to do with it.

Jerri: How is vertical SEO or search marketing different from general SEO?

Bloomfield: I actually haven't dealt with anything that's not vertical SEO. Everyone has to target according to their market. Even in dealing with Yahoo! you're targeting one of the different verticals within Yahoo!. If you're targeting general SEO, you're going to spend a lot of money and you're not going to get much. Almost everything you do is highly targeted and vertical.

I haven't really had a case where someone came to me and said "I need everything." It's really a case of "here are my targets, here's what I need, and here's how I'm going to get it."

Jerri: What tips would you give an organization just going into SEO?

Bloomfield: You've got to have control of your web site. One of the big issues is that everyone has good plans, but they don't have the ability to carry out those plans. Determine what your approach is. Focus on what you can change and what you can't change.

Know about what pages you're dealing with and what you should change and what you shouldn't. I'll say, "Here are my pages, I'm really concerned with how the search engines see them and how customers see them." Then I just need to have a good strategy for creating and deploying content and then stick with it. I have to have a good plan on how I can continually add these pages and keep my content fresh.

It's so important that you have a plan in place to keep this going, because you spend all that money and if you don't keep up with it you'll have spent that money for nothing.

Jerri: Is there anything else about SEO that you think might be important for my readers to know?

Bloomfield: It's tough. For an SEO it's about staying current, because it's such a changing field. There's always a need to stay on top of search engine trends. It's about staying ahead of that curve and making sure that whatever changes the search engines make, you are able to make changes very quickly, too. It's having ability to make changes in a continuously changing environment.

Jessica Bowman, Director of SEO, Business.com

Jessica Bowman is the director of SEO for Business.com and does independent consulting. She relishes the human side of SEO, the art of SEO — getting people to do what you need to be done.

Bowman has managed search engine optimization for up to seven different divisions across the North America and Europe, in five different languages. Her diverse experience in project management, web-site usability, and process analysis has given her unique insight into working with IT to get things accomplished — one of the biggest challenges for in-house search marketers.

Business.com is the leading business-to-business search engine, directory, and pay-per-click advertising network. Business.com helps business decision makers quickly find what they need in order to manage and grow their businesses, and enables advertisers to reach them across the business Internet through premier partners, including the *Wall Street Journal Online*, *Forbes*, *BusinessWeek*, *Hoovers*, and more.

Jerri: How does having your search marketing in-house differ from hiring someone to help you with your search marketing strategies?

Bowman: The overarching tactics that need to be executed are the same for both search marketing in-house and outsourced.

The key differences are:

- The innovativeness of your strategy due to differences in experience/knowledge of doing your search marketing. Many in-house search marketers fell into their role and/or are fairly new to the world of search marketing. Their challenge is to compete in the SERPs with competitors who have hired a more experienced search marketing person or agency.

- When bringing search marketing in-house with dedicated resources, you now have someone there 40 hours a week, in the halls and at meetings, who is able to represent and champion search marketing, keep it top-of-mind and high in the priority list. In contrast, when you hire an agency, then the selling of search marketing changes is left to someone who has other things on their plate.

Jerri: Is there anything about search marketing that's more difficult when you're doing it in-house?

Bowman: Yes, you're busy in meetings! When you're in-house, there is a lot of networking and schmoozing that has to happen to get and keep search marketing efforts a high priority and not removed from projects. Just because you know what needs to be done to boost your organic rankings does not mean it's easy to implement — there are priorities, politics, and red tape that must be overcome, and some people are just resistant to the changes needed for search marketing. It is a challenge to be the person in meetings, networking and schmoozing, and also the person who has to execute the search marketing tactics. It can be done, it is just challenging.

The second thing is that some companies (or even particular individuals/departments within a company) seem to give more trust in what a consultant says versus what an employee says. Any in-house search marketer could give you examples of how they pitched changes again and again and received opposition; however, once a consultant recommended that same change, it suddenly became a wonderful idea that is technically feasible. This is one of the reasons that I recommend in-house search marketers have an SEO consultant available for outside counsel.

Lastly, when your rankings drop, or traffic decreases, you don't typically have other sites that you can compare with to see if they saw something similar. Whereas when you work with an agency they work with many clients and can compare you with a number of sites to see if there was a big change in the formula that affected many companies, or it is something that specifically affected you.

Jerri: Do you ever work with outsourcers on parts of your search marketing?

Bowman: Yes. I love to outsource portions of a project. I have a short list of preferred vendors for keyword research, directory submissions, troubleshooting, copywriting, site audits, question and answer, code reviews, and there is even one someone I use to keep me up to speed on industry news when I get extra busy.

Jerri: What suggestions would you make for organizations that are considering bringing their search marketing in-house?

Bowman:

- Know what you're getting into. There are many ways to bring search marketing in-house and structure the team, tactics, etc. Search marketing in-house will not likely reach its fullest potential if your in-house search marketer is also allocated on other things. You typically spend about 80 percent of your time selling SEO and 20 percent actually doing SEO work. Also, bear in mind that, while the agency you hired only worked 20 hours per week, outside of your billable hours the consultants kept up with trends and news outside of that 20 hours. Also they live and breathe search marketing all day, making them far more productive than a typically isolated in-house search marketer. Also, your outside consultant wasn't responsible for getting the changes through the IT department.

- Budget for outside counsel, a more experienced consultant to reach out to when you have questions.

- Make it a priority to attend search marketing conferences, at least two conferences per year. When you're in-house you tend to lose perspective and put on your "corporate-tinted glasses." Conferences bring you back to the search marketing reality and keep you grounded.

Jerri: Is there anything particular that an organization should avoid if it's managing its search marketing in-house?

Bowman: Don't work in isolation. It's very easy to get so caught up in busy work that you lose touch with changes in the industry. At one time cloaking was accepted, now it can get you banned. Just last year buying links worked, now Google penalizes when they know a site is buying links (and they have asked people to report it).

Don't get so busy that you don't have time to stay abreast of the industry happenings and continuously expand your knowledge. I now have the expectation that I will spend two hours a day reading about the industry — while no one else on my in-house team spends this much time, your most senior search marketer should.

Jerri: What changes do you see coming that will affect the way organizations use search marketing in the future?

Bowman:

1. Brand Protection and Management. Search engines are where people go for information about a company, product, service, or an answer to their question. They use search engines like a question-and-answer machine. Search engines display a wide variety of sources of information for users, some of it favorable, and some of it unfavorable. In coming years companies (e.g., PR departments) will finally catch on that there are things you can do to influence the search results just as there are things you can do to influence the media in the offline world. You just go about it in a completely different manner, but the goal and results are similar.

2. Videos. Google now displays highly relevant videos in their regular search results. This means that companies have the opportunity to have a video in front of Google users, displayed as an image — a rare and highly valuable commodity in the Google SERPs. It's an eye grabber and will give your company far more visibility than any other company on the search results page — even if you aren't listed in position one. We are already starting to see search marketers dabble in videos more than ever before. In the next few years companies will get more involved, offering useful interviews, how-tos, and entertaining videos for their target audiences. The risk for the late adopters is that by the time they join the online video market, online videos will be quite mature and there will be little room for error without receiving public criticism. The benefit of being an early adopter is that everyone is still trying to figure out what is successful; therefore errors are more acceptable.

Jerri: What kind of changes will these trends require for in-house search marketing?

Bowman: They need to adopt and get involved in new media — social media and online videos for sites like YouTube.com.

It's funny, back in the early days of SEO large companies weren't on the bandwagon and small businesses could easily overtake larger businesses in the search results. Now larger companies have caught on, and it's now more difficult for the smaller businesses to outrank larger businesses for many search terms. Social media today is like SEO in the early days — large companies aren't on the bandwagon. There are far more risks and challenges that prevent big companies from going in this direction. For large companies, doing nothing seems like less of a risk than diving in and risking a backfire or no

ROI. What they don't realize is now is the time to backfire. It's going to be more acceptable to mess up now than it will be in five years when they're ready to start getting involved.

Jerri: Is there anything else you think might be important for organizations to understand about in-house search marketing?

Bowman:

- My biggest advice is for the same for any company. Search marketing is not a project. It is like marketing and public relations, it never ends. Once you get high rankings, you need to maintain your high rankings. And in order to continue growing your search marketing traffic, you need to go after new opportunities (new niche phrases, video optimization, local search, brand protection, etc).

- Know the in-house life cycle.

- Understand that just because you build the team, it does not mean high rankings and traffic increases will come. Your in-house search marketer needs to work with many people and several departments to get search marketing changes out the door, and they are competing with many other high profile projects for resources and priority. If the changes don't launch, you are not going to meet your goals. I find that management is on-board with SEO; it is the lower level managers and technical leads that have opposition and cause delays in launching changes.

- Just because you bring search marketing in-house, it does NOT mean your outsourcing days are over. Search marketing in-house is like an on-staff corporate attorney — there are times when you will need to reach to outside counsel for sound advice.

The in-house lifecycle as defined by Jessica Bowman.

Source: SEMinhouse.com

Brian Combs, Founder and VP of Services, Apogee Search

As an online marketing expert and Internet pioneer, Brian Combs specializes in bringing measurability to marketing. Before founding Apogee Search with William Leake in 2002, Combs was director of marketing and business development for Journyx, the leading provider of web-based time- and expense-management solutions. At Journyx, he oversaw all marketing and strategic partnership activities.

Since 2004, Apogee has grown to become one of the 20 largest SEO/PPC firms in the country, with clients in the hundreds. The company has achieved top Google rankings for clients on horrendously competitive keywords with high search volumes in spaces like consumer and auto finance, home security, consumer-packaged software, online education, and insurance-type products.

Jerri: Where do you see the current state/importance of SEO?

Combs: The industry is still in the "Wild West" stage, but beginning to mature. As the ROI of SEO is difficult to track (although not impossible), many SEO firms (and individual SEOs) are able to get away with providing the appearance of value, while providing very little actual value.

SEO, of course, can be a very effective marketing technique, but like all marketing, efforts must be made to track the results so that improvements can be made.

Jerri: What can organizations do right now to improve their SEO?

Combs:

- Install a tracking system. Find out what actually works.
- Run a PPC campaign for 30 days to prove which keywords matter. Optimizing for keywords with no search volume will not provide any benefit.
- Put those keywords as the FIRST thing in their title tags.
- Start link building.

Jerri: What should they be focusing on for future improvements?

Combs:

- Better content.
- Create compelling "link bait."
- Continue link building.
- Invest more in a keyword selection testing campaign (PPC).

- If you're trying to master hundreds to thousands of keywords, work with the content management system to programmatically automate much of the content-driven SEO (e.g., dynamically populating title tags with database-provided keywords).
- Stay on top of, and take advantage of, emerging trends in social media.

Jerri: Are there any strategies that organizations might know about but are not implementing that might help with SEO results if they did?

Combs: So many organizations believe that the content part of SEO means generating page after page of keyword-stuffed copy. People should focus on creating copy for a web site's visitors, not the search engines. Use one's keywords in the copy, but use them naturally.

Concentrate on regularly creating new, quality content for your web site. This will help both with SEO, and with building the traffic of your site.

Jerri: What is one facet of SEO that most small and mid-sized business don't do well, and how can they improve that?

Combs: There are two facets:

1. How they choose keywords (don't do it on visibility metrics, don't do it based on industry-speak).
2. Lack of link building (SMBs typically have even less in the way of trust rank or link infrastructure with which to work than the big dogs; therefore link building is even more important to them).

Jerri: What changes in SEO are coming as the result of the growth of social media?

Combs: Social media provide a tremendous extension of ability to create and rapidly promote link bait, including new sources of links. These new link sources can also be great sources of native traffic and potentially cause huge changes in the *way we search*, and thus a potential threat to the Google hegemony.

Jerri: Are there any other coming changes that will affect SEO?

Combs:

- Mobile and local advertising.
- Video content.
- Google's never-ending thirst for new revenues, and dislike of the SEO industry (a change agent).

Jerri: Is there anything I haven't touched on that might be important for small to mid-sized organizations to know about SEO?

Combs: Most "SEO experts" are no more SEO experts than the organization they work for. Much can be self-achieved with proper research. This industry is enough of a snake pit of vipers, that it really does pay to do a bunch of research yourself (and even potentially some of the work yourself) before you buy from a vendor. Bad SEO can really really hurt you, and cause you to lose multiple years of marketplace momentum.

Lastly, make sure you focus on the real results. Rankings alone don't pay the bills. In most cases, neither does web traffic. Track and analyze the results of your SEO efforts, making sure that you are increasing leads and/or sales.

Rhea Drysdale, Internet Marketing Manager, MPS Group

Rhea Drysdale is the Internet Marketing Manager for MPS Group, a Fortune 1000 staffing and consulting company. She's also an associate editor for Loren Baker's *Search Engine Journal* and the co-founder of a local SEM association.

MPS Group is a leading provider of staffing, consulting, and solutions in the disciplines of information technology, finance and accounting, law, engineering, and healthcare. MPS Group delivers its services to government entities and businesses in virtually all industries throughout the United States, Canada, the United Kingdom, and Europe. A Fortune 1000 company with headquarters in Jacksonville, Florida, MPS Group trades on the New York Stock Exchange.

Jerri: What do you see as the current state of SEO?

Drysdale: The current state of SEO…I think that SEO is experiencing a major evolution with the recent universal search update on Google and new Ask.com user interface changes. However, it's still in its infancy compared to other forms of marketing. With that in mind, I think marketers are still trying to figure out what they can do with it. And unfortunately, the "rules" for SEO change on a daily basis, which makes it difficult to keep up with those changes and provide formal education in a classroom setting.

As search engines evolve, I'm really interested in seeing how search behavior changes accordingly. I think users are going to get smarter about how they search, which will challenge marketers to be more savvy in the methods they use to reach those users.

Jerri: What are companies doing well in SEO?

Drysdale: At this moment I think the experienced companies are doing an excellent job of tracking results and justifying the SEO return, something that hasn't been easy in the past. As an in-house SEO, my biggest challenge is educating companies on an invisible marketing technique. Even if the return is less, most companies would prefer to spend their ad budgets on a banner ad than SEO. There's something sticky about visuals whereas SEO feels a bit like smoke and mirrors to those that aren't intimately familiar with it. So companies that are able to translate results and track return are rising to the top, while the more money-hungry spammers are crumbling. This is great for both the SEO reputation and companies seeking quality campaigns.

Jerri: What are some of MPS's challenges and successes in SEO?

Drysdale: With my background in e-commerce, the biggest personal challenge has been tracking leads, which requires human interaction to document return. Previously, I could tie my efforts to specific dollars, but now, the source is much more difficult to discern.

As for successes, I think MPS does an excellent job of bringing new acquisitions up to certain standards of design, usability, and optimization. From there we work with them to develop a marketing approach they can easily maintain that targets opportunities best suited to their business model.

I think that's the key. A lot of companies like the concept of SEO, but they don't have the infrastructure to support it and it fizzles out over time. You have to have a unique approach with every company or client to see phenomenal success. Some will do better with a certain strategy than others, since certain target markets just aren't going to be receptive to different techniques. It's a matter of understanding your customers — how they search and how they think, what words do they use when they search? What phase of the buying or information gathering cycle are they in when they get to your site? And once you understand the customer, it's much easier to reach them.

Jerri: What kind of changes to you think that social media are going to have on SEO?

Drysdale: With recent updates on Google and Ask, I think it's more apparent than ever before that certain industries need to make a concerted effort to be everywhere! This means developing videos, blogs, generating news articles, and having a presence on social networks. When we talk about social media, most people think about MySpace and Facebook, but there are hundreds of specific niche networks that are worth marketers' attention. For example, Café Mom and Stylehive are terrific networks for the beauty and fashion industry. Would you rather spend thousands on poorly targeted MySpace ads or hundreds on a highly targeted presence that will generate much greater conversions?

If marketers can start a conversation on those networks, beyond ads, the return is even greater. They will naturally build a following, which will in turn produce qualified backlinks and content. The SEO implications are huge if social media campaigns can be successfully implemented and maintained.

Jerri: How important do you think that vertical markets will be in the future?

Drysdale: I don't see them going anywhere if that's what you mean. Verticals offer a more targeted method of finding information. So I think people will use them, and they will continue to grow. I know that Google is trying to organize all of the world's information, but ultimately, if users can narrow their search right from the start, they will, and verticals make that possible.

A quick side note, Google's reliance on backlinks for rankings limits them when it comes to highly relevant, recent web content. The universal search update should allow for postings of recent news and blog articles, but if I'm looking for something specific that's just a few weeks old, more often than not I have to resort to creative search behavior or verticals to find the information. So, until Google or the other engines can account for new content, I see verticals maintaining or increasing in popularity.

Jerri: What other trends do you think will affect SEO over the next 18–24 months?

Drysdale: I'm a little concerned about personalized search but not immensely so. I think it's still in its infancy and the search engines are dabbling in it to see what they can do. It's a little disconcerting as a marketer, because I can't tell how the search results differ for a user in Montpelier, Vermont, versus San Jose, California, or even in my own city if they have radically different search behavior from other users. From an SEO standpoint, you can't tell where traffic comes from and how it reaches you, which makes it difficult to track changes. I'm all about the numbers and if I can't see the numbers I feel like I'm flying blind, which is never a good thing.

As for universal search and the compartmentalized UI at Ask.com, I'm very interested in how this will affect search behavior and interaction with the results pages. I was really amazed by a recent eye-tracking study from Gord Hotchkiss of Enquiro who found that the "golden triangle" is broken as images are introduced. This sounds somewhat obvious, but the implications on paid search and emphasis of top position natural rankings might be less intense as marketers discover where users are clicking.

I'm also interested in seeing the evolution of "link bait" and bloggers. I think the time and knowledge involved in implementing a high quality viral marketing campaign will leave many marketers scratching their heads. As for bloggers, their credibility is often called into question, but more importantly, the amount of noise on the Web is unbearable. I'm hoping that over time we see a decline in the number of bloggers and an increase in their quality.

With both bloggers and viral marketing, I think that companies that embrace these campaigns early on will do much better in the long run than those that wait for a proven return and "safe" approach.

Paul Dyer, Senior Account Executive, Marketwire

Paul Dyer is an expert in SEO and other advanced Web technologies. As Marketwire's new-media specialist, Dyer brings a breadth of technical knowledge and field experience in social media, search engine optimization, web design, and Web 2.0 product development. He is a frequent speaker on SEO and public relations for social media, having recently presented at *Bulldog Reporter's* PR University, PRSA Los Angeles, a national PRSA teleseminar, the University of Southern California Annenberg School for Communication, the PR Online Convergence Conference, and as part of a professional development series for several top-100 PR firms.

Marketwire is a full-service partner to IR, PR, and MarCom professionals seeking premier distribution, media management, multimedia, and monitoring solutions. Marketwire's corporate philosophy focuses on infusing its business with the following core attributes: precision, adaptability, innovation, and simplicity. The company delivers its clients' news to the world's media and financial communities.

Marketwire also offers innovative products and services — including social media, search engine optimization, dashboard mobile financial, news dashboard coverage reports, exclusive access to networks such as the Canadian Press Wire Network, Easy IR and Easy PR workflow solutions.

Jerri: How are social media changing the way organizations reach their customers on the Web?

Dyer: In the Web 1.0 world, organizations built a web page that had information about themselves, their purpose, their product, or whatever information they wanted to convey to their customers. For the savvier organizations, there was a halfway point between Web 1.0 and Web 2.0 in which search engine optimization of the organization's main web page took priority for reaching their customers online. Now in Web 2.0, with social media, organizations have a plethora of online forums where they can reach their customers. Places like YouTube, MySpace, Flickr, Digg, and Facebook are carrying the flag for social media, but niche communities and social sites are popping up almost daily. These sites are dramatically changing online communications from being primarily "pull" communications (trying to pull your customers through the search engines) to a push/pull combination that previously never existed. Organizations can now push their message through these communities, as well as pull their customers who are conducting keyword and tag-based searches. In the search engines, organizations are also finding these social media sites do half the SEO work for them. Sites like YouTube and MySpace have such high volume of traffic and backward links, they can achieve strong search rankings — normally much stronger than small or startup companies with little resources. All companies have to do is target their content in these communities for the keywords they want a search engine presence for.

Jerri: And how will that shift in communication affect SEO?

Dyer: Traditional SEO focuses on driving search engine traffic to a corporate page. With social media, SEO can apply to any number of other sites, but the purpose is to build not just a web site, but a web PRESENCE. This is accomplished by syndicating content in a plethora of web destinations — blogs, social networks, social bookmarks, image and video galleries, and more. By syndicating keyword-rich content in these destinations, organizations can cast a much wider net with their message and maybe even spark that ever-illusive dialogue with their key audiences.

Jerri: What aspects of SEO should small and medium-sized businesses focus on most closely at this time?

Dyer: First things first — small companies need to be strategic about the keywords they go after. With SEO and online advertising budgets creeping ever higher, few small companies have the resources to compete for keywords that have monthly search volume in the millions. Instead, small companies should focus their efforts on a few highly specific search terms for which users will definitely be interested in their company's content. At that point, organic SEO for these key terms becomes critical, and SEO releases are a great first line of attack. SEO releases have been available for several years now, but still remain one of the strongest ways for small companies to receive valuable and highly ranked links from pages on which they control the content.

Jerri: What upcoming SEO technologies and strategies should these organizations begin to focus on?

Dyer: There are a number of up-and-coming technologies, but I will focus specifically on SEO releases, as that is where my real expertise lies. A properly conceived SEO release can be a powerful tool for driving traffic to your site and increasing your site's search ranking. The best strategy is to craft a release for every key term that is central to your business. This release should be written specifically for that key term and include it in positions of prominence like the headline, meta tags, and first paragraph. It should also use the term in a high keyword density — 2 percent or higher. This term can then be hyperlinked to a key-term-specific landing page on the company's web site. For instance, linking Product A as a key term to the landing page for Product A. Doing this alone will increase the backward links and the keyword relevance of your site for this term. To take the campaign to the next level, companies can then distribute a second release that is targeted for the very same key term. For this release, in addition to linking the term to a specific landing page, it can also be linked to the original press release at the distributor's web site (on Marketwire.com for instance). Doing so will drive the original press release up the search rankings for that term as well as your company site and allow you to hold down more than one position in the search engines.

Jerri: What's the most frequently missed aspect of SEO for social media?

Dyer: The most frequently missed aspect is strategy. Many companies are dipping their toe into the social-media pool, but few are doing so strategically. Instead, companies are doing what I like to call "Throwing Hail Mary's." They are posting videos into YouTube, building MySpace pages, uploading image galleries to Flickr, and getting involved in the blogosphere, but they are doing so blindly and without any continuity. Success in social media and the way to achieve strong search results comes through regularly updating content and creating a web of information. If you have keyword-rich content in social sites, you will achieve strong search results by networking (linking) that content together. There has to be a strategic and continuous connection between all of your company's social efforts.

Jerri: What's the most important aspect of SEO for social media?

Dyer: The most important aspect of SEO for social media is syndication. This means making sure all of the regularly updated content on your corporate site as well as the social sites you participate in is available via RSS and linked together to form an online network that encompasses your organization's total web presence. Not only will this build readership and relationships in these communities, the RSS feeds will have a positive impact on the search rankings of all your various locations with content.

Jerri: Do you have any specific message for readers about social media and how they will affect SEO now and in the future?

Dyer: The most important thing for people to realize is that social media represent a fundamental shift in the way people meet, communicate, and interact. It is not a passing trend or a "here today, gone tomorrow" fad. Like e-mail and the mobile phone before it, social media is a new conduit through which people communicate.

Miki Dzugan, President, Rapport Online Inc.

Miki Dzugan believes that online marketing efforts should produce positive bottom-line results. That comes from many years of general management experience. Dzugan brings more than 30 years of experience in the fields of manufacturing, software development, computer hardware marketing and sales, computer software consulting, property management, education, and hospitality management into her position as president at Rapport. Her varied background enables her to quickly grasp the management goals of companies, and then define ways for them to integrate the use of the Internet into their marketing communications functions.

Rapport Online Inc was founded as an outgrowth of many years of Internet marketing and website development experience. Building rapport aptly describes the power that Internet communications tools bring to doing business.

Rapport encompasses "branding" and believes that branding online is not achieved through advertising, but rather through experience and "buzz." Rapport stresses direct communication and harmony in its environment, and strives to provide these to its customers.

Jerri: What do you see as the current state of SEO?

Dzugan: For many SEO experts, the SEO/search engine relationship is a game of chess, us vs. them. They try to game the search engine to get their client to the top of the heap by taking advantage of what they can understand of the search engine algorithms. This may be done without respect to whether the site really belongs at the top of results. In other words, the search engine has the objective to produce the most useful result for the searcher and the SEO is working to push his/her client in the searcher's face.

SEOs that work against the best interest of the search engine are killing the golden goose. If the search engine does not produce good results, it will not be used.

Working with the best interest of search engines and searchers as well as our clients produces lasting results. Sites that are optimized to rank high in results where they provide the best value are not as vulnerable to changes in search algorithms. Clients that were optimized years ago still retain high position in results even for quite competitive search terms.

You will find SEO divided into black hat and white hat with a big gray area that the experts debate. My thought is that if you are helping search engines to serve the searchers well, you are behaving ethically and effectively in the long term.

Jerri: What do you mean by helping the search engine serve searchers well? Are there specific activities that organizations should be doing?

Dzugan: The worst case of *not* serving the searchers well is to optimize a porn site to come up on top for a search for "candy land" for example. This kind of abuse is really hard to get past search engines now. It is easier to identify activities that organizations should not be doing — there is a whole list of spamming activities that can still sometimes succeed, temporarily. Organizations should stake out their keywords carefully and aim for those that are realistically achievable. For example, a web site selling shoes has a better chance of achieving top results on a phrase, such as "women narrow shoes" or "child sport shoes" than if they go after "shoe" and "shoes."

As part of this method of SEO I stumbled upon the concept of branding through search results. I'm beginning to hear more of this idea in industry discussions. I think this will be the next big thing in SEO.

Jerri: Explain how branding through search results works.

Dzugan: We use the kind of narrowing of keywords described above to reinforce our client's brand. For example, my own company, Rapport Online, is very small, and how do you compete on keywords like "search engine optimization" without a staff member to work on that full time? We are staking out the concept of building rapport as the online marketing approach. Our site ranks on the first page of Google results for "keyword ad calculator" and other more specific phrases that relate to a cost-per-customer-acquired approach to online marketing.

Jerri: What strategies should companies be using to create their brand in search results?

Dzugan:

- Stake out the desired keywords.
- Use pay-per-click advertising to get your sales pitch across.
- Optimize top-level pages for the desired brand keywords.
- Get linked in to the most popular and industry-related directories, using the brand concepts in the description.

And are there some branding opportunities that are better than others?

Certainly, less competitive brand concepts and more differentiating concepts are better. Our client Powder Technology, Inc., produces test dust for testing of engines, filters, etc. We have staked out the keyword "test dust" (not as easy as it sounds) and if you search on that keyword in Google you see that they pretty much own the top of the first page of results.

Niche brand concepts are easier opportunities than more general concepts, such as "best shoes" but, if you can pull it off, the more general concept will get much more traffic because more people will be using it in search. Just remember that if you are promoting your product as the "best" and it is inferior, you undermine consumer confidence in your company and the search engine that was used.

Jerri: What are the coming trends that you see affecting search engines over the next 12–18 months?

Dzugan: Ask Google. People have been waiting for mobile search to take off and maybe that will finally happen. It is hard with the small screen to effectively browse the net — it's a whole different animal.

Google is working on personalized search, but I'm not keen on that concept, because I don't really think the desired search result can be effectively predicted on past searches — not if you use search for a variety of reasons.

Jerri: Is there anything else you think is important for readers to understand about SEO?

Dzugan: SEO is still a buyer-beware industry. When considering SEO assistance, don't fall for the slick presentation or guarantee. Get references. And never buy from a company that approaches you through unsolicited e-mail.

Rand Fishkin, CEO and Co-Founder, SEOmoz

Rand Fishkin has been involved with Internet technologies for almost 15 years. He began working with a company called Marketlink International and eventually moved to a web-development startup firm with Gillian (who happens to be his mother). Since coming together, Gillian and Rand have changed the model of their business, to arrive at the current iteration of SEOmoz.

SEOmoz provides companies around the world with consulting, Internet marketing, and search engine optimization services. Some of its clients include AllBusiness, Benchmark Capital, Drivl, National Public Radio, and Shoe-Store.net. Rand and SEOmoz are well-respected names in the SEO industry. You may have seen Rand at an SEO conference if you've attended one in the last few years. Even if you didn't know his face, you should be able to pick him out. He's the one wearing yellow Pumas.

Jerri: What do you see as the state of the SEO industry today?

Rand: That pretty broad. From a growth standpoint, I think the industry is positive. It continues to grow at a steady pace.

From a maturity standing, I think we still have a long way to go. There's been a lot of bad press, bad companies, and snake-oil salesmen that need to be dealt with. And a lot of companies get caught up in bad contracts. The industry is still very young, and we have a long way to go before it becomes mature.

Jerri: What's the difference between SEO and search marketing?

Rand: Technically speaking, SEO always leans toward the organic side of search marketing — it doesn't include paid services. Search marketing as a whole is anything that you do to market your web sites through search.

Jerri: So how is social media marketing different from SEO?

Rand: Social media marketing refers to a couple of big techniques. The first is viral-content creation and promotion. There has always been some form of viral content; however, the appearance of portals like NetScape, Spin, and others has enabled social media to spread like never before.

An example of how this has changed would be the linking structure of a blog. A blog post goes out, people link to it, those links are spread and before you know, the post is linking to thousands of other web sites. It's one of the ways that you can use to grow a link structure very quickly.

The second side of social media marketing is social network marketing and reputation management. There are more ways available now for companies to grow their reputation. You need to have a presence on sites like Facebook, LinkedIn, and MySpace. It's brand marketing — you can build and share your brand over the Web.

Jerri: How can organizations use social media to improve their business?

Rand: First, you have to have a great deal of familiarity with the space. You have to have a deep understanding of the community, and you have to become part of the community, sharing content, creating content, tagging content, and interacting with other people in the community. If you aren't familiar with this space or you don't participate in the space, you won't be successful.

How much time is spent participating in this space depends on your specific needs as an organization. Some organizations only need to devote a few hours a week. Three or four, because social media isn't that important to their organization. There are companies, though, like AllBusiness, where social marketing is more important and it's nothing for them to spend 80 hours a week participating in social marketing. It's all determined by your business and what your business needs are.

Jerri: What do you see as trends in the SEO space?

Rand: It would be foolish to ignore what Google calls "universal search" and we call "vertical search." It's in vertical search that companies find highly qualified traffic, and there's going to be a significant amount of traffic in these areas. So, vertical search can include:

- Local search
- Product search
- Instant answers (like Ask.com. That's a rapidly growing area of search.)
- Image search
- News search
- Travel search

And there are many more. All of those are vertical that can lead you closer to the customer that you want to reach.

Jerri: What are your thoughts on what's being called "human-powered search"?

Rand: Basically, I think it's a joke — less than useless. A waste of time. It doesn't scale, results are of considerably worse quality than an algorithmic search, and there is very little hope that it would take off in the next few years. I could be wrong, too, but in my opinion it will never achieve results that have the quality which engineers can put into algorithmic results.

Jerri: Where do you see that organizations are performing poorly in search marketing?

Rand: That's really a story of two different worlds. Less than 10 percent of small and medium-sized business in the U.S., and less around the world, have paid any attention to search marketing and are deriving any value from it at all. And they don't really care. Many small and micro business owners don't know how the Internet can impact their business, and they don't care.

But then there are a very small number of tiny web-based businesses that have come to it over time that have seen phenomenal results. Etsy.com is an example. But mostly smaller businesses have no interest in search marketing.

It's in the larger companies where we generally tend to see great hunger for knowledge from users. And even then, a great number of larger businesses have still not begun to focus on search marketing. These companies usually do one thing, like pay-per-click marketing, and nothing else.

Jerri: Is there anything else about search marketing that you think might be important to mention?

Rand: There are thousands of topics we haven't touched on. And there are lots of tips that I could give you. But if I had to choose one, I would say that companies should look at widget strategies, and try to design and deploy a high-demand widget that can be plugged into a blog or browser. When done successfully, widgets are really great. You can get phenomenal amounts from traffic and links to your site when you have a good, high-demand widget.

We're also fond of link-baiting strategies and content strategies as a means of providing relevant information to your site visitors.

Duane Forrester, Founding Co-Chair for the In-House Committee with SEMPO

Duane Forrester is an in-house search marketer for a sports media company in Canada. He's also a private search marketing consultant and a co-chair on the In-House Committee and a board member of SEMPO (Search Engine Marketing Professional Organization), a professional organization for search marketers.

SEMPO is a global non-profit organization serving the search engine marketing industry and marketing professionals engaged in it. Its purpose is to provide a foundation for industry growth through building stronger relationships, fostering awareness, providing education, promoting the industry, generating research, and creating a better understanding of search and its role in marketing.

Jerri: Does being an in-house search marketer change the way that you approach SEO and search marketing?

Forrester: Being in-house doesn't change it, my perspective does. And my perspective is that I treat my company as if they are my client and I am their consultant. I am a consultant. But when I start getting into the nuts and bolts of search marketing, it's no different than if I was at an agency. I would approach search marketing the same way, I just wouldn't know the client as well as I know the client that I'm an in-house marketer for.

There are some differences worth noting between smaller and larger companies, however. Smaller businesses usually have fewer stake-holders in a given project, making it much easier to be heard at the table and ensure the right bits get "baked into" the search optimization pie from the very beginning.

Because our organization isn't large, I can sit down with a product manager and say, "Here's what I need and here's why I need it." They can then build the product around those needs, making the entire process more efficient.

So one benefit is that it's much easier, since I'm in-house, to get exactly what we need integrated very early in the development cycle.

Jerri: What would you consider the state of search marketing today?

Forrester: There's a lot of offshore growth in search marketing and a proliferation of search engine software. Lots of seemingly knowledgeable search marketing experts take a software application and spin it to make it appear to meet more needs than it does. It's a very lucrative business.

But if I were going to hire a search marketing company and planned to spend $7,500 to $10,000 a month for that service, I would expect the effort to be based around knowledge, not just a software tool. There should be some level of personal experience and interaction as well.

It is so expensive to hire a search marketing company now that I would shy away from any consultant or business that relies on a software program to guide them. For the same budget, there are some great search marketers who have a lot of experience — experience makes the difference, not software.

Many search marketing consultants are expensive and they rely on diagnostic software to do the job that should really be done by an experienced person. Using the software, they will do a basic examination of the site and give you a report on their findings.

Then, based on their understanding of your site, your needs, and where you are currently, they will provide a series of recommendations that may or may not be accurate. The state of search marketing when the software was built and the state of search marketing when the software is used often changes — subtly and dramatically. There can be a large discrepancy there.

So what happens is companies hire these search marketing organizations and it's just money out the door. The money is spent and the company finds that they get little or no value from the investment — no usable return. So, they're out the money and they still don't have the help that they need.

Relatively few people have a large amount of experience in search marketing. For the handful that do have considerable experience (more than three or four years, which is often the minimum requirement when an organization is hiring a search marketing consultant) trying to recover from the damage done by these services becomes an image protection mechanism.

I want the industry to look good. If it doesn't, I suffer because my potential customers still remember when they got burned. I have to come up against the bad stuff and try to overcome it. This is part of the reason why I take on so few clients.

So I would say that when you're looking at search marketing capabilities, you need to know what questions to ask. If you don't know what questions to ask you're going to find yourself in a position to spend money and never receive results. You're going to get a lot of pitches from people who don't know what they're doing. Asking the right questions will help to let you know if they're experienced or just someone who thinks they can handle search marketing because they bought some software.

Jerri: What should organizations be focusing on to improve search marketing?

Forrester: Training is one area that is still being developed in this industry. I'm a bit biased, but I think the SEMPO curriculum is one of the best available today. It's not an endorsement of a person's capabilities. When they finish a course, they receive only a certificate of completion. Other programs offer a "certification," which can lead potential clients to feel the person is not only knowledgeable, but ethical, too. Though no program could ever hope to certify an individual's ethics, it comes down to perception and presentation. If someone says they are "certified" and you don't understand exactly what that certification entails, it's easy to assign more credit to an individual than they deserve.

There are other training options besides SEMPO. I tend to gravitate toward the broader theory-based components of education as opposed to the "here's a tool and here's how to use it" method. But some people work better with theory and others work better with tools. Personally, I don't use tools in search marketing, or I use them as little as possible, and if I do have to use a tool, I only use it for specific tasks. Keyword research and link management are two areas that come to mind. I use specific tools to help me manage workloads in those areas, but I'd never put my trust in software that claims to "optimize my site" for me — software like that is only as good as the programmer who built it, and only as current as the last update. Miss an update and you may be in dangerous territory.

The search marketing industry is still very young. There are not a lot of experienced SEMs with seven-plus years of experience, and those who do have it are expensive to employ or contract with — though their experience leads them to be able to perform, so many are easily worth it.

Those seeking to build in-house teams of SEMs in their own businesses tend to seek a lower number of years of experience. Typically, in other industries, to reach the management level or the director's level and above, five to seven-plus years of experience are required. I see lots of search marketing management jobs posted each week where management level positions are seeking only two to three years of experience.

Most smaller companies cannot afford to hire a six-figure SEM to get the best. They need to strike a balance, so less experience is often acceptable. This is not a reflection on a company's level of professionalism, but rather a statement of the relative youth of our industry. There just aren't that many deeply experienced SEMs floating around — and those there are command higher salaries. The critical point for companies to remember is this — while learning the basics of search marketing can be compressed into a short period of time, and a person can be theoretically competent, it's often the better network that the more experienced person has that makes a difference.

Jerri: How are organizations budgeting for search marketing?

Forrester: The budget for search marketing has continued to grow over the last two or three years, but no additional funds have been added to cover that budget. Instead, companies take that budget from other areas like e-mail marketing and pay-per-click advertising. Organizations are already worried about marketing strategies like PPC because of click fraud. That's a serious concern, because it's very real and hard to control.

So what we see is organic SEM budgets that are growing at the expense of other areas of marketing. Many companies feel organic search offers the best ROI — it's a long term investment that can be comparatively low-cost. Large PPC campaigns can easily run into the millions of dollars each year. By comparison to a PPC campaign that requires a constant influx of money to perform, organic search marketing needs are often met after a number of months of work, effectively moving a web site to a new baseline level of inbound traffic. This type of effort will continue to perform long after the last bill to an effective SEM consultant is paid.

Jerri: If organizations are taking away from their e-mail and PPC marketing budgets, then what are they doing to ensure that potential customers are seeing them?

Forrester: There are two models for the marketing that companies are doing: organic and paid. In paid, money is being shuffled around so that organizations are bringing their search marketing in-house or they are hiring third-party vendors to manage their search marketing efforts.

On average, the overall marketing budgets are not growing. Companies are looking for what are profit centers, so they need to allocate existing budgets differently. The money has to come from somewhere, and it usually comes from other marketing efforts.

For example, if a company's marketing budget for PPC has been $100,000 a year in the past, and they begin to use a consultant or vendor that requires $10,000 a month for six months, that leaves just $40,000 a year for PPC marketing. And that's one area where budgets are being shuffled. Companies understand that an agency will likely help them get better converting traffic for their investment, either by providing better converting traffic or by reducing the cost of existing search marketing campaigns. And most search marketing agencies are very good at what they do. Many larger agencies do not practice "churn and burn" tactics. They know if they perform for a client, the client will come back. Short-changing a client for the sake of immediate profits is always a poor business model, yet is sadly still popular with many of today's "instant experts" who use software to manage everything and claim to understand what they're doing.

We are also slowly beginning to see some of the older, larger advertising agencies toying with the idea of doing search marketing now. As traditional advertising spending has dropped consistently, these larger organizations are beginning to realize that their customers want more options for marketing, and the online channel brings good results for less investment. So the larger agencies have begun to realize that they could be holding onto a portion of their clients' spending if they are offering the search marketing capabilities that those clients want. But these older companies are kind of behind the eight ball now, because search marketing companies have already been established and they're good at what they do, so these more traditional agencies will have a hard time breaking into this space.

Jerri: What tips would you give an organization looking to hire a search marketing consultant or firm?

Forrester: First, get a list of past clients, and not just anyone in the organization. Request the contact name and number for the person who was responsible for the SEM agency relationship. Then, meet with them and ask them the hard questions. Ask how the relationship went. Ask if and how quickly the company responded to their requests. And the most important question to ask is, "If you needed work done again, would you still hire this company?"

The agency's job is to make you look like a hero, but if they are overloaded, you end up in a situation where you're just left hanging. So, if a reference says they would prefer to do their search marketing in-house or would not hire the company again for any reason, then you should reconsider whether you want to hire the company or not. It's a telltale sign when a previous customer won't hire the company again, but if they say they would, then that's a good endorsement for the company.

In the end, it's a leap of faith — at some point you'll need to pony up the cash to get the program up and running. Just make sure that whoever is handling the agency relationship in-house understands enough of the various facets being worked on to know if the agency is getting the job done properly. If you are a marketing manager tapped to manage this effort, get cracking on learning about organic search and paid search marketing yourself. Even a basic level of understanding can be enough to spot problems and get this sorted properly for you.

Jerri: If you find that your relationship with a search marketing organization isn't working, how do you get out of that relationship?

Forrester: Contracts, contracts, contracts. Make absolutely certain there are performance clauses in the contracts before you sign them. And because search is a long-term investment, clarify how long it will take to reach the results that you're being promised by the search marketing firm. Then you can incorporate a provision to pay a percentage of the fee up front and the balance of the fee when the performance goals are reached. If the organization is doing a good job with meeting their promised performance goals, then they should have no problem allowing this type of clause in the contract that they ask you to sign.

The most important part of hiring a search marketing firm is vetting them as a vendor. Ask for at least three references and then speak to them. If, for some reason you can't reach one of the references, then go back to the vendor and request another one. Successful agencies should have plenty of customers waiting to tell others how good they are, and in fact larger agencies have a list that's as long as your arm of people who have praises for them.

One final thought:

If an agency or consultant *ever* promises you they can get you ranked as number one for any organic efforts, run, don't walk away from them. No one can guarantee results in the world of organic search results. We don't know the actual algorithms the engines use to rank sites, so making guarantees such as #1 is just a sales tactic, nothing more.

Results should be measured on actual metrics — inbound traffic from each search engine, conversion on the site, those types of things.

Stephen Harris, Consultant, SPH Associates

Stephen Harris has been involved in the Internet marketing space since the late 1990s — initially as director of e-business technology at ADP, creating the first e-business platform for small business payroll services. Since then, Harris has designed and managed affiliate marketing programs and worked at DigitalGrit, an online marketing agency. For DigitalGrit he devised and provided project management processes to search marketing for large-scale, big-brand companies.

Harris's hands-on experience with SEO and online marketing has been as a consultant for the firm he started — SPH Associates. The firm is focused on small businesses. And this venue has led to his beliefs about conversion-based thinking for SEO.

Jerri: Where do you see the current state/importance of SEO?

Harris: SEO is very important . . . at least that is what business owners think. I receive calls where they say they need SEO — but in truth we learn that they need more effective web design and even paid-click programs. This does not mean to dispel the value of a top ranking — for credibility and indeed traffic — as per the EyeTool/Did-It study. (You can find this study at `http://www.eyetools` `.com/inpage/research_google_eyetracking_heatmap.htm`.)

I also see a ton of snake-oil salespeople, or people who simply give the client what they asked for without actually listening to what they need. There are people who claim they will submit your web site to the top 200 search engines. There are some that say they guarantee top listing on a few of the top 200 search engines but would never make such a claim for Yahoo!, Google, or MSN ([those companies] represent around 98 percent of all searches). These snake-oil salespeople make it hard for legitimate SEO professionals to earn trust in the small and mid-sized business space.

However, it is clear that the top three or four search engines are so ingrained into our way of life — we use Google as a verb — that it is important for businesses to design their web sites not only for effectiveness and usability, but to get long-tail benefits.

Jerri: Could you please explain to me what you mean by long-tail benefits?

Harris: It just means that well-written, readable, and relevant content will help the site appear highly ranked on obtuse or lesser used search terms. But in accumulation all these "little used" terms can add up big-time. I think that natural, well-written content that speaks to the reader will allow for long tail — rather than content that is gamed (or abused) for the top keyword that the SEO specialist is trying to achieve results for.

Jerri: What can organizations do right now to improve their SEO?

Harris: Work backwards — examine your web site and make sure your house is in order. Make sure your content is quick and tight but yet readable — and do the SEO basics (title tags, image tags, and the like). This all by itself will help your site to be relevant and relevancy is key to Google success and of course conversions.

I am more of an on-site optimizer. I find some off-site linking to be dubious. I think the winds may be changing, causing highly linked sites not to be as relevant unless the links are truly relevant.

I provide suggestions to my clients on how to get effective links and provide them with linking code to give to their peers and customers. I do employ someone that does linking since it still works, even though I don't fully agree with pursuing linking strategies.

Just create a relevant and compelling site. Make me want to be there and everything else will work out.

Jerri: What should web-site owners be focusing on for future improvements?

Harris: From an SEO standpoint [web site owners should] become thought leaders in their space, using blogs, writing articles, and posting on the Web. [You should also] create a Web 2.0 stickiness to your site. Give people a reason for being there and wanting to come back. This in itself is not an SEO play, but by having strong content that is frequently updated and extended, you give the robot spiders plenty of reason to want to come back time and again.

Jerri: Are there any strategies that organizations might know about but are not implementing that might help with SEO results if they did?

Harris: I have been trying to figure this out, [looking for] some technology that enhances SEO beyond what we all know already. Unfortunately, some of these [technologies] tend to come back as black hat, which I am not a party to. The only black hat area I think should be *carefully* allowed is creating a clone for heavily flashed sites. But that is a tough one to call.

The key is Web 2.0 — social integration, updated, frequent, and relevant content, and thought leadership. This all goes back to Google's principles on relevancy! Make it relevant and they will come . . . and come again.

Jerri: What do you consider a strong, viable web site and how does that impact SEO?

Harris: Well, I am such a content purist sometimes — I believe that one should have a brief but good strong content strategy that tells me who you are, what makes you great or special, why should I be here, and how do I learn more (which falls under permission marketing). I can live without a lot of Flash and images. But I always lose that argument and concede the need for aesthetics.

Seriously, a good balance of content and attractiveness will rule the SEO day. Too much Flash and gee-whiz does not help conversions nor relevancy except in some unique cases. A well-designed, well-written web site will do well from all perspectives.

Jerri: What changes in SEO are coming as the result of the growth of social media?

Harris: There are some tough decisions coming here. The power of Adobe Flex and Ajax is making web sites much better usability-wise — more like an application than a web site — but this is causing tracking people to freak out (pageviews are passé in this genre), and of course these are not very white-hat SEO-able. But it can be done — and we do know Google and Adobe are talking (I am actually participating in this interview from the 360Flex conference in Seattle).

I think the biggest changes are again that balancing act between the visual and the content, and how to balance them effectively.

But here is a radical thought — SEO may not be as important for a strong social site, whereas word of mouth and viral marketing will be what delivers the visitation. Could social sites be able to thumb their nose at the search engines?

Jerri: Are there any other coming changes that will affect SEO?

Harris: Well we think that Flex and other tools will become SEO-friendly. We hope people get it — and write their sites to focus on the visitors, not the robot spiders. To my knowledge, no sales have come from the spider . . . but they do come from the visitors.

We also are well aware of strong vertical search engines, and this may be an area where the rank-and-file SEO specialist is not focusing — to optimize for vertical search engines that are within the space of the client web site.

Jerri: Is there anything I haven't touched on that might be important for small to mid-sized organizations to know about SEO?

Harris: Cost . . . cost is a huge issue. Education is another. I spend so much time discussing maintenance programs and the need to keep doing SEO monthly. It is not a one-time thing. And of course educating people that you do not need to pay people to submit your web site and that no one can guarantee a top position on the top three search engines.

Again, back to cost. Small businesses have been educated that they need SEO, but they find they cannot easily afford it. Even mid-sized businesses feel this way. The issue is that SEO is still mystical — whereas they know paid-click programs work, or if it doesn't work they can stop it quickly. The snake-oil people aren't helping.

My approach recently has been more common sense–based, as discussed earlier. When someone asks me about SEO, I immediately ask them about their web site. Is it working for them? Then I look to see if it is effective and usable. I also try to manage their expectations. I had someone ask me to get them top-ranked for the word "diamonds," and they ended up not hiring me because I said they should consider more realistic targets like "quality diamond earrings" or something similar. Of course, for $100,000 maybe I could have gotten them top rankings [for such a broad term] but they only wanted to spend $5,000.

I am coming up with a product called SEO Lite which provides basic usability and web effectiveness, along with SEO best practices and education about what a web-site owner can do on their own for optimization.

I do hear of major companies that have stopped their SEO initiatives. It's all about results and costs.

Jerri: In what circumstances would a company stop their SEO initiatives?

Harris: When they feel or perceive that they are not getting any real results from their ranking vs. the cost of the maintenance fee. I think that this is often a perception that maintenance fees bleed site owners dry, especially where it takes a long time to achieve high ranking for a top keyword. I think showing the long-tail increase may help stem this kind of maintenance remorse. It also may be a lack of clear communications with the client, or it could be specialists that get lazy and then the client does not feel there is any real effort occurring.

Jerri: If they are not focusing on SEO, what are they focusing on to improve site visits and conversions?

Harris: Site usability, implementation of Web 2.0, paid-click programs. And I think these are or could be even more important for clients initially, as they can achieve an immediate kick in visits and establishment of retention/loyalty. If the site is built using SEO standards, then over time the long tail effect and time can naturally lift the site. I have not done any meaningful changes to my own site (`http://www.stephen-harris.com`) in many months, yet it is top-ranked! And in some very competitive keywords!

Ryan Hoppe, Director of Product Marketing, Fast Search

Ryan Hoppe serves as director of product marketing for Fast Search & Transfer, responsible for FAST's products and solutions in the media and e-commerce sectors. Before joining FAST, Ryan managed product marketing for Microsoft Office Enterprise 2007 as part of Microsoft's Information Worker Division. Ryan has also held product marketing and marketing communications positions at Groove Networks, Bose Corporation, and the communications consultancy Brodeur Worldwide. Ryan holds a bachelor of science degree in communications from Cornell University.

Fast Search offers enterprise search solutions. The company was started in Norway in 1997 and has grown rapidly to become a global organization with offices across six continents. Fast Search is committed to building lasting customer partnerships and a positive reputation. The company caters to clients all over the Internet. In fact, if you've used site search — the search capabilities within a web site — then chances are you've seen what Fast Search can do.

Jerri: Could you give me an overview of what you're calling site search?

Hoppe: SEO is about driving traffic to destination sites on the Web. But when someone arrives at a destination site and wants to explore its content, that's where site search kicks in. You'd be surprised how many sites are powered by FAST. We index all of the content on a site — and sometimes content off the site — and allow the customer to easily search that data.

For example, *TV Guide* is a FAST customer. So if you went to the *TV Guide* web site and did a search for the show "24," in the past you would just get TV listings. Now, when you search for "24" on the *TV Guide* site powered by FAST, you might see premium content such as interviews or relevant blog results from offsite locations — all included with the search listings. Providing that additional, relevant content helps build loyalty and keeps people on the site, which in turn helps boost search engine rankings.

There was an interesting study released recently that was done by Susan Feldman at IDC. Her study indicated that up to 70 percent of searches on the Internet occur at destination sites. That means that only about 30 percent of all search goes through general web search engines like Google or Yahoo!. That gives you sense of how large site search is.

Jerri: Does site search fall into the category of vertical search?

Hoppe: Not necessarily. Vertical search is still a web search engine; it's just crawling vertical-specific content and then using a tuned relevancy model to highlight relevant content in that vertical. The knock against Google and Yahoo! is that their web search relevancy model is too broad and is not really tuned to niche content. Vertical search engines better understand your context and tune their relevancy models appropriately.

For example, if you're looking for financial data on "bonds" using a vertical search engine, and you search for the word "bond" you would receive information (in the vertical) about financial bonds. But if you typed that same search into Google you might get James Bond very near the top of the results. The web search engine had no idea that you were looking for financial bonds, whereas the vertical search engine understood your context.

Jerri: Is there any value in SEO for site search?

Hoppe: Site search does some bad things and good things related to SEO. I'll give you the bad first.

Site search provides users with a truly dynamic experience versus static web pages that are preprogrammed. Landing pages and category pages, for example, traditionally have static content that is chosen by a marketer or merchandiser. Web crawlers are much better at crawling these types of pages with static content and keyword-friendly URLs. A search engine results page, on the other hand, is truly dynamic. It didn't "exist" before you typed in the search query and hit return. The page — and its content — is rendered on the fly. Web search crawlers sometimes have a hard time indexing dynamic pages because they are not part of the site map; they are created at the moment of need.

Now the good. FAST does several things to help improve SEO. First, we can rewrite the URLs of search results pages to make them easier to crawl, inserting search keywords into the URLs. Second, we can work with our customers to create "topics pages" — landing pages focused on a specific topic that use search to draw in the most recent, relevant content on that topic. Let's go back to the *TV Guide* example. *TV Guide* could create a topics page for the show "24." One area of the page could be a "latest news" box that is using site search to pull in the most relevant news headlines on the show "24" from *TV Guide*'s internal sources and sources across the Web. It could have a premium content area where *TV Guide*'s marketing staff can promote their own content. It could have an area on the most recent blog postings. Topics pages help boost SEO because they are part of the standard site map, yet have dynamic, rich content that should help generate significant link activity.

Jerri: What's a tag cloud?

Hoppe: Tag clouds are usually boxes on a web page that help users explore other content related to a topic. We have a feature in our product, FAST ESP®, called Contextual Insight®. It can look at a piece of content (a news article, for example) and extract certain key attributes related to this content (e.g., persons, places, and things) and then associate those attributes with the content. For example, when FAST ESP indexes a news article on the show "24," it may extract "Jack Bauer" and "terrorists" as attributes from the article. These attributes can be pulled out and made into a tag cloud that is generated dynamically when someone searches on "24" and clicks on the article. Typically the words in the cloud all have different sizes and boldness, so some words would have more emphasis than others, based on their relevancy or weight to the original topic.

Jerri: Is there anything we haven't touched on that would be important for people to understand?

Hoppe: SEO and site search are very distinct. However, one thing we haven't discussed is how site search can boost SEO purely by creating a better user experience. A web site that has advanced site search helps build a loyal community of visitors by enabling people to easily find what they are looking for on the site, and helping them explore and discover related content. It also helps recommend content to users as it gets to know them, based on their previous search and site interaction habits. By having a loyal base of users who come back to the site more and more, a web site should increase its inbound links, which in turn will drive up SEO. Though this is an indirect benefit, it is important to point out how search is becoming less of a "utility" for users and more of a way to create rich, dynamic site experiences that keep people coming back.

Diane Kuehn, President, VisionPoint Marketing

Diane Kuehn founded VisionPoint Marketing after holding numerous executive sales and marketing positions with, among others, Cox Communications, SourceLink, High Speed Net Solutions, and ADVO — the country's largest direct marketing firm. Today, she's what the company calls the "lead brainiac."

VisionPoint Marketing is a marketing solutions agency providing integrated programs — interactive and/or traditional tactics — for mid-sized organizations in a variety of industries including higher education, health care, biotech/life sciences, pharmaceutical, high tech, and business services.

Jerri: What's the big deal about SEO? Why is it suddenly the "must have" strategy for web sites?

Kuehn: I really think this is not new. I think that it's just a matter of people figuring out the Web. There are a lot of organizations that are just beginning to realize there has been a paradigm shift in the last 12–18 months.

I'm not sure the "must have" is a recent focus. I think that a lot of organizations have spent the last five to ten years figuring out what to do with their web site first. Now, as most are considering how the Web has changed, especially over the past few years, and they need to do a re-design, organizations realize that if they want to optimize their sites for the search engines, they need to start that process when they are re-designing and building their site.

This is the time to start the SEO process. I think SEO hasn't been something that they've focused on in the past as much, because they haven't focused on web-site redesign. A lot of things are happening now that are causing people to refocus at this time.

The cost of search is zero. Since search is free we are no longer basing our decisions on Yellow Pages. And search is even faster than word of mouth. Google search result pages are better than having perfect retail space on Main Street or a perfect billboard, so by optimizing your web site you can really do so much more and you can get better results and it doesn't cost as much as it has in the past. Before, you had to spend a lot of money on all those other marketing outlets. Now if you can be good at organic SEO, you have a jump start on getting people to your site.

Rather than marketing — intrusive marketing — at your customer, prime customers (those who are ready to buy and are specific to your niche), you need to make sure they find you. Using search marketing you can meet their needs rather than hitting them with intrusive marketing. And if you are ranking well organically, there is an assumed authority that you are a leader in a specific field.

The last research I saw is that conversion from organic click vs. paid click is three to one overpaid. And B2B [business-to-business] clients do know the difference. They're savvy enough in general to know the difference.

Jerri: What are some of the most frequently ignored strategies for implementing SEO? How does ignoring those strategies hurt organizations and how could improving them help?

Kuehn: A company or organization really needs to understand that ranking well in search engines is not about paying an agency to just do it. They have to build content. It truly is about building valuable content on your web site or out in the community

It comes down to content versus search. People are finding things faster; they search for stuff and find it, and then when they get there, they're interacting more. So sites built for the search engine — search engines are getting smarter so they recognize when a site isn't built for people. Then, when the people come to the site and see it's built for a search engine, they won't stay. Focusing on building for search engines doesn't work. You have to provide the audience with the content that they want.

Some companies don't understand that they need to build content. I just saw some research yesterday that talks about how time spent on content as an activity on the Web has increased by 37 percent, while search as an activity has decreased by 35 percent over the past four years. Focusing on simply getting top results in rankings on the engines isn't going to get you new customers. You need to build content that helps you get top rankings on the engines *and* positions your organization as a thought leader or provides your audience with the content that they want.

Blogs, tutorials, high-quality tips and tricks . . . companies need to have the mindset that giving away info that is truly valuable is the best strategy. When you have good content that's linkworthy, then people are going to link to it.

Another thing that companies need to think about is the navigation: how pages on your site interlink, and how the site works when you are dropped in the middle of it. If you're doing it right, people are coming into your site from all different places. Your design needs to be such that they know where they are in the site and they know how to get around. I have found a lot of organizations think that the old standbys, such as pages that are about us, or contact pages and the like, are sufficient. They're not thinking about "when I land in the middle of the site, I still want to know how to get around." It's just assumed that I'm coming in from the home page and that's not always what happens.

Jerri: Are there other aspects of SEO that organizations could improve upon?

Kuehn: The biggest strategy that we find is undervalued or ignored, that not only helps SEO but also makes a site more user-friendly, is its information architecture. Planning out your site's navigation in such a way as to allow someone who drops right into the middle of the site from a search engine results page to still know where they are, how to find additional information, and motivates them to take the call to action is extremely important. Once again, it's not about getting top rankings on the search engine results page; it's about getting the right people to your site and then engaging them.

Jerri: In what areas is SEO being handled well?

Kuehn: People are starting work in modern coding standards and that is good for SEO. We build all of our sites in xHTML. That means that it can work extremely well for the user in all of the different browsers, but also it's read the best by spider, and mobile devices display it just like it's supposed to be displayed. Now I'm starting to see customers that are starting to recognize that this is an important thing. And other firms that are also starting to code that way.

Jerri: What's coming for the future of SEO and how can organizations begin to prepare for those coming changes now?

Kuehn: I think that what's happening with the Web . . . if you think of the evolution of search engines and the search engine algorithms, they have to stay a couple of steps ahead of the search engine spammers. So we're starting to see search results or weighting a site more by using a human editor. For example, there is some indication that Google may begin weighing Digg results into the authority given to a web site.

We are also going to see more and more content that is built specifically for SEO being removed from search engine result pages. Social search — Mahalo is a good example — wikis of search results and other methods of human-filtered content are becoming popular. And it will work especially well if you can develop a way to use other search tools like Google and Yahoo! and filter out all the useless information.

Google is best suited to figure this out. So while there are sites out there like Digg and you're using them to vote as to whether a site is good or not, I think that Google could start to figure out how to weigh human input into their algorithm, then that's essentially what's going to happen. The future is going to be more about "let's not focus so much on the search engine, let's focus on what's valuable content."

It's like the saying, "If you build it they will come." I think humans as opposed to a machine might think about your site and how valuable your site is and that's going to be much more important than anything else that you can do. So if you can get people to drink the Kool-Aid on that — if you build it, they will come.

Jerri: How do you see vertical SEO going?

Kuehn: I think we're a little bit far off from that right now . . . that being where you want to spend a lot of time. Of course it depends on how niche your business focus is. Let's use real estate as an example. If you're in real estate, you're going to want to focus on major search engines because that's where your audience is. Your audience isn't going to be something niche.

It depends. There are sites like Knowledge Storm where you see a lot of tech things and you can pay to be on there. That can be very effective from the marketing perspective of participating on that, but right now the money and focus should be on where people are going, and right now they're still on the major search engines. I think it's a ways off before people are going to their own niche area.

If Google can figure out how to (in specific vertical or niche areas) deliver me good results, why would you try something else? Why would you split your searches up into different areas?

Matt Naeger, VP and General Counsel, IMPAQT

Matt Naeger graduated from Duquesne University Law School and applies his legal training and expertise to the search industry in a multitude of ways — specifically as they relate to online client branding, as well as trademark and copyright issues. He spent six years managing large-scale direct marketing analysis projects for Fortune 500 clients before the start-up of IMPAQT in 1999. Naeger is also recognized as a true "thought leader" in search, frequently speaking at leading industry events and summits, as well as being considered a go-to source for search analysts and media.

IMPAQT was founded in 1999. The company redefined search marketing and stays at the forefront of the industry with a combination of innovation, strategy, expert staff, and analytics. IMPAQT's offerings include search engine optimization services, paid-search management, search education services, agency partnerships, search analytics, strategic consulting, customized reporting, and online/offline data integration. The company currently services Fortune 1000 corporations with data intensive search marketing needs in the B2B, finance, insurance, pharmaceutical, retail, and travel industries.

Jerri: What do you see as the current state of SEO?

Naeger: During 2002 and 2003, people were starting to back away from SEO, but over the last 18–24 months, there has been a much more prevalent view of optimization. SEO has once again become the in-vogue tactic for marketing.

People are also starting to look at how organic optimization works with paid-search marketing strategies. In the beginning there was a more siloed [compartmentalized] approach to search engine optimization and search engine marketing. Many organizations saw it as two different programs, and it was either one or the other. But now people are beginning to realize they have to do both together. When both are implemented, we have seen that they support each other and each becomes significantly more successful than when they operate independently.

Jerri: How does SEO fit into overall search marketing?

Naeger: To begin with, users still don't necessarily understand that a sponsored link is paid for. Even a lot of marketers don't understand. We find that many organizations are doing either one or the other, but they don't do both. The way that it should be is that SEO should be a core component of any online marketing strategy. The opportunity to capture a very large audience at what is comparatively a small cost is something that should never be overlooked by a marketer in today's world. SEO should also be utilized as a means of growing the depth of understanding of what users are wanting from your site and your company. By optimizing your web site to appear within organic search results, you can then evaluate the relevant terms associated with your site for potential purchases in engines where your placement may be lacking. As you evolve your online marketing strategies, SEO and SEM should both be looked at not only as a way to capture customers, but also as a way to understand them and in extension a way to understand the effects of your total brand marketing efforts.

Jerri: What are organizations not doing that would improve their SEO if they did do it?

Naeger: Organizations are not educating people internally enough to allow them to understand what effect SEO and SEM can have on the marketing of their brand. This education should be done across the entire organization and not just within the marketing group that is responsible for the effort. To implement SEO effectively and successfully, multiple departments and third-party agencies must be involved, educated, and completely aligned.

They should educate the content team that, "this is why the content should be done a different way," and show them how content can affect SEO.

They should educate the public relations department that a press release is not just a single document. It should be linked to the corresponding page on your web site.

Organizations should also look at SEO and SEM in order to build a web site that doesn't have to have changes made to it to keep up with any marketing changes that are made. That's where content management systems can help to integrate content into the site in a way that's relevant. They should build the site within the content management system, so that it can automatically integrate that press release or piece of content into the site in a quick and efficient manner.

One more thing is that people are turning a blind eye to other types of media. Search is a channel that is dramatically affected by both online and offline marketing. Companies should consider their overall media mix, and measure the results of that media by both online and offline effects.

Something that some organizations don't understand is that just because you're placing an ad on a search engine doesn't mean that ad has to be a click-to-sale effort. It's also a method that you can use to look at the data provided through search. The data collected during search can help uncover what the intent of the customer was, based on how they search and what they searched for. This is where the industry will turn next: complex data analysis and leveraging all of its intellectual value across all ad media.

Finally, a third capability that search marketing gives you is the ability to see how your competitors' advertising, both online and offline, can drive the awareness of the category and therefore may affect your marketing efforts as well. As you enhance the sophistication of the way you utilize online and offline tracking data, you will be able to react to and take advantage of the efforts of your competitors in ways that have not been possible in the past. As an example, using your search marketing results, you can learn what specific feature interests consumers developed out of a new product launch, and using this information you can gain insight into the consumer mindset that can then be utilized to build how you market your product in the future.

Jerri: What about social media marketing, how will it change SEO?

Naeger: Social media marketing helps you to build brand advocacy and lets you learn how consumers feel about your marketing efforts.

We will continue to see some big numbers on the growth of social media marketing until it reaches a maturity level. But it's not mature yet, and more and more people are finding it's useful. Social media change the way in which people find information. They don't want to spend as much time searching anymore. Social media give consumers the ability to find the information that they need based on recommendations from their friends and colleagues as opposed to the message that the marketer is trying to send to them through their advertising.

The big question in the industry is, how can social media marketing affect search engine results pages? Until recently, social media haven't shown up in search engine results, but now we're starting to see more and more social media sites showing up under general research-based search terms. This is the reason that the search engine marketing industry began to take notice of social media.

The next evolution of the question right now is, "How can we as search marketers understand and influence what is driving the inclusion of these results with the search landscape?" Marketers want to understand how pages are showing up on their brand and what those pages are saying about them. A good example of a site that is driving a lot of search visibility for brands is Wikipedia. Wikipedia consistently ranks well in Google searches, and in particular for those searches relative to brand information. So marketers are trying to figure out how to use social media to rank well, and how to control social media search results algorithmically in order to help control the view of the brand that a searcher is presented with inside of organic search results.

Jerri: How long will it be before we see this algorithmic control and ranking of the influences that social media have on web sites?

Naeger: We probably won't ever see ultimate control, but I think within the next six to eight months people will find a way to influence search results with social media. There's also a lot more talk about vertical search, and even in social media marketing I think the search world will become more verticalized.

Verticalized search is where people are finding other places they want to search. I think the next evolution of search is of a person telling a search engine how, where, and what to be told and then utilizing the engine to deliver on that request. What this means is that people are starting to utilize different search engines for different types of content, and in the future this will also extend to using different search engines for different categories of information as well.

The next 15 to 18 months will be critical in growing a more qualified audience in vertical search. If you tell users to tell you what they want you to tell them, they will. Especially as it applies to organic SEO, consumers are saying they want information that's not necessarily of the brand yet is specific to a particular type of content area or format. If vertical engines can deliver on this request in a fashion that is easy to use, then they will have the advantage over the personalized search features of the major search engines.

Jerri: Is there anything else that I haven't touched on that you think is important?

Naeger: The big thing is that the data and learning that you derive from what people do inside a search engine has an effect that we can't even fathom yet. There are ways to look at, track, and understand that data that are still in development. And when we figure out how to do that, we'll have the ability to provide users the information they need through not only customized search programs, but also through the customization of all marketing efforts.

There's an adage used in the search space that goes, "He who has the most data wins." But that's only effective if you can look at the data, understand what it is telling you, and apply that understanding to your campaign. And I think that's where improvements for the future need to, and will be, focused.

Simon Otter, Technical Manager, thebigword

Simon Otter is the group technology manager at thebigword, with overall responsibility for the technology and the associated processes used in creating integrated, efficient translation services.

Much of Otter's role involves working with customers to understand their technical and process requirements and adapting technology to fit their needs. An early starter in IT, Otter began programming at the age of eight and after graduating in software engineering, held several IT positions with the Ford Motor Company, creating localized public-facing software solutions, among many other projects. He is a Chartered IT Professional, member of the British Computer Society, and a Chartered Engineer.

Thebigword is one of the largest translation companies in the world. Its web site is translated into nine different languages, and the company offers translation services to more than 3,000 clients in 77 languages.

Jerri: Tell me about your perspective on SEO localization.

Otter: We have been thinking about and developing how we should handle SEO for clients asking us to localize their web sites. It's quite a dark art, and everyone thinks different about SEO. For some, it's just keywords and meta tags, and those customers want them translated, but there's much more to it. There are many different inputs that go into the mix of how to choose one keyword or another.

Typically, SEOs try to expand their keyword lists to other related keywords and compound phrases or terms and then build the needed content around these. And when you're doing it in one language, there's an almost subliminal process that goes into finding synonyms and related keywords, because it's your language and you recognize the keywords and phrases that will work for less money. There is a lot of careful selection and discarding of keywords.

When you're working with a multi-lingual site, it isn't that easy. When you go into another language, you immediately have a language barrier. What we propose to do is find the people who are enabled to translate but are also able to interpret the results once they're translated to see what words are still relevant.

As it stands, if an English-based company were to translate their site into German, the keywords could be translated, but the company wouldn't know what the words were. They could see the metrics for them, but they can't read the words, so it's difficult to tell if they're the right keywords.

Once you translate something to another language, there is a usually a choice of words. Some of those words will have the same meaning as the English keywords, but others will not. And you don't want to use the keywords that don't translate into your message.

We propose to work within an SEO environment in a multi-lingual environment. We could translate the keywords into another language and then an SEO coordinator could review that translation and discard the words that are not relevant. Once you've translated the words, and expanded your [second language] keyword list, then you must see if the words are still relevant, and if they are back translated — translated back to English — are they also still relevant?

Our thinking is around liberating the SEO environment. Once translated, then we could build a glossary that whenever you translate one word, this is what you should use for this word in this language. Then you could write all of the content around those keywords. And it would be based on the keywords that have already been examined and carefully chosen.

Jerri: Does the localized way people think affect how they consider SEO localization?

Otter: The way people think does play a role in localization. I think it does. An American might not think of localization as much as people in other countries do, but that's changing. A lot of education is required to help people understand the need to present localized web sites, but I would say it varies by corporate culture.

We suggest that you find an SEO partner when you're localizing your web site. We don't recommend hiring an individual, because in our experience, individuals aren't equipped to handle localization. Find a partner that specializes in translation, because a company like that has more resources and can return a translation to you that's been validated or approved.

Once you've decided what keywords you want, you can build a glossary of those terms so the next time a word comes up, the proper translation for that word is already decided upon. Another tool you can use is a translation memory.

A translation memory allows you to analyze your pages against the translation memory to leverage existing translations. This is a method that's often used in translation to speed the process and to keep the content consistent.

Translators come and go. But you need consistency and you need to achieve the correct translations as quickly as possible.

We also work with our clients to understand their link structure. Links are important in SEO, but translating a link is a little more difficult than translating a word or phrase. So we work with clients to understand their link structure. So we do essentially a translation of the links on a page to make it possible to contain a link hierarchy.

Sarah Skerik, VP Distribution Services, PR Newswire

Sarah Skerik is the vice president of distribution services for PR Newswire. In this role, she is responsible for managing the core wire product, content syndication, media relations, customer reporting, and targeted distribution products. PR Newswire Association LLC (http://www.prnewswire.com) provides electronic distribution, targeting, measurement, and broadcast/multimedia services on behalf of tens of thousands of corporate, government, association, labor, non-profit, and other customers worldwide.

PR Newswire provides electronic distribution, targeting, measurement, translation, and broadcast services on behalf of tens of thousands of corporate, government, association, labor, non-profit, and other customers worldwide. Using PR Newswire, these organizations reach a variety of critical audiences including the news media, the investment community, government decision-makers, and the general public with up-to-the-minute, full-text news developments. Established in 1954, PR Newswire has offices in 11 countries and routinely sends its customers' news to outlets in 135 countries and in 40 languages.

Jerri: What are some of the misconceptions about public relations from an SEO perspective?

Skerik: First, let me put a finer point on my perspective. Public relations is not separate from SEO, it is a component of SEO. I'm thinking about all of PR Newswire's clients, which range from large to tiny. The large companies do SEO really well, and the small companies do SEO really well. Where the missed opportunity lies is in those mid-range companies that are large enough to have silos between the marketing and public relations departments.

Today, companies are spending a lot of time optimizing their sites. And in doing that, there are so many opportunities to really leverage press releases. But it requires a little shift in thinking. For example, about a month ago I was talking to a customer about SEO, and I was trying to understand their different departments and services. And what I found is that each person focuses on a different aspect of the company, but no one owned or took responsibility for the public.

Traditionally, press releases have been focused on delivering a message, not on how that message can be connected to search as part of their marketing campaign. And for that to take place what really needs to happen is for organizations to develop an understanding of SEO across the organization. What keywords are relevant? What landing pages are relevant? All of this should be applied to press releases.

These are more involved than just what sits in the marketing department, because at the end of the day, the message is across the organization. Search engines put a lot of emphasis on content. So it's important to look at press releases not just as press releases, but as content.

For most organizations, content is a problem. That's one of the reasons that social media has become so popular. Blogs are a power indicator that there's fresh content here. And if a search engine sees that you've got regularly updated, fresh content, then they'll return to index your site more often.

My favorite advice to tell our customers is to stand back and really get a good understanding of how customers talk about your company and products. Then try to reach your customers using the way they speak and think. You can't change human behavior. Instead you need to change the content to reach the people.

I would suggest that you march right over to the person in charge of SEO about any keyword research they have done. This helps you determine what keywords your customers are using, and then you can integrate those into your press releases.

Jerri: In integrating your press releases with the rest of your search marketing efforts, should you include links in them?

Skerik: Yes. You have to think of press releases as part of your content, not separate entities. It's absolutely fabulous to include the keywords that have been identified as productive for what you're marketing. And you can add extra emphasis to those keywords by linking them to corresponding pages on your web site.

The best practice is to link your press release to a page on your web site that's related to the keyword. The search engine then infers that the keywords, press releases, and links are all related and relevant.

Be careful, though, because you can dilute your efforts if the keyword is linked to a page on the site that doesn't contain that keyword. For example, if your keyword is "hot dog" and you decide to link it to a section on your page about hamburgers, reasoning that people who like one would be interested in the other, you actually risk diminishing your audience. Linking to a page that doesn't strongly support your message is a mistake, because search engines won't make the connection, and your ratings can suffer as a result.

The search engine will see the press release, see the link, and follow that to the web page to see that there's nothing related to the keyword. If the search engine doesn't see something related, then that page won't get a powerful reciprocal connection.

This is where press releases can be really powerful. You send out a press release with links back to your site and it's widely distributed. The results will be links back and forth to your site. So the search engines will see the connection and it lends credibility to your site. Web sites that have the highest visibility are those that have hundreds of links back and forth. Here again, this is an opportunity to strengthen your SEO because linking helps to build the overall authority of your site.

Jerri: You said there had to be a shift in the way that organizations think about using press releases. Does there also need to be a shift in the way companies think about using SEO as a means of gaining visibility for the message?

Skerik: Yes. Writing a press release is where some difference in thinking comes into play. Headlines are one area where you can gain a lot of mileage for SEO. Headlines are so important that the *New York Times* is training their writers in SEO techniques so they know how to write headlines that are search engine-friendly. Instead of the catchy headlines that most media organizations use, the practice now is to use contextual headlines that are relevant to the subject of the press release and that contain keywords.

Search engines read from the top down just like people do, and information at the top of a press release has the most importance. If you don't use keywords in your headlines, then you can lose really important real estate.

Clear writing, writing from the top down, including important information at the top of the press release, and writing in a natural style are all important to search engines, too. These are the same strategies that work to make content both people-friendly and search engine friendly.

One more mistake that some people make is to try to write a press release to appeal to everyone, and that just doesn't work. It's not search engine friendly and so is not meaningful to SEO. Focusing your message is the better practice, from both the SEO and news writing standpoints.

Andrew Wetzler, President, MoreVisibility

Andrew Wetzler co-founded MoreVisibility eight years ago. Today, the company, which started with three people, has grown to more than 40 and has been named to the Inc. 500 list two years in a row. MoreVisibility targets small and mid-sized business in niche markets, helping them create strategies for SEO and SEM. Some of their clients include the Metropolitan Museum of Art, Sony Disk Manufacturing, Clemson University, GarageTek, and Hagerty Insurance.

Wetzler is a member of MSN's Search Advisory Council and is the membership chair of the Direct Marketing Association's Search Engine Marketing Council.

Prior to MoreVisibility, his background includes 10 years of direct-marketing consulting where he taught organizations how to better utilize multiple channels to improve campaign performance. Andrew serves on the board of directors for Jambase.com. He holds a B.A. in economics from Tulane University.

Jerri: What do you see that organizations are doing well in search engine optimization today?

Wetzler: I think the first line in the sand is where in the process SEO comes into the mix. There are several categories: those companies that already have a web site and know they need SEO and also those companies that are about to invest in a major redesign and want to integrate SEO into the redesign. The second category is companies that have it in their head that they want SEO in the future, and they are planning their site around SEO principles.

Organizations are trying to create a balance between the search engine experience and the human experience — they're trying to decide which is most valuable and on which they should focus more of their attention.

I say they are both valuable. Organizations need to build a web site that first accomplishes the objectives. But you ought to have an understanding of the elements of SEO and how to use those to improve your search engine ranking.

Jerri: In what aspects of SEO are organizations not doing so well?

Wetzler: There are a couple of areas. Content is one area because organizations see content for search engines differently than content in general.

We try to get our clients to narrow the scope of their content on a page so there are not too many ideas on a page. This focus makes content more valuable and more relevant. And more focused content means that you continually have fresh material on your site, which is better because search engines see the content change more often and will revisit the site more often.

Jerri: What trends do you see that organizations should focus on now which will have impact in the future?

Wetzler: Again, I think that organizations need a careful balance of the bells and whistles with the notion of what a search engine needs to see.

Also, organizations should be thinking about making a web site that is easy for search engines to navigate but is also appealing to the user. And as new technologies evolve and begin to be implemented, organizations should carefully research and understand the impact those technologies will have on SEO.

Going back to the previous question for a minute, another situation where things get tripped up is when a smaller organization is a separate entity, but part of a larger organization. Often we see that a satellite office has a clear picture of what they want from SEO, but they are often without the ability to achieve that picture because their hands are tied by the corporate organization.

For example, we talked with a small local office of a large non-profit organization. They wanted to incorporate better SEO into their site, but when we looked at their site we found there was a lot of duplicate content across the web site. But fixing that has to come from the top down, so our hands were tied. Because the larger organization wouldn't change the way they did things, the duplicate content couldn't be removed.

If the SEO goals of the larger organization don't fit with the SEO goals of the smaller organization, there are limits to what can be done.

Jerri: Is there anything else that you think is important for organizations to understand about SEO?

Wetzler: There is one thing that I think some organizations miss. The organization should not look at SEO as the whole picture. SEM should be part of the bigger picture. Small to mid-sized businesses are looking for a solution that gets their ranking up naturally, but it takes more than just organic SEO. SEO efforts should be combined with marketing efforts in order to achieve the best possible exposure.

There are also some companies that have incredible natural search engine results that want to know why they should invest in a paid program like pay-per-click. The combination of SEO and SEM is more effective than either of them alone.

Jill Whalen, Founder and CEO, High Rankings

In the early 1990s, Jill Whalen was a housewife and mom who discovered a passion for the Internet and building social media and social communities on the Web. Twelve years later, she's involved in SEO daily and is a well-known SEO expert at her consultancy, High Rankings.

Whalen prides herself on providing close, personal care to her clients through High Rankings. Through her SEO strategies, Whalen helps clients such as Geico, Breeders.net, Proctor & Gamble, the Log Homes Council, and the Discovery Channel reach better search rankings.

Jerri: What usually brings a client to you?

Whalen: Being a pioneer in the search marketing industry for 12 years and having a newsletter subscription base of 25,000-plus subscribers has built a lot of credibility and trust around the High Rankings brand. Many of our clients have been newsletter subscribers for many years, and they want confirmation that what they've been doing on their own is sufficient. Often our first contact is with the Internet marketing manager of a small to mid-size B2B company who simply doesn't have the time to keep up with everything in the SEO space.

Jerri: What do you see as some of the least successful practices in SEO?

Whalen: There are a number of things in SEO that people believe are necessary, but which in reality have little to no actual effect on bringing highly targeted search engine traffic. For instance, submitting your web site to the search engines has no effect on whether your site will be indexed or ranked well. Putting keywords into the meta keyword tag is not needed if you are concerned with Google. Optimizing for keyword phrases that nobody actually searches for in the engines is another common SEO practice that yields no results.

Jerri: What are some of the most successful practices?

Whalen: Successful practices include carefully researching keyword phrases and systematically choosing the pages of the site in which they should be targeted. Then it's simply a matter of working them into the pages in a natural way.

Jerri: Are there any strategies that small and mid-sized business know they should be using but don't? Why?

Whalen: We often find that the actual architecture of a site should be changed for best results in the search engines. But since this can often mean a fundamental redesign of the entire web site, it's not something that can always be done and "workarounds" have to be found instead.

Jerri: What guidelines would you give a small or mid-sized business that is just beginning to implement SEO strategies?

Whalen: I'd highly suggest thinking about their SEO at the very beginning of their web site development, or at least while they're in the process of a redesign. If they do that, they can get things right from the very start. Many small to mid-sized companies spend tens of thousands on a redesign, and then they try to hire a company such as High Rankings for SEO. At that point, it can sometimes be too late, or certainly not as cost effective as it could have been had they consulted with an SEO firm during the redesign process.

Jerri: What changes have you seen in search engine optimization and search engine marketing over the last few years?

Whalen: The greatest changes have been in how companies measure the success of their SEO campaigns as well as the advent of social media marketing as a link-building tool.

For measuring success, it used to be done via search engine rankings; however, as rankings have become far less static, it's actually an impossible measurement. Search engines are no longer showing the same thing to everyone anymore. Most search results are personalized as well as geo-targeted. Today's measurement for success is in search engine traffic, conversions, and sales.

With social media marketing, web sites such as Digg and del.icio.us as well as numerous other popular online communities enable savvy search marketers to get their clients' products and services noticed in a completely new way. Since having numerous high-quality links pointing to your web site is a big factor in getting found in the search engines, "link baiting" has become a popular new form of viral marketing that can really help an SEO campaign get off the ground.

Jerri: Will SEO even be possible as social media grows? If so, how will it change the way that SEO is achieved?

Whalen: Yes, as in the previous answer, it has already changed things to a certain extent. However, social media alone are not going to be half as effective if you have a "broken" web site. At High Rankings, we like to say that we "fix" web sites to be the best they can be for the users as well as the search engines. You'd be surprised how much good usability goes hand-in-hand with good on-page SEO. Very often, the things that make a web site better for its users also make it better for the search engines. After all, Google wants to find the best web sites for their users — the searchers.

Jerri: Any other changes that companies considering or even already using SEO should be aware of? How are those changes likely to affect SEO in the future?

Whalen: I'm of the SEO school of thought that the more things change, the more they stay the same. The same fundamental principles I've written and talked about since the early 2000s are still often the same ones we talk about today. The search engines want the same things they've always wanted — the most relevant web site for the search query at hand. The trick, if you will, is making your site actually be the best, and then getting the word out to others about it.

Jerri: Is there anything I haven't touched on that you think is important for small and mid-sized businesses to understand about SEO?

Whalen: The greatest difference we see today is that you can't fake being the best anymore. There is simply too much competition out there. The best way to set yourself apart from all the others is to truly be creative and unique. If you're just going to offer the same product or service as everyone else, you don't stand a chance of making it in the search engines anymore.

Appendix C

SEO Software, Tools, and Resources

When you begin working with your SEO strategies, you'll find you need all kinds of resources. Most of those will be available on the Web, but it might take some searching to find them.

Rather than sending you off to use a search engine, this appendix provides the URLs for dozens of tools that will help you optimize for search engines. You'll find everything from search engines and directories to keyword tools, and other resources, all of which can either be used to improve your SEO in some way or to submit your site when you're ready.

Some of the tools included in these pages are free, and the fees for others will vary dramatically from very low (under \$.05 per click) to very high (over \$10,000 for the application). Obviously all of the tools won't be for you. But if you're looking for something specific, these links should at least give you a place to start looking.

This listing of resources is by no means all-encompassing. There are many other services and applications available to you, but because of space, we can't include all of them in this book.

Major Search Engines and Directories

There aren't tons of major search engines any more. Since all of the consolidation in the industry, there are only a handful of really large search engines and directories. But there are hundreds of smaller ones that range from very

IN THIS APPENDIX

Major search engines and directories

Secondary search engines

Meta search engines

Keyword tools

Content resources

RSS feeds and applications

Search engine marketing resources and articles

Registration services and programs

Link resources and software

Pay-per-click

general to very specific in nature. Those are the big ones. Secondary search engines are listed in the next section.

Google: www.Google.com

Yahoo! Directory: http://dir.yahoo.com/

Yahoo! Search Engine: www.yahoo.com/

Open Directory Project: www.dmoz.org

Microsoft: www.live.com

Ask: www.ask.com

Secondary Search Engines

The listings allowed in secondary search engines and directories can be general or specific. This list doesn't differentiate the search engines from the directories, and they aren't separate by types of listings. But there's still a pretty comprehensive list here, so you should be able to find enough places to list your site to keep you busy for quite some time.

AlltheWeb: www.alltheweb.com (same index as Yahoo)

AltaVista: www.altavista.com (same index as Yahoo!)

Simpli: www.simpli.com/

Slider: www.slider.com/

7Search: http://7search.com/

GoClick: www.goclick.com/

Miva: www.miva.com/us/

Search123: www.search123.com/

SearchFeed: www.searchfeed.com

All the Internet: www.alltheinternet.com/

Windows Live: www.live.com/

MySearch: www.mysearch.com

Alexa: www.alexa.com/

HotBot: www.hotbot.com

Netscape: www.netscape.com

SearchIt: www.searchit.com/

Wisenut: www.wisenut.com/

Lycos: www.lycos.com/

Findtarget: www.findtarget.com/

Towersearch: www.towersearch.com/

Entireweb: www.entireweb.com/

LiveSearching.com: www.livesearching.com/

Scrub the Web: www.scrubtheweb.com/

All-websearch.com: www.all-websearch.com/

SearchHippo: www.searchhippo.com/

ExactSeek.com: www.exactseek.com/

Information.com: www.information.com/

Nutch: www.nutch.com/

123World: www.123word.com

ExactSeek: www.exactseek.com

Jayde: www.jayde.com

LinkMaster: www.linkmaster.com

Qango: www.qango.com

Xoron: http://xoron.com

ZenSearch: www.zensearch.com

1800Miti.com: www.1800miti.com

Aesop: www.aesop.com

AXXASEARCH: www.axxasearch.com

BigLocate: www.biglocate.com

Claymontt: www.claymontt.com

Cozy Cabin: www.cozycabin.com

Infotiger: www.infotiger.com

WhatUSeek: www.whatuseek.com

Where2Go: www.where2go.com

SearchKing: www.searchking.com

Splat: www.splat.com

Genius Find: www.geniusfind.com

01 Web Directory: www.01webdirectory.com

Yeandi: www.yeandi.com

So Much: www.somuch.com

Start4all: www.start4all.com

Wow Directory: www.wowdirectory.com

Business.com: www.business.com

Gimpsy: www.gimpsy.com

Go Guides: www.goguides.org

JoeAnt: www.joeant.com

Skaffe: www.skaffe.com

Web-Beacon: www.web-beacon.com

Beaucoup!: www.beaucoup.com

Complete Planet: http://aip.completeplanet.com

LinkClix: www.linkclix.com

AlltheBizz.com: www.allthebizz.com

Find Hound: www.findhound.com

AbiLogic: www.abilogic.com

BizWeb: www.bizweb.com

Directory Archives: www.directoryarchives.com

Mavicanet: www.mavicanet.com

Re-QUEST do net: www.re-quest.net/

SuperSeek: www.superseek.org/

Web World Index: www.webworldindex.com

Bigall.comwww.bigall.com

International Business Directory: www.internationalbusinessdirectory.com

Premium Quest: www.premiumquest.com

Cipinet: http://directory.cipinet.com

The Safety Search: www.thesafetysearch.com

America's Best: www.americasbest.com

B2Business.net: www.b2business.net/

LCN2000.com: www.lcn2000.com

At Home Business Portal: www.athomebusinessportal.com

BizWeb.com: www.bizweb.com

BamInfo.com: www.baminfo.com

Ioma: www.ioma.com

Christ Engine: http://christengine.com

Among Stars: http://amongstars.com

Meta Search Engines

Meta search engines are those that search search engines. This listing of meta search engines will point you in the direction of the most used ones. You can't submit your site to most meta search engines. Instead, for your site to appear in these rankings, it will have to appear in the top listings in several other search engines.

DogPile: www.dogpile.com

MetaCrawler: www.metacrawler.com/info.metac/

Kanoodle: www.kanoodle.com

7MetaSearch: http://7metasearch.com/

Ixquick: www.ixquick.com/

iZito.com: www.izito.com/

Vivisimo: http://vivisimo.com/

kartOO: www.kartoo.com/

Mamma: www.mamma.com/

SurfWax: www.surfwax.com/

Clusty: http://clusty.com/

CurryGuide.com: http://web.curryguide.com/

Excite: www.excite.com/

Fazzle: www.fazzle.com/

Gimenei: http://gimenei.com/

IceRocket: www.icerocket.com/

Info.com: www.info.com/

InfoGrid: www.infogrid.com/

Jux2: www.jux2.com/

metaEureka: www.metaeureka.com/

Turbo10: http://turbo10.com/

WebCrawler: www.webcrawler.com/

Keyword Tools

You could spend half your life and most of your budget trying to figure out which keywords will work best for your site, for your content, and for your search engine rankings. Tools, like the ones listed here, will make optimizing those keywords at least a little easier.

Google Keyword Tool: https://adwords.google.com/select/KeywordToolExternal

WordTracker: http://freekeywords.wordtracker.com/

SEO Book Keyword Suggestion Tool: http://tools.seobook.com/general/keyword/

Submit Express Keyword Suggestion Tool: www.submitexpress.com/keytracker.php

Global Promoter Keyword Suggestion Tool: www.globalpromoter.com/seo-tools/keyword-suggestion-tool.cfm

McDar Keyword Analysis Tool: www.mcdar.net/KeywordTool/keywordtool.asp

Overture Keyword Selector Tool: http://inventory.overture.com/d/searchinventory/suggestion/ (Note: Although Overture is now part of Yahoo! this keyword tool is still available.)

BRL Keyword Suggestion Tool: www.build-reciprocal-links.com/keyword-suggestion/

Trellian: Search Word Suggestion Tool: www.keyworddiscovery.com/search.html

Microsoft adCenter Labs Keyword Research Tools: http://adlab.microsoft.com/ResearchPaidSearch.aspx

Keyword Intelligence: www.keywordintelligence.com/

The Permutator: www.boxersoftware.com/thepermutator.htm

Keyword Typo Generator: http://tools.seobook.com/spelling/keywords-typos.cgi

SEMPhonic: http://semphonic.com/

Digital Point Solution Search Engine Ranking Tools: www.digitalpoint.com/tools/keywords/

Keyword Density Analyzer: www.keyworddensity.com/

Search Engine Ranking Report: www.top25web.com/cgi-bin/report.cgi

Web Site Keyword Suggestions: www.webconfs.com/website-keyword-suggestions.php

Content Resources

Because content is such an important part of your web site (and your web-site optimization), you'll need to know where to find it. The links in this section not only take you to content providers, but also to content syndicators and to other content tools that will have the text on your page working overtime to keep visitors on your site.

ArticleDashboard: www.articledashboard.com/

Creative Commons: http://creativecommons.org/

OpenContentList.com: www.opencontentlist.com/

Ezine Articles: http://ezinearticles.com/

FreeSticky: www.freesticky.com/stickyweb/

GoArticles.com: www.goarticles.com/

IdeaMarketers.com: www.ideamarketers.com/

World Wide Information Outlet: http://certificate.net/

AbleStable Syndication: http://ablestable.com/content/syndication.htm

FeatureWell.com: www.featurewell.com/

Thomson Gale: www.gale.com/

MagPortal: www.magportal.com/

Moreover: http://w.moreover.com/

OSKAR Consulting: www.electroniccontent.com/

Pages: www.pagesmag.com/

Uclick: http://content.uclick.com/

YellowBrix: www.yellowbrix.com/

Hot Product News: www.hotproductnews.com/

Internet News Bureau: www.internetnewsbureau.com/

M2 Communications: www.m2.com/m2/web/page.php/home

OnlinePressReleases.com: www.onlinepressreleases.com/onlinepr/index.shtml

PR Newswire: http://prnewswire.com/

PR Web: www.prweb.com/

USANews: www.usanews.net/

RSS Feeds and Applications

In today's world of constantly changing content, RSS feeds and applications can contribute to your site optimization by keeping your content in front of prospective customers at all times. The content resources included here will help you set up all of the RSS options that your site needs.

Feedster: www.feedster.com/

Lockergnome: www.lockergnome.com/

NewsGator: www.newsgator.com/

NewsKnowledge.com: www.newsknowledge.com/home.html

Syndic8: www.syndic8.com/

Freshmeat: http://freshmeat.net/

SourceForge.net: http://sourceforge.net/

Search Engine Marketing Resources and Articles

We could talk about SEO and SEM for hours and still not cover all there is to know about it. That's why it's good for you to immerse yourself in the culture of SEO. That way you can keep up with what's going on in the industry and changes that might be made to the way SEO and SEM are achieved most effectively.

Search Engine Watch: http://searchenginewatch.com/

All Search Engines: www.allsearchengines.com/

SearchEngines.com: www.searchengines.com/

ShortKeys: www.shortkeys.com/

Pandia: www.pandia.com/

HighRankings.com: www.highrankings.com/

Search Engine Spider Simulator: www.webconfs.com/search-engine-spider-simulator.php

WebCEO: www.webceo.com/

Search Engine Simulator: www.delorie.com/web/ses.cgi

Measuring Up: www.measuring-up.com/seo-reference/seo-resources.html

ClickTracks: www.clicktracks.com/

Similar Page Checker: www.webconfs.com/similar-page-checker.php

Search Engine Saturation Tool: www.marketleap.com/siteindex/default.htm

Internet Marketing Tools: www.webuildpages.com/tools/internet-marketing-page.htm

Meta Keyword Tool: www.apogee-web-consulting.com/tools/keyword_tool.php

Top Ten Analysis SEO Tool: www.webuildpages.com/cool-seo-tool/

Advanced Meta Tag Generator: www.optimization-services.com/meta.asp?ID=4

Meta Tag Generator: www.searchbliss.com/free_scripts_metatag.htm

Search Engine Spider Simulator: www.webconfs.com/search-engine-spider-simulator.php

Registration Services and Programs

After looking at that huge list of search engines and directories at the beginning of this appendix, submitting your site to all of them might seem like an overwhelming task. If it does, the links in this section will take you to services and programs that can help to automate your submission and registration processes.

AddPro: www.addpro.com/

Ineedhits: www.ineedhits.com/

Dynamic Submission: www.dynamicsubmission.com/

Web Position: www.webposition.com/

Submit Wolf: www.webposition.com/

Directory Submission Tool: www.123promotion.co.uk/directorymanager/

Domain Registry Checker: www.123promotion.co.uk/directory/

URL Rewriting Tool: www.webconfs.com/url-rewriting-tool.php

Link Resources and Software

Links are nearly as important as the content on your site, so you'll need some additional tools to help you stay connected with your linking strategies, and to help you gather links to your site or push links out from your site.

LinkPopularity.com: www.linkpopularity.com/

MarketLeap: www.marketleap.com/

AntsSoft Link Popularity Checker: www.antssoft.com/linksurvey/index.htm

Xenu's Link Sleuth: http://home.snafu.de/tilman/xenulink.html

Link Alarm: www.linkalarm.com/

Backlink Anchor Text Checker: www.webconfs.com/anchor-text-analysis.php

Backlink Builder: www.webconfs.com/backlink-builder.php

Backlink Summary Tool: www.webconfs.com/backlink-summary.php

Reciprocal Link Checker: www.webconfs.com/reciprocal-link-checker.php

Link Popularity Checker and Link Quality Assessment: www.elixirsystems.com/tools/linkpopularity.php

Broken Link Checker: www.dead-links.com/

Reciprocal Link Spider: www.recip-links.com/

Site Link Analyzer: www.seochat.com/seo-tools/site-link-analyzer/

Link Appeal: www.webmaster-toolkit.com/link-appeal.shtml

Link Popularity Check: http://uptimebot.com/sql/one.php

Robots Txt Generator: www.123promotion.co.uk/tools/robotstxtgenerator.php

Robots.txt Syntax Checker: www.sxw.org.uk/computing/robots/check.html

Pay-per-Click

Pay-per-click will likely be a large part of your marketing efforts for your site. PPC goes hand in hand with SEO, so the links in this section should help you find all of the PPC tools that you need. There are even some PPC services included in these listings.

FindWhat: www.findwhat.com/

Espotting Media: www.espotting.com/

Enhance Interactive: www.enhance.com/

EPilot: www.epilot.com/

PayPerClickSearchEngines.com: www.payperclicksearchengines.com/

Social-Media Tools

Social media is the next major shift in SEO that's happening right now. Web 2.0 is all about the social nature of the Internet, and if you don't tap into that social aspect, the SEO on your site will quickly be out of date. Using social-media tools, however, you can get a jumpstart on your social-media strategy.

Social Tagging Tool: www.elixirsystems.com/tools/sociable/

Del.icio.us: http://del.icio.us/

Digg: www.digg.com

Furl: www.furl.net/

Appendix D

Worksheets

SEO Plan

Goals and Strategies	Notes
Primary goal	
Secondary goal	
Secondary goal	
Secondary goal	
Description of marketing strategy	
Who are your best customers and why?	
Who is your competition? (Include URLs.)	
What's the geographic scope of your marketing?	
Web Site Design	
Corporate history, news, PR, or current events?	
Executive bios?	
Product and service information?	
Customer support/live help?	
Online requests for information or contact forms?	
Membership-only content?	
Contact information?	
Forums?	
Educational materials?	
Links or resources?	
Archived content?	
Unique title tags on each page?	
Meta keyword tags?	
Meta description tags?	
Headers?	
Alt tags?	
Anchor text?	
Links and linking strategies?	
Keyword density? (Suggested 3–7 percent.)	

SEO Plan *(continued)*

Goals and Strategies	Notes
Keyword Considerations	
Keyword brainstorming	
Initial keyword list	
Keyword research	
Pay-per-click strategies	
Content Considerations	
Well-written and reader friendly?	
Keywords included in body text?	
Keywords included in titles?	
Keywords included in directories?	
Keywords included in file names?	
Keywords contained in images? (Should be avoided.)	
Keyword variation?	

SEO Checklist

Current State

Check your rank in the major search engines.

Don't overuse or misuse rank-checking automation.

If it works, don't "fix" it unless the fix will improve your SEO efforts.

Keep your site fresh and persuasive.

Keyword Research

Use your visitors' words, not just your own.

Focus on phrases.

What key phrases are most popular?

What relevant key phrases have less competition?

Web-Site Design

Is your site visually attractive?

Is your site's topic apparent at first glance?

Are your file names based on relevant keywords?

Try to avoid frames. If you can't or don't want to, use appropriate workarounds

Include a site-map page.

Include a robots.txt file.

Avoid delays and dead ends.

Write Clean Code

Put your indexable content as early as possible in the source code.

Put heavy JavaScript and CSS code in external files.

Include spider-friendly navigation.

Make Use of Tags and Attributes

Title tag.

Description meta tag.

Keywords meta tag.

Alt tags.

Headlines and headers.

Keyword-based links.

Table Summary tags.

SEO-Approved Content

Create unique content.

Make content as effective as possible.

Examine and adjust keyword density.

Avoid invisible text.

Avoid very tiny text.

Optimize your entire site.

Optimize your interior pages.

Give each page its own focus.

Manual Submissions

Submit to search engines and directories.

Know what your submission software does before you begin to use it.

Do not over-submit.

Do you have a site map?

Linking Strategies

Cultivate quality links.

Avoid garbage links.

Offer accurate, enticing descriptions.

Ask for key-phrase or keyword discount.

Allow return links sparingly.

Links from third parties?

Conversions

Improved sales conversion often outweighs improved SEO performance.

Keyword Worksheet

Keyword or Phrase	Number of Impressions	Search Popularity	Estimated Click-Through Rate	Estimated Conversion Rate	Cost per Conversion	Landing-Page URL

PPC Keyword Worksheet

Keyword or Phrase	Category	Bid	Estimated Click-Through Rate	Estimated Cost	Estimated Conversion Rate	Landing-Page URL	Ad Title	Ad Description	Notes

Keyword Checklist

Brainstorming? (Enter preliminary keyword list here.)

Review competitors' sites? (Look specifically for HTML tags like the title tag and meta tags.)

Check multiple keyword suggestion tools? (Enter the suggested terms below.)

List final keywords below.

Keyword tagging throughout web site?

Keyword testing? (Describe testing and methods used.)

Keyword Performance Worksheet

Keyword or Phrase	Cost Per Click	Cost Per Sale	Brand Awareness	Lifetime Keyword (Yes or No)	Products Per Customer Value	Customer Loyalty Index	Notes

A/B Testing Worksheet

Factor/Attribute Tested	Control PPC Ad	Testing PPC Ad	Notes About Testing
Item number/description			
Goal page			
Completed goals			
Percent completed			
Percent change			
Paid (ads)			
Paid conversions			
Conversions and percent change			
Income from keywords			
Percent changed			
Average cost per conversion			
Testing results			

PPC Competition Worksheet

	URL	Competitor 1* Visible Keywords Links	Number of Inbound Page Rank (in more than one search engine)
Main page			
Page 2			
Page 3			
Page 4			
Notes about web site			
SERPs rank			
PPC sponsorship assessment			
Notes			

*Repeat this information for each competitor.

Link-Tracking Worksheet

URL	Requested Landing Page	Contact: E-mail and Web Site	Date Requested	Link Received	Landing Page	Notes

Rank-Tracking Worksheet

URL	Baseline	Month 1	Month 2	Month 3	Month 4

Glossary

8 bit UCS/Unicode Transformation Format A variable-length character encoding for Unicode. It is able to represent any character in the Unicode standard, yet the initial encoding of byte codes and character assignments for UTF8 is consistent with ASCII.

A/B Testing A method of advertising testing by which a baseline control sample is compared to a variety of single-variable test samples.

Ad groups A group of ads that target one set of keywords or sites.

Adversarial search A search algorithm that looks for all possible solutions to a problem, much like finding all the possible solutions in a game.

Affiliate programs A method of promoting web businesses in which an affiliate is rewarded for every visitor, subscriber, customer, and/or sale provided through his/her efforts.

alt attributes HTML tags that provide text as an alternative to the graphics on a web page.

alt tags See **alt attributes**.

Analytics Measurement of web-site statistics such as the number of visitors, where they arrived from, and how much time they spent on a web site.

Anchor text Text that is displayed as a link instead of the URL for the link being displayed.

Anonymous FTP A file transfer protocol that allows a user to retrieve documents, files, programs, and other archived data from anywhere on the Internet without having to establish a user id and password. By using the special user id of "anonymous," the network user will bypass local security checks and will have access to publicly accessible files on the remote system.

Automated bid management A process that uses software to monitor and manage the amount bid on a keyword or key phrase.

Bait and switch A deceptive method of drawing users to a web site by providing the search engine with a highly optimized web page, but serving the user a different page.

Behavioral targeting A technique used by online publishers and advertisers to increase the effectiveness of their campaigns. The idea is to observe a user's online behavior anonymously and then serve the most relevant advertisement based on their behavior.

Bid jamming Placing a keyword bid that is just one penny below the highest bidder in an effort to force the advertiser to consistently pay a higher amount for the keyword.

Black-hat SEO Unethical SEO strategies.

nBlog A web site where entries are written in chronological order and commonly displayed in reverse chronological order.

Blogroll A list of links to other blogs or web sites that the author of the blog regularly likes to read.

Body text The text that makes up the body, or main section, of a web page.

Boolean search techniques Search techniques formed by joining simple terms with "and," "or," and "not" for the purpose of limiting or qualifying the search.

Glossary

Bounce The term that's used to describe how a website visitor lands on a web page and immediately clicks away from it.

Brand keywords Keywords that are associated with a well-known brand.

Bread-crumb trail A text-based navigation strategy that shows where in the site hierarchy the currently viewed web page is located and your location within the site, while providing shortcuts to instantly jump higher up the site hierarchy.

Broken links URLs or text-based links that do not lead to the expected page.

Buzz The "talk" that is going around the Internet about a product or service.

Cascading style sheet (CSS) CSS is a style-sheet language used to describe the presentation of a document written in a markup language. Its most common application is to style web pages written in HTML and XHTML, but the language can be applied to any kind of XML document.

Click bots Software applications that run automated tasks over the Internet. Typically, bots perform tasks that are both simple and structurally repetitive, at a much higher rate than would be possible for a human editor alone.

Click fraud A type of Internet crime that occurs in pay-per-click online advertising when a person, automated script, or computer program imitates a legitimate user of a web browser by clicking on an ad, for the purpose of generating a cost per click without having actual interest in the target of the ad's link.

Click-through rate A way of measuring the success of an online advertising campaign. A CTR is obtained by dividing the number of users who clicked on an ad on a web page by the number of times the ad was delivered.

Closing tag An HTML tag that indicates that a previously executed command should stop.

Code jockey A person who is highly trained in computer languages and writes programming code full time.

Constraint satisfaction search The process of finding a solution to a set of constraints. Such constraints express allowed values for variables. A solution is therefore an evaluation of these variables that satisfies all constraints.

Container tags A set of HTML tags that "contains" a full command. Usually indicated by the opening and closing tags (that is, <b>Bold</a>).

Content management systems A software system used for content management. Content management systems are deployed primarily for interactive use by a potentially large number of contributors.

Content-rich doorways Doorway pages that contain lots of heavily keyword-optimized content.

Content scraping A technique in which a computer program extracts data from the display output of another program.

Contextual targeting The term applied to advertisements appearing on web sites or other media, such as content displayed on mobile phones, where the advertisements are selected and served by automated systems based on the content displayed by the user.

Cookies Parcels of text sent by a server to a web browser and then sent back unchanged by the browser each time it accesses that server.

Copyright infringement The unauthorized use of material covered by copyright law, in a manner that violates one of the original copyright owner's exclusive rights, such as the right to reproduce or perform the copyrighted work, or to make derivative works that build upon it.

Cost per acquisition The amount it costs for a web site to acquire a new visitor or customer.

Cost per click A bid, placed on a keyword advertisement, that is charged each time a visitor clicks the advertisement.

Cost per conversion The average cost of acquiring a conversion, or goal.

Crawl Frontier The URLs that a crawler can follow from a given point.

Crawlers Search engine programs that "crawl" from one site to another, following the links given to them or included in the page they're examining.

Cross-channel tracking A feature that allows PPC users to track their PPC programs on different computers, and with different cookies.

Dangling link A link to a page that contains no other links.

Database A collection of information stored in a computer in a systematic way, such that a computer program can consult it to answer questions.

Dayparting The practice of dividing the day into several parts, during each of which a different type of radio programming or television programming appropriate for that time is aired.

Deep submission tool A tool that submits even the "deep"-level pages of your site to a directory or search engine.

Demographic targeting Targeting a specific group of people for advertisements, based on a particular demographic trait.

Deprecated tags Older HTML tags and attributes that have been superseded by other more functional or flexible alternatives.

Directory A way of organizing files and other directories.

Domain cloaking A strategy that allows you to redirect users to your existing web page while maintaining your URL in the browser's address bar.

Doorway pages Web pages created for spamdexing, that is, for spamming the index of a search engine by inserting results for particular phrases with the purpose of sending you to a different page. They are also known as bridge pages, portal pages, zebra pages, jump pages, gateway pages, and entry pages.

Dynamic web pages Web pages that are created on the fly in response to specifics that are associated with a specific web site.

Edited directories Directories that are monitored and edited by humans.

Entity escape Characters used to replace symbols when the search crawler is stopped by a specific character.

External navigation A navigational structure that leads users off your web site.

False Internet When traffic is redirected to another web site, that looks and feels the same way as the intended site, but is actually designed and created as a method of redirecting traffic for criminal reasons.

Flash A popular authoring software developed by Macromedia, is used to create vector graphics-based animation programs with full-screen navigation interfaces, graphic illustrations, and simple interactivity in an anti-aliased, resizable file format that's small enough to stream across a normal modem connection.

Forbidden search terms Words used in search that are censored by search engines.

Frameset An HTML file that defines the layout of a Web page that is composed of other, separate HTML files.

FTP (File Transfer Protocol) A common method of moving files between two Internet sites.

Gadgets Small applications designed to run on a desktop or toolbar. The applications can be any useful "gadget," from a clock to a note-taking application.

Generic keywords Keywords that are broad in nature.

Geo-targeting Serving of ads to a particular geographical area or population segment.

Goal conversion Achieving a preset goal. In SEO, a goal conversion occurs when a site visitor completes a task you have defined for him/her.

Google Analytics A web-site statistics measurement program.

Google bombing An attempt to influence the ranking of a given site in results returned by the Google search engine.

Header tag The HTML tag that denotes the header of a web page.

Heuristics Heuristics are rules of thumb people follow in order to make judgments quickly and efficiently.

Hidden pages Article pages that are outside the standard navigational structure.

Hybrid directory A directory that uses both directory listings and search engine listings.

img tags An HTML tag used to define alternative text in place of a graphic in the event the graphic cannot be displayed.

Impressions The number of times that people see a web page or advertisement.

Inbound links Links to your web site from someone else's.

Inclusion protocol A protocol that tells search engines what they should include in their indexes for your site.

Informed search Search that applies to a regular search using directing properties.

Internal linking The links that lead from one page to another within the structure of a single web site.

Invisible keyword stuffing Creating keywords on a page that are made to be the same color as the web page's background to make them invisible to people, but detectable to search crawlers.

JavaScript A system of programming codes, created by Netscape, that can be embedded into the HTML of a web page to add functionality. JavaScript should not be confused with the Java programming language. In general, script languages such as JavaScript are easier and faster to code than more structured languages such as Java and C++.

Keyword density The frequency with which chosen keywords or phrases appear on a web page compared to the other text on the page.

Keyword performance indicators Elements of keyword performance that are used to weigh the effectiveness of a given keyword.

Keyword poison Keywords that reduce the effectiveness of the keywords with which you have chosen to market your web site.

Keyword spamming The practice of overusing keywords in an attempt to trick search engines into ranking a web site better in search results.

Keyword stuffing Adding more keywords to a web page, either in text or in the HTML tags, than is appropriate.

Keyword testing A method of testing individual keywords to learn which keywords are the most effective for your marketing efforts.

Landing pages The web page to which visitors are directed when they click through an advertisement.

Link farms Web pages that contain only links to other pages in an attempt to draw search crawler attention.

List search The ability to search for multiple terms by separating each term with a comma.

Manual bid management The practice of managing your keyword bids on your own, without the assistance of software.

Mashup A web application that combines data from more than one source.

Meta refresh An HTML meta element used to specify a time interval (in seconds) after which a web browser should automatically refresh the current web page.

Meta tagging HTML elements used to provide structured metadata about a web page.

Monitored directories Directories in which the submissions are read by human editors, but are rarely changed by those editors.

Multi-submission tool A submission tool that will submit your web site to multiple search engines.

Natural language A language that is spoken, written, or signed by humans for general-purpose communication, as distinguished from formal languages such as computer programming languages.

Negative keyword tool A keyword tool that suggests keywords that you would not want included with the key phrases you are searching for.

noframes tag An HTML tag that indicates the content of a framed web site, but ignores the frames.

Open directory project A directory that is populated by volunteers.

Opening tag An HTML tag indicating that a command is coming. The opening tag usually takes the form of <b>.

Organic SEO Strictly speaking, SEO efforts that are integrated with web-site design and do not require a monetary investment.

Page jacking A way of spamming the index of a search engine. It is achieved by creating a rogue copy of a popular web site, which shows contents similar to the original, to a web crawler, but redirects web surfers to unrelated or malicious web sites.

Page saturation The number of pages that a search engine recognizes for your web site.

Paid directory review A fee-based service in which a web site is reviewed for a directory more quickly than others. A paid review does not guarantee inclusion or rank.

Paid-inclusion service A service that connects search directories to consumers who will pay to have their web site added to that directory.

Paid placement A method of improving search engine ranking. The web-site owner pays a fee to have a site listed in a search engine or directory, but that fee does not guarantee the search engine ranking for that site.

Post-search ads Advertisements that are served to web-site users upon their exit from a web site, based on the pages they looked at while navigating through that site.

Primary search engines One of the big search engines that are more general in nature.

Return on investment A mathematical calculation that illustrates how much profit is made in return for the investment that was made.

Robots Computer programs that visit a web site based on links and other criteria set out by the search engine algorithm.

Robots exclusion standard A file that tells robots, or web crawlers, what not to look at while they're on your site.

Robots meta tag A simple mechanism to indicate to visiting web robots if a page should be indexed, or if links on the page should be followed.

robots.txt The file that is used to tell robots and crawlers what not to crawl on your site.

RSS feed A syndication feed that grabs news, blogs, or other activities and presents the reader with up-to-date content.

Scrape To copy web-site materials from another web site in an effort to create a false web.

Scraper bot Software that crawls around the Internet looking for content to steal.

Scraper site The web site where scraper content is collected.

Search Algorithm A mathematical equation used to define what words or phrases someone is looking for and how the collected results should be returned to them.

Search engine An application that indexes and serves content to an Internet user who is looking for something specific.

Search engine optimization (SEO) Improving a web site in an attempt to attract search engine crawlers.

Search engine results pages (SERPs) The pages of results that are returned after an Internet user searches for a specific word or topic.

Search engine spam The process by which some people try to artificially influence the search engine into indexing their site and ranking it higher in the results.

Search profiling A method by which marketers can use the behaviors and actions of Internet users to target other users with similar interests and lifestyles.

Search query The string of words and characters used to perform a search engine search.

Secondary search engines Search engines that are more targeted in nature than primary search engines. These search engines are also smaller than primary search engines.

Seeded The process of "loading" a search crawler with URLs to examine.

Server-side include An easy server-side scripting language used almost exclusively for the Web. As its name implies, its primary use is including the contents of one file in another, via a web server.

Server-side redirection A method of URL redirection using an HTTP status code issued by a web server in response to a request for a particular URL. The result is to redirect a user's web browser to another web page with a different URL.

Simple directories A basic web directory that usually allows users to perform a search.

Site map A document that outlines where every link leads. Also a document that's included in the HTML code for a web page that directs crawlers where to go.

Site mirroring Including an exact duplicate of a web site in another location, usually stored on another server.

Social bookmarking A way for Internet users to store, classify, share, and search Internet bookmarks.

Social-media optimization A set of methods for generating publicity through social media, online communities, and community web sites.

Social networks A social structure made of nodes (which are generally individuals or organizations) that are tied by one or more specific types of relations, such as values, visions, ideas, financial exchanges, friends, kinship, likes or dislikes, conflicts, trade, web links, sexual relations, disease transmission (epidemiology), or airline routes.

Source code The basic code around which a program or application is designed.

Spamdexing The process of spamming a search effort.

Spiders Web crawlers that examine and index web pages.

SQL search An alternative search module that offers an advanced search operand; searching by taxonomy term, user, and date; filtering within results; and an advanced search page.

Static web pages Web pages that stay the same all the time.

Stop words Forbidden words that will cause a search engine to stop crawling your web site.

Submission tools Software applications that automatically submit a web site to search engines and directories.

Subset (data) A small portion of an overall group of data.

Syntax The rules governing the construction of search expressions in search engines and directories.

Table summary tags HTML tags that provide a summary for a table in the event that it cannot be tagged properly.

Targeted search engines Search engines that are targeted to a specific audience.

Text delimited Excel files Excel files that retain data formatting.

Throw-away domains Domains that are purchased specifically for the purpose of having a referring domain. When these domains are discovered, they are deleted.

Tree search The process of searching data in a very logical way.

User agent The client application used with a particular network protocol; the phrase is most commonly used in reference to those which access the Web.

UTF–encoded See 8 bit UCS/Unicode Transformation Format.

Viral content Content that is spread through a self-replication viral-type process.

Viral marketing Marketing techniques that use pre-existing social networks to produce increases in brand awareness, through self-replicating viral processes, analogous to the spread of pathological and computer viruses.

Virtual include See Server-side include.

Web 2.0 A perceived second generation of web-based communities and hosted services such as social-networking sites, wikis, and folksonomies, which aim to facilitate collaboration and sharing between users.

Webmaster A person who designs and maintains web sites.

WHOIS Information A database of information that lists who owns what domain name on the web.

XML inclusion XML tags that tell a search crawler what should be included in the crawler's index for that URL.

Index

H

Harris, Stephen, 321–324
header tags, 376
    content, 106–108
heuristics, 11, 61–64, 376
hidden links, 187–188, 240
hidden pages, 56, 376
hidden text, 186, 241
hijacking, 242
Hoppe, Ryan, 325–327
human-powered engines, 34
hybrid directories, 213, 376
hybrid engines, 34

I

img tags, 49, 376
impressions, 376
inbound links, 198–200, 376
    social media and, 253
inclusion protocol, 376
inclusion services. *See also* paid inclusion (PI)
    business model of, 221–222
    contracts, 224
    fee-based, 220
    hiring, 223–224
    managing, 222–223
    when to use paid, 221
inconspicuous links, 241
informed search, 376
internal links, 206–207, 376
    organic SEO and, 26
invisible keyword stuffing, 376

J

JavaScript, 52–53, 376
Jughead, 4

K

key features, click-through rates and, 149
keyword advertisement text, 116–119
keyword list, finalizing, 93–95
keyword pay-per-click programs, 77–78
keyword poison, 90, 376
keyword spamming, 376
keyword stuffing, 24, 241, 376
    avoiding, 70–71, 123
keyword suggestion tools, 81–88
keyword testing, 93, 376
keyword tools, 353
keywords
    auctions, 135
    bid management
        automated, 137–140
        manual, 136–137
    bidding for, 73, 135
    budgeting, 133–136
    costs, CPA, 92
    density, 67–69, 376
    generic, 376
    importance of, 59–61
    invisible keyword stuffing, 376
    list, creating, 88–89
    metrics for, 134
    negative, 145
    organic, 70
    performance indicators, 376
    placement, 97
    selecting, 65–66
    tracking, 140–143
Kuehn, Diane, 329–331

L

landing pages, 115, 376
    creating, 119–121

The books you read to succeed.

Get the most out of the latest software and leading-edge technologies with a Wiley Bible—your one-stop reference.

0-471-78886-4
978-0-471-78886-7

0-470-04030-0
978-0-470-04030-0

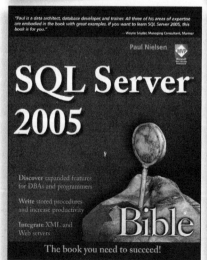

0-7645-4256-7
978-0-7645-4256-5

0-470-10089-3
978-0-470-10089-9

Available wherever books are sold.

Wiley and the Wiley logo are registered trademarks of John Wiley & Sons, Inc.
All other trademarks are the property of their respective owners.

WILEY
Now you know
wiley.com